THE WEHRMACHT

The German Army of World War II
1939–1945

The Great Armies

A series of books that examines the great armies of history. By looking in detail at the separate components of each army, and how these components combined effectively, each title presents a unique view of a particular army, and explains why it was so successful in battle. Each volume analyzes the various elements required to make an army a battle-winning force: an efficient supply system, good chain of command, effective tactics, good equipment, high morale, and fine leadership. But these separate elements are only effective when combined successfully, and so each volume analyzes how they interacted to forge an effective fighting force, and why a particular army under examination did it more effectively than its opponents.

THE WEHRMACHT

The German Army of World War II
1939-1945

Tim Ripley

FITZROY DEARBORN

An Imprint of the Taylor and Francis Group

New York ● London

Published by

Fitzroy Dearborn
An imprint of the Taylor and Francis Group
29 West 35th Street
New York, NY 10001-2299

and

Fitzroy Dearborn
An imprint of the Taylor and Francis Group
11 New Fetter Lane
London EC4P 4EE

*British Library and Library of Congress
Cataloging-in-Publication Data are available*

ISBN 1-57958-312-1

For Brown Partworks Limited

Editors: Peter Darman, Matt Turner
Designer: Mike LeBihan
Cartographer: Darren Awuah
Picture research: Susannah Jayes
Managing editor: Lindsey Lowe
Production manager: Matt Weyland

Printed and bound in Hong Kong through
Asia Pacific Offset, Inc.

Picture credits:
All photographs the Robert Hunt Library

With Thanks

I would like to thank the following
individuals for helping to make this book
possible. Arthur Grant for his help
translating Wehrmacht documents; Neil
Tweedie and Mickey Brooks for their
insights into global strategy; the records
staff of Imperial War Museum, London,
for their help with research into German
World War II records; the British Army
Staff College, Camberley, for allowing me
access to numerous German World War II
records in its possession; Stewart Fraser for
proof-reading my text; Pete Darman, of
the Brown Reference Group plc, for giving
me the opportunity to fulfil my long-held
ambition to write about the Wehrmacht;
Major Hasse Resenbro of the Danish
Guard Hussar Regiment for his assistance
during my visits to the battlefields of the
Ardennes; Richard Cartright for his help
with Wehrmacht uniforms and medals;
and Miss Hayley Griffiths and Dr. Johnny
Grey for morale-boosting supplies of cake
at key moments.

Dedication

This book is dedicated to the men of Royal
Air Force Bomber Command and the US
Army Air Forces, who took the Allied war
effort into the heart of Hitler's Third Reich
in the dark days of World War II.

Contents

Key to Maps

Military Units – Sizes

XXXXX
Army group/front

XXXX
Army

XXX
Corps

XX
Division

X
Brigade

III
Regiment

II
Battalion

Military Units – Types

Infantry

Armored

Panzergrenadier

XX
Fortress

Mountain

XX
Parachute

Airlanding

Marines

Cavalry

National Colors

German

Soviet

United States

British & Commonwealth

Belgian

Finnish

Dutch

Romanian

French

Italian

Norwegian

Polish

Hungarian

General Military Symbols

Minefield

Airfield

Machine guns

Parachute landing

Army Movements

Attack/advance (in national colors)

Retreat (in national colors)

Frontline (in national colors)

Heavy defense line (in national colors)

Defense line (in national colors)

Geographical Symbols

River

Road

Railroad

Urban area

Town

Capital city

Marsh

Trees

Bridge

Mountains

International border

Foreword

The November 11, 1918, Armistice allowed the German Army to march home intact in good order, thus signaling the end of World War I. The subsequent failure of the war-weary Entente powers to carry the war into Germany—after all, in November 1918 not a single Entente soldier stood on German soil—prevented them from bringing home to the German people either Germany's primary responsibility for the outbreak of World War I or the reality that Germany had been defeated. Consequently, in Germany there was little of the utter revulsion against the barbarity and futility of modern industrial war that emerged during the interwar years in the rest of Europe. Instead, the German military was able to consolidate its position as the guardian of the German nation, which gave rise to the "Stab in the Back Legend"—the fallacy that the German Army had never been decisively defeated in the field in 1918. Thus German militarism did not die in the trenches of Flanders, but instead flourished in interwar Germany. The seeds of World War II were thus laid by the peculiar circumstances that ended World War I.

There is no doubt that Hitler's Wehrmacht was one of history's great armies. Its victories and defeats will continue to be studied by soldiers and scholars for years to come for insights into the art of war. Equally compelling is the story of how the German Army sold its soul to one of the most evil regimes to emerge in the 20th century.

This book is not a blow-by-blow account of every battle fought by the German Army in World War II. It aims to give readers an overview of the war and then analyze why the Wehrmacht won its great victories and suffered massive defeats. Although the term Wehrmacht encompassed also the German Air Force and Navy, this study concentrates on Germany's land forces. Air and naval power was of key importance in the war, but the German Army was the power house of Hitler's war machine and its fate decided the eventual outcome of the war.

The story of the Wehrmacht is intertwined with the fate of a number of key individuals. The names Guderian, Rommel, and Manstein are as synonymous with the German Army as the words panzer and Blitzkrieg. It is one of the abiding lessons of military history that individuals are more important to the course of events than any amount of military hardware. Hitler's army rode to victory because of such men and their moral weakness in the face of the Nazi regime was a major factor in Germany's ultimate defeat.

Tim Ripley
Lancaster, December 2002

Introduction

The purpose of this book is to ascertain why the German Army of World War II was so competent on the battlefield, and thus why it deserves the title "great army." Millions of words have been written about the German Army between 1939 and 1945, though many of them have merely reinforced the many myths that have arisen around the Wehrmacht. The Blitzkrieg, for example, has been elevated into a type of magical military formula, armed with which the German Army was able to crush its enemies with relative ease between 1939 and 1942. Similarly, because much of the information mined by authors regarding the war on the Eastern Front was drawn mainly from German sources, especially in the 1950s and 1960s, assembling accurate data pertaining to battles and campaigns in Russia was, until the 1990s, fraught with difficulties.

Fortunately, a wealth of new information about the war on the Eastern Front has become available thanks to the opening of Russian archives. The historian David Glantz has carried out extensive research on the war in Russia, and his published works have been widely used in the Eastern Front chapters in this work. In addition, the works of James Lucas contain many German first-hand accounts of fighting on the Eastern Front, and they provide a useful insight into how the German Army operated in Russia.

Other essential sources used to compile this volume are the writings of those who held senior command positions in the German Army during World War II. Thus the writings of Guderian, Manstein, Rommel, Senger und Etterlin, Stadler, and Toppe form the bedrock of this work. Additionally, the reader is strongly advised to consult the German Army titles of J.J. Fedorowicz Publishing Inc. and Schiffer Publishing Limited, which contain many first-hand accounts from junior officers and rank-and-file members. Those extensively made use of are listed in the bibliography.

The campaigns of the German Army in France, the Low Countries, North Africa, and the Balkans have been examined in great detail since the end of World War II. Due to the openness of British, American and French archives, plus a plethora of individual memoirs that have been published in the West since 1945, there is little controversy concerning the sequence of these campaigns.

In pursuing the goal of establishing why the German Army was such an excellent fighting force, the individual campaign chapters are each divided into two sections. The first section in each chapter provides an analysis of a particular campaign, while the second section analyzes factors that determined how the army conducted the campaign. Thus the chapter on the war in North Africa examines the impact of armor, antitank weapons, the generalship of Rommel, desert tactics, the Tiger tank's performance, and the influence of logistics. What emerges from these chapters is an army that often triumphed against numerically superior opponents, and reveals that a combination of excellent leadership and highly trained soldiers was able to exploit Blitzkrieg tactics to the full, throwing the enemy off-balance and denying him the space and time to reorganize. Ironically, close analysis of these campaigns also reveals that technological superiority was often negligible or indeed non-existent.

Armies are the product of the social, economic and political environments in which they operate, and the German Army was no different. The third part of the book therefore examines the army's relationship with its Nazi masters and the Waffen-SS, the Nazis' ideological soldiers. It never forgets that the German Army served one of the most murderous regimes in history, and its record must be judged accordingly. However, though National Socialism did infuse many levels of the army, Nazi ideology never exceeded a sense of duty toward the Fatherland as a motivation for military service. This explains why the professionalism of the officer corps and rank-and-file operated to the very end, allowing the army to function as a fighting organization after all hope had disappeared.

A problem for any scholar of battles and campaigns of World War II is the question of numbers: troops, casualties, tanks, artillery pieces, and production figures. There is a danger, particularly when relying upon German sources, and especially memoirs of German soldiers who fought in Russia, to fall into the trap of exaggerating numbers. Fortunately, the research undertaken by David Glantz, Martin van Creveld, Thomas Jentz, Hilary Doyle, Peter Chamberlain, and R.H.S. Stolfi has cleared away the mists of uncertainty regarding the numbers issue. The works of these authors used in this work are listed in the bibliography.

There are many color maps throughout this book, which are essential for showing the movement of forces. The two main sources for the maps are those made available on the United States Military Academy West Point website—www.usma.edu—and the excellent *Historical Atlas of World War II* compiled by the late, and much lamented, Dr. John Pimlott, former head of war studies at the Royal Military Academy Sandhurst.

The appendices make extensive use of the works of George Nafziger, who has spent years compiling his German orders of battle from captured German documents held in American archives. The reader is advised to consult his works for further detailed information on individual German divisions that participated in the war.

PART 1
CREATING THE MACHINE

Genesis of the War Machine

After World War I the German Army was reduced to a 100,000-man force called the *Reichswehr*. However, in the 1920s and 1930s it reorganized itself to become a formidable military machine. But the process was both haphazard and fractious.

The bitter legacy of defeat in 1918 stimulated vigorous scrutiny and innovation in the interwar German military that paved the way for the great German Blitzkrieg (Lightning War) victories during the early years of World War II. That the German military had such a prominent place in German politics and society ensured that a cultural climate receptive to both defense spending and military reform flourished between the two world wars, even during the traumatic socioeconomic catastrophe of the 1929 Great Depression.

The victorious Allied powers imposed in 1919 the Treaty of Versailles on a vanquished Germany. This peace settlement sanctioned the democratic Weimar Republic that had come into being after domestic revolution had compelled Kaiser Wilhelm II to abdicate. The Versailles treaty, however, reduced Germany's ground forces to a 100,000-man volunteer internal security and frontier defense force – the *Reichswehr* – which was forbidden to field aircraft, armor, antiaircraft and antitank guns, heavy artillery, or chemical weapons. Versailles also severely restricted German deployment of heavy weapons and prohibited armaments importation or production. The Allied powers hoped that such restrictions would limit German military capabilities and therefore prevent Germany from conducting a war of aggression in the future. However, the Treaty of Versailles failed to incapacitate the German military and, ironically, served only to facilitate and to fuel the dramatic triumphs of 1939–41.

Smarting under what many viewed as a punitive peace unfairly imposed on an undefeated people and army, most Germans bitterly resented the peace dictated at Versailles and sought its repudiation. Throughout the interwar years, therefore, German politicians and generals alike remained committed to resurrecting a

German Panzer II tanks on a prewar exercise. Typical of German interwar tank design, it was a compromise between an armored fighting vehicle that could be produced quickly and in high numbers and something that could fight on the mechanized battlefield. By the time of the invasion of Poland in September 1939, Panzer Is and IIs made up virtually the whole German tank arm. However, their thin armor and light armament meant they were rapidly phased out of frontline service after 1940.

strong military that could defend Germany's borders. That said, the idea that the army spent the years between 1919 and 1939 preparing for another Europe-wide conflict is erroneous. It was only after Adolf Hitler and the National Socialists (Nazis) came to power in 1933 that war became much more likely. Hitler was determined to incorporate all Germans living outside Germany's borders into his Thousand Year Reich, and provide his people with *Lebensraum* (living space) in the Slav lands of the East, specifically Poland and the Soviet Union.

Germany resisted the Versailles treaty throughout its 16-year existence. First, it evaded treaty restrictions by dismantling and hiding large amounts of weapons – including 350,000 rifles, 12,000 machine guns, and 675 howitzers – in secret arms caches throughout Germany. Second, the German Army smuggled ordnance overseas, including 1,500 howitzers ostensibly purchased by Blessing, a Dutch subsidiary of Krupp, the famous German armaments company. In the mid-1920s the German Army covertly rearmed as it drew on these stockpiles, developed forbidden weapons abroad, and later secretly within Germany. The German firm of Rheinmetall, for example, acquired the Swiss company of Solothurn and used the latter's prototypes to develop the 20mm Antiaircraft Gun 30 (designated the 20mm Flak 30 by the Germans). This weapon would later prove critical to the antiaircraft armament of the panzer divisions, being deployed to provide devastating defense against low-level aircraft attacks. On May 10, 1940, for example, panzer divisional Flak shot down 13 of 32 British Fairey Battle light bombers for almost no damage inflicted.

The German Army also maintained clandestine troop and ordnance reserves well in excess of treaty limits. Enforcement of the treaty also proved lax as the

The German Army returns to the Fatherland following the end of World War I. Four years of war had resulted in defeat; humiliation would follow as the army was reduced to a mere 100,000 men – the *Reichswehr*.

victorious Allies squabbled among themselves as a result of competing visions of how to build a new European order, and as they turned to address domestic, social, and economic problems long neglected due to the imperatives of war.

The interwar German Army searched for new ways to prevail against potential future aggressors, especially as the *Reichswehr* numbered only 100,000 men. It was necessary for Germany to maximize the limited combat forces and equipment allowed her by Versailles. The German Army therefore extensively analyzed the lessons of World War I in order to fight as effectively as was possible within the constraints of the treaty. German officers wrote after-action reports on their experiences during World War I, produced detailed campaign and battle studies, published scholarly articles in Europe's leading military journals, and participated in extensive wargaming to examine the conduct of the war's most important operations. As a result of this effort, the German military examined World War I more extensively than did any other participant. While the interwar British Army desperately attempted to exorcize the ghosts of the Somme and Passchendaele by jettisoning the knowledge and expertise it had gained at such cost in lives on the fields of Flanders, the German Army studied and learned from both its World War I successes and failures. In contrast, much of British military thought during the 1920s focused back on the traditional British strategic preoccupation of policing a vast colonial empire with grossly overstretched forces.

The Lessons of 1914–18

German examination of World War I demonstrated that the well-trained Imperial General Staff had created a flexible command ethos that fostered individual in-itiative within the framework of a uniform and universal doctrine. This tradition enabled the army to adapt tactically and operationally throughout the war. Realizing that this flexibility was an important advantage, the interwar German Army sought to enhance the considerable tactical and operational skills that its predecessor had shown. Study also revealed the importance of firepower superi-ority and quality training for offensive success, and that the army's determination to retrain in the field during ongoing combat had allowed it to adapt continually to developments in the character of the fighting. The lessons the Germans derived from World War I thus reinforced the army's belief in the principles of flexibili-ty, tactical superiority, and operational skill.

The Germans also reviewed in detail the aerial operations undertaken during 1914–18, and came to the conclusion that the strategic bombing attacks Germany had launched with Zeppelin airships and Gotha and Riesen bombers against Great Britain had largely failed. More successful was the development of purpose-built ground-attack aircraft and then committing them as central elements of the combined-arms storm troop attacks launched on the Western Front during the spring of 1918 (see Chapter 2). The interwar German Army thus concluded that World War I demonstrated a future tactical role for aircraft in direct support of ground forces. Such a conclusion reinforced the natural German predisposition toward a future ground-support air force – an attitude engendered both by Germany's geographic situation as a central European power and by the emasculated nature of its ground forces after 1919. The German military thus emerged from World War I with a more accurate reading of the future capabilities and roles of air power than did its enemies.

Close scrutiny also revealed that Germany lost the wartime struggle in terms of technology. Her failure to develop an effective tank, in particular, had contributed to defeat, after-action reports emphasized. Thus the interwar German Army committed itself to remaining at the very forefront of interwar weapons development and procurement, despite the restrictions imposed by Versailles. It also remained determined to replicate the technical achievements of its potential enemies. So the Germans avidly recorded and reviewed the new developments in weapons technology throughout the 1920s, and sought to gain access to and replicate these advances. The Germans then built on the achievements of their enemies in their own research and design. The result was a slew of innovative new ordnance between the wars that combined firepower and mobility (two qualities that would be crucial to the success of Blitzkrieg), and which was well-adapted to the kind of maneuver war the German Army of the 1920s expected to fight in the future. Thus during the 1920s Germany produced many modern, quality weapons that the Nazi government would mass-produce after 1935. This weaponry included the MG 13, a rapid-fire light machine gun, from which during the mid-1930s Germany developed the famous MG 34 general-purpose machine gun, capable of employment in both a light and a heavy role. Indeed, German infantry firepower was built around the MG 34, which was estimated to be the equivalent of 20 riflemen in terms of volume of fire.

New Weapons

During this period the German Army also developed unrivaled modern infantry guns that combined mobility and firepower, such as the 75mm Light Infantry Gun 18 (75mm le IG 18), as well as the rugged and mobile 105mm Light Field Howitzer 18 (105mm le FH 18). Infantry guns were allocated to infantry battalions to provide them with light artillery support – the guns were light enough to be physically dragged across country by the infantrymen.

The army also designed the 100mm Heavy Cannon 18 (s 100mm K 18), a quality piece of long range and accuracy, and the horse-drawn 37mm Light Antitank Gun L/45 (37mm Pak L/45), later to become the widely used Light Antitank Gun 35/36 (Pak 35/36). Finally, German armaments firms also produced outstanding air defense guns, including the famous 88mm Antiaircraft Gun 18 (88mm Flak 18). The "88" had a high muzzle velocity, which meant it had long range and good penetrative powers. In addition, like all Flak guns, it could fire armor-piercing (solid shot) and high-explosive shells. Thus, it could fulfill two roles: it could knock out tanks and shoot down aircraft. It was also comparatively light – 4.82 tons (4.9 tonnes) – compared with the British 3.7in. gun, which weighed 10.3 tons (10.46 tonnes).

Testimony to the ruggedness and dependability of these weapons was the fact that most of them remained in production throughout World War II. The interwar German Army's roll call of technological innovation also extended beyond armaments to encompass modern portable short-wave radios and the Enigma encoding machine that encrypted radio transmissions. Consequently, Germany inexorably edged ahead in the interwar technology race, and it would not generally be until late in World War II that her opponents were able to close this gap.

The political and cultural climate of interwar Germany clearly promoted both militarism and military innovation. Cultural militarism and nationalism ensured that the military remained widely respected and admired in Germany after 1918 despite defeat, and therefore it had to justify neither itself nor defense spending. Rather, its social prestige grew as it acted as a bulwark against communism, thus reinforcing its traditional standing as the preserver of the nation and of the German way of life. The standing of the military in German society allowed the interwar German Army to focus on its political mandate for reform with far less distraction from political opposition or from domestic popular resentment and suspicion. Thus, despite the enduring economic difficulties of the 1920s, Weimar Germany was able to maintain high levels of defense spending. In fact, the Weimar government of the 1920s spent more per capita on defense than any other Western military, particularly when one allows for the "black budget": the hidden funds that were secretly channeled to the military. Thus, financial constraints never shackled military reform in Germany nearly as much as they did in Britain, France, and the United States between the wars.

At the same time, the German Army of the 1920s remained the best informed army in the world regarding the force structure, capabilities, and intentions of likely future rivals. Such effective intelligence helped the interwar German Army to stay ahead of other powers in the arms and technology races. Thus, it standardized, for example, the 105mm Light Field Howitzer 18 (105mm le FH 18) as the mainstay of its artillery during the 1920s, many years before other European nations, such as the French, standardized their pieces on the 105mm caliber. The 105mm le FH 18 was an average weapon but it was very versatile, firing all types of projectile and even being able to knock out tanks at short ranges.

Another of the German Army's key strengths between the wars was its insistence on integrating the lessons learned from World War I into revised doctrine. In the early 1920s it published a new doctrinal manual, *Command and Battle,* which presented a holistic, modern, integrated approach to war. It presented doctrine that emphasized offensive concentration and rapid deep-penetration followed by encirclement, achieved through close combined-arms cooperation. In addition, the interwar German Army frequently updated doctrine to take into account technological advances. Thus it revised doctrine to

German armored cars during maneuvers in the 1920s. During this period the *Reichswehr* used large numbers of armored cars, indicating that it was serious about motorizing its units. Under the Nazis the process was accelerated.

accommodate the impact of steadily improving aircraft and armor capabilities. While *Command and Battle* demonstrated a continued skepticism about the effectiveness of aircraft and armor on the modern battlefield – a product of Germany's own World War I experience – as more capable tanks and aircraft emerged in the 1930s, the German Army devised a new *Troop Leadership* manual during 1933–34 that emphasized the importance of armor and mobility as the army finally began to mechanize. A word about combined arms: in German doctrine it means the combined efforts of various arms – tanks, artillery, infantry, antitank guns, and aircraft – to defeat the enemy. Support is the key: the panzers would be supported by motorized infantry (either in lorries or halftracks), motorized engineers, artillery fire, and aircraft. It was never envisaged that the panzers alone would rupture the enemy line; the advance would consist of numerous, small attack groups (*Angriffsgruppen*), made up of armor, infantry, and

artillery. Then combined-arms battle groups (*Kampfgruppen*) would conduct the pursuit. Overhead, aircraft would attack enemy artillery, tanks, and reserves. Combined arms thus required an understanding between the various branches of how each of them operated to achieve the maximum results.

The clear exposition of a progressive, comprehensive, realistic, and flexible doctrine in a single *Troop Leadership* manual that was universally inculcated upon all German soldiers irrespective of branch of service lay at the heart of German military effectiveness throughout World War II. For it ensured that German troops of all the combat arms possessed an understanding of the functions and value of other arms and their individual places in the combined-arms team. As a result, it was easier for German troops to develop combined-arms expertise. The ability of German commanders at every level of command to quickly and often seamlessly throw together grenadiers, pioneers, gunners, and tankers to form cohesive and flexible battle groups remained one of the greatest strengths of the wartime German Army.

German dummy tanks in the 1920s. Forbidden tanks by the Treaty of Versailles, the *Reichswehr* had to improvise. They may look comical, but for the purpose of getting troops used to operating with armor they had all the mannerisms of real tanks.

German doctrinal emphasis on mobility, decentralization, speed, surprise, and exploitation ensured that Germany entered World War II with realistic, balanced, and offensively oriented doctrine and forces. The panzer division, for example, was a versatile fighting formation. It comprised motorized infantry regiments, a motorcycle battalion, an artillery regiment, an antitank battalion, a reconnaissance battalion, and an engineer battalion, in addition to its tank regiments.

The extensive use of large-scale exercises helped familiarize units with doctrine. By the end of the 1920s these exercises had become sophisticated and the army's skill on maneuvers unsurpassed, and by the early 1930s it had even begun to devise operational and tactical methods for employing mobile forces. Moreover, in general the Germans took maneuvers more seriously than did other Western armies and intensively studied and acted upon the recommendations that emerged from after-action reports. The result was a rapid restoration of the high standards maintained by the Imperial Army prior to World War I. Through regular maneuvers the interwar German Army progressively improved its organization and proficiency, developed procedures and mechanisms for controlling and employing motorized and mechanized troops, instilled in soldiers the ability to coordinate with other arms of service, and investigated the practical problems of mechanized warfare.

Defensive Doctrine

The German Army also refined defensive doctrine during the 1920s to take account of changed circumstances and capabilities. The Versailles treaty restrictions prevented it from conducting the doctrine of defense in depth that the Imperial Army had devised during the latter stages of World War I. Instead, it developed the doctrine of delaying defense in which outnumbered German forces would conduct a delaying withdrawal, utilizing terrain advantages, speed, and concentration of force to inflict crippling losses on the enemy, while at the same time preserving its own limited strength. Once an enemy had been bled dry and his offensive fought to a standstill as a result of the combination of vigorous defense and the inevitable friction of offensive warfare, German reserves would concentrate to launch a counteroffensive designed to throw back the aggressor. The interwar German Army recognized that to prevail against more powerful opponents via delaying defense, however, required combat arms to coordinate closely to ensure that the sum of their fighting power was greater than that of the individual parts.

The man most responsible for molding the German Army of the 1920s was its commander in chief, Hans von Seeckt (see page 22). Seeckt believed that an offensive-defensive strategy implemented by fast-moving forces could offset numerical and material inferiority. Thus, during 1920–26 he initiated the motorization of the army and sought to encourage the offensive. In stressing maneuver war, Seeckt drew on the extensive mobile operations the German Army had undertaken on the Eastern Front during World War I. He modernized the German cavalry and transformed it into a mobile, offensive, semimotorized, combined-arms force for deep-penetration operations: it became the army's "fire brigade." The mobility and fast-paced offensive orientation that Seeckt instilled in the interwar German Army played an important role in Germany's dramatic victories during 1939–41. As important, in the long term, was the initiation of limited mechanization during 1929–31 by Seeckt's successor, Wilhelm Groener.

Nevertheless, at the coming to power of Hitler's National Socialist Party in Germany in 1933, the German Army (now known as *das Heer*) remained a lightly equipped, horse-drawn, 10-division garrison force incapable of unleashing the devastating aggression it demonstrated just six years later. The fruits of the experimentation and innovation of the 1920s, however, finally bore full fruit in the late 1930s, and eased the burden of the massive, ill-planned expansion and rearmament on which Hitler embarked. For the hard work and preparation of the 1920s had created a cadre of future leaders, which allowed the army to expand into a large, modern, offensive-oriented field force during the late 1930s far more quickly than would have been otherwise possible. Hitler's rise to power thus brought a dramatic acceleration in the pace of both military growth and reform as, during 1933–35, clandestine expansion and broad rearmament began, despite the continuing Versailles restrictions. Hitler covertly expanded the army to 24 divisions and secretly put into production the quality ordnance developed in the 1920s, such as the 75mm Light Infantry Gun 18 (75mm le IG 18).

Hitler and Rearmament

In 1935 Hitler openly abrogated the Versailles treaty, an action that received enormous popular endorsement. The new Führer (Leader) promptly reintroduced conscription, and publicly began simultaneous massive rearmament and expansion. In July 1935, the Reich Defense Law redesignated the German armed forces as the Wehrmacht and formally recognized the existence of an hitherto clandestine air force (the Luftwaffe). That same year Germany put into production its first light tanks (see below) and raised its first three armored (or panzer) divisions. Armed with the fruits of interwar German Army research, design, and technological innovation, the elite German mechanized spearhead possessed a technological edge over its opponents during the early years of World War II. Thus, German medium tanks had crews of five so the men were not overworked (French tanks had one-man turrets), while German designs made better use of armor: providing extra thickness where needed (at the front) and using thinner armor elsewhere. Moreover, the maintenance of secret weapons stockpiles in contravention of the Treaty of Versailles throughout the 1920s allowed the German armed forces to expand at an otherwise impossible pace. The World War I weapons it had secreted away allowed the army to train large annual intakes in the mid-1930s until sufficient new production became available. And given that expansion continued to outstrip production, the new divisions that Germany mobilized for war in September 1939 could only be equipped with these World War I weapons, such as the Kar 98 bolt-action rifle, many of which continued to offer sterling service throughout World War II.

At the same time, Germany's militaristic culture facilitated rapid military expansion, since few Germans opposed the reintroduction of conscription, and political and public sentiment supported rearmament. German business eagerly embraced rearmament, which provided unprecedented employment opportunities to a Depression-ridden economy. New careers in the military – which had always conferred societal respect and status in Germany – and in the defense industries restored individual and national pride as the Nazi regime spent its way back to full employment, offering the people new levels of social mobility in the process.

But rearmament brought problems as well as benefits. The German Army's cohesion and combat effectiveness initially eroded during expansion as formations reorganized, divided, absorbed new recruits, and redivided in turn. In total, the German Army underwent a 20-fold expansion in a mere six years. Such rapid, massive expansion inevitably brought growing pains and teething problems. During 1935–36 the army completed its second stage of expansion to

36 divisions, but growth temporarily eased in 1937 as the army struggled to complete a five-fold expansion in just three years. Rapid and massive growth brought rushed training in the late 1930s that saw an inevitable decline in quality from admittedly high German standards. Such rapid expansion also disrupted logical progression in training and caused enormous difficulties in terms of maintaining the general training of instructors.

Reichswehr cavalry on exercise. The US military attaché in Germany in the 1920s, Colonel A.L. Conger, described the *Reichswehr*'s troops as the "100,000 best soldiers on the continent." The Treaty of Versailles allowed Germany to retain three cavalry divisions, which Seekt then transformed into the army's "fire brigade."

Though Hitler pushed the pace of expansion and rearmament, his long-term strategic goal of *Lebensraum* had little impact on the development of German tactical or operational doctrine. In fact, it was Generals Freiherr Werner von Fritsch, the army commander in chief, Ludwig Beck, the chief of the General Staff (CGS), and Erich von Manstein, the deputy CGS, who were mainly responsible for the development of the army. An important key to the German Army's wartime success was its receptiveness to ideas outside the main rearmament effort as senior commanders gave wide latitude and freedom to innovators to develop novel weapons, tactics, and doctrine. This quality led the army to develop a tank arm, the air force tactical aviation, and the navy a submarine force: these novel arms subsequently proved to be Germany's most effective military instruments. Of course, the largely unlimited funding and full support of the Nazi regime naturally allowed such largesse and latitude to flourish (though it did encourage interservice rivalry).

The most ominous portent of future events was that in the 1930s Germany usurped Great Britain's position as the pioneer in armored warfare. Germany had lagged well behind Great Britain in the development and employment of tanks during World War I, and the Treaty of Versailles had forbidden the interwar

Hans von Seeckt

Infantry General Hans von Seeckt (left) was the commander in chief of the German Army from 1920 to 1926. As such he played a pivotal role in shaping the evolution of the interwar German military. Confronted with the reduction of German military capabilities imposed by the draconian Versailles settlement of 1919, Seeckt utilized his experience of mobile warfare on the Eastern Front during World War I to pursue his belief that an aggressive defense conducted by mobile forces could defeat a numerically and materially superior enemy. It was Seeckt, therefore, who initially pushed motorization in the interwar German Army as he sought to inculcate offensive spirit in German troops. The Treaty of Versailles allowed Germany to retain three cavalry divisions, which the Western powers viewed as an anachronism useful only for internal policing duties. Yet Seeckt modernized the German cavalry, adding motor transport and firepower and transformed it into a mobile, offensive, semimotorized, combined-arms force for deep-penetration operations. Under Seeckt's guidance, the cavalry therefore became the interwar army's "fire brigade," designed to rush from one battlefield crisis to another. The mobility and fast-paced offensive orientation that both Seeckt and – inadvertently – the Versailles settlement instilled in the interwar German Army played an important role in Germany's dramatic Blitzkrieg victories during the early years of World War II.

German Army from retaining, developing, or producing tanks. This did not stop Germany during 1925–28 from secretly building a tiny number of tanks, deceptively titled the Light Tractor and Large Tractor to disguise their military usage. During 1928–32, the Germans covertly tested these seven vehicles in tactical exercises conducted at the Kazan training grounds in the Soviet Union, after the two pariah states of the post-Versailles international system had concluded a military cooperation agreement. That these two politically opposite states should cooperate with each other may seem surprising. However, their respective military doctrines had much in common. The Red Army was the product of a revolutionary process, and under such leaders as M.V. Frunze and Mikhail Tuchachevski the revolutionary spirit was translated into military doctrine. They drew on the mobile warfare that had characterized the Russian Civil War, and so advocated a highly mobile army, in Frunze's words "impregnated in the spirit of bold and energetically conducted offensive operation." These words could also have been spoken by Seeckt and Guderian.

In addition, the interwar German Army examined, absorbed, and refined British ideas on armored warfare, blending them with traditional Prussian military concepts (see Chapter 2) to develop its own embryonic armored doctrine between the wars. The Nazi rise to power energized mechanization, as many leading Nazis favored motorization. In October 1934 a Mobile Troops command and Germany's first independent mechanized formations emerged, based around the army's motor transport troops and its semimotorized cavalry arm. In 1935, the establishment of Germany's first three panzer divisions followed. One contributor to this process of armored development was Heinz Guderian (see page 29), who in 1937 published

Achtung! Panzer!, a polemic that promoted the use of the German armored arm as an instrument of strategic penetration. Hastily written, the book synthesized the contemporary ideas of Europe's leading mechanized warfare proponents.

This development was more a natural evolution of German strategic, operational, and tactical thought than revolutionary change, however. For the panzer division concept was a logical outcome of the trends of mobility, offensive-mindedness, and deep-penetration deeply rooted in pre-existing German doctrine and operational art. The combined-arms panzer division was a logical progression from the storm troop units and tactics evolved during the latter stages of World War I. Such novel forces could be relatively easily adapted to prevailing German strategic tenets of deep-penetration, encirclement, and annihilation to forge the Blitzkrieg strategy that transformed the European balance of power in the first three years of World War II. This reality helps explain why Germany more easily and effectively absorbed armored ideas between the wars than did Great Britain.

From their genesis the panzer divisions were combined-arms, rather than simply tank, formations that trained to cooperate together. In August 1935, the German Army conducted its first large-scale tank maneuvers; it also closely scrutinized British evaluation of their Experimental Mechanized Force (EMF) of 1928 and learned more from its exercises on Salisbury Plain than the British did. Though its panzer formations were modeled on the British EMF, the German Army gradually came to recognize, through regular exercises, the strategic – rather than tactical – potential of its mechanized forces.

After 1936 the expansion of the panzer arm lost some momentum as it both generated opposition and invited grasping hands. Such resistance, however, focused on the viability of deep-penetration operations, rather than on the value of the tank *per se*, on which there was a consensus. In fact, it was the broad acceptance of the utility of the tank throughout the army that led Germany to raise two panzer brigades in the late 1930s for infantry support, four light divisions to replace the cavalry for reconnaissance and raiding operations, and four motorized infantry divisions to hold captured ground. Recognizing the strategic potential of mechanized warfare, the German Army consolidated these formations into three motorized corps in January 1938.

Historians have argued that the early wartime success of German armored forces was due in part to German refusal to build this new arm around the cavalry, as occurred in the British Army. However, historians have underemphasized the importance of the German cavalry in the creation of the panzer arm. Not only was the German Army's first mechanized division built around the cavalry, but the latter provided most of the personnel for Germany's first armored divisions. The key difference was that the interwar German Army trained its cavalry during the 1920s as a combined-arms, deep-penetration force. Thus the incorporation of German cavalry into the armored force proved far less detrimental to its future than was the case in the more conservative British Army, for example.

German Armor

In 1933–35, Germany produced its first two tanks: the Panzer I and Panzer II. These were light, mass-produced training vehicles intended to be quickly superseded by larger and more effective battle tanks. A 5.3-ton (5.4-tonne) vehicle operated by a two-man crew, the Panzer I possessed 0.2–0.5-in. (6–13-mm) thick armor, and mounted two 7.92mm MG 13 machine guns. The tank was powered by a 57-bhp Krupp M305 B4-cylinder gasoline engine that permitted a

maximum road speed of 23 mph (38 km/h). The Panzer II weighed 8.8 tons (8.9 tonnes), possessed 0.6-in. (14.5-mm) thick armor, and mounted the 20mm KwK 30 L/55 gun. These early German tanks, however, not only remained excessively light, undergunned, and poorly armored, but also mounted inadequate optics. Every combat tank, however, did possess communication receivers, although these remained rudimentary, while command tanks mounted powerful radio transmitters. The ability of the panzers to communicate on the battlefield – unlike many tanks fielded by Germany's future enemies, especially France – clearly augmented the offensive combat power possessed by the German Army's spearhead panzer divisions.

Equipment shortages, inexperience, and rapid expansion all inevitably hindered the development of German armor in the 1930s, however, so that it was not until 1938 that the first medium tanks – the Panzer III and Panzer IV – entered service; even then lack of manufacturing expertise meant that production remained slow. The German tank force at the start of World War II was therefore not a well-balanced, formidable force. These deficiencies were only partly ameliorated when, in March 1939, the German Army acquired both of the Czech Army's main tank models – redesignated the Panzer 35(t) and 38(t) in German service – after the German occupation of the rump Czech state. The more numerous Panzer 38(t) weighed 14.7 tons (15 tonnes), possessed 1.4-in. (35-mm) thick welded armor and mounted the 37mm KwK L/45 gun. What is worth emphasizing, however, is relative capabilities: while the German panzer force of 1939 remained deficient, the weaknesses that dogged the armored forces of Germany's opponents were even greater.

The stunning German ground victories of 1939–41 notwithstanding, German rearmament in the late 1930s was neither easy nor particularly effective.

Adolf Hitler (giving raised arm salute in leading car), Nazi Party leader and chancellor of Germany. De facto dictator of the country, he speeded up rearmament and reintroduced universal conscription in 1935. He recognized the propaganda value of the tank. In 1935, during a visit to the Kummersdorf army ordnance testing ground to review his panzers, he stated: "That's what I need. That's what I want to have." The fact that Hitler regarded Guderian, the general of panzer troops, as reliable facilitated the growth of the panzer arm.

It was hurried and poorly planned, and the regime failed to gear rearmament toward a strategic blueprint. Rather, Germany pursued rearmament in breadth not depth. Each service pursued independent, uncoordinated, and virtually unlimited rearmament. Such a policy inextricably bound the German military to the National Socialist regime, but did so at a heavy price. Broad rearmament coupled with the construction of the West Wall (Siegfried Line) fortifications – a defensive line that extended from the Netherlands to Switzerland; it consisted of hundreds of pillboxes with interlocking fields of fire, supported by an extensive system of command posts, observation posts, and troop shelters, and its man-made obstacles, such as the antitank "Dragon's Teeth," were integrated with the terrain – almost bankrupted Germany during 1938–39. It was only the annexation of Austria and Czechoslovakia that prevented German financial and economic collapse. Moreover, several inescapable strategic limitations constrained German rearmament, most significantly Germany's dependency on raw material imports, especially petroleum products and heavy metals, as well as its shortage of foreign exchange capital.

Interservice Squabbles

Within these constraints, however, Germany prepared for war to the maximum extent possible. Unconstrained rearmament promoted considerable innovation – thus the army pursued its panzer force, the air force the Stuka dive-bomber, and the navy a submarine force – alongside the more conventional ground forces, air assets, and surface fleet. Yet it also simultaneously removed central direction from rearmament, which encouraged interservice rivalry to flourish. Bitter squabbles, for example, emerged between the army and the air force over control of the fledgling paratrooper arm and of antiaircraft artillery. Equally, the army and the navy bickered over coastal artillery and coastal defense. The character of the National Socialist regime with its numerous competing authorities (which was encouraged by Hitler as part of his social Darwinist "survival of the fittest" beliefs) merely fueled the interservice rivalry inherent in all military organizations. Broad, virtually unlimited rearmament may have reduced rivalries, but it could not eradicate them entirely as, for instance, the infantry, artillery, and cavalry all clamored for their own tanks in the late 1930s. An inability to resolve these squabbles eventually led to considerable duplication of effort both in terms of force structure and weapons development. Thus while the air force maintained control of paratroopers and antiaircraft artillery, the army responded by creating its own force of glider-borne infantry and light army antiaircraft artillery units. When the artillery was denied armor, it pursued its own independent program to develop a fully-tracked "assault gun" vehicle equipped with a low-velocity, high-caliber weapon for infantry support. The culmination of this process was the StuG III (see page 103).

Ironically, massive unplanned rearmament gave the West a false impression of German strength that contributed to appeasement and the Munich Agreement (an agreement signed in September 1938 between Germany, Italy, Great Britain, and France that ceded the German-speaking Sudetenland of Czechoslovakia to Germany). In fact, the Allies consistently underrated German military capabilities in the early 1930s, but conversely came to overestimate them during the period of open rearmament and expansion after 1936. Moreover, the Nazis manipulated propaganda effectively to inflate Western perceptions of German military strength, which helped to instill political uncertainty among Germany's potential rivals. In reality, German rearmament was window dressing: raw material and foreign exchange limitations placed a ceiling on rearmament.

Expansion, therefore, consistently outstripped both production and training facilities. Even in the spring of 1939, for example, the army remained seriously deficient in weapons, especially mortars and heavy artillery, and only had an estimated 15-day stockpile of munitions. Underlying this, massive rearmament increased Germany's dependency on raw material imports, which left her severely short of petroleum reserves.

While Germany's ambitious and expansionist foreign policy goals created a fertile environment for military innovation, both policy and geography directed innovation toward offensive ground warfare to prevent a repetition of Germany's defeat during World War I. Thus the army widely adopted radio to allow rapid and effective communications among its fast-moving offensive army. Indeed, Germany developed the best radios in the world between the wars, but she failed to capitalize on the potential of radar because its value was seen as largely defensive to an offensive-oriented military.

Military Exercises

Hitler thus expanded the German Army at a tremendous pace, but forced expansion fragmented and rushed training and reduced its quality. Massive expansion of combat units also unbalanced the army's force structure, restricted its operational flexibility, and left it extremely short of nondivisional army troops and support services. That said, the German military's tradition of open, honest, and critical self-examination limited the detrimental effects of excessive expansion. Even in the middle of massive growth and restructuring after 1935, the German Army continued regular and extensive exercising. The July 1935 exercises saw the first maneuvers by an entire mechanized division and demonstrated the potential of armored warfare.

In September 1936 the largest German maneuvers since 1913 took place, and in the following year an even larger exercise occurred. These maneuvers revealed many flaws in German preparation and led to a reversion to basic training. The Czech crisis led to a scaling back of the 1938 maneuvers, though troops exercised intensively in preparation for war with Czechoslovakia. Moreover, the German Army evaluated in detail its combat readiness and mission potential, and gathered extensive intelligence on likely future enemies. German military attaches and observers closely monitored the exercises and maneuvers conducted by foreign armies and presented reports on these experiences, while German officers posing as "tourists" also gathered information on foreign military activities. In addition, German staff officers systematically scrutinized foreign newspapers and military journals to digest the most recent views on tactics and equipment. Hard work and sensible application characterized German military preparation throughout the interwar period, and such professionalism helped to minimize the deleterious effects of forced expansion.

Such efforts notwithstanding, the German Army underwent considerable prewar growing pains. It experienced a severe and insurmountable officer shortage which reinforced the army's traditional reliance on its noncommissioned officers (NCOs). Yet the shortage of NCOs in the late 1930s was even more acute. The German Army thus went to war in September 1939 under-officered, a situation that steadily worsened throughout the war as losses mounted. Moreover, rushed training and its offensive orientation left troops inexpert at defense, while a constant turnover in personnel delayed the acquisition of combat readiness and eroded cohesion.

That the German military of 1939 had gained some recent operational experience helped partially to offset these deficiencies. This combat experience derived from the participation of the German Condor Legion during the Spanish Civil War of 1936–39. The German armed forces learned important lessons from this conflict. In Spain, the Luftwaffe conducted the first large-scale strategic airlift in history, pioneered carpet bombing when Heinkel He 111 medium bombers demolished Guernica, first used the Junkers Ju 87 Stuka dive-bomber in a tactical ground-support role, and developed an embryonic command and control system for air-to-ground attack. The ground fighting also provided important lessons, including the notable antitank capabilities – high velocity, long range, great accuracy, and rapid rate of fire – of the German heavy 88mm Antiaircraft Gun 18 (88mm Flak 18), as well as both the potential and limitations of Germany's first generation of tanks.

Germany's peaceful annexations of Austria and the Sudetenland in March and October 1938 respectively, plus that of the rump Czech state in March 1939, gave the German armed forces additional operational experience. These campaigns were highly instructive dress rehearsals that identified numerous and glaring deficiencies in German equipment, training, and organization. These annexations witnessed progressive improvement in German mobilization that followed a disastrously muddled and chaotic mobilization for the peaceful re-occupation of Austria in March 1938. Considerable confusion accompanied mobilization for the annexation of Austria and German forces straggled into Vienna strung out and in some disorder, despite the fact that they had conducted

German troops march into the previously demilitarized Rhineland in 1936. The operation involved only 20,000 troops and a contingent of local policemen. In a plebiscite held on March 29, 1936, 98.8 percent of the German population voted in favor of Hitler's action.

an unopposed march. After-action reports were highly critical of doctrine, troop performance, training, and discipline. Undertrained reserve and auxiliary forces mobilized in disorder, march discipline remained poor, and the German advance into Austria fell well behind schedule. Moreover, SS paramilitaries, armed police, and air force units that had not conducted joint exercises with the army caused major disorder. Post-campaign analysis revealed that the most serious operational limitation was not non-army units but inadequate fuel provision for the mechanizing German Army. So short of gasoline were German forces that they were repeatedly compelled to stop off and fill up their vehicles from Austrian gas stations en route to Vienna!

Due to the intensive German preparations for war with Czechoslovakia and the absorption of lessons learned from the Austrian debacle, the October 1938 annexation of the Sudetenland went more smoothly. Nevertheless, continued serious deficiencies hampered operations and required intensive training to correct in the months thereafter. The fruits of German labor were revealed during the March 1939 occupation of the rump Czech state. This operation witnessed further improvement in German mobilization as reforms and reorganizations introduced in response to previous failures finally paid off. In particular, these operations provided Germany with its first practical experience with armored forces off the training grounds, and they ironed out many kinks in German organization, preparation, and mobilization.

German Infantry

Despite the historical focus on the development of the panzer arm in the 1930s, most of the German Army remained infantry. An integral, but often underrated, element of the German Blitzkrieg success was the skill, quality, and aggressiveness of German infantry in the early war years, which will become apparent in subsequent chapters. Though often depicted as a conservative opponent of armor, the chief of the General Staff, General Ludwig Beck, rather than opposing the development of armor, favored the creation of a well-balanced fighting force. He therefore pushed the parallel enhancement of the German infantry arm in the 1930s. This investment contributed both to the German triumphs of the early war years and to the prolonged defense the German Army offered in the last two years of the war. Examination of the lessons of World War I during the interwar period revealed that the German infantry arm had collapsed during late 1918 under the strain of four years of total war.

The interwar army thus embarked on a major rehabilitation of the infantry. These reforms, promoted in particular by Seeckt, imbued the German infantry of the 1930s with the doctrine of mobile offense that Seeckt had himself championed. Senior German commanders overhauled infantry training to build an aggressive infantry arm. Training emphasized individual initiative, the highest caliber squad leaders, and maximum physical fitness (this last quality would enable infantry divisions to march great distances to seal and reduce pockets created by the motorized columns). Rigorous training built obedience and discipline, while preparing squad leaders to be intelligent leaders rather than mindless automatons. Notwithstanding the popular image of German soldiers as unthinkingly obedient, German training taught recruits not simply to embrace the accepted "school" solution, as was often the case with other armies, but to adopt originality. The result was a broadly competent infantry arm capable of thinking and acting independently as part of a fast-paced, combined-arms team.

Heinz Guderian

A cavalry leader turned staff officer in World War I, Heinz Guderian was an ardent anticommunist who in 1919 served with the *Freikorps* in defense of his native East Prussia against the Bolsheviks. When he resisted official recall orders, the German Army High Command transferred him to the 7th Motor Transport Battalion at Munich. Here he met Oswald Lutz, a leading proponent of mechanized warfare. From the mid-1920s Guderian envisioned a future strategic role for Germany's armored forces. Then, in October 1931, Guderian became Lutz's chief of staff, when the latter became Inspector General of Motor Transport Troops and then head of the Motorized Troops Command in 1934, renewing a partnership crucial to the future evolution of the panzer arm. In 1935 Guderian took command of the 2nd Panzer Division, and then in 1937 he published his major work on armored warfare, *Achtung! Panzer!*

After war broke out in September 1939 Guderian daringly led XIX Motorized Corps in the deepest penetration the German Army achieved in Poland. Subsequently, during May 1940, he commanded his XIX Corps in its audacious penetration of the Ardennes and its subsequent breakthrough to the coast that isolated the BEF at Dunkirk and forced its evacuation. Between June and December 1941, Guderian led the Second Panzer Group in Operation Barbarossa as it rampaged through the Soviet Union right up to the gates of Moscow. His inability to halt the enemy during the Soviet winter counterattack, however, led Hitler to dismiss him in late December 1941. It took the dire emergency that followed the annihilation of Colonel-General Paulus's Sixth Army at Stalingrad for Hitler to recall Guderian during the spring of 1943. The Führer gave him unprecedented authority to reorganize and revamp the panzer arm that had been savaged during the bitter Eastern Front battles. Guderian both rationalized and dramatically expanded German armored production to restore some of the panzer arm's lost combat power. He also skillfully maneuvered his way through the July 20, 1944 attempt on Hitler's life, and the inevitable repression that followed. Consequently, Hitler immediately rewarded him with promotion to the office of chief of the General Staff of the German Army. In the last six months of the war, Guderian tried – but usually failed – to mitigate Hitler's increasingly irrational strategic leadership and bizarre attempts to tactically micromanage frontline German units. In the spring of 1945, having quarreled once again with his Führer, Hitler sent Guderian on extended "medical leave," bringing the wartime military career of Germany's leading tank theorist and practitioner to an inglorious end. He died in 1953.

Prewar infantry preparation also gave much attention to effective field camouflage, and throughout World War II no other army came close to challenging the German Army's mastery of this craft. In addition, prewar training also stressed discipline and through harsh exercises conditioned troops to a broad range of likely combat conditions that they might encounter on the field of battle. Training was realistic and not confined to good weather and daylight, and troops trained long and hard to condition themselves to the privations of war. German infantry between the wars also routinely practiced small-unit tactical drills involving combined-arms assault groups (*Stosstruppen*), and flexible, ad hoc groupings that forged a cohesive, disciplined, and flexible infantry arm prepared for fast-paced, combined-arms offensive warfare. German infantry were therefore prepared for the rigors of cooperating and interacting with troops of other arms of service, though inevitably no amount of peacetime preparation could adequately prepare troops for the realities of actual combat.

Recognizing the infantry arm as a battle-winning instrument in its own right, the interwar German Army also improved infantry mobility and firepower. It introduced two revolutionary new weapons – the 75mm Light Infantry Gun 18 (75mm le IG 18) and the versatile 150mm Heavy Infantry Gun 33 (150mm sIG 33) – that combined the firepower of an artillery piece with the mobility of the 77mm field gun of World War I vintage. Horse-drawn and capable of being broken down into half-a-dozen packs for easy transport, these weapons gave the German infantry the kind of mobile firepower that they had often lacked in World War I. The Germans also greatly augmented their use of both the 50mm Light Mortar 36 (50mm le GrW 36) and the 80mm Mortar 34 (80mm GrW 34) during the interwar period. The trench mortar, introduced during World War I, had proved to be one of the most effective and deadly infantry weapons of the conflict, a fact the Germans were among the first to recognize. The German Army also began to motorize the heavy weapons, communications, and headquarters of infantry units to enhance mobility and give them some capability to keep pace with mobile mechanized forces. Thus the German infantry that went to war in 1939 was better equipped and trained than its counterparts. Most importantly, it was better prepared than its opponents both for fast-paced offensive operations and for cooperation with other arms of service.

German Artillery

The German artillery arm of the 1930s, however, remained less progressive than the panzer or infantry branches. The Treaty of Versailles severely reduced the German artillery arsenal and banned mobile heavy artillery. As a result, the artillery arm struggled to meet the explosive growth of the army during the 1930s. It was slow to motorize and lacked heavy artillery – a term that generally

Ju 87 Stuka dive-bombers in Spain during the civil war. "Stuka" was derived from *Sturzkampfflugzeug*, meaning dive-bomber. The Ju 87 was useful because bombs dropped from aircraft diving upon their target have greater accuracy than bombs dropped from aircraft flying straight and level. Sirens were fitted to each Stuka to produce a terrifying, high-pitched scream, thus adding to the psychological effect of the attack.

applied to weapons of 160mm caliber and above, although the Germans rather inconsistently designated the 100mm Cannon 18 (s 100mm K 18) as a heavy weapon. Overexpansion meant that even in 1938 army heavy artillery remained both largely horse-drawn and in short supply. Nonetheless, in the early 1930s the German Army raised experimental motorized and chemical mortar batteries. Moreover, the mobile 105mm Light Field Howitzer 18 (105mm le FH 18) standardized in the 1930s proved well-suited to fast, mobile operations.

The German Army's strategic emphasis on fast-paced warfare, though, militated against the establishment of a centralized artillery arm. In fact, the structure and organization of German artillery reflected continued doubt that massed artillery fire could make a decisive contribution to offensive victory on the modern battlefield (the lessons of World War I, when bombardments that had lasted for days ultimately proved largely futile, except in turning the ground into a lunarlike landscape of earth craters that hindered the attacking infantry but aided enemy machine gunners who could mow down the slow-moving infantry with ease, had been very much taken to heart). Instead, the German Army envisaged the decentralized forward employment of artillery at the battalion and regimental level to disrupt and to harry – rather than smash – an enemy already outmaneuvered and unbalanced by fast-paced, deep-penetration ground attacks.

The sustained research and development of the 1920s by the German Army ensured that a variety of high-quality artillery pieces entered service in numbers during the late 1930s to equip units. These included the so-called Heavy 100mm Cannon 18 (s 100mm K 18) that possessed a very long range and proved an extremely effective counterbattery and interdiction weapon. In addition, the German Army received delivery of the modern and lightweight 75mm Mountain Gun 36 (75mm GebG 36), and developed prototypes of the 105mm Mountain Howitzer 40 (105mm GebH 40), some of the first purpose-built alpine artillery constructed in Europe since World War I.

Air Support

The lessons of World War I led the Luftwaffe to devote greater resources to creating an air superiority fighter force; and Germany's geostrategic position compelled the German armed forces to approach air-to-ground cooperation with greater openness and less interservice rancor than other militaries during the interwar period. The Germans had also gained some, albeit limited, experience of the problems inherent in air-to-ground communication in the Spanish Civil War. German aerial doctrine thus advocated a more integrated approach to war and recognized the need for air power to assist the land battle. In effect, the Luftwaffe became an arm to assist ground units, and though it did possess bombers, the strategic bomber concept never got off the drawing board. During the campaign in the Soviet Union this would have grave consequences, as the Luftwaffe was unable to strike at Soviet industry located beyond the Urals.

The Spanish Civil War gave the Luftwaffe practical experience of the problems of air-to-ground coordination, from which it drew important lessons. The static warfare that dominated the civil war – due to well-matched and rather amateur ground forces – led the Condor Legion to develop a primitive close support capability. While demonstrating the accuracy of the Stuka dive-bomber as a precision bombing platform, however, the Luftwaffe gained no experience in Spain of the provision of close support to fast-moving mechanized forces conducting deep-penetration operations. Thus, in September 1939 the Luftwaffe

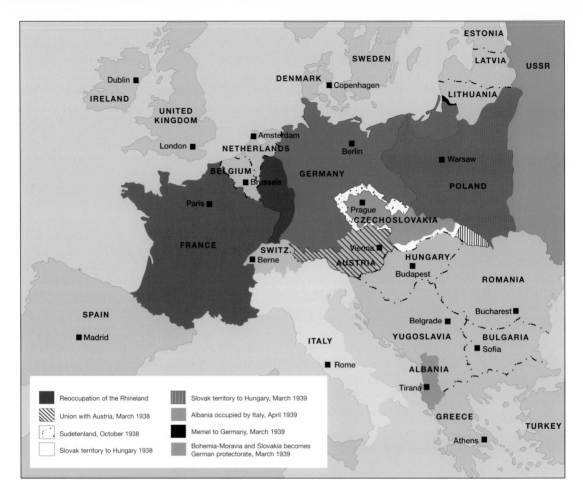

had only a very limited close support capability. For the Polish campaign it allocated to direct support a single wing of obsolete aircraft relegated to this task because they were unsuited for more important missions. Moreover, the Luftwaffe lacked tested procedures for operating in support of armored forces, and structurally the German system of air-to-ground coordination left much to be desired. Thus serious tactical, organizational, equipment, and training deficiencies hampered execution of the air-ground battle. Expansion of the air force and navy also fueled interservice rivalry as these services sought to acquire ground force capabilities.

In September 1939 Hitler mobilized a "window front" army, in which Germany committed all its ground forces to the field. The German order of battle displayed an impressive 103 divisions, but all were under strength and underequipped. Only half the army comprised trained combat troops, while the rest were either reservists or *Landwehr* troops – World War I veterans who had undergone hasty refresher training. German reserves remained almost nonexistent and supply stocks negligible – a mere six weeks of munitions, for example. The munitions situation was not an immediate problem, as Blitzkrieg was designed to defeat an enemy speedily, but if a campaign became prolonged logistical frailties would become critical.

Not only was everything in the shop window, but the army was heavy on "teeth" and short on "tail" as Hitler committed everything in an effort to quickly

Germany's territorial conquests up to the outbreak of World War I in September 1939. As well as the increase in the manpower pool, the seizure of Czechoslovakia gave the German Army vast amounts of excellent munitions, including nearly 400 tanks.

overwhelm Polish resistance. Support services remained inadequate, reflecting traditional German disdain for rear-echelon services and the German orientation toward offensive ground warfare to overwhelm opponents.

The outbreak of war thus found Germany quite unprepared for protracted war, and consequently its armed forces remained weak long-term instruments of aggression since Germany lacked the raw materials and industrial capacity necessary for a lengthy conflict. Only by overwhelming its neighbors one by one before they were prepared could Germany acquire the material, economic, and financial base necessary to launch Hitler's bid for European domination. Moreover, despite its aura of modernity, most of the German Army remained horse-drawn. The strategic weakness of the German petroleum industry, the relatively small number of automobiles in Germany, the limited supply of tanks, and adherence to an as yet unproven armored doctrine; all placed real constraints on the extent of mechanization. The limited size of the German armored force in September 1939 therefore reflected genuine strategic constraints far more than it did any significant conservative opposition to change.

Nonetheless, Germany had started rearmament several years before her neighbors, and while the German armed forces suffered from many deficiencies, relatively, it remained far better prepared than its rivals. In September 1939 Hitler thus gambled that this imperfect instrument could quickly overwhelm Germany's ill-prepared neighbors before they could mobilize their resources, rearm, and eliminate the German lead. The result – which materialized as much by default as by rational planning – was the Blitzkrieg strategy of the early war years that transformed the global balance of power.

A Receptive Environment

Germany's strategic and political environment therefore created a climate conducive to military expansion and innovation between the wars. A combination of personalities, experiences, and the character of German military culture made the interwar German military receptive to new ideas. The root of the brilliant German successes of 1939–41, therefore, lay in the bitter experience of defeat in 1918 and in the army's determination to learn the operational and tactical lessons of World War I. The interwar German military explored and disseminated these lessons diligently, flexibly, and with receptivity to new ideas. Moreover, its awareness as to who Germany's future enemies were and where they would be fought both eased the task of innovation and focused it toward offensive ground warfare: the result was the Blitzkrieg.

The theory of Blitzkrieg warfare presented less of a challenge to the German military because it believed that Germany had fought World War I with sound operational and strategic principles. Consequently, the new German armored forces offered a solution to the problems of implementing effectively what was firmly believed to be a solid doctrinal basis; it had been these difficulties of execution, rather than intrinsically flawed doctrine, that had led to Germany's defeat in 1918. Intellectual and doctrinal accommodation of the tank was thus somewhat easier in Germany than it was in interwar Great Britain. This reality explains why by 1939, despite opposition in both countries, armored warfare had become a firm tenet of German military doctrine but had failed to become similarly established in Britain. Accommodation of armor within a realistic combined-arms doctrine allowed Germany to succeed during 1939–41 despite the fact she devoted no more resources to mechanized forces than did her European enemies.

Blitzkrieg: Myth and Reality

The Blitzkrieg stunned the world when it was first unleashed in September 1939. The speed and shock of mechanized units and air power were its attributes, but its doctrinal elements were firmly rooted in the tactics used by the armies of Prussia and Imperial Germany.

The Blitzkrieg in action – German troops march past a burning American halftrack during the Wehrmacht offensive in the Ardennes in December 1944. Secret concentration, surprise, and poor visibility over the area of operations allowed the Germans to make gains during the first few days of the offensive.

The term Blitzkrieg (meaning "Lightning War") is invariably linked with the German Army in World War II. It is an emotive term, recalling as it does in the layman's imagination massed armored formations smashing through enemy defenses to spread panic and destruction in rear areas, while overhead hundreds of Junkers Ju 87 Stuka dive-bombers strafe enemy columns and refugees. Laying aside the fact that massed tanks cannot break through fixed defenses without massive losses – the experience of the Fourth Panzer Army at the Battle of Kursk in July 1943 being a case in point – the German Army in the 1930s did not develop a new war-winning strategy; rather, it developed already existing doctrines to assimilate the use of armored fighting vehicles (AFVs). The historian Matthew Cooper puts it succinctly: "German military manuals both before and during the war may be scoured in vain for any mention of it [Blitzkrieg], and it is seldom found in even the post-war memoirs of the generals who were supposed to have evolved and practised its methods." Heinz Guderian stated: "As a result of the successes of our rapid campaigns ... our enemies coined the word Blitzkrieg." Hitler himself said "the expression is an Italian invention; we picked it up from the newspapers."

The aim of this chapter is to examine the military doctrine of the German Army of Nazi Germany to separate the myths from the realities regarding what is called Blitzkrieg warfare. However attractive it may be to historians and laymen to portray the German Army of World War II practicing revolutionary tactics, the reality is that the army was the heir to a long and proud military tradition, and that the tactics it employed between 1939 and 1945 were the product of an evolutionary process. A comparison between the doctrine of the Blitzkrieg and the warfare waged by previous Prussian and German armies will illustrate the point. First, however, we need to answer the question: what is Blitzkrieg? Put simply, it is a method of warfare that aims to win a campaign by decisive offensive action rather than by attrition. By employing a combination of fire and movement, friendly forces first encircle and then destroy enemy formations. To do this requires massing a superiority in both numbers and firepower at a specific point of the front to effect a breakthrough. This location is the point of main effort – the *Schwerpunkt*. Once the offensive is launched, the emphasis is on speed, boldness, and firepower both to maintain the momentum of the advance and keep the enemy off-balance. Breakthroughs are reinforced by follow-on reserves, while a well-prepared logistical system ensures a steady supply of ammunition, fuel, and food to keep the spearheads moving. Beyond the spearheads, Luftwaffe bombers and dive-bombers pound enemy reserves, communications, and headquarters to paralyze the enemy's "brain" – his High Command. Every effort is made to encircle enemy troop formations, not drive them back. This allows follow-on infantry divisions to encircle and then destroy these pockets of resistance.

Concentration and Maneuver

A casual glance at German history reveals that her generals have always employed maneuver to surprise and defeat enemies. Germany's geographical position in many ways dictated such a doctrine. Located in central Europe, she has always been faced by potential enemies in both east and west. As such, her forces have always been potentially numerically outnumbered. Her generals have thus had to search for ways to deploy their military resources to maximize their often quantitatively inferior forces against opponents. At the Battle of Leuthen in December 1757, for example, Frederick the Great marched his army toward the Austrian right flank, then changed direction obliquely to the right and marched behind a range of low hills to deliver a devastating attack against the Austrian left flank. The result was a spectacular Prussian victory that Napoleon described as a "masterpiece of maneuver and resolution." Over 100 years later, Field Marshal Helmuth von Moltke, commander of Prussia's armies, was using rapid mobilization of reserves, surprise concentration of overwhelming strength by utilizing convergent lines of march, and the tactical use of railways for movement and supply to give the Prussian Army a series of stunning victories over the Danes, Austrians, and French. During the 1870 war with France, for example, Moltke gathered 475,000 men in four armies, executed a gigantic turning movement to sweep behind the French, and drove them against the Belgian frontier. The offensive was so successful that Prussia was able to separate the French armies and defeat them in turn, at Metz and Sedan, thus ensuring French defeat.

Maneuver and boldness, two essential ingredients of the Blitzkrieg, can also be found in the strategy of Alfred Graf von Schlieffen, chief of the General Staff, who devised a strategy for a simultaneous war with France and Russia. His plan was based on an extreme but calculated risk: estimating that Russia would take up to six weeks longer than either France or Germany to mobilize for war, he left one army in the East, and a further three to cover the Franco-German border, while the remaining and strongest four would be used to envelop the left flank of the French Army by a massive wheeling movement through Belgium. The armies would engage and defeat the French within the six-week breathing space, and then he would be able to transfer his victorious armies eastward to meet and defeat the Russians. This was the plan that was put into operation in August 1914, and

The triumph of maneuver over attrition: motorized elements of the 4th Panzer Division in open country in France on May 17, 1940. Having broken through the Allied front in the Ardennes, the panzer divisions were free to strike for the English Channel to cut off Allied armies in Holland and Belgium from the rest of France. The confusion and panic this caused among both military and civilian Allied personnel acted as a force multiplier for the Blitzkrieg advance.

which nearly worked, though its failure condemned Germany to an attritional two-front war – the very thing Schlieffen had spent his life trying to avoid.

The trench deadlock of World War I was a nightmare scenario for the German Army. Against more numerical opponents (especially following the entry of the United States into the war in 1917), Germany could not hope to win a war of attrition, the more so since the Royal Navy's blockade of Germany deprived her of valuable food and raw materials from overseas. The Germans, like the British and French, attempted deep and massive penetrations to break the deadlock in northern France; they were nearly always disastrous and costly in terms of manpower. Both sides looked at ways to solve the problem. For the Allies the answer seemed to have been found in the tank, whose caterpillar tracks allowed it to cross barbed wire, shell-blasted terrain, and trenches. The German General Staff, first under General Erich von Falkenhayn, and then under Paul von Hindenburg and Erich von Ludendorff, sought a tactical answer.

The size of a German division was reduced from four regiments to three, while drills were developed around small, more mobile units, i.e. battle groups

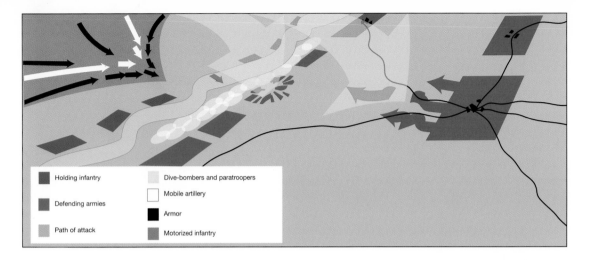

within each company. The units would employ surprise in the attack: secret troop concentrations (made at night and at the last moment) and short, intense, and accurate artillery bombardments would precede the attack. The tactical unit was the squad of between 14 and 18 men, and each squad would have its own fire base – a light machine gun and mortar. Specially trained assault infantry – storm troops – would advance and probe the enemy for weak spots. Strongpoints would be bypassed at all costs; the overriding principle was to maintain the momentum of the attack. Behind the assault units, reserves would be committed to the point of greatest progress to reinforce the breakthrough, while other reserves would reduce surrounded pockets of enemy resistance. Meanwhile, regiments and divisions would enlarge the penetration by attacking into and behind the newly created enemy flanks on either side of the breakthrough. Artillery would move forward behind the infantry to maintain a constant rolling barrage, while aircraft would strafe and bomb enemy pockets and reserves. That was the theory, but would the tactics work on the battlefield?

The Blitzkrieg Phase One: holding infantry engage defenders' attention along the front. As dive-bombers attack reserves and frontline artillery, armored spearheads, with sappers, cross the river.

Phase Two: assault troops and demolition squads knock out enemy strongpoints and widen the bridgehead. Armor passes through them and advances into the enemy rear, followed by motorized infantry and artillery. Dive-bombers clear a path ahead.

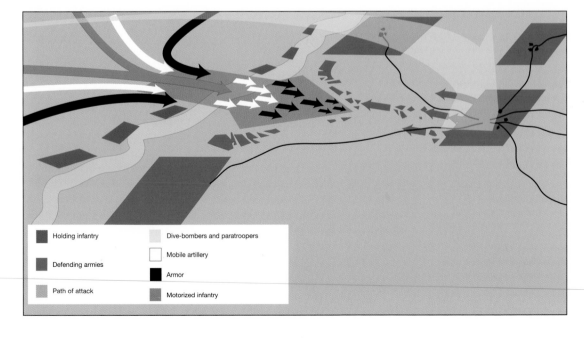

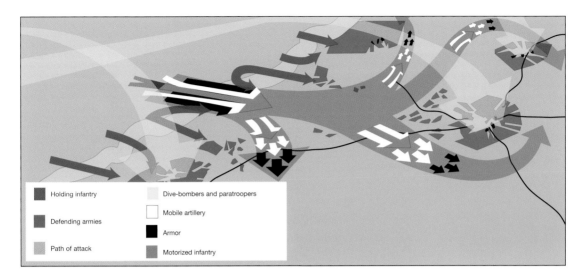

Holding infantry

Defending armies

Path of attack

Dive-bombers and paratroopers

Mobile artillery

Armor

Motorized infantry

Phase Three: armored spearheads fan out and bypass enemy strongpoints. Panzers sweep around key road and rail junctions, paralyzing enemy supply, reserve, and command elements.

Phase Four: Geran spearheads drive deep into enemy territory as marching infantry moves up to surround and then reduce pockets.

In September 1917, the German Eighth Army, commanded by General Oskar von Hutier, was outside the Russian-held town of Riga, which had been invested for a considerable amount of time and had resisted all attempts to take it. Using the new tactics, Hutier attacked the town on September 1. Following a short but intense bombardment, his infiltration units went forward. Riga fell two days later – "Hutier Tactics" were born. However, as the military historian Trevor Dupuy has noted: "There was no dramatic innovation in the new tactics. All the commanders since 1914 had been trying to apply the principles of war under modern conditions to achieve surprise, to make a breakthrough, and then to exploit it. What the Germans did was to devise systematic and practical ways in which these things could be done under the new circumstances of combat, and to provide detailed procedures for training and supporting the men who were to do the job."

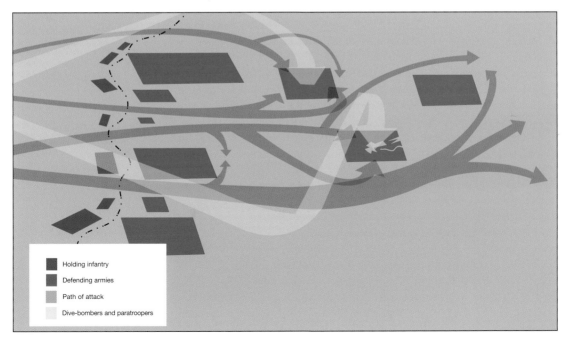

Holding infantry

Defending armies

Path of attack

Dive-bombers and paratroopers

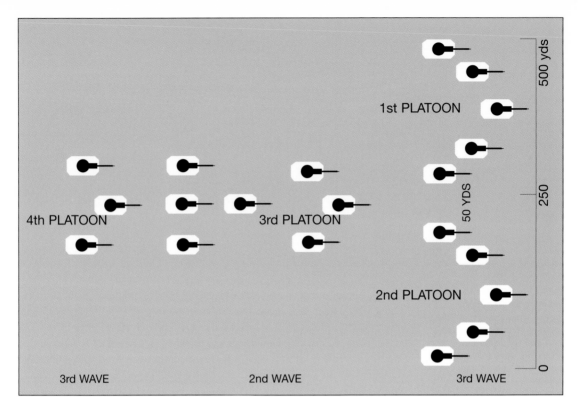

1st PLATOON

4th PLATOON

3rd PLATOON

2nd PLATOON

500 yds

250

0

50 YDS

3rd WAVE   2nd WAVE   3rd WAVE

The new tactics were tried on a larger scale in Flanders in 1918, when Ludendorff launched Operation Michael. Beginning on March 21, his storm troops went forward and began to achieve spectacular results. Bypassing strongpoints, they smashed through weak resistance. The front of the British Fifth Army was ripped apart. However, the Germans soon discovered that tactical success could not be turned into strategic victory. The army was unable to keep supporting artillery reinforcements and supplies immediately behind the advancing storm troops. This, combined with tenacious Allied defense, especially from the relatively fresh Americans, blunted the offensives. The five German offensives inflicted massive losses on the British and French, but by the end Ludendorff had lost most of his storm troops. The army's morale was weakened by the loss of its best troops, which made it easier for the Allies when their own counteroffensive came on August 8, 1918. Germany was de facto defeated.

In defeat the much-reduced army of the Weimar Republic continued to analyze the lessons of World War I, the results of which would be to lay the foundations for the success of the Blitzkrieg in the 1940s. Under commander in chief General Hans von Seeckt, no fewer than 57 committees were established to examine the lessons of World War I. The lessons were taken to heart, and under leaders such as Seeckt, Chief of the General Staff Ludwig Beck, and Chief of the Army Command General Werner von Fritsch, German military doctrine became based on flexibility, initiative at all levels, exploitation, and aggressive leadership. Adolf Hitler may have instituted a massive rearmament program, but he did not interfere with strategy or tactics. The new field service regulations issued in 1933, the year the Nazis came to power, entitled *Truppenführung* (*Troop Leadership*), contained many old regulations that laid stress on simplicity of orders, the need for combined-arms warfare in both attack and defense, and the pivotal role of

Diagrammatic representation of a panzer company in a "blunt wedge" formation. The primary mission of the panzers was to break through and attack the enemy's artillery and antitank guns, as opposed to his tanks.

leadership. Combined arms were essential to success: "Attack aviation supports the tanks by attacking hostile defense weapons, artillery, and reserves. Planes flying deep into hostile territory can maintain communications between the troop commander and the tanks and can warn of hostile tank attacks." In addition, tanks were to be used in conjunction with motorized infantry, antitank guns, and artillery, never alone. These were the hallmarks of the Blitzkrieg, but they had not been devised by the Nazis; rather, they were at the end of an evolutionary process. "By the time Hitler came to power in 1933, the German Army had already laid down the entire theoretical groundwork for Blitzkrieg. It is true that Hitler's declaration of rearmament in 1935 allowed tanks to be produced in the open and panzer divisions to be formed for the first time, but it is equally true that he had absolutely nothing to do with the origin of Blitzkrieg as a military doctrine." (Robert M. Citino, *The Path to Blitzkrieg*).

Bearing the above in mind, the creation of panzer divisions was less revolutionary than some commentators, such as Heinz Guderian, would have us believe. Guderian, the "Father of the panzer divisions," had become the army's leading specialist in armored warfare and had worked clandestinely to develop armored doctrine, organization, and techniques for Germany. In June 1934, a new Motorized Troops Command was created under General Oswald Lutz, with its chief of staff being Guderian. The first three panzer divisions were created on October 15, 1935, with Guderian being given the command of one of these divisions. However, the *Reichswehr* had begun experimenting seriously with armored tactics in 1922–28, and other figures were more prominent than Guderian. First there was Ernst Volckheim, who wrote *German Tanks in the World War* in 1923 and *Tanks in Modern Warfare* a year later. Then there was Guderian's commander, Lutz, who propounded ideas that subsequently became associated with Guderian: concentration of armor, the use of armor in mass, and the importance of surprise. Lutz conducted a series of exercises involving dummy tank battalions at the Jüterbog and Grafenwöhr training grounds in 1931 and

Diagrammatic representation of a panzer battalion in attack formation. The panzers aided each other by fire and movement: medium or heavy tanks (Panzer IIIs and IVs) would take up hull-down firing positions (behind obstacles or rises in the ground) to give covering fire while the faster tanks (Panzer Is and IIs) would advance to the next commanding feature. Then the latter would give covering fire to the former moving forward to their next bound.

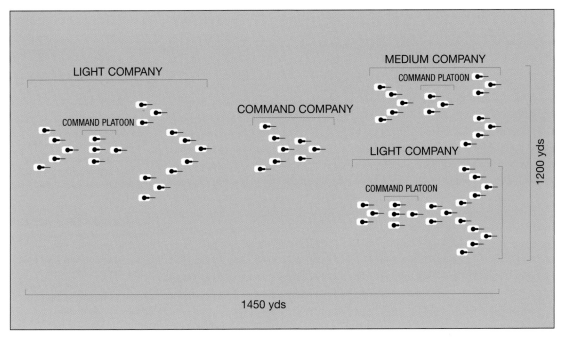

1932, which have been seen as the "true birth of Blitzkrieg" (Citino). But again it was the result of an evolutionary process, rather than a radical break with the past. What was revolutionary was the harnessing of technological developments to existing tactics, which would make the Blitzkrieg all the more irresistible when it was launched.

Every campaign in war is different, presenting as it does a unique set of challenges to those who have to plan and carry it out. During World War II it was the same with the Blitzkrieg. Each of the three great Blitzkrieg campaigns – the invasion of Poland in 1939, the invasion of the West in 1940, and Operation Barbarossa in 1941 – was affected by different considerations regarding geography, logistics, manpower, vehicles, and political motives. Nevertheless, certain common characteristics can be discerned among all three that allow us to construct a model to illustrate the "typical" course of a Blitzkrieg campaign,

Motorized units on the advance in Belgium in May 1940. Halftracks were used to tow artillery, antitank and Flak guns, which could be quickly deployed to erect a Flak screen against enemy aircraft or a "Pak front" against counterattacking enemy armor. In this way the combined-arms panzer division was a potent military formation that could react to rapidly changing tactical conditions.

though the reader should always bear in mind Moltke's words that "No plan survives the first contact with the enemy."

First came the planning phase. The Germans, as aggressors, had many advantages here, as they were allowed to select the point of main effort, the *Schwerpunkt*. Enemy dispositions generally made the process of selecting a breakthrough point relatively easy. In Poland, for example, the High Command placed the bulk of its forces along the German–Polish border in an effort to hold the whole of the country. Similarly, in France and the Low Countries in 1940, Allied planners endeavored to hold the entire line from the English Channel to the Swiss border – in effect, to be strong everywhere. This meant they were weak at the objective points chosen by the Germans, specifically in the Ardennes. They had effectively diluted their combat power before the campaign had started. Prior to Operation Barbarossa, the invasion of the Soviet Union, the Red Army, though it had its forces arrayed in three successive belts along the Soviet border, again made the mistake of concentrating its units too far forward (and the invasion of Poland in 1939 meant many Red Army units were positioned west of Soviet frontier defensive systems when the German attack came). In addition, the Soviet High Command was mistaken in believing that the main Wehrmacht thrust would be made south of the Pripet Marshes. It therefore concentrated its forces in the southwest, which meant it was off-balance when the bulk of the German mechanized forces attacked to the north of the marshes. This is not to say that deficiencies in enemy plans and dispositions were solely responsible for the success of the Blitzkrieg – far from it. In 1940, for example, the Wehrmacht had a superb plan of attack conceived by Erich von Manstein, who was chief of staff to Field Marshal Rundstedt's Army Group A. Hostile to repeating the World War I strategy of a strong right-wing wheeling movement through the Low Countries and into France, Manstein favored transferring the bulk of the armored forces from the north (Army Group B) to the south (Army Group A). These forces would be used to punch through the forested Ardennes region, force a crossing of the Meuse River, and then press on to the coast. This would sever the Allies' lines of communications which stretched back into central France. Although Manstein's plan was rejected several times by the General Staff, it was eventually accepted as a viable strategy.

Reconnaissance and Surprise

Once the plans had been finalized regarding the point, or points, of main effort, next came the reconnaissance phase. This was crucial to the success of the attack, for it provided the High Command with precise information regarding the location and strength of enemy units and defenses. Prior to the invasion of the Soviet Union, for example, the Luftwaffe conducted over 300 reconnaissance flights over Soviet territory. The information was put to good use: within four days of the German invasion the Soviets had lost over 3,000 aircraft to Luftwaffe attacks. Prior to the assault in the West, Brandenburg commandos – specially trained troops who operated behind enemy lines in civilian clothes or uniforms of opponents – made safe demolition charges placed on Luxembourg's bridges that may have held up the advance of Guderian's panzers.

Concealment was another crucial factor during the build-up phase of the Blitzkrieg. However inevitable German offensives may appear with the benefit of hindsight, at the time the High Command was at pains to deceive the enemy as to its intentions until hostilities were under way. For example, prior to Operation Barbarossa, *Oberkommando der Wehrmacht* (OKW), the Armed Forces High

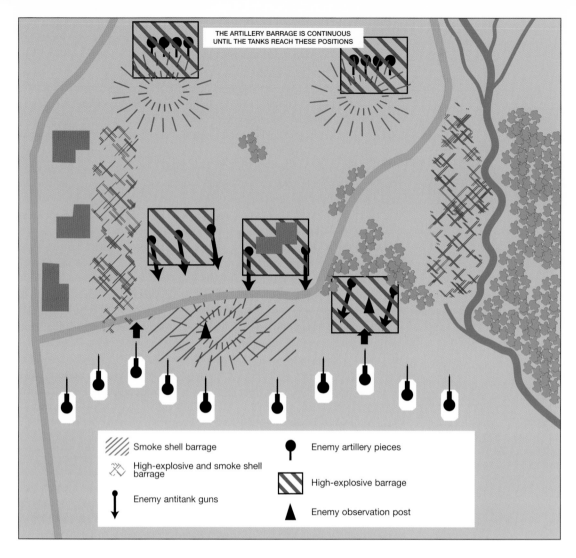

THE ARTILLERY BARRAGE IS CONTINUOUS
UNTIL THE TANKS REACH THESE POSITIONS

//// Smoke shell barrage

⬤ Enemy artillery pieces

High-explosive and smoke shell
barrage

High-explosive barrage

Enemy antitank guns

▲ Enemy observation post

Command, informed Moscow that the build-up of forces in the East was a deception aimed at the British, and that the German Army needed to practice for Operation Sealion (the codename for the invasion of Great Britain) beyond the range of British bombers and reconnaissance aircraft (one wonders what the Soviets thought of the German reconnaissance flights conducted over their territory). In addition, most of the Luftwaffe units assigned to Barbarossa were kept in the West or in Germany until the beginning of June 1941. However, within three weeks the various air fleets moved swiftly into the bases prepared for them, and as soon as they arrived they were moved to their dispersal areas and carefully camouflaged.

Surprise gives an attacker many advantages in war, and thus with the Blitzkrieg the precise time and date of the attack was concealed from the enemy. When it did come, the fear, uncertainty, and chaos that resulted all aided the German advance. Thus, in the West in May 1940 surprise attacks by ground and air units were made against the neutral countries of Holland, Belgium, and Luxembourg. Similarly, against the Soviet Union in June 1941 the German attack was not preceded by a declaration of war, and prior German deception measures

Diagrammatic representation of a panzer attack against enemy artillery and antitank guns. Artillery support was of decisive importance to a successful tank attack. During an assault the missions of the artillery were: counterbattery fire, blinding enemy observation posts, engaging antitank defenses, screening the flanks with smoke, and delaying the movement and deployment of enemy reserves, especially tanks.

meant that enemy units and staffs were like rabbits transfixed in a vehicle's headlights: unsure what to do and vulnerable. This gave the Germans precious time in which the full fury of the Blitzkrieg could be unleashed.

Though the staggering victories of the panzers and infantry divisions on the ground in 1939–41 attest to the brilliance of the Blitzkrieg, it was the Luftwaffe that decided whether the army would be victorious in each campaign – and the first few days decided between success or failure. Total air superiority was critical to German success, and thus the air force committed the majority of its assets to the opening of the campaign. For the invasion of Poland in September 1939 the Luftwaffe committed 70 percent of its bombers, all of its dive-bombers, and 50 percent of its fighters to the attack. The Luftwaffe had two main roles in the Blitzkrieg. First, to destroy the enemy's air force, preferably on the ground before it had a chance to mobilize and get airborne. In Poland this was achieved in two days, for on September 3 the emphasis of air attacks switched to Polish aircraft and munitions industries. The second role, which could be carried out only when air superiority had been established, was close support for ground units. Air support for the army was crucial for a number of reasons: to offset the vulnerability of concentrating units against enemy air attack, to supplement artillery fire (as artillery units would be "leapfrogging" forward during the attack), and to protect the exposed flanks of the advancing columns. During ground-support operations, Luftwaffe aircraft concentrated on interdicting enemy supplies and communications, and hitting masses of enemy reserve troops and retreating units.

Luftwaffe Operations

The effects of fighting against an enemy with air superiority was graphically described by General Kutrzeba, commander of the Polish Poznan Army: "Every movement, every troop concentration, and all march routes were taken under annihilating fire from the air ... it was Hell come to Earth. The bridges were destroyed, the fords were blocked, the antiaircraft and part of the other artillery forces were annihilated. ... Continuation of the battle would have been nothing but a matter of holding out, and to have remained in position would have posed the imminent threat that the German Air Force would have turned the whole place into a graveyard, since antiaircraft defenses in any form were completely lacking."

In France in May 1940 the Luftwaffe's role remained the same, though there was a slight variation in that some German aircraft were used from the beginning to support ground operations, and the large number of bombers needed to strike French ground troops precluded their use for other missions. Once again the effects on the enemy were devastating. Marc Bloch was a French Army officer during the 1940 campaign: "The effect of bombing on the nerves is far-reaching, and can break the potential of resistance over a large area. It was doubtless with that end in view that the enemy High Command sent wave after wave of bombers to attack us. The result came up only too well to their expectations."

To the use of bombing and strafing must be added the employment of airborne forces. Used during the 1940 campaign in Norway and the West, paratroopers and air-landing forces had a powerful physical and psychological effect on the enemy out of all proportion to the numbers actually used. The glider-borne attack on and capture of the Belgian fort of Eben-Emael, reputed to be the strongest in the world, was a massive blow to the Belgium morale. Similarly, the use of paratroopers against airfields and bridges in Holland spread both panic and confusion, and diverted Dutch military assets to searching for imaginary German airborne forces numbering thousands of men instead of concentrating them at the front.

On the ground, once the Luftwaffe had begun its operations, the army would launch its attack at the *Schwerpunkt*. Following a brief but intense artillery bombardment, the attack was launched. Since it was essential to effect a breakthrough, commanders would deploy a large amount of resources to ensuring success. During the crossing of the Meuse at Sedan in May 1940, the Luftwaffe committed 12 squadrons of Stukas to support the river crossing made by infantry of the panzer divisions in rubber boats. The attack was made at 0400 hours and was completely successful. The Germans established a bridgehead on the western bank of the Meuse through which the panzers poured. True to Blitzkrieg doctrine, follow-on forces advanced to gain ground for the achievement of a breakthrough. General Gamelin, commander of French land forces, stated: "It was a remarkable maneuver. But had it been entirely foreseen in advance? I do not believe so – any more than that Napoleon had foreseen the maneuver of Jena, or Moltke that of Sedan [in 1870]. It was a perfect utilization of circumstances. It showed troops and a command who knew how to maneuver, who were organized to operate quickly – as tanks, aircraft, and wireless permitted them to do. It is perhaps the first time that a battle has been won, which became decisive, without having had to engage the bulk of forces."

Blitzkrieg and Enemy Paralysis

Having effected a breakthrough, the doctrine of the Blitzkrieg called for the maintenance of the advance, both to prevent the enemy from recovering and to achieve the campaign's objectives as quickly as possible, which would also minimalize casualties. Using Operation Barbarossa as an example, one can appreciate the results that could be achieved when the momentum was maintained. "Sixteen hours after the opening of Operation Barbarossa the German Army in the east had virtually unhinged two Soviet fronts, the Northwestern and Western. At the junction, the Soviet 11th Army had been battered to pieces; the left flank of the 8th Army and the right flank of the 3rd Army had been similarly laid bare, like flesh stripped from the bone which lay glistening and exposed. The covering armies in the Soviet frontier areas were being skewered apart." (John Erickson, *The Road to Stalingrad*). Guderian's Second Panzer Group – nine divisions, including four panzer and two motorized – advanced 273 miles (437 km) into Soviet territory in seven days. Reaching the city of Bobruisk along the Berezina River, Guderian linked up with Hoth's Third Panzer Group to the north and trapped 32 enemy rifle divisions and eight tank divisions in the Minsk Pocket. Some 25 days into the campaign, Guderian's panzer group had penetrated 413 miles (661 km) into enemy territory and had surrounded a further 185,000 Soviet troops in the Smolensk Pocket. The pace and depth of the Blitzkrieg prevented the Soviets from forming coherent defensive fronts, leaving isolated pockets to be cut off and destroyed.

"By mid-month in August 1941, Russian forces defending along the Smolensk–Moscow highway stood swaying, like a punch-drunk fighter waiting for the knockout blow. With no coherent front and their own rear services in shambles from incessant air attacks and panzer raids, the Soviet units facing von Bock [commander of Army Group Center] represented but broken fragments of the proud formations that had stood on the Bug only weeks before. Though German strength declined with every step forward, relative to their opponents the

The flanks of German mechanized formations were always vulnerable during the Blitzkrieg. The following tactic was used to neutralize this threat. The main attack (thick purple arrow) is engaged in the flank by strong enemy forces (red arrows). The Germans, having gathered intelligence concerning enemy movements, launch a separate force to sever the base of the enemy attack (thin purple arrow).

German troops retained an absolute superiority in striking power throughout the summer and early fall. Supreme in the air, dominant on the ground, with all the advantages of the initiative and unchecked success, the final operational bound from Smolensk to Moscow against a shaken and demoralized enemy was surely within their grasp, as the German generals themselves argued so vehemently." ("Reinterpreting Operation Barbarossa," R.D. Hooker, *Parameters*, Spring 1999)

The French Army was similarly "shaken" and "demoralized" in May 1940. Guderian, commander of the panzer corps that broke through at Sedan, recorded the effect on the French of having masses of enemy tanks in their rear: "Everywhere enormous numbers of bewildered, demoralized French troops were beginning to give themselves up, often with the perplexed complaint '*Trahison!*' on their lips." Rommel, commander of the 7th Panzer Division, wrote of the same breakthrough: "Civilians and French troops, their faces distorted with terror, lay huddled in the ditches, alongside hedges, and in every hollow beside the road." Here, wireless communications came into their own, for commanders such as Guderian and Rommel were always far forward with the advancing panzer columns, but could remain in contact with higher headquarters. In this way the Germans could react faster to fluid situations than could their adversaries. This gave bold commanders a decisive edge in receiving information and in making and communicating decisions. In addition, the Germans had broken the French codes in October 1939, thereby giving them a clear picture of the French order of battle. However, it is important to realize that the crucial element was bold and innovative commanders and not technology: German panzer commanders reacted to changing tactical situations very quickly, rather than wait for orders to arrive via their radios. This contrasts sharply with the British and French during the 1940 campaign, when opportunities presented themselves to the Allies to strike the vulnerable flanks of the advancing panzers, but were not acted upon.

It is important to note that the panzers during the Blitzkrieg assumed the role of cavalry, i.e. pursuit and exploitation. There was no place in the Blitzkrieg for armor-to-armor clashes, except where German success was guaranteed. It is worth remembering that in France in 1940, the army employed over 500 Panzer Is, whose armament consisted of only two 7.92mm machine guns, and which were certainly inferior to many French and British tanks. Rommel's 7th Panzer Division was temporarily halted by British tanks at Arras – an indication that head-on armored clashes were often far from desirable.

The Final Phase

Having pushed the disorganized and demoralized enemy into isolated pockets, the final phase of the Blitzkrieg was the reduction of those pockets. Invariably this was the job of the infantry divisions and artillery regiments, who moved at a slower pace than did the mechanized panzer and motorized infantry divisions. Those troops herded into pockets were invariably short of ammunition, supplies, and, most importantly, the will to carry on the fight. At Kiev in September 1941, for example, the Wehrmacht surrounded a force of over 600,000 Soviet troops. Though some units attempted to break out of the encirclement, they were shot to pieces by German artillery and machine guns (in these cases the high rate of fire of the MG 34 machine gun – 900 rounds per minute – came into its own). For five days the fighting continued, then Soviet resistance collapsed, and over 600,000 Red Army troops entered German captivity. It should be pointed out that the reduction of these enemy pockets was not a mere formality: there was still a lot of hard fighting to do, and on Eastern Front during 1941 Soviet formations often launched desperate attacks in an attempt to break out. In addition, the panzer commanders were always wanting to leave these pockets to the infantry and continue the advance into enemy territory; this meant the German perimeter was often dangerously thin.

This, then, was the Blitzkrieg. A doctrine of maneuver based on having quantitatively inferior forces when compared to the enemy. However, as theorists such as Guderian realized, maneuver acted as a psychological multiplier to the forces employing it. When one realizes that the 1940 campaign in France was in effect won by 10 panzer divisions, one can appreciate the power of the Blitzkrieg. The aim of the latter was always the destruction of the enemy's mental cohesion and will, rather than the reduction of his physical assets.

PART II

THE YEARS OF ATTACK

Honing the Weapon

The invasion of Poland was characterized by high-tempo operations spearheaded by elite armored forces, which crushed Poland in three weeks. However, the Wehrmacht's first major campaign revealed several areas of weaknesses that needed to be rectified.

On September 1, 1939, Adolf Hitler unleashed the German armed forces (Wehrmacht) in an invasion of Poland that initiated World War II. Poland, which was sandwiched between the much more powerful nations of Germany and Russia, had long experienced a precarious existence. After 123 years of foreign occupation, an independent nation reemerged in 1918 to fill the power vacuum left by the disintegration of the German, Russian, and Austro-Hungarian empires. The result, however, was to leave festering revanchist ambitions among the German and Soviet leaderships, both of which desired to dismember the "upstart" Polish state. Hitler viewed the Slavic peoples of Poland as racially inferior and therefore unworthy of statehood. The Führer also coveted the German minority in Poland and viewed as unacceptable the physical separation of East Prussia from the rest of Germany by a narrow neck of land – the "Polish Corridor" – created by the victorious Allied powers at the Treaty of Versailles in 1919.

After his political success in exploiting the German minorities in question to achieve the absorption of Austria (1938) and the Czech Sudetenland (1938), which was followed by the outright occupation of the rump Czech state in March 1939, it was only a matter of time before Hitler turned his expansionist ambitions eastward to Poland. While happy to reacquire the Baltic port of Danzig and the Polish Corridor through intimidation short of war, Hitler believed military conflict to be the final arbiter of national destiny and was prepared to risk war to fulfill his foreign policy agenda. Thus, during the fall of 1939 Hitler set his as yet unblooded war machine to prepare for a decisive settlement of the Polish question.

The basis of German strategy as devised by Hitler was to launch a massive all-out offensive that would commit the bulk of Germany's military assets to an attack

A Junkers Ju 87 Stuka dive-bomber releases its bombs during the opening of the war against Poland. The Luftwaffe quickly established air superiority over the theater of operations and was soon interdicting Polish Army supply and reinforcement columns making their way to the front.

intended to overwhelm and destroy Poland before Great Britain and France could intervene on the thinly defended Western Front. In fact, based upon Anglo-French appeasement at Munich and their failure to respond militarily to the German conquest of Czechoslovakia in March 1939, Hitler – recognizing the implausibility of the Anglo-French pledge to defend Polish sovereignty – believed that Britain and France would again back down and acquiesce to a German conquest of Poland. If they did not, however, he planned immediately to redeploy his forces, after crushing Polish resistance by sheer weight of numbers, to the Western Front to thwart any Anglo-French counterinvasion. Correctly reading the parlous state of military preparedness in Britain and France, as well as their general aversion to embroilment in another major continental war, Hitler believed that the limited German forces left in the West could successfully hold up any Anglo-French counteroffensive until the bulk of the German Army, victorious in Poland, could be redeployed westward.

German Deployments

Hitler ordered general mobilization on August 25, 1939, and this was largely complete by September 1, since the Germans benefited immensely from the earlier mobilization rehearsals during the Austrian and Czech crises (see Chapter 1). The problems and chaos that had bedeviled these earlier mobilizations remained less prevalent in September 1939, as the Germans – having learned through trial and error – had improved significantly the mobilization process. German forces formed up in two major concentrations: Colonel-General Fedor von Bock's Army Group North, with the Third and Fourth Armies under command, which operated from East Prussia and Pomerania; and Colonel-General Gerd von Rundstedt's larger Army Group South, which deployed in Silesia and the German puppet state of Slovakia, with the Eighth, Tenth, and Fourteenth Armies under command. The German High Command intended that Rundstedt's command would form the main offensive strike force of the invasion.

Hitler committed all of Germany's panzer, motorized, and light mechanized divisions to the attack, together with the bulk of his active infantry divisions and a host of smaller frontier defense forces. Overall this force amounted to the equivalent of some 70 formations, including 55 divisions. Hitler left a mere 30 divisions in the West, only 12 of which were active infantry divisions. He therefore took a tremendous gamble as he threw the bulk of the German Army into a rapid campaign to overwhelm Poland before the Western militaries mobilized and launched operations against Germany. In total the German invasion force amounted to 559 infantry battalions, 5,805 artillery pieces, 4,019 antitank guns, and 2,511 tanks. The Germans thus achieved at the outset a marked numerical superiority: 50 percent in infantry, 180 percent in field artillery, 420 percent in antitank guns, and 430 percent in armor. The German qualitative edge served only to accentuate their numerical advantage.

To each army group the German High Command assigned an independent strategic mission. Army Group North was to seize the Polish Corridor, restoring a direct land link with East Prussia, then swing through Prussian territory and attack toward Warsaw from the north. Army Group South's main strike force, spearheaded by the Tenth and Fourteenth Armies with four armored and four light mechanized divisions under command, was to smash through the Polish frontier defenses and advance on Warsaw from the southwest. Meanwhile, other elements of the Fourteenth Army were to defend the southern flank of this main thrust while

The most viable Polish strategy when confronted with a German invasion was to have rapidly withdrawn from the frontier and assumed defensive positions along a north–south line that connected the Bug, Narew, Vistula, and San Rivers, utilizing existing fortifications. Such a defensive strategy took into account the limitations of the Polish forces that precluded large-scale offensive action. However, this plan required sufficient advanced warning of an impending invasion so as to give time for an ordered mobilization and concentration of the Polish Army – a process that required at least two weeks. Because the Poles correctly perceived that Hitler would launch a surprise attack, the efficacy of this defensive strategy was called into question. Another major drawback was that this Polish strategy would relinquish the bulk of western Poland, where most of the Polish industry and population were concentrated.

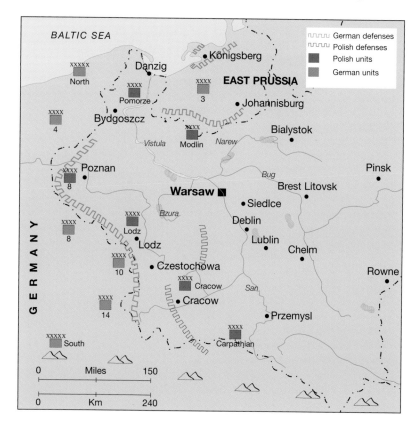

simultaneously pushing toward the northeast to link up with Army Group North east of Warsaw. The linking up of these two forces would isolate the Polish capital and – the Germans also hoped – the bulk of the Polish Army as well. Army Group South, the largest of the invasion groups, deployed some 886,000 troops, 323 infantry battalions, 3,725 artillery pieces, 2,453 antitank guns, and 1,944 tanks on September 1, 1939. What is most noticeable about this strategic blueprint is that Polish dispositions and intentions played directly into German hands, this making a bad sitation worse for the Poles.

The other branches of the German armed forces also had roles to play in the invasion. German strategy offered a limited role for the German Navy, since Poland was actually landlocked once the Polish Corridor was severed, as it inevitably would be. German naval assets were to assist in the initial assault and submarines would blockade enemy ports to deny any operational freedom to the small, largely coastal forces Poland possessed. Hitler assigned a much larger and more aggressive role to the Luftwaffe, and it was in air power that the greatest disparities between the two protagonists lay. The German Air Force deployed some 2,085 aircraft against Poland, including 648 bombers, 219 Stuka dive-bombers, and 426 fighters; Poland had 360 combat aircraft. Thus the German air assets committed to the campaign outnumbered the Polish Air Force by a factor of four to one and represented, given the qualitative differences between the respective air forces, more than sufficient to establish immediate aerial superiority, which spelt disaster for the Polish Army. Once this primary air superiority mission had been achieved, the German Air Force would concentrate on tactical missions – interdiction, close air support, and reconnaissance – to aid the unfolding ground campaign.

The MG 34 Machine Gun

Although the MG 34 dual-role machine gun had entered German Army service back in 1934 and had been employed in the Spanish Civil War, Hitler's fall 1939 invasion of Poland proved the first significant period of high-intensity combat during which the weapon's capabilities could be truly tested in a sustained fashion on the hard anvil of war. The potent firepower of this weapon, which formed the basis of every German infantry squad, provided the latter with a resilience that was to prove an important contributing factor to the success obtained by the Wehrmacht in Poland, as well as that secured in Norway and the West during 1940. The dual-purpose MG 34 could be employed in both a light and heavy role, providing German infantry sections with greater tactical flexibility. Because of its use in a light role, the weapon possessed the weight-saving system of an air-cooled barrel ventilated by holes in the sleeve, rather than the heavier jacket used to water-cool earlier heavy machine guns. Since air-cooling remained less efficient than water-cooling, however, the relatively lightweight MG 34 was designed so that soldiers could easily change its barrel in the field. The gun possessed an impressive

rate of fire of 820 rounds per minute (rpm) and could deliver rounds to an effective range of 6,564 ft (2,000 m). The weapon fired its rounds from either a 50-round belt or a saddle magazine. All in all a formidable infantry weapon, the MG 34 provided the German infantry squad with tremendous organic firepower that augmented powerfully both the offensive and defensive fighting power of infantry units. Though it remained in production throughout the war, from 1943 the MG 34 became increasingly replaced at the frontline by the even more devastatingly potent MG 42.

The Polish government feared that a too-rapid surrender of western Poland would have deleterious ramifications in London and Paris, upon which Poland depended for rapid military intervention if the country was to withstand Nazi aggression. Moreover, Polish leaders remained afraid that the early mobilization required for such a strategy to have a chance of success might be misconstrued in London and Paris as a Polish provocation: such a perception might delay Western military intervention. In addition, the Polish elite feared that the adoption of such a strategy might embolden Hitler to grab small parcels of disputed Poland, just as he had done with the Sudetenland, and thus dismember Poland piecemeal.

Poland plumped for an alternate strategy – Plan Z – that called for a more forward deployment to defend the economically vital region of Polish Silesia. These forward forces were to conduct a fighting withdrawal to buy time for the full mobilization of the Polish armed forces. Once reserves had assembled, they would counterattack any German penetration of the frontier armies and restore a firm defensive front. Vigorous forward defense would encourage a more rapid and energetic Western military intervention that would, Polish leaders hoped, siphon off German forces to reinforce the Western Front. If this plan failed, the Poles intended to conduct a phased withdrawal back into southeastern Poland, where the Polish military planned to make a final stand.

Unfortunately, Plan Z had several serious flaws. The frontier was so long that forward defense ensured that nowhere was the Polish Army strong enough to oppose a concentrated German advance. The length of the front to be held also compelled commitment of the Polish cavalry brigades – the bulk of the army's reserves – to the front, which wasted their mobility and added little to overall defensive strength due to their lack of firepower. Plan Z also understated the speed, pace, and fighting qualities of the mechanizing German Army – a failure shared by many British, French, and even some German generals! For skepticism remained among many senior German generals about the potential and efficacy of the panzer divisions. The September 1939 German strategic deployment against Poland reflected such skepticism, since it did not concentrate the available mechanized forces for truly independent strategic operations.

Polish Force Structure

For the campaign Poland deployed seven field armies and five smaller operational groups. The Polish Army remained predominantly an infantry force organized in 30 infantry divisions plus the equivalent of 18 less effective second-echelon divisions. All these formations, however, remained generally inferior in both quantity and quality of equipment, training, mobility, firepower, communications, and fighting power in comparison with German infantry divisions. In antitank, antiaircraft, and field artillery, the Polish formations also remained less well equipped than the Germans. Next to the infantry, the cavalry was the second most important arm of the Polish Army. The Poles organized their anachronistic horsed cavalry in 11 brigades. The cavalry's chief strength was its mobility, which gave it some survivability and endurance on the modern battlefield, even though it lacked firepower. The Polish Army also remained badly deficient in armor, deploying a total of 887 tanks, most of which were obsolete tankettes (small, lightly armed tanks) that were dispersed in "penny packets" for infantry support. Thus Poland had no strategic armored reserve and only two embryonic mechanized brigades that lacked firepower, training, effective doctrine, and organization. These deficiencies inevitably relegated Polish armor to a subsidiary role.

Artillery, the queen of the battlefield, comprised the bulk of Polish firepower and was neither insubstantial nor outmoded. Yet, in general, Polish artillery batteries had less firepower than comparable German ones, and possessed inferior communications, inadequate ammunition provision, and less sophisticated fire control systems than the enemy that faced them. Polish equipment was generally older and less effective than that fielded by the Germans, with much of it being of World War I vintage. Just one Polish weapon proved superior to its German equivalent: an antitank rifle that fired tungsten-cored rounds.

The Polish Air Force and Navy could likewise make only a limited contribution to the defense of their country. The air force remained both materially and doctrinally unprepared for offensive operations and, as part of the army, was geared toward defensive ground-support operations. The Polish High Command parceled out what aircraft were available for infantry support, and for both defensive air and offensive air missions: this deployment spread the small air force too thinly to pursue any of these missions effectively. It was also widely dispersed in small packets at airfields all across Poland, which further hampered its operational employment. The Polish Navy was similarly small and in addition vulnerable to air attack, and thus did not contribute significantly to the defense of Poland, beyond committing naval troops to ground fighting.

The German invasion of Poland began on the morning of September 1, 1939, with heavy air force attacks on Polish airfields, rail centers, and communications links. The first clash on the ground occurred when a naval assault company from the old German battleship *Schleswig Holstein*, aided by

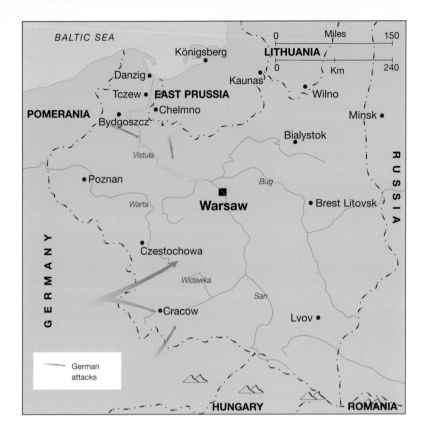

The Polish campaign September 1–5. The most significant German achievement on the first day of the war was the seizure of Danzig by Brigade *Eberhard* in the face of little opposition. As the German Third Army crossed the border from East Prussia, however, it encountered strong enemy resistance. The Fourth Army simultaneously attacked from Pomerania across the Polish Corridor toward East Prussia with the mission of restoring a direct land link between the two German territories. It encountered only limited resistance, as the opposing Pomorze Army conducted a fighting withdrawal, the Polish High Command having deemed the corridor to be untenable.

local paramilitaries of the SS Home Defense Force *Danzig*, launched an abortive attack on the Polish military installations at the Westerplatte on the outskirts of the Free City of Danzig. When the personnel of the Polish post office armed themselves and resisted, the SS troops subsequently executed some of the postal workers after they had surrendered. The first German foray into Poland thus set the stage for four years of brutal occupation and repression.

Army Group North spearheaded the battle for northern Poland. On September 1, the Third Army debouched from East Prussia and advanced south toward Warsaw and southwest toward Brest Litovsk.

Rapid Gains

During September 2, the significant numbers of 37mm Antitank Gun 35/36 (37mm Pak 35/36) pieces available to the German Third Army were called upon to provide sterling defensive fire to repel several strong Polish counterattacks spearheaded by TKS tankettes. Though the Pak 35/36 possessed only modest penetration capabilities, it proved more than adequate in halting the assaults launched by the lightly armed Polish tankettes. Subsequently, during the late afternoon of September 2, the Third Army approached the city of Graudenz after it had broken through the Polish defenses east of Mlawa and now sought to envelope the outflanked enemy. Meanwhile, that same day the German Fourth Army crossed the Brde River and cut off the rear guard of the Pomorze Army in the corridor, before linking up with spearheads of the Third Army at Nowe Swiecie the following day.

In the Polish Corridor, meanwhile, German advances pushed back the Polish defenders to the outskirts of the port of Gdynia. Then, on September 4, the

Third Army captured Graudenz after a stiff struggle and threw back the Polish defenders, while the infantry of the Fourth Army mopped up the residual Polish forces as they endeavored to escape out of the corridor.

With the Polish Corridor entirely cleared by September 5, Colonel-General von Bock's Army Group North had completed its first mission in the campaign. Immediately this command began to redeploy the Fourth Army eastward into East Prussia to attack toward Warsaw alongside the most eastern formations of the German Third Army. On September 6, the Third and Fourth Armies effected a new juncture south of Graudenz, and so confident of success had the Germans become that Bock relocated his headquarters to Allenstein in East Prussia. From this location he could oversee the subsequent German operations launched deep into the interior of Poland. Having reinforced its strength in East Prussia, Army Group North launched the second stage of its planned operations as it struck south in strength on September 7, 1939, toward Lomza.

Operations in the North

Meanwhile, in northern Poland the German Third Army forced a crossing over the Bug River on September 10, and two days later turned to pen and invest the bulk of the Polish forces in and around Warsaw from the east while simultaneously advancing southwest toward Siedlce. That same day Fourth Army headquarters finally disengaged itself from operations in western Prussia and redeployed to East Prussia, where it assumed command of the eastern drive on Bialystok. The Third Army continued its advance to the southwest until it drew up to the Vistula River on September 16, south of Warsaw. The following day it laid siege to the eastern Warsaw suburb of Praga. At the same time, the German Fourth Army became operational east of Lomza and accomplished the rapid occupation of Bialystok. Between September 14 and 17 the Third Army battled to storm Brzesc, where it encountered stiff resistance as the Poles continued to fight valiantly.

On September 17, 1939, Soviet forces invaded eastern Poland in accordance with the terms of the secret protocol added to the August 1939 Ribbentrop–Molotov non-aggression pact between Germany and the Soviet Union. Consequently, Bock not only ordered Army Group North not to advance past a line that ran from the Bug River via Brzesc to Bialystok, but also simultaneously recalled those forces that had already crossed this line. The Soviet intervention represented the death-knell to Polish resistance in eastern Poland, which rapidly disintegrated. The Soviet invasion of September 17, and the meeting that same day of the vanguards of Army Groups North and South across the Vistula River at Gora Kalwarja, which isolated the bulk of the remaining Polish forces in and around Warsaw, therefore marked the culmination of the second stage of Army Group North operations in Poland.

The stage was set for the final phase of Army Group North operations: the capture of Warsaw itself. This stage of operations effectively began on September 26, when the Polish garrison rejected German capitulation overtures. The success of the subsequent German ground operations against the city owed much to the effective massed bombing attacks undertaken by the Luftwaffe on September 15, which had weakened to some degree the previously fierce Polish resolve. On September 18, Bock's forces resumed operations against Warsaw with a vengeance. The German Third Army attacked in conjunction with the Tenth Army from Army Group South, powerfully supported by artillery fire and also by both aerial interdiction and tactical air sorties flown by the Luftwaffe.

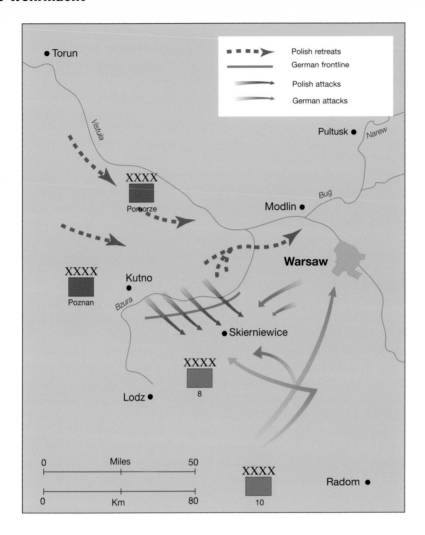

The Battle of the Bzura. On September 11, the German Eighth Army systematically began to eliminate the Polish forces about Kutno, which amounted to 12 divisions, or about one-quarter of the entire Polish field force. So began the Battle of the Bzura, in which the isolated Polish forces stubbornly resisted German efforts to subdue them. The Eighth Army thwarted vigorous Polish breakout attempts toward the east during September 11–12, and three days later the Tenth Army assumed command of the German forces endeavoring to reduce the Bzura Pocket from the east, and thwarted the final Polish breakout attempt on September 16. The failure of this foray demolished lingering illusions among the Polish troops that they might escape encirclement, and consequently their resistance finally disintegrated on September 17. Over the next few days the Tenth Army mopped up residual Polish resistance, and by September 20 the Poznan Army was no more.

Yet the German drive met spirited resistance in northern and eastern Warsaw as the Germans found themselves embroiled in bitter and protracted street fighting that negated their advantages in firepower. The advance thus quickly degenerated into a slow and methodical crawl that increasingly took its toll on the attackers. For the first time since World War I German troops experienced the difficulties of urban warfare. The numerous buildings not only provided excellent cover for enemy ambushes and sniper fire, but also hampered German artillery fire direction and observation. Gradually, however, the sound training and resilient fighting spirit of the German troops tipped the balance and enabled them to push back the Polish defenders as the latter's supplies ran increasingly low. On September 26, Army Group North supported the final attack on Warsaw spearheaded by the Eighth Army. The following day the remnants of the Polish garrison capitulated.

Throughout September Army Group North also fought a less glamorous secondary campaign to subdue Polish resistance at Gdynia and in the Hel Peninsula. But the force that spearheaded this campaign – Corps *Kaupisch* – had much more limited means than those at the disposal of the besiegers of Warsaw. By September 9, Kaupisch's forces had captured Puck and had established a tight investment around Gdynia and the neighboring low-lying Oxhöfter Heath. Gdynia finally fell on September 14, yet the largely Polish naval forces, isolated on the Hel Peninsula, continued to offer stiff resistance as the Germans endeavored to push down the narrow sand spit toward the port of Hel at the tip of the peninsula. After a stubborn, protracted defense that inflicted heavy casualties on the enemy, the Polish garrison finally capitulated on October 1, bringing Polish resistance in northern Poland to an end.

The main thrust of Army Group South was mounted by the Tenth Army with the bulk of the German armor against the boundary of the Polish Lodz and Cracow Armies. Its aim was to reach Warsaw. Through the second day of the invasion, the Polish positions mainly held in heavy fighting. But by September 4 the German onslaught had smashed the Polish 7th Infantry Division and forced it back, allowing German forces to press rapidly forward. Meanwhile, on the flanks of the main thrust the Eighth Army advanced toward Lodz while the Fourteenth Army thrust toward Cracow and into Galicia, capturing the strategic Jublunka Pass after a hard fight.

A horse-drawn German supply column on the move toward the front in Poland. The bulk of German artillery was pulled by horses, while the overwhelming majority of infantry divisions marched on foot. The small number of panzer and motorized divisions, supported by air power, held the key to more mobile operations.

On the second day of the invasion the Fourteenth Army encountered stiff resistance at Katowice from outnumbered Polish forces that nevertheless fought long and hard. The Eighth Army crossed the Prosna River that same day, while the Tenth Army shouldered its way across the Warta River to capture Czestochowa in the face of determined Polish opposition. In the south, however, the beaten Poles began a general withdrawal in accordance with their preconceived strategy as the German attacks battered the Cracow Army. By September 5, Tenth Army was across the Pilica River, and the next day the

Fourteenth Army captured the key city of Cracow. This completed the first phase of Army Group South operations, and after five days of intense offensive operations Rundstedt's command paused to regroup and replenish.

Notwithstanding these timely German reactions, the countermove of the Poznan Army demonstrated that the Polish forces continued to fight hard and could not yet be written off. The Polish counterthrust also demonstrated the Polish High Command's determination to defend their capital at all costs. The stage was thus set for the Battle of Warsaw.

Unfortunately, the Polish counterthrust pushed the Poznan Army ever deeper into a noose as German forces now converged on the environs of Warsaw from three directions. The Polish countermeasures therefore merely served to hasten the envelopment of the Poznan Army at Kutno as it was outflanked to the east by the German XI Corps, which established a bridgehead across the Bzura River.

The End of the Campaign

At the same time as the Battle of the Bzura was reaching its climactic finale, the Tenth Army had launched a second envelopment operation against Radom, which fell on September 11. After another brief pause Tenth Army resumed its advance toward Lublin two days later. From September 15, the Tenth Army participated in the siege of Warsaw and simultaneously pushed eastward toward Lublin, which fell two days later after a brief but spirited defense. Meanwhile, the Fourteenth Army crossed the San River on September 10, invested Lvov two days later despite fierce enemy resistance, and then captured Przemysl after a stiff day-long fight during September 15. The Eighth Army continued its mopping-up operations in and around Warsaw, while the Tenth Army flushed out Polish stragglers east of the Vistula, and the Fourteenth Army occupied the San River line. The final organized Polish resistance in the Army Group South sector ended at Kock on October 6, 1939, bringing to an end the Polish campaign after 36 days.

Notwithstanding the tremendous victory achieved, the Polish campaign demonstrated manifold flaws in German preparation, training, doctrine, and organization. One of the key strengths of the German Army, however, was its determination not to equate victory with excellence in performance. Thus the Germans quickly examined in detail the lessons of the Polish campaign. In honest and far-reaching self-criticism, German officers – senior and junior alike – criticized their own performance, and in so doing identified a host of deficiencies. Unlike other armies – particularly the British – where criticism was often equated with disloyalty to superiors, the culture of the 1939 German Army ensured that even lieutenants and captains felt free to criticize openly doctrine, training, equipment, and tactics.

Some German commanders displayed great flexibility and composure in the face of crisis. The second day of the invasion, for example, witnessed the unsuccessful attempt of German assault engineers from Group *Medem* to seize the Vistula River bridge at Tczew. Fortunately, advancing ground troops secured crossings at Gniew and Marienwerder intact as field commanders deftly modified their operational plans once the intended coup de main on Dirschau had failed. Here, the flexibility of local German commanders, schooled in the command and control ethos of Mission Analysis (*Auftragstaktik*), and willing to exercise their initiative, ensured that the setback at Dirschau did not upset the unfolding German invasion. Such responsive leadership ensured that German soldiers typically fought effectively even in unforeseen and rapidly changing tactical

A short-barreled Panzer IV in
Poland in September 1939.
When used properly the
panzers were devastatingly
effective; when used poorly
the results could be
disastrous. In its rush to
capture the Polish capital as
quickly as possible, the
German Army ill-advisedly
committed unsupported
armor to the Warsaw street
fighting, where it suffered
heavy losses. Of the 81
tanks lost during the whole
campaign by the 4th Panzer
Division, the bulk were
destroyed in the street
fighting that raged in
Warsaw. Indeed, the majority
of German armored losses
had occurred in the Warsaw
fighting, including virtually all
of the 19 heavy Panzer IV
tanks lost.

situations, and this contributed directly to the spectacular success the Wehrmacht achieved during the Polish campaign.

Similarly, on September 7 the Eighth Army resumed the German attack toward Lodz and the Tenth Army launched a new offensive intended to envelop Radom. Meanwhile, the Fourteenth Army fought its way across the Vistula River, the main Polish defensive position, to cut the main Polish route of retreat, and then advanced to Lvov. To control its widening front as German forces fanned out into the interior of Poland, Army Group South headquarters moved on September 7 to Lubliniec, just inside the Polish frontier. The next day the Eighth Army reached the suburbs of Warsaw from the southwest. This thrust toward the northeast exposed the German left flank, and so on September 10 the Poznan Army counterattacked the over-extended, open flank of the Eighth Army and threw back the German flanking forces, causing a brief panic amid German units that lacked training in defensive tactics.

Rapid redeployment of local German reserves, however, quickly restabilized the front the following day and blunted the Polish thrust. Such timely tactical responsiveness typified the effective reactions of German junior officers and NCOs in the Polish campaign. The flexible use of initiative – within the parameters of the commander's intent – that German training ruthlessly inculcated in its troops went a long way to explain the rapidity and effectiveness of German tactical responses.

Throughout the Polish campaign, Germany infantry carried out a secondary – albeit still vital – role in the invasion. The horse-drawn German infantry units followed up the more mobile mechanized spearheads and carried out three broad tactical missions; they engaged and neutralized isolated or bypassed centers of enemy resistance, they protected the vulnerable flanks of the armored divisions, and they occupied ground.

In these unglamorous, yet important, tactical missions, the German infantry benefited significantly from the potent offensive and defensive firepower possessed by the standard infantry section. The tactics typically employed by the German infantry squad in Poland revolved around the awesome power of the MG 34 machine gun (see text box page 54). In infantry platoon attacks against Polish defensive positions, the supporting fire from several well-sited and superbly camouflaged MG 34s (fieldcraft proved a skill at which many German soldiers excelled) powerfully assisted the forward momentum of the German assault. This proved to be the case when, on September 2, German forces stormed the town of Czestochowa in the face of fierce enemy resistance. In addition, the standard German practice, initiated during the Polish campaign, of allocating the firing of the MG 34 to the most experienced and reliable soldier in the squad ensured that the troops used this potent weapon to maximum effect. When this effective tactical employment of the MG 34 was combined with rigorous training and use of initiative, German infantry squads often – yet not universally – proved adept at neutralizing the resistance of Polish forces bypassed by the swiftly advancing panzer divisions.

Triumph of the Infantry

The success enjoyed by German infantry in thwarting the desperate efforts of Polish forces to escape from the Bzura Pocket owed much to the rigorous and realistic training all German soldiers underwent in this period. Basic training, for example, involved strenuous day and night-time tactical exercises that included live firing. Indeed, the German Army remained prepared to accept a one-percent fatality rate during training as the inevitable price of creating resilient soldiers who were more likely to survive on the actual battlefield. Through realistically replicating the conditions of combat these exercises both tested fully the ability of recruits to cope in this hostile environment, and simultaneously developed their use of initiative. Such training also prepared recruits to assume the responsibilities of their immediate superiors, so that if those leaders fell in combat, one of their subordinates could immediately fill the gap in the command hierarchy. As a result of this rigorous training, many of the German infantrymen who fought in the Polish campaign proved tough, flexible, and resourceful. The favorable contribution such qualities exerted on the outcome of tactical encounters was demonstrated repeatedly during the Polish campaign.

It was not all good news, however. Deficiencies in German training were also exposed during the campaign. Several fierce night-time counterattacks by Polish marines at Gdynia and Hel had routed panicked German troops, demonstrating the inadequacy of German night-fighting tactics and techniques. These setbacks in fact revealed that night fighting was a skill neglected in prewar training drills. Realization of this deficiency resulted in an increased emphasis on night fighting during the intensive refresher training programs that German troops, then preparing for the campaign in the West against France and the Low Countries, undertook during the winter of 1939–40.

In addition, German after-action reports also demonstrated a lack of aggressiveness in certain infantry units, which senior generals generally rated as inferior to their World War I predecessors. The infantry often proved reluctant to

The following labels appear on the map:

Kovno, Vilna, Königsberg, LITHUANIA, Bulow, Danzig, XXXXX North, XXX XIX, EAST PRUSSIA, Grodno, Kolberg, 10 XX, Marienwerder, XXI XXX, Chelmno, XXXX 3, Stettin, Bydgoszcz, Neidenberg, XXX, XXX, XXX XXI, Neize, XXX II, Torun, Warta, XXX 4 XXXX, Kustrin, Modlin, Oder, Vistula, XXX XIX, POLAND, Kutno, Kompinos, Bialystok, Frankfurt, Warsaw, XXXX Modlin, Neize, XXXX Poznan, XXX X, Lowitch, XX 30, Lodz, Brest Litovsk, Pripet Marshes, Glogau, XXXX 8, XXX XIII, Radom, Kock, Wlodawa, Breslau, XXX X, XXX XVI, XXX XIV, XXXX Cracow, Bug, XXXXX South, Tornowice, 10, Vistula, IV XXX, XV XXX, San, XXXX, Lvov, Carpathian, Gleiwitz, XXX VII, XXXX, Tarnopol, XXX VIII, XXX XVII, Gracow, Gorlice, XXX XXII, XXX, 14, Teschen, XXX XXII, XXVIII XXX XVIII

German units

Polish units

0 Miles 100

0 Km 160

The situation in Poland on September 14. The campaign saw the first application of Blitzkrieg warfare, which combined traditional Prussian *Kesselschlacht* encirclement strategy with revolutionary new mechanized forces. The German Army employed its six armored divisions, backed by other motorized formations, as instruments of strategic penetration. The brown circles represent fragmented Polish formations; those with outer purple circles represent trapped Polish pockets.

press the attack without extended artillery preparation and support, in contravention of prevailing doctrine. During the September 15 German attack on Podsosnina Lukowska, for example, the dearth of artillery fire support – just four 105mm Light Field Howitzer 18 guns – resulted in a rather half-hearted infantry assault. The German Army rectified this "stickiness" with new squad-level tactical drills and increased emphasis on individual initiative. Commanders also concluded that general standards of coordination had proven inadequate. This was true even of the élite panzer forces. Despite a heavy emphasis during training on combined-arms operations, the Germans realized that no amount of peacetime preparation could adequately prepare troops for the real difficulties of effective battlefield coordination. The refresher training undertaken that fall turned once again to hone and perfect combined-arms coordination.

The panzer divisions proved a great success in Poland, though only if used properly. For example, when Army Group North launched the second stage of its planned operations as it struck south in strength on September 7, its reinforcements included Heinz Guderian's XIX Motorized Corps, which moved to the far eastern flank of the Third Army and on September 9 threw itself against the weak Polish Narew Group in an effort to outflank Warsaw from the east and link up with the advancing spearheads of Army Group South. Guderian's troops crossed the Narew River and pushed on toward the Bug River until they found themselves heavily engaged at Zambow during their attempt to cross the Nurzyck River on September 10. Guderian's well-trained mobile forces, pushed relentlessly forward by their energetic commander, set an example that other commands sought to emulate, thus raising the overall tempo of German operations. Not surprisingly, the defending Polish forces found it extremely difficult to cope with the unexpectedly rapid development of the unfolding German invasion. On Guderian's left flank, Group *Brand* began an advance on Bialystok on the extreme eastern flank of Army Group North, and screened his exposed left flank as his forces advanced farther southward.

Panzers in Poland

In consequence, armor played a major role in the German victory over Poland as mechanized forces, occasionally supported by highly effective tactical air strikes, penetrated deep into the Polish rear to disrupt their communications and paralyze the enemy until infantry and artillery could arrive to annihilate them. This combination allowed the Germans to rapidly overrun Poland at a light cost in terms of lives lost, at least by World War I standards. In addition, the relatively effective all-arms cooperation enacted within the six spearhead German armored divisions contributed greatly to the spectacular German success achieved in the Polish campaign. These formations were reasonably well-balanced divisions that included – in addition to the armored component – motorized infantry, mobile artillery, reconnaissance forces, armored signals vehicles, and all the required support services. In particular, the ability of German motorized infantry (panzergrenadiers) to cooperate intimately with the panzers on the tactical battlefield contributed significantly to the fighting effectiveness of these élite formations. In Poland, the organic German motorized infantry units incorporated within the armored divisions – then grouped in a rifle brigade – operated primarily in trucks. In addition, a tiny number of halftracked armored personnel carriers (APCs) were available for these troops. During the campaign German motorized infantry tactics saw both these types of vehicles used simply to transport the infantry to the edge of the tactical battlefield. There the panzergrenadiers would debus and support the attacking armor by assaulting enemy positions on foot, particularly those held by Polish infantry equipped with potent antitank rifles, or by mopping up isolated pockets of resistance.

However, after-action reports showed the German Army's inadequate preparation for urban warfare. The lessons of the Battle of Warsaw, for example, would be absorbed by German commanders, who came to appreciate the vulnerability of tanks to close-combat destruction in urban environments. These lessons were taken to heart: in May 1940 Hitler would halt rampaging German armor short of Dunkirk and Calais out of fear that they would suffer heavy losses akin to those suffered in Warsaw. This delay aided the escape to Great Britain of the bulk of the British Expeditionary Force (BEF), as well as a sizable number of French troops, from the beaches of Dunkirk. However, two years later the Führer forgot that it is both time-consuming and costly to engage in urban combat when he committed the Sixth Army to the battle for Stalingrad.

Polish prisoners under guard following the end of the campaign. At a cost of some 16,000 killed and 32,000 wounded, the Germans had conquered Poland. Given the Soviet invasion in the rear and the failure of Anglo-French forces to make any kind of meaningful counteroffensive action in the west beyond a mere demonstration, Poland was doomed from the outset.

Contrary to popular myth, the German Army's conquest of Poland was not an easy campaign. Not only did the Poles fight hard and long but the German Army was not yet the well-oiled war machine of later years – the Germans did make numerous blunders. Stiff Polish resistance and German combat inexperience combined to ensure that the German military, despite its overwhelming numerical and material advantage, incurred significant equipment losses. The Wehrmacht suffered 674 tanks so badly damaged that they required factory renovation, 217 of which were write-offs. This represented one-quarter of the total tank force involved. German air losses were also heavy, particularly when one considers the disproportionate strength in air assets. The Luftwaffe lost 285 aircraft shot down, and a further 279 had to be written off due to heavy damage. This represented a 20-percent loss rate; quite heavy considering the short

Warsaw – the Lessons of Urban Warfare

The Battle of Warsaw was the first German experience of urban warfare since World War I, and it was the first ever involving mechanized forces and air power. The long, bitter, and costly battle for the Polish capital revealed German inexperience and lack of preparation for the unique difficulties of urban warfare. The Germans realized from their experiences in Warsaw that city buildings and infrastructure both obstructed observation and reduced the effectiveness of artillery and aerial bombardment; they also came to see the vulnerability of unescorted armor in urban settings. Indeed, the Germans lost the bulk of the tanks destroyed in the Polish campaign during the street fighting that took place in Warsaw. German armor proved vulnerable to close-combat destruction by determined Polish defenders, who attacked tanks from their more vulnerable flanks and rear with antitank guns, flamethrowers, Molotov cocktails, mines, and satchel charges. German tank commanders also proved highly vulnerable to Polish snipers ensconced in high-rise buildings. The subjugation of Warsaw therefore taught the German Army to respect the inherent difficulties of urban warfare and to recognize that built-up areas could not be captured quickly or easily. Instead, they required methodical preparation and systematic reduction. The lessons of Warsaw would lead Hitler in late May 1940 to halt his rampaging panzers short of Dunkirk and Calais out of fear that they would suffer an even worse drubbing than that which the 4th Panzer Division had suffered at Warsaw (a lesson he forgot two years later at Stalingrad). Such a fate undoubtedly would have occurred if the panzers had plunged into towns held by a desperate enemy that was better equipped than the Poles had been, and which remained determined to hold the embarkation points to allow the evacuation of British, French, and Belgian troops from the beaches at Dunkirk. Instead, Hitler allowed Göring's air force to pound the towns to soften up enemy resistance. This halt allowed the British Expeditionary Force (BEF) to escape from Dunkirk and has been hailed by historians ever since as a disastrous German strategic error. When one appreciates the important lessons the German High Command derived from the Battle of Warsaw, however, Hitler's decision becomes more intelligible.

duration of the war and the very modest forces encountered in the skies. Thus there is little doubt that the Polish Air Force fought courageously with the limited means at its disposal.

Poland was thus the perfect training ground and classroom for the German Army. Post-battle study demonstrated that the army had failed to concentrate its armor sufficiently for independent strategic operations, and that the rudimentary mechanisms of air-to-ground coordination might not work so well against a better prepared and stronger aerial opponent. Just two mobile air signal detachments were available to work with the six armored divisions, in what represented a far from adequate situation. In addition, these detachments could not deliver requests from armored divisional commanders for close air support back to air corps headquarters. Instead, such requests had to go via army headquarters to air wing commands, a slow and relatively unresponsive process. As a result, once the battle for aerial superiority over Poland had been won, the Luftwaffe tended to support army ground operations with both aerial interdiction to seal off the battle area from enemy reinforcements, and reconnaissance missions, rather than by tactical air strikes (or "close air support"). Indeed, the latter remained relatively uncommon when compared with the high number of interdiction sorties. At the very least, however, the army and air force both gained valuable practical experience of air-to-ground cooperation during the campaign in Poland, which they used to improve the effectiveness of their interservice operations.

Self-evaluation revealed organizational defects, such as the insufficient armor and cumbersome nature of the German light mechanized divisions that rendered them too unwieldy and lacking in firepower to perform adequately the cavalry roles of reconnaissance and screening for which they were intended. Consequently, during the winter of 1939–40 the German Army upgraded these four formations into fully fledged panzer divisions. Likewise, after-action reports

The entry of Soviet forces into Poland on September 17, 1939, led Army Group South to order an immediate halt to its eastern advance. Three days later the Army Group ordered all of its forces to withdraw west of the Vistula–San Line, in accordance with the provisional demarcation line delineated by the two governments. This decision compelled the Germans to abandon the siege of Lvov and leave its reduction to the advancing Red Army. As the Germans withdrew, however, the Lvov garrison hastily capitulated to prevent themselves falling into Soviet hands. Several clashes materialized between retiring German and advancing Soviet forces during the days of the general withdrawal to the demarcation line. No sooner had Army Group South retired to these positions than political negotiations between the German and Soviet governments led to the eastward movement of the demarcation line once again. Consequently, on October 1, Rundstedt's troops advanced once again to occupy the positions they had previously held along the San and Bug Rivers.

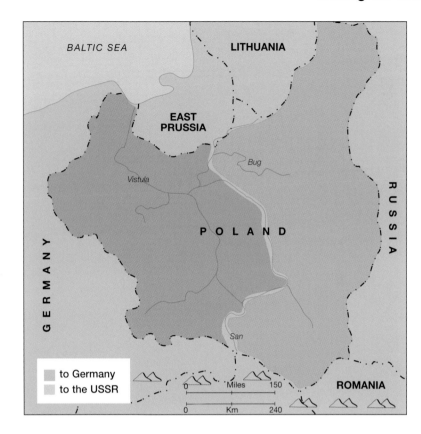

highlighted the lack of punch evident within the German motorized infantry divisions. Not only did they lack the firepower to justify their mobility, but lack of motor transportation had ensured a light establishment with only two, instead of the normal three, infantry regiments. It became clear from experience in Poland that these formations lacked the staying power necessary to perform the spearhead role of accompanying panzer divisions on deep-penetration advances. Therefore, German Army responded by beefing up the firepower and adding more infantry to its motorized divisions prior to the 1940 campaign in the West (see appendices).

Despite all the failings, Germany had won the first of what would prove to be a devastating series of military victories that shattered the European balance of power and created a Nazi "New Order" on the continent that Hitler and his cronies expected to last a millennium. Central to this German success was the German Army's willingness to evaluate its performance critically and honestly, to absorb combat lessons, and to retrain, reorganize, and reequip to enhance its combat effectiveness (the British and French armies drew no new conclusions from the Polish campaign). This determination helped Germany acquire a central European hegemony despite a weak strategic base and the absence of an economy organized for war. However, the campaign in Poland was also detrimental to the army, for its stunning success convinced Hitler that it could be unleashed against any opponent and in any set of circumstances and still achieve victory. His senior commanders did not initially appreciate their Führer's thinking, but they would during subsequent campaigns in the Soviet Union when Hitler made unreasonable demands upon German armies that were understrength and ill-equipped to carry out his orders.

The Campaign in Norway

Victory in Norway was one of the German Army's most impressive achievements, but it fostered dangerous delusions of invincibility. There would come a time when inspired improvisation and the inherent qualities of German fighting units would no longer suffice.

German troops on the water outside Oslo. The invasion benefited from almost total surprise, thanks to thorough security precautions, stormy weather, widespread fog, and a dismaying series of oversights and misinterpretations by both the Anglo-French and the Norwegian armed forces.

Germany's April–May 1940 conquest of Norway – which virtually coincided with the onslaught against the West – was one of its most surprising and daring victories, yet it was one that neither Hitler nor the German armed forces intended until shortly before the fact. The Führer's agenda did not initially encompass Scandinavia, and the Norwegian government declared its neutrality on the outbreak of war in September 1939. The German leadership generally regarded this as a satisfactory state of affairs. British naval superiority appeared so overwhelming that the Germans counted themselves lucky that Anglo-French forces did not immediately press their advantage in northern waters. A crucial consideration for Hitler was the export of Swedish iron ore to Germany, which in winter had to pass through the northern Norwegian port of Narvik. From there, shipping could reach Germany in relative safety by remaining within Norwegian territorial waters. The then British First Lord of the Admiralty, Winston Churchill, pressed repeatedly for action to close this loophole in the blockade of Germany; but the dilatory nature of Prime Minister Neville Chamberlain's War Cabinet and Anglo-French politics repeatedly delayed any such decision.

Two events during the winter of 1939–40 changed the situation. One was the Soviet invasion of Finland, which offered a possible pretext for Anglo-French intervention in Scandinavia. Churchill directed planning for the occupation of several Norwegian ports, including Stavanger, Bergen, Trondheim, and Narvik, ostensibly for the purpose of establishing a line of communications to aid Finland. The primary objective, however, was to open a new theater of war against Germany. Although these plans proved fruitless when Norway and Sweden refused to cooperate, the Germans now realized that they could no longer take Norwegian neutrality for granted. Another dramatic episode, meanwhile, emphasized this point further: the *Altmark* incident of February 1940, in which British destroyers intercepted and boarded a German naval auxiliary inside Norwegian territorial waters. Norway's failure to offer even token resistance to the British incursion helped to convince Hitler and the German Armed Forces High Command (OKW) that Norwegian neutrality offered little further benefit for

German infantry advance through a burning Norwegian village. The Norwegian campaign offered a number of operational and tactical lessons. For the most part German equipment and training proved excellent, and German initiative stood in sharp contrast to Anglo-French hesitation. Occasional reverses, however, pointed to certain weaknesses in defensive doctrine, particularly under winter conditions as in the cases of Norwegian ski-borne attacks. As individuals, Norwegian soldiers generally proved better marksmen as well as skiers, but German superiority in automatic weapons generally compensated for this. Again, as after the Polish campaign, the Germans conducted a thorough evaluation of these and other issues. This time, however, also in light of the overwhelming victory in France, there seemed little need for substantial corrective action.

Germany. Vidkun Quisling, leader of the politically insignificant Norwegian equivalent of the Nazi Party, also helped to persuade Hitler that the socialist government in Oslo was already secretly in league with London.

Besides forestalling an Anglo-French occupation and securing the vital flow of iron ore, the Germans sought two other basic goals when they began to contemplate their own attempt on Norway. One was to obtain air and naval bases for operations against Great Britain (even Hitler did not expect to achieve rapid and total victory over France in the spring of 1940), and the navy wanted northern ports to avoid being bottled up in the North Sea as it had been during World War I. The other goal was to secure Germany's northern flank in anticipation of the eventual invasion of the Soviet Union, which would have been virtually impossible with British and French forces in control of Scandinavia.

Planning began as early as December 1939 with a tentative study by the German Naval Staff, which initially discouraged the idea due to Great Britain's overwhelming naval superiority. Hitler nevertheless ordered further planning by an ad hoc interservice staff, under the codename *Weser* Exercise. Directly following the *Altmark* affair, Hitler increased the tempo of preparations and appointed Lieutenant-General Nikolaus von Falkenhorst to command the operation. Falkenhorst's main qualification apparently was his prior service in the German expedition to Finland in 1918, but in fact he knew little about Norway and later admitted that his first step on learning of his new assignment was to go to a bookstore and purchase a tourist guide! Although the operation eventually involved nine divisions and a variety of lesser units, Hitler totally excluded the German Army High Command (OKH) from both planning and command. Instead, the Führer subordinated Falkenhorst's headquarters (XXI Corps, later redesignated Group XXI) directly to OKW, through which Hitler would exercise personal command over the invasion.

The German Plan

Hasty but effective improvisation characterized the preparations for *Weser* Exercise, which would have to commence before the extended hours of Arctic daylight made surprise impossible. The plan was extremely risky, for it invited German forces to be defeated in detail since the principle of concentration was to be ignored. However, two factors combined to reduce the risk for Wehrmacht forces. First, the professionalism and aggressiveness of German units and commanders, which meant units that became isolated would not suffer from paralysis and indecision. Second, the slowness of the Allies to react to initial German vulnerability.

The invasion force included six groups. The northernmost force – Group 1 – consisted of the 139th Regiment of the élite 3rd Mountain Division, embarked in 10 destroyers with only minimal supplies and equipment. In command was Major-General Eduard Dietl, a fox-faced Austrian in whom Hitler placed considerable confidence. Dietl's mission was risky at best: to seize and hold Narvik until relieved by friendly forces advancing from southern Norway. This link-up would depend on the success of Group 2, consisting of the 3rd Mountain Division's other regiment, the 138th, which had to seize and hold Trondheim. Farther south, Group 3 consisted of two battalions of the 69th Infantry Division, with Bergen as their objective. A company of the Luftwaffe's 1st Parachute Regiment, meanwhile, would seize the vital Sola airfield near Stavanger. Groups 4 and 6, whose mission was to secure the ports of Kristiansand, Arendal, and Egersund on Norway's south coast, consisted of several small detachments of the 163rd Infantry Division. Finally, the High Command allocated to Group 5 the most important objective: the capture of Oslo, the Norwegian capital. The assault wave would consist of two battalions of the 163rd Infantry Division aboard the pocket battleship *Lützow*, the heavy cruiser *Blücher*, a light cruiser, and various smaller craft. The Germans also assigned two parachute companies to seize Fornebu airport slightly west of the city. Follow-on waves would then reinforce Oslo and advance north and west to link up with the other groups. In a subsidiary operation, *Weser* Exercise South, two German infantry divisions and a motorized rifle brigade would simultaneously occupy Denmark.

Surprise was essential both to avoid interception by the Royal Navy and to seize the key objectives before Norwegian forces could mobilize. In relative terms, the Norwegian armed forces were extremely weak, lacking both training and equipment after two decades of budget cuts and general neglect. Nevertheless, Norway's geography presented excellent opportunities for defense of critical points such as the airfields and narrow approaches to the harbors, most of which were covered by coastal artillery emplacements. Given enough warning to mobilize reserves amounting to a total of roughly six divisions, even these brittle defenses might well have broken the teeth of the audacious German assault. If all went according to plan, however, the Germans hoped to avoid any major combat by seizing the Norwegian government as well as nearly every key military

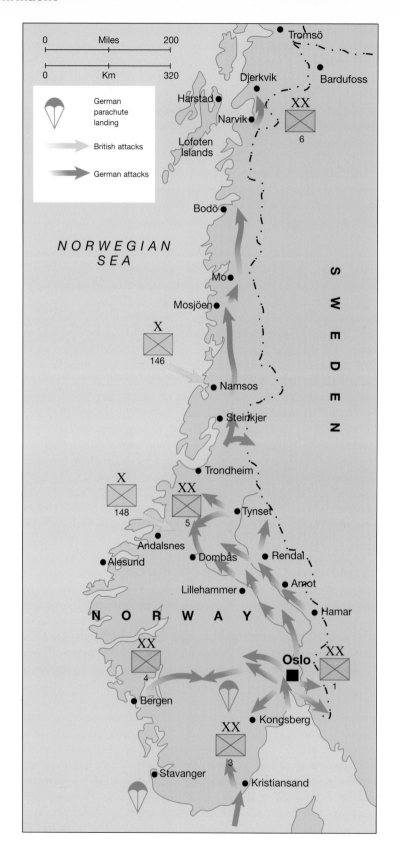

Norway is an elongated, rugged country, whose major population centers are located on its coastline. This ruggedness favors the defense, but only if it is speedily and properly organized. Conversely, as the Norwegians discovered to their cost, the same feature lays the defense open to defeat in detail because of the scarcity of communications between the separated and exposed centers of population. This disadvantage is compounded if, as happened in April 1940, an attacker achieves surprise.

installation within a few hours of H-hour – 0415 hours on April 9, 1940 – thus presenting the Norwegian public with a *fait accompli*. Ironically, Churchill had finally gained approval for a limited operation to mine Norwegian waters on April 8, and strong British forces were at sea. In response to sketchy contact reports, however, they proceeded on the false assumption that the Germans were attempting a raiding foray into the North Atlantic shipping lanes. In Oslo, meanwhile, the government was paralyzed by indecision and failed to order general mobilization.

At Narvik the destroyers of Group 1 sank a pair of antiquated Norwegian coastal defense vessels, and Dietl's mountain troops seized the port and rail terminus virtually unopposed (one of Quisling's associates was in command of the local garrison). In two successive naval actions on April 10–13, however, the British destroyed all 10 German destroyers, and the German hold on Narvik appeared tenuous at best as elements of the Norwegian 6th Division moved south from Finnmark to contain the landing.

Initial German Strikes

At Trondheim, Norwegian batteries at the entrance to the fiord failed to score any hits on the German ships before they penetrated the narrows and landed their troops, which promptly took the defenses from the rear and seized the undefended town itself. As at Narvik, the local Norwegian commander proved entirely passive, allowing the Germans to occupy a crucial airfield east of Trondheim on April 10. German interservice cooperation proved remarkably effective as naval gun crews promptly manned the undamaged Norwegian guns, driving off an attempt by British destroyers to enter the fiord on April 12. The period of extensive German retraining undertaken during the winter of 1939–40 was paying off, at least in regard to effective amphibious joint operations.

Group 3 had a somewhat more difficult time at Bergen, where the Norwegian naval commander showed more initiative. Although they were unable to prevent the Germans from seizing the town, Norwegian batteries did inflict considerable damage on the light cruiser *Königsberg*, which British dive-bombers finished off on April 10. Norwegian destroyers managed to sink two unescorted supply ships en route to Stavanger with heavy equipment, but the German airborne assault succeeded in taking Sola airfield. By the end of that day, the Germans had managed to transport by air two full battalions of reinforcements to Sola. The small detachments at Egersund and Arendal also secured their objectives as planned.

The German operation at Kristiansand nearly failed when poor visibility delayed the initial landing, and effective fire from the Norwegian coastal batteries repulsed several attempts to enter the harbor. The Luftwaffe helped to retrieve the situation, however, with a heavy bombardment that suppressed and demoralized the coastal artillery, finally allowing the landing to proceed. Once again, German ground-to-air cooperation was more effective than during the Polish campaign. By the end of the day the Germans had secured both the nearby Kjevik airfield and Kristiansand harbor.

The most serious setback of the entire German invasion occurred at Oslo, where plans called for Group 5 to dash up the long, narrow fiord by sheer bluff, in order to secure the capital so quickly that the Norwegian government would have no opportunity to escape or issue mobilization orders. Unfortunately for the attackers, the main Norwegian fortress in the fiord mounted three old, but still powerful, 280mm guns (ironically manufactured by Krupp), as well as a recently overhauled battery of shore-launched torpedoes. The fortress commander held his fire until the leading ship, the *Blücher*, was only 1,640 ft (500 m) away, too close for even the poorly trained Norwegian crews to miss. The cruiser suffered fatal damage and took nearly 1,000 men to the bottom, including much of the 163rd Division's headquarters and various special detachments designated to secure key objectives in the capital.

The surviving German vessels withdrew to land their troops farther south in the lower regions of the fiord. To make matters worse, the German air assault on Fornebu airfield nearly failed as well when transports carrying the paratroops failed to locate the objective. Showing remarkable initiative, however, the commander of the second German wave, carrying infantry reinforcements, ordered his aircraft to land regardless of enemy resistance. Hence, through a combination of sheer boldness and the use of initiative engendered by the Mission Analysis (*Auftragstaktik*) command ethos, the Germans not only took the airfield but marched into Oslo before the Norwegian armed forces could organize any sort of effective defense.

The Germans Consolidate Their Grip

Nevertheless, the delay in taking Oslo proved critical because it gave the government time to evacuate north and to issue orders for mobilization and resistance. The decidedly pro-British King Haakon helped to rally the wavering cabinet, and on April 10–11 they promoted Colonel Otto Ruge to command what remained of the Norwegian Army. Ruge moved quickly to deal with rampant confusion and defeatism among his scattered troops. Based on the reasonable assumption that strong Anglo-French forces would arrive soon, Ruge concentrated on delaying the German advance north of Oslo. With British and French assistance he hoped to retake Trondheim and Narvik, thus securing northern Norway as a basis for the eventual liberation of the rest of the country.

German air power largely nullified Anglo-French naval superiority. The occupation of Denmark had proved an unqualified success, and with Danish as well as Norwegian bases the Luftwaffe was able to dominate southern and central Norway. Consequently, on April 9 German bombers successfully engaged the British Home Fleet west of Bergen, inflicting little physical damage but scoring an important psychological victory by demonstrating the threat to warships operating near the coast. Henceforth the British Admiralty exercised great caution and risked only submarines to interdict German shipping en route to Oslo, with little success. German aircraft also subjected enemy ground movements to almost constant harassment during the long hours of daylight, thus hampering enemy reactions to the German invasion and facilitating the advance of the well-trained ground forces.

As German reinforcements poured into Oslo by sea and air, Falkenhorst lost no time in forming them into improvised battle groups to fan out from the initial bridgehead. Having failed to achieve the bloodless coup envisaged in the original plan, he concluded, it was imperative to break the resistance of Norwegian troops through ruthlessly executed rapid operations. Elements of the 181st and 196th Infantry Divisions soon followed the 163rd, while units of the 214th Infantry Division reinforced Stavanger. By April 16, the Germans deployed around Oslo had succeeded in mopping up substantial pockets of Norwegian troops in both the relatively flat region southeast of Oslo and in the Setesdal Valley north of Kristiansand.

Mountain (*Gebirgs*) Divisions

Training of German mountain infantry had begun under Seeckt, who ordered one battalion per division to be trained as *Jägers* (light infantry) and equipped with mountain hardware. A July 1924 decree established two types of mountain unit: those specially trained for high-mountain (alpine) work, and those with equipment for mountains of medium height. Though it took time to create dedicated mountain units, the army instigated an intensive training program that included mountain-climbing, abseiling, skiing, and firing drills for mountains and snow conditions. The training was also long, and included four weeks of alpine exercises (marching and firing within the company or battery) that began in May, followed by further training in the fall. The latter was more individualistic, with an emphasis on patrol work. The incorporation of Austria into the Third Reich boosted the mountain arm. The 2nd and 3rd *Gebirgs* Divisions, for example, were both created from former units of the Austrian Army and included expert mountaineers and skiers.

A typical *Gebirgs* division comprised a headquarters, two rifle or *Gebirgsjäger* regiments, an artillery regiment, and support units, including a battalion of signallers, reconnaissance troops, antitank gunners, and engineers – around 13,000 men in all. As the troops were trained for combat in inhospitable terrain, there was a high proportion of mules and horses, and support weapons were lighter than normal for easy breakdown into man-portable loads. The medium artillery battalion, for example, had 105mm guns in place of 150mm pieces. The Germans found that a personal load of 40 lb (18.1 kg) was the maximum that could be carried – heavier loads impaired individual speed and mobility. Fire discipline is crucial in mountain warfare, as units rely

on the ammunition they carry. Weaponry was tailored to the terrain in which the men fought; a plentiful supply of ammunition for a few weapons is preferable to a wide range of weapons with little ammunition. Since firefights usually occurred at close ranges, small arms with a high cyclic rate of fire were more important than accuracy. Thus the submachine gun was ideal. Interestingly, egg-shaped grenades were preferred to stick types, as the latter snagged on rocks (though deep snow rendered grenade bursts harmless).

German progress toward Bergen and Trondheim, however, proved more difficult. With its main base located about 20.5 miles (45 km) east of Bergen, the Norwegian 4th Division was able to mobilize relatively unmolested and thus had little trouble containing the German lodgment there. Though severely hampered by the disrupted state of mobilization, elements of the Norwegian 2nd Division also established blocking positions north of Oslo and succeeded in checking the Germans at several points. One such reverse occurred on April 15–16 at Bjrrgeseter, where a Norwegian ski battalion executed a flanking attack and forced a road-bound German column to retreat in near panic. Meanwhile, a German parachute company had to surrender at Dombås when units from Oslo were unable to link up with it.

These were exceptions, however, and elsewhere the well-motivated German troops almost always retained the initiative. On April 16, for example, the 196th Infantry Division commander General Pellangahr personally led a surprise attack across the frozen Lake Mjrsa, a bold move that outflanked and dislodged an otherwise strong Norwegian blocking position at the southern end of the lake. The first detachment of German light tanks in Norway also went into action that

same day and proved devastating against the Norwegians, who possessed no antitank guns. Although geography inevitably channeled the advance into only a few narrow valleys, German units developed an effective tactical pattern for breaking the succession of Norwegian blocking positions in their path. Close behind a spearhead platoon of light tanks would follow a platoon of assault engineers in armored trucks, a motorized infantry company, and an artillery battery for direct-fire support. While narrow frontage generally prevented the Germans from exploiting their numerical superiority with lateral maneuvers, they exploited it in depth by rotating units to maintain a high tempo of operations that soon wore down the Norwegians as much by exhaustion as by actual combat.

British and French ground forces finally appeared in central Norway on April 18, 1940, when the British 148th Brigade landed at Andalsnes. Composed of poorly trained Territorial Army soldiers, however, it promptly disintegrated when committed to hold what should have been a strong position at Tretten gorge on April 23. German progress slowed considerably against the regular British 15th Brigade that followed, but their advance continued and prevented Anglo-French forces from attacking Trondheim from the south. Another large force, composed mostly of French troops, landed at Namsos north of Trondheim to form the other half of an intended pincer movement. The Germans again seized the initiative, however, when the outnumbered force at Trondheim staged a small-scale amphibious landing at Steinkjer in the upper reaches of the Trondheim fiord. Effective heavy bombing by the Luftwaffe virtually obliterated the ports held by

German Nb Fz medium tanks in Oslo in April 1940 (only five were built in total). Apart from naval losses, German casualties in Norway amounted to 1,028 killed and 1,604 wounded, a remarkably small proportion of the roughly 100,000 troops engaged. In operational terms, *Weser* Exercise had proved a stunning success; yet there were some significant costs and failures as well. The German Navy had sustained severe losses, including three cruisers and 10 destroyers, which reduced the possibility of invading England in summer 1940. The Germans succeeded in securing the iron ore route, but severe damage to the port and rail facilities at Narvik prevented shipments for many months to come.

the Anglo-French forces, and by April 28 the British and French had decided to withdraw from central Norway. Reinforced by air, the Germans at Trondheim launched their own breakout and linked up with forces from Oslo on April 30. The British and French completed their evacuations from Andalsnes and Namsos on May 2–3. In a hopeless position, the remaining Norwegian forces in central and southern Norway now started to surrender.

It remained doubtful, however, whether the Germans could exploit these victories in time to relieve Dietl's isolated force at Narvik, which Hitler had already written off after receiving news of the destruction of the destroyers on April 13. In fact, Dietl's men temporarily regained the initiative with an audacious spoiling attack against advancing Norwegian forces at Gratangen on April 25–26, which virtually destroyed an entire battalion. By mid-May, however, Anglo-French and Norwegian forces had deployed the equivalent of two divisions around Narvik, forcing the Germans into an ever-smaller perimeter. Narvik finally fell to a combined assault by Allied units on May 27–28, but Dietl succeeded in withdrawing his remaining troops to a last-ditch position at Bjrrnefjell on the Swedish border, where they could still accept internment as an alternative to surrender.

The End of the Campaign

Relief forces from Trondheim made remarkably swift progress, led by the crack German 2nd Mountain Division, which repeatedly broke or outflanked a series of Norwegian and British blocking forces south of Bodö, sometimes advancing 13.5 miles (30 km) per day through what the British had considered "impassable terrain." Such an impressive rate of movement was only possible thanks to the excellent physical resilience of German soldiers, engendered by the rigorous training programs they had previously undertaken. The German relief force surely could not have broken through in time, however, if not for the unexpected turn of events in France. The dramatic success of the May 10 German offensive in the West had forced Churchill, who was now Prime Minister, to abandon the campaign in Norway and concentrate all available units for the impending Battle of Britain. The Anglo-French forces at Narvik and Bodö therefore carried out a methodical evacuation between May 25 and June 8, meanwhile completing the assault on Narvik mainly just to facilitate their embarkation. The Norwegians kept up relentless pressure on Dietl's position, both to cover the Anglo-French withdrawal and to score a final moral victory by forcing the Germans into Sweden. Falkenhorst concluded that Dietl's command was nearly finished, while Dietl himself reckoned that his men could not have held their positions for more than another 48 hours. As it turned out, however, the Germans still occupied a small pocket on the Norwegian side of the border when the Norwegian government agreed to a ceasefire on June 8.

Norway was conquered, and Hitler's personal leadership gained further vindication despite his virtual nervous collapse over the crisis at Narvik in April, which foreshadowed many such later episodes. Norwegian bases would prove useful against the Soviet Union beginning in 1941, but Norway became a drain on German resources as Hitler continually reinforced the garrison against a British invasion that never materialized. In addition, the failure to capture the Norwegian government on April 9 contributed to German problems in the long term, as the government-in-exile established in London fostered patriotic resistance and subversion.

Western Triumph

The conquest of France and the Low Countries in 1940 was perhaps the German Army's greatest victory. In six weeks the Wehrmacht defeated the French, Dutch, and Belgian armies and British Expeditionary Force in an archetypal Blitzkrieg campaign.

Three interconnected factors contributed to the stunning German success obtained in the West: an excellent plan that ruthlessly exploited pre-existing Allied maldeployment to achieve strategic surprise; the shock action imposed by the unprecedented fast tempo of advancing massed German mechanized formations which prevented Germany's enemies from responding effectively on the battlefield; and the tactical effectiveness of German all-arms and interservice cooperation (facilitated by good training, resilient and well-motivated soldiers, and swift and responsive leadership at all levels, and by the solid foundation of reliable, if not markedly superior, equipment).

On October 9, 1939, Hitler stunned his senior generals by ordering an imminent attack on the West, timetabled for November 12. OKH was horrified by this prospect, since it was acutely aware of the numerous tactical deficiencies the Polish campaign had exposed. It remained convinced that German forces were simply unready to invade France successfully, and hence used delaying tactics to stall Hitler's intentions while it conducted rigorous retraining of its forces. Nevertheless, Hitler's insistence led to the development of Case Yellow, the future attack on Belgium, Holland, and France.

The principal flaw of the original German scheme was that – unlike the 1914 Schlieffen plan – it did not offer the prospect of decisive success. The obvious frontal assault into central Belgium had already been anticipated by French strategy, which the latter sought to counter through the D-Plan. If the Germans had launched their May 1940 invasion along these original lines, it is probable that the British, French, and Belgian defense of the Dyle Line would have successfully held the German onslaught in central Belgium, and consequently the

Armored cars and motorcycles of Guderian's panzer corps (note the "G" painted on the vehicles) advance through France in May 1940. The attacking German forces fielded some 2,574 tanks out of their total arsenal of 3,380 machines, many of the uncommitted vehicles being the scarcely combat-worthy Panzer I light tank. The idea that the Germans had an overwhelming superiority in tanks is a myth: they just used their vehicles more imaginatively than did the British and French.

campaign would have degenerated into a static, attritional conflict. Fate was about to take a hand, however.

On January 10, 1940, just one week before the revised target start date for the invasion set by Hitler on December 28, 1939, paratroop Major Hellmuth Reinberger took a briefcase of top-secret documents relating to the German invasion plan with him on his aerial journey to a key staff meeting. Reinberger's pilot became lost in bad weather and crash-landed his aircraft just inside the Belgian border at Mechelen. Belgian police apprehended Reinberger, and within hours the vital information contained in his case was in French hands. Needless to say, on Reinberger's repatriation to Germany, a furious Hitler instructed the Gestapo to arrest him as a traitor.

In March 1940 the French, after concluding that the intelligence obtained at Mechelen was genuine, amended their existing strategy. The French commander in chief, General Maurice Gamelin, simply reinforced the forces committed to the Dyle Plan and extended its geographical scope to create the Breda Variant. French forces were now to advance farther – 102 miles (164 km) – to reach the town of Breda in southern Holland to reinforce the Dutch Army. To achieve this new mission, Gamelin increased the forces committed to the maneuver from 20 to 32 divisions, largely by stripping the French strategic reserve of its mobile divisions and allocating them to General Giraud's Seventh Army in its coastal dash to Breda.

Once Hitler had canceled the compromised original German plan in the spring of 1940, the High Command's growing awareness of the weakness of the French strategic reserve led it to look more closely at an alternative plan of attack that originated from the ideas of Major-General Erich von Manstein. This plan advocated a strategic infiltration of German mechanized forces through the supposedly impassable terrain of the Ardennes.

The Manstein Plan

Back in October 1939 the High Command had appointed Colonel-General Gerd von Rundstedt and his chief of staff, Major-General von Manstein, to command Army Group A, the center force within the projected German invasion of the West. Manstein remained unhappy with the original plan, which he believed did not offer the prospect of decisive success. Consequently, he began to develop his own plan, which he repeatedly pestered his superiors to consider. The High Command resented Manstein's meddling, and refused to present his plan to Hitler. However, through a chance remark the Führer came to hear of Manstein's plan and summoned the officer from Stettin to explain his ideas. Afterward, a much impressed Führer ordered OKW to develop further Manstein's concept. This final plan – subsequently termed the *Sichelschnitt* (Cut of the Scythe) – moved the German point of main effort farther south. The plan envisaged a swift surprise advance by concentrated mechanized formations through the Ardennes.

The new German plan, however, remained extremely risky. The terrain of the Ardennes was very restrictive for large mechanized forces. The narrow, winding roads with steep banks on each side, the heavily forested and hilly ground, and the numerous fast-flowing rivers severely hampered movement. To move seven panzer divisions with 1,900 tanks, 41,000 motor vehicles, and 175,000 men through these communication routes – often only on a single vehicle frontage – would involve march columns that were 100 miles (160 km) long! To make the

A diagrammatic representation of the forces arrayed by both sides at the beginning of May 1940. In terms of numbers of divisions they were evenly matched. The French deployed nearly 50 divisions held in or immediately behind the Maginot Line along the Franco-German border. To keep these French divisions fixed in the south long into the campaign, the Germans undertook a deception scheme that feigned an intended attack by Army Group C against the line. In a clever *ruse de guerre*, the Germans leaked false information through double agents that suggested that the Germans would launch an outflanking attack on the Maginot Line by violating the neutrality of northwestern Switzerland. Again, this constituted a clever deception: by appearing to threaten the obvious Achilles' heel of this supposedly impregnable defensive barrier, the Germans cleverly tapped into the sensitivities of a military command that had nearly bankrupted the French economy constructing the line in the first place.

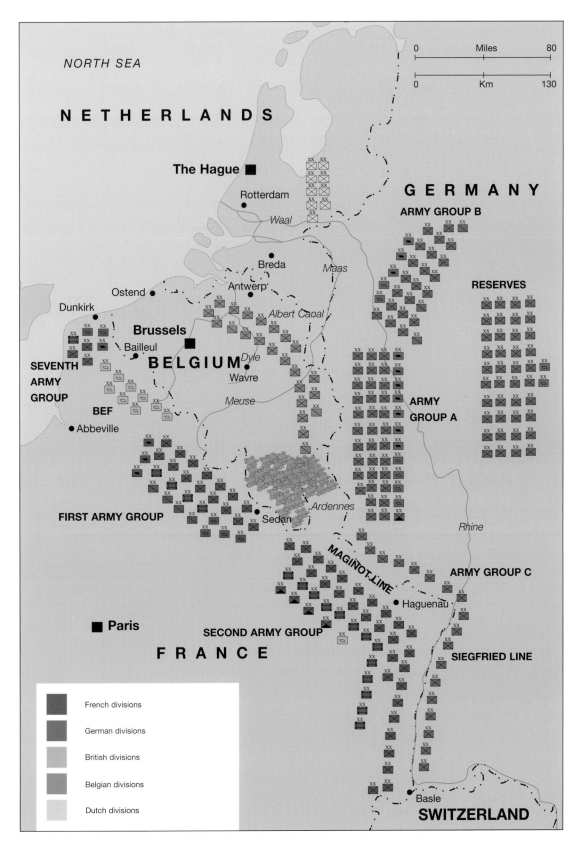

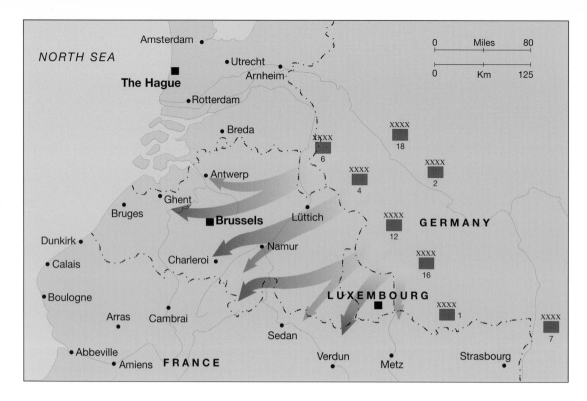

plan work, the Germans needed the closest possible integration of their respective air and ground efforts. In particular, they needed to achieve swiftly aerial superiority over the Ardennes.

To maximize the destruction of hostile air power, the Germans hoped to catch the enemy unawares and hit their aircraft on the ground, while at the same time cratering the runways to prevent the remaining intact planes taking to the skies. Above all, the Luftwaffe had to prevent massed French aerial formations from flying over the Ardennes to attack the vulnerable German armored columns.

On May 10, 1940, the German Army comprised 157 divisions, 49 more than it had at the start of World War II. Some 136 were committed to the invasion of the West, although the High Command held back 44 of these to form a strategic reserve. Against this force of 136 divisions Germany's enemies could muster 135 divisions – 96 French, 10 British, 21 Belgian, and eight Dutch.

Along its northeastern border the French Army deployed 3,563 tanks out of its total available force of roughly 4,000 vehicles. The French "penny-packeted" 1,485 of these tanks in 33 infantry support battalions each with 45 vehicles. A total of 110 French tanks served in three cavalry divisions, a further 582 in three mechanized divisions, and the remaining 1,386 vehicles in three (plus one forming) armored divisions. In addition to this French armor, the British Expeditionary Force (BEF) deployed 196 tanks, the Belgians 60, and the Dutch 40, to produce a grand total of 4,296 Allied armored vehicles in the northeastern theater. Approximately 2.9 million German soldiers faced the three million troops fielded by the Allies.

During the early hours of May 10, 1940, 92 German divisions commenced their invasion of Belgium, France, Holland, and Luxembourg. Surprise was total (Hitler ensured that his forces only learned about the impending attack 20 hours before it commenced). The lead elements of Colonel-General Fedor von Bock's

The original German attack plan in the West took the form of a cautious assault that bore strong similarity to the 1914 Schlieffen plan. The German Army would outflank the French forces deployed along the fortified Maginot Line by a sweep into neutral Belgium. However, unlike 1914, this time the Germans intended simultaneously to violate Dutch neutrality. In truth, this plan remained an unimaginative one with little to recommend it. After a successful push into central Belgium, for example, the planners intended simply to leave it to the field commanders on the spot to recognize a tactical opportunity that they could exploit.

The final German plan advocated a concentrated mechanized strike through the weak French center, which disposed just 14 divisions for its defense. If the French sent large forces into Belgium and Holland to implement the Breda Variant, as German intelligence believed they would, this redeployment would aid the Manstein plan by sucking British and French forces to the north away from the center. To be able to infiltrate through the weak French center, the Germans needed to encourage the existing French maldeployment. Hence, they planned to launch a powerful secondary effort into northern Belgium and southern Holland. The German Army High Command assumed that the French would regard this as the main German effort. The Germans therefore expected that substantial French and British forces would be drawn away from the center by this deception attack in the north. Once these forces had redeployed north, this powerful German secondary attack could fix these forces there in a contact battle, while the main German offensive lanced through their rear.

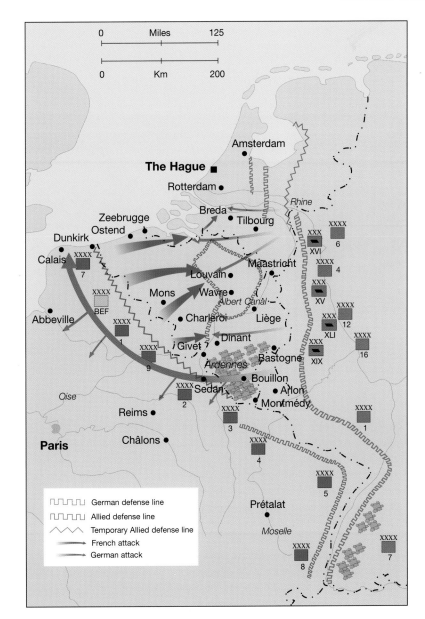

Army Group B advanced into southern Holland and northern Belgium. The German spearheads soon pushed the relatively weak Dutch Army back toward "Fortress Holland," the latter's planned main defensive position in the west of the country. Viewing these operations as the anticipated German main effort, Gamelin instructed the 32 divisions of General Billotte's First French Army Group to implement the Breda Variant by crossing into Belgium. These forces, plus the BEF, began to move to their designated positions around Breda and thence south along the River Dyle in central Belgium down to Sedan. The Luftwaffe did not undertake major efforts to hinder this movement, since it actually played into German hands by removing powerful enemy forces from the decisive central sector. The divisions fielded by the German Army Group A would subsequently keep these British, French, and Belgian forces locked in the north of the theater by relentlessly attacking the Dyle defenses.

As the three panzer and 26 infantry divisions of Bock's Army Group B pushed west in the northern sector of the theater during the early hours of May 10, Rundstedt's Army Group A commenced its crucial operations in the center. Spearheaded by three motorized corps, commanded by Generals Guderian, Reinhardt, and Hoth (the former two subordinated to Motorized Group *von Kleist*), Army Group A began to move into the weakly defended Ardennes region. General Hermann Hoth's XV Motorized Corps controlled Hartlieb's 5th and Rommel's 7th Panzer Divisions. This corps formed the northern axis of Rundstedt's armored wedge with a thrust from Stadtkyll, via Malmédy, to the River Meuse at Dinant. Following up Hoth's advance came the 12 infantry divisions of General Hans von Kluge's Fourth Army. In the center, General Georg-Hans Reinhardt's XLI Motorized Corps deployed the 6th and 8th Panzer Divisions along an axis from Prüm to the Meuse at Monthermé.

Along the southern axis, the strongest corps, General Heinz Guderian's XIX Motorized, fielded the 1st, 2nd, and 10th Panzer Divisions as well as the élite motorized *Grossdeutschland* Regiment. This corps would advance through Luxembourg and onto the Meuse at Sedan. Guderian's command needed to be the strongest of the three motorized corps, for upon his troops would fall the onerous burden of fending off any French attacks against the vulnerable southern flank of this concentrated armored penetration. In total, Rundstedt's three motorized corps fielded 1,900 tanks – over three-quarters of the total committed to the invasion. Farther to the south, below the Ardennes region, the 18 infantry divisions of Colonel-General von Leeb's Army Group C masked the Maginot Line.

During the 72 hours of May 10–12, Rundstedt's three motorized corps successfully advanced through the weak Belgian and French forces in the Ardennes. The speed with which the Germans accomplished their infiltration through the Ardennes owed much to the air-landed forces dropped in front of the

Major-General Erwin Rommel, commander of the 7th Panzer Division (on the right of the group in the far left of the photograph), observes a river crossing exercise before the Western campaign. Despite the adverse terrain the Germans needed to advance swiftly through the Ardennes, otherwise the French would be able to redeploy forces to block any German egress onto the plains beyond. To ensure momentum, the Germans utilized effective all-arms cooperation. A key component of this was the practice of utilizing Mission Analysis (*Auftragstaktik*). This flexible ethos gave considerable leeway to subordinate commanders and obviated the need to pause during operations to await further orders from above. On several occasions the command vehicle used by Rommel was the lead vehicle in his division – allowing him to make rapid and well-informed tactical decisions.

armor to secure key bridges and road intersections. Once the German armor had successfully infiltrated through the Ardennes, the next important step in the German attack plan was to get swiftly across the Meuse River before the French could recover. At Sedan, which Guderian's corps approached during the evening of May 12, the Germans faced a tough assault river crossing against prepared enemy defenses. The main contingent of the defending French force was the 55th Infantry Division, which occupied powerful fortified positions along the southern bank of the Meuse River. In addition, they had the fire support of heavy artillery, and also benefited from the superb field of vision obtained from the Marfée Heights south of the German crossing sectors.

At 1500 hours on May 13, Guderian's artillery unleashed a two-hour artillery bombardment, supported by the direct fire of his 700 panzers lined up along the German-held bank of the river. Although the inability of the often horse-drawn German artillery to keep pace with the rampaging armored spearheads restricted the contribution it made to German victory in 1940, at Sedan it helped significantly to soften up the resolve of the French defenders.

On May 14, as Guderian's forces, having launched an infantry and engineer assault river crossing supported by massed aerial, artillery, and tank fire, consolidated and deepened their bridgehead south of Sedan. Allied resistance was beginning to crumble: in the north, the decimated Dutch armed forces surrendered after being forced back by the 9th Panzer Division and the Eighteenth Army to western Holland. The Dutch Army alone had incurred nearly 3,000 killed and 7,000 wounded in the previous five days of combat. The imminent Dutch surrender, however, did not prevent the Luftwaffe from undertaking a terror bombing attack on Rotterdam which inflicted some 1,200 civilian casualties and left 78,000 homeless. The Dutch capitulation allowed the Germans to bring the full force of their thrust into southern Holland to bear on the northern flank of General Blanchard's French First Army positioned around Breda and Antwerp.

German infantry crossing a river during the invasion of Belgian. During the campaign German commanders displayed greater initiative than their opponents. At Dinant, for example, where elements of Hoth's corps attacked, Rommel's 7th Panzer Division only managed to get across the Meuse in the face of heavy French resistance thanks to the rapid improvisation of their divisional commander, who, as normal, was right up with the frontline troops. Rommel witnessed intense French fire repulse the attack mounted by his crack motorized infantry employing inflatable boats to cross the river. Instantly recognizing the need for smoke to conceal their attempted crossing, he quickly instructed uncommitted soldiers nearby to set light to the buildings on the German side of the river. With a favorable wind, the smoke drifted across the river and the German assault troops this time successfully established a bridgehead on the other side.

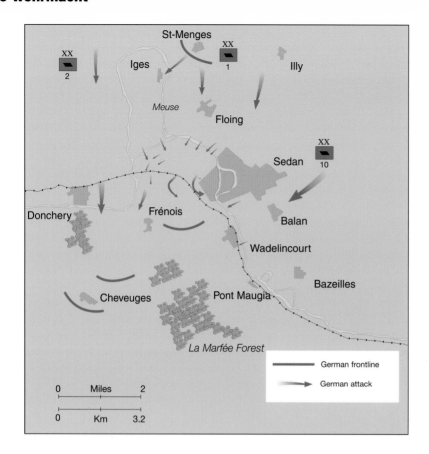

St-Menges

XX
2

Iges

XX
1

Illy

Meuse

Floing

XX
10

Sedan

Doncherry

Frénois

Balan

Wadelincourt

Bazeilles

Cheveuges

Pont Maugia

La Marfée Forest

German frontline

German attack

0   Miles   2

0   Km   3.2

The Battle of Sedan, May 13–15, 1940. The audacity and aggressiveness of the German attack, combined with French indecision and ineptitude, ensured Guderian victory at this critical German attack axis.

In central Belgium, Reichenau's infantry divisions (Sixth Army) attacked Allied defenses along the Dyle River, while Hoepner's armor (XVI Motorized Corps) charged west toward the open ground of the Gembloux Gap. Meanwhile, Hoth's and Reinhardt's motorized corps also undertook assaults on the Meuse River, at Dinant and Monthermé respectively. On May 14, Reinhardt's motorized corps finally managed to establish a small and precarious bridgehead across the Meuse at Monthermé after being repulsed the previous day. Hoth's corps managed to push 30 miles (48 km) west beyond Phillippeville to Sivry, despite encountering a fierce riposte by the surviving elements of the French 1st Armored Division. This resistance caused Kluge, commander of the Fourth Army, serious anxiety. Consequently, he instructed his subordinate to slow the advance the following day.

By May 15, one German motorized and six infantry divisions of the Fourth Army had also managed to reach the Meuse and successfully cross. This was a dangerous development for the French, because as these forces filled the 20-mile (32-km) gap that existed between Hoth's corps and the Motorized Group *von Kleist* to the south, it reduced enemy opportunities to hit the armor in the flank. By the night of May 15/16, these three motorized corps with six armored divisions, supported by seven other formations in ancillary thrusts, were striking rapidly west in a concentrated armored corridor some 47 miles (76 km) wide into the rear of the French center held by the by now rapidly disintegrating French First and Ninth Armies.

In addition, this critical German armored advance deep beyond the Meuse between Sedan and Namur threatened to turn the southern flank of the still-cohesive British, French, and Belgian forces deployed on the Dyle River and in the Gembloux Gap down to the Meuse at Dinant. Late on May 15, Gamelin ordered the forces along the Dyle Line to commence a staggered withdrawal over four days to new positions on the Escaut River, some 45 miles (72 km) farther west. By May 17, the full extremity of France's plight had permeated the High Command at Vincennes. For the French had committed all their reserves to the sectors located north and east of the German armored penetration, and a proportion of these reserves had already been badly battered in contact battles. The French Army now possessed no reserves to stop the panzers from advancing on Paris. Having falsely perceived that the three German motorized corps would swing east behind the Maginot Line, on May 17 the French perception altered – again incorrectly – to assume that the Germans would turn southwest toward Paris.

To stem any German drive toward the French capital, that day the commander of the Northeastern Front, General Alphonse Georges, ordered that a coordinated, six-division counterattack against the southern and northwestern flanks of the German panzer salient be launched as soon as possible. However, the six earmarked divisions found themselves too pressed defending their own sectors to disengage. In addition, these formations were too battered, too dispersed, were experiencing too many transportation problems, and remained too busy reacting to the continued German advance to carry out Georges' order. That day, apart from a few unsuccessful minor countermoves, the only significant counterattack that materialized was the unsuccessful thrust initiated by Colonel de Gaulle's newly formed 4th Armored Division against Guderian's XIX Corps at Montcornet.

During the next day, May 18, in western Belgium, the BEF and the northern flank of Blanchard's French First Army successfully fell back to the Escaut River.

French artillery in action in the Ardennes. In general, and though it was convinced that the dominance of firepower would decide battles, the French Army's artillery in 1940 performed poorly. Manstein, commander of XXXVIII Corps in France, had this to say of French artillery: "Their shooting was not adaptable enough, and their speed in putting down strong concentrations of fire fell far short of the standard required in a war of movement. What was more, they had not developed forward observation technique to anything like the same extent as we had, nor were their specialists in this field of the same quality as our own observation battalions."

Erich von Manstein

The then Major-General Erich von Lewinski Manstein (1887–1973) rose to prominence within the German Army in 1940 while chief of staff of Army Group A poised to attack the West. Erich von Manstein put forward an alternative plan for the attack, but in so doing so infuriated his superiors that he was packed off to the Polish border to command a reserve formation. Yet, through a stroke of luck, Hitler heard of the new plan and ultimately ordered his senior commanders to carry out the Manstein scheme. This excellent plan made a strong contribution to the stunning German success achieved in the West and ensured that Manstein's career prospered. During 1941–42 he commanded the Eleventh Army first in its attack on the Crimean peninsula in southern Russia and then in its operations around Leningrad. Promoted to command Army Group Don in November 1942, he failed to rescue Colonel-General Paulus's encircled Sixth Army at Stalingrad. The high-point of his career came in the spring of 1943, when he combined a skillful elastic defense in the Ukraine with an audacious armored counterstroke around Kharkov that temporarily wrested back the strategic initiative from the Red Army on the Eastern Front. In March 1944, Hitler relieved Manstein of his command after losing patience with the field marshal's attempts – however operationally sound – to conduct a mobile defense on the Eastern Front in defiance of the Führer's prohibition on tactical withdrawals.

Meanwhile, in the center, the panzer divisions resumed their rapid advance west toward the coast and again, through bypassing the pockets of resistance that they encountered, managed to advance a further 40 miles (64 km). In the process, the panzers managed to sweep through several of the halt lines General Georges had ordered even before the allocated French forces could fall back to occupy them. Guderian's forces crossed the Somme River, while both Reinhardt's and Hoth's corps advanced beyond the Canal de St-Quentin in the St-Quentin–Cambrai sector. Once again, the only responses the shaken French Army managed that day were a few uncoordinated, unsuccessful, small-scale counterattacks against the "panzer corridor."

To augment this German armored punch further, Hoepner's corps redeployed southwest toward the Sambre River to link up with Hoth's corps in a four-division armored wedge. It was this continuation of the rapid armored thrust through the French center on May 18 that finally convinced the French High Command that the Germans were intent on reaching the Channel, but this realization had come a critical three days too late. In retrospect, a further advantage of the Manstein plan was that by offering the Germans three possible axes of advance once Sedan had fallen – southeast to the Maginot Line, southwest to Paris, and west to the coast – it helped maintain the element of surprise long after their crossing of the Meuse.

During May 19 the German armored corps made less spectacular gains, with Guderian's forces pushing on just 15 miles (24 km) to Péronne. Once again, as on May 17, the slackening panzer advance owed much to logistic shortages as the German combat support services struggled desperately to keep the panzer spearheads supplied. In addition, two French ripostes slowed Guderian's advance. Colonel de Gaulle's weakened division managed to counterattack from Laon toward Crécy to strike Guderian's exposed southern flank, while the battered 2nd Amored Division also hit Guderian from the north at Saint Quentin. However, the successful penetration of the French center represented a French military disaster. An operational setback of this magnitude needed a sacrificial victim to provide some atonement. Consequently, late on May 19, Premier Paul Reynaud sacked French Commander in Chief Gamelin and replaced him with the 72-year-old General Weygand, just returned from the Middle East.

The German Victory

On May 20, Guderian's and Reinhardt's panzer divisions reached the Channel coast at Abbeville, just seven days after they had crossed the Meuse. They had covered 240 miles (386 km) in a week, at an incredible average rate of advance of 34 miles (55 km) per day. Then they began to push forward toward Calais and Dunkirk to seize the embarkation ports that represented the sole means of escape for the British, French, and Belgian troops trapped against the coast by the German advance. During the next day, however, the repercussions of the shock inflicted at Arras (see page 105) now critically influenced the unfolding German invasion. Hitler's twin concerns about the threat posed by enemy counterattacks against the weak German flanks and the high losses likely when the panzers entered defended urban areas led him to order the panzer divisions to halt for 48 hours. During this pause the Luftwaffe pounded the isolated British, French, and Belgian forces to further weaken their battered cohesion.

Between May 27 and June 4, 1940, British, French, and some Belgian forces resolutely defended the shrinking defensive perimeter they held around Dunkirk to permit the evacuation of a large part of these isolated forces. In the nine-day "Miracle of Dunkirk," some 861 small boats transported 226,000 British and 112,000 French and Belgian soldiers to safety. But they left most of their equipment behind: 2,472 guns and 84,427 vehicles.

In the subsequent fighting in France, the French hoped to secure an early armistice before the Wehrmacht had occupied the whole of France, but the Germans remained in no mood to negotiate. Army Group C started to attack the vaunted Maginot Line from the rear, while the panzers, having broken through French defenses on the Aisne and Somme, were running amok. Although France retained a puppet state in the south that avoided German occupation – the Vichy regime – the settlement was as much a "dictated peace" as the 1919 Treaty of Versailles had been.

In just six weeks the Wehrmacht had conquered Belgium, France, Holland, and Luxembourg, and driven the BEF off mainland Europe. All this was accomplished with modest casualties: 156,000 killed and wounded. In comparison, the Allies had suffered 300,000 killed and wounded plus a further two million captured. All that Hitler required now was to either conquer Britain or drive her out of the war so that he would be free to turn east and repeat these glorious martial achievements against the Germans' true ideological enemy: the Bolshevik Soviet Union.

Though the campaign was a triumph for the fast-moving panzers, ironically it had been fixed defenses that had determined its conduct. Given that the final

German plan had successfully exploited pre-existing Allied strategic maldeployment, any account of the success the Wehrmacht obtained during the 1940 campaign in the West has to consider carefully the nature of French strategy. World War I had devastated northeastern France, and from this the French military concluded that in the next major war the defensive firepower of artillery and the machine gun would dominate the tactical battlefield. Consequently, France based its interwar military strategy on a defensive posture, an orientation encapsulated by the construction of the Maginot Line during 1930–35. This orientation also reflected French reaction to the huge casualties they had suffered during World War I, which had significantly reduced the country's adult male population.

Forts and Defense Lines

Supposedly the most formidable static defensive position ever constructed, the Maginot Line ran along the Franco-German border from Switzerland to Luxembourg. An undertaking as immense as the construction of the line naturally proved a massive burden on the French economy. The purpose of the line was – at best – to deter Germany from any future war with France by closing off the traditional movement corridor through Alsace-Lorraine north of the Vosges mountains. At worst, if the Germans did attack, the existence of the line would force the German Army first to invade and conquer Belgium in order to attack northeastern France from southern Belgium.

To counter this anticipated enemy move, French strategy prior to 1936 planned to send forces into central Belgium to help the latter resist the German onslaught, which brought France the added benefit that the devastation inflicted on the countryside during the process of halting the Wehrmacht would take place on Belgian territory. In the first half of the 1930s, therefore, French strategy took the form of the D-Plan – the "D" referring to the Dyle River, the geographical barrier in central Belgium to which the French forces would advance and then assume defensive positions alongside Belgian units.

It was this anticipated Franco-Belgian military cooperation that prompted the French not to continue the Maginot Line from Luxembourg along the Franco-Belgian border to the North Sea. If French strategy intended to assist the Belgians by moving 20 divisions onto their soil, the construction of the world's most powerful defensive barrier along the Franco-Belgian border would hardly have sent the right message to the Belgian government. The fact that the construction of the existing 225 miles (362 km) of the Maginot Line had already virtually bankrupted France also influenced this decision not to extend the fortifications to the coast.

Given what is now known about the form that the German invasion of 1940 took, much retrospective criticism has been made of France's failure to extend the line to the coast. In reality, however, during 1940 the line served its intended purpose. The fortifications forced the Germans to attack elsewhere – into Belgium. The fatal flaw in the line was not the failure to extend it to the coast, but the failure of French strategic planning to contemplate the German intent to launch a major mechanized attack through the difficult terrain of the Ardennes. Moreover, on the few occasions when German artillery did engage the Maginot Line during the campaign, it found that even its heaviest guns could not destroy the French bunkers. On June 18, for example, when infantry units of Army Group C attacked the Fort de Formont, they found that the supporting fire of even their heaviest guns

The "panzer corridor," May 13–20. By the late afternoon of May 12, all three German motorized corps had begun to exit the hilly Ardennes terrain and move onto the approaches to the Meuse River. This geographical feature represented the last substantial obstacle between the German armor and the open plains of central France beyond. Early on May 15, Reinhardt's 6th and 8th Panzer Divisions successfully burst out of their bridgehead across the Meuse. By evening the corps had advanced rapidly west an incredible 31 miles (50 km) to Montcornet against disintegrating French resistance. In the process, Reinhardt's armor extended north the critical hole that Guderian's armor had ripped through the French center. Unfortunately for the French, only a few scattered reserves now stood in front of this armored German thrust west to the sea.

– the 210mm Mortar-Cannon 18 (210mm Mörser 18) and the ex-Czech 305mm Mortar (305mm *Mörser*) – proved ineffective, and consequently the attack failed with heavy casualties. Clearly, any sustained direct attack on the strongest parts of the line would have cost the Germans severe casualties. As it was, the French failure to anticipate the German infiltration through the Ardennes enabled the latter to simply bypass the line. Consequently, these potent defenses played an insignificant role in the campaign.

Given that the French decision not to extend the line to the coast was based on their desire to cement future Franco-Belgian military cooperation in the advent of a German attack, Belgium's 1936 decision to declare its neutrality proved ironic. In part, this decision reflected both internal political tensions and fears that closer Franco-Belgian ties would only increase the likelihood of a German invasion of Belgium to gain access to northern France. This said, the fact that in 1914 the German Army violated Belgian soil to attack France hardly made it certain that Belgian neutrality after 1936 would successfully keep away the ravages of any future European war.

After 1936, Belgian neutrality proved a major obstacle to intended French strategy. The French rightly considered that if the Germans violated Belgian neutrality, the latter would immediately seek French military assistance. Consequently, the French retained their pre-1936 strategy, although now they could not discuss with the neutral Belgians the practicalities of the Dyle Plan. These problems would come to haunt the French on May 10, 1940, when they found the roads into Belgium from France blocked to their troops by Belgian police who had not yet received orders to allow the French to come to Belgium's assistance!

The Belgian fort of Eben Emael also figured large in German attack plans. Back in the fall of 1939, German planners had concluded that this powerful Belgian fortress remained vulnerable due to its lack of antiaircraft defenses. Consequently, they formulated a daring plan to land by surprise a glider-borne force onto the roof of the fort – the first time such a tactic had ever been

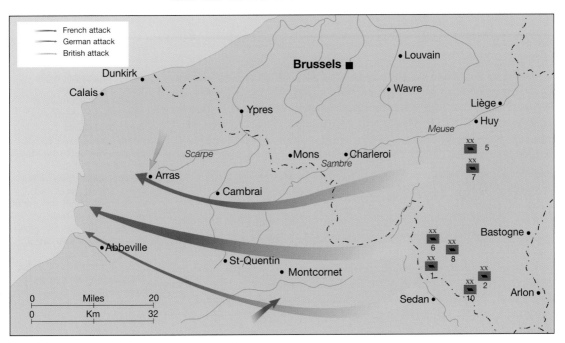

attempted. Once on the roof, the German troops would use a novel lightweight weapon – hollow-charged rounds – to blast through the thick concrete walls of the fort. Consequently, some minutes before the German invasion commenced in the early hours of May 10, a group of 11 gliders, flown by the best pilots available, landed on the roof of Eben Emael. The remote chance of German success in this risky operation had been increased by the fact that the 78 volunteer assault engineers of Detachment *Koch* had trained and rehearsed under conditions of maximum secrecy for as much as six months just to successfully complete this single mission.

After 10 of the 11 German gliders had successfully landed on the roof of Eben Emael, the pioneers quickly overran the surprised defenders and captured the fortress. This success owed much to the effectiveness of German training in inculcating flexibility and willingness to assume vacant leadership roles when necessary. For initially, the only glider not to arrive contained the force commander, *Leutnant* Witzig. Yet this loss did not jeopardize the mission, because the senior NCO present, *Oberfeldwebel* Wenzel, promptly took command and effectively carried out the vital task of employing the hollow-charge explosives to seize the fort. Capturing the fort was only half the mission, however, for the German engineers then had to defend it against Belgian counterattacks until the advancing armor of General Hoepner's XVI Motorized Corps relieved them, which they successfully accomplished. Therefore, a combination of audacious planning, the utilization of new weapons and novel tactics, the achievement of surprise, the tactical initiative shown by Wenzel, and the extremes of top-secret training and preparation undertaken, ensured that this special operation secured the critical Belgian defenses at Eben Emael both quickly and with minimal casualties.

German paratroopers in training prior to the campaign in the West. In 1940 Germany possessed only 4,500 trained paratroopers, and 4,000 of them were used in the attack on Holland. But the psychological effect on the Dutch armed forces and civilian population was out of all proportion to their numbers. The fear and panic they caused greatly aided the German advance, not least by the Dutch allocating army units to hunt down what turned out to be non-existent German airborne units.

With the crucial obstacle of Eben Emael removed through such a daring special operation, Hoepner's panzer corps – with the 3rd and 4th Panzer Divisions under command – raced toward the strategically vital open terrain of the Gembloux Gap.

One of the chief reasons the Wehrmacht triumphed in 1940 was the aggression and boldness displayed by German corps and division commanders during the campaign. At Sedan, for example, the French High Command expected the Germans to wait at least eight days to build up sufficient force for a

A destroyed gun position at Eben Emael. In the most spectacularly successful German special operation of the campaign in the West, a 78-man glider-borne force of assault pioneers landed on top of the powerful – and supposedly impregnable – Belgian fort, which dominated the German route of advance into central Belgium. The German paratroopers, using explosive charges, had soon neutralized the fort's guns and forced the surrender of the garrison.

set-piece attack on the position, and planned to use this valuable time to prepare their defenses and move up reinforcements. Unfortunately for the French, in 1940 German armored commanders like Guderian conducted their operations at a higher tempo than those the French had experienced during 1918. Consequently, late on May 12, both the audacious Guderian and his superior General Ewald von Kleist agreed that XIX Corps should attack across the Meuse River the next afternoon with whatever forces were available. The speed and ferocity of the German assault at Sedan caught the French off-balance and successfully imposed shock action upon them. Some 15 miles (24 km) to the northwest, the other component of the Motorized Group *von Kleist* – Reinhardt's corps – was also to assault the River Meuse at Monthermé that same afternoon.

On May 15 Guderian, against the advice of his more cautious superior Kleist, then made one of the most crucial decisions of the campaign. Aerial reconnaissance had informed him that General Flavigny's French XXI Corps, with the 3rd Armored and 3rd Motorized Divisions under command, was moving up toward his bridgehead from the east to launch a counterattack in the area of Stonne. Despite this information, Guderian nevertheless decided to launch his armor west toward the Channel coast. Although prior to May 10, German operational planning had not decided which axis of advance its forces would develop once Sedan had fallen, Guderian privately had always intended to head west for the coast to split the French armies in two. In an example typical of the extemporized and devolved German approach to operations, the High Command now permitted Guderian, as the commander on the spot, to decide his own axis. In an audacious example of risk-taking, Guderian left just the 10th Panzer Division to protect the bridgehead against Flavigny's approaching two French divisions, until both of Wietersheim's follow-up motorized divisions reached Sedan to reinforce the bridgehead.

In the meantime, Guderian swung his remaining two armored divisions through a right angle and unleashed them west toward the Channel coast. He instructed his formations to advance to their last drop of petrol and to maximize their momentum through simply bypassing enemy centers of resistance. His 1st and 2nd Panzer Divisions advanced an impressive 37 miles (60 km) toward Montcornet and Rethel. In so doing, Guderian created a critical penetration deep into the rear of the weakly held French center. Yet on the morning of May 15 the strong-willed Guderian had only won the freedom to initiate such bold offensive operations after a bitter argument with his superior, Kleist. For on that morning the serious underlying tensions that had existed since early spring within the German High Command over the conduct of the campaign now became overt. The more cautious High Command, and Hitler in particular, harbored grave misgivings about the dangers associated with the audacity displayed by panzer commanders like Guderian, Hoth, and Rommel. That morning, much to Guderian's fury, Kleist initially instructed the corps commander merely to expand and consolidate further the Sedan bridgehead during 15 May, while the two follow-up motorized divisions raced to reach the area. Indeed, only after vigorous and protracted argument did Kleist defer to Guderian's dogged insistence that he be allowed to advance west.

Command Disagreements

In mid-May, Guderian again received explicit orders from Kleist that he exercise greater caution by slowing his advance and shoring up his vulnerable flanks with forces taken from his armored spearhead. During another acrimonious row, Kleist vehemently ordered Guderian to halt, except for reconnaissance, while the latter insisted that he be permitted to conduct his corps with audacity. In addition to sending his resignation up the chain of command, Guderian partially circumvented Kleist's unwelcome halt order by sending large elements of his two panzer divisions on reconnaissance missions.

These command disagreements, together with the serious logistical problems that had arisen due to the speed of the German advance, meant that during May 17 the panzers made more modest advances of up to 10 miles (16 km). But this slackening pace did allow two German motorized divisions from Wietersheim's follow-up XIV Motorized Corps to reach Sedan and take defensive positions on the southern flank. These reinforcements relieved the 10th Panzer Division from its defensive duties and enabled it to begin to head west to join Guderian's spearhead. That day, OKH also ordered the three armored divisions of Generals Hoepner's XVI and Schmidt's XXXIX Motorized Corps to be detached from the German advance into central Belgium to reinforce the drive through the center; within a few days, therefore, all 10 German panzer divisions would be concentrated against the by now crumbling French center.

Clausewitzian Chance

Carl von Clausewitz's book *On War*, published in 1832, is now regarded as one of the finest examples yet produced of an all-embracing theory of the Western view of warfare. One of the concepts that Clausewitz puts forward in this work is that war – more than any other human activity – is inextricably bound up with the influence of chance. Helmuth von Moltke's famous dictum that no plan survives the first point of contact with the enemy reflects his acceptance of Clausewitz's assertion. No commander can avoid the influence that chance events might exert on operations, given the unpredictability of human reactions (whether by enemy or friendly forces), as well as the uncertainty and confusion that pervades every action carried out as part of the application of military force. The 1940 German campaign in the West illustrates well the influence that chance can exert. If it were not for two chance events the Germans may well have proceeded with their original October 1939 plan of invasion. Although it is dangerous to descend into counterfactual "what if?" history, the evidence from the actual campaign suggests that if they had attacked with their original plan, a decisive victory may well have eluded them and, consequently, World War II may have unfolded quite differently than it did. The first chance event was the airplane crash at Mechelen on January 10, 1940, that compromised the German invasion plans. The second was Hitler's chance hearing of a remark concerning Manstein's plan, after its author had been banished to the Polish border to command a reserve formation. Without these two fortuitous events, the Germans may not have adopted the Manstein plan, consequently may not have conquered the West in just six weeks, and as a result may have found themselves in a situation that would have prevented them from invading the Soviet Union in June 1941.

The effects of morale on the French Army and its inability to deal with rapid German advances were critical to the Wehrmacht success in May 1940. At Sedan, for example, Guderian's corps faced a tough and risky mission, but his chances of success were increased by the enormous scale of Luftwaffe support he received. The air force employed no fewer than 900 aircraft to support his attack at Sedan, which the German High Command correctly recognized as representing the campaign's decisive point and thus demanded the concentration of the maximum possible force. During the morning of May 13, the Luftwaffe carried out sustained aerial attacks using Dornier Do 17 bombers in the hinterland beyond Sedan to isolate the battle area. Then, from midday, five hours of attacks by bombers and Stuka dive-bombers on the French defenses helped soften up enemy resistance and assisted the German ground assault that commenced at 1500 hours. Although the physical destruction wreaked by these continuous aerial attacks remained modest, they nevertheless powerfully undermined French morale, particularly among the artillery units in the area.

The French commander at Sedan had contemplated ordering a counterattack against the still-weak German bridgehead on May 13. At 1800 hours, however, he received the disturbing news that German tanks had been seen 2.5 miles (4 km) south of the Marfée Heights around Bulson. Subsequently, it emerged that this information was untrue – no German tanks had yet managed to cross the river, and in reality the vehicles seen at Bulson were French. Nevertheless, this rapidly spreading rumor caused widespread panic among some French infantry units and artillery batteries that evening. Consequently, hundreds of French soldiers fled back to the rear areas in mass hysteria. The panicked French artillery abandoned 50 guns, and the loss of this support crucially undermined the defensive power of the infantry units.

It was this collapse of morale that enabled the Germans to break through at Frénois that evening and seize the vital Marfée Heights. The unfortunate coincidence that at this very moment of French weakness, the headquarters of the 55th Division was in transit to a new location, only hampered French attempts to restore cohesion in this sector. Although the panic died down that night, many smaller and less spectacular examples of French morale collapse continued throughout the night and into the next day around Sedan. These events, in addition, overshadowed the fierce resistance that certain French units offered that evening and night. Perhaps most significantly, these signs of morale fragility shattered the faith of the French High Command in the determination of their troops to resist the German onslaught. In the chaos that resulted during the night of May 13/14 from this break in morale, the French at Sedan found it extremely difficult to organize a swift counterattack against the still-vulnerable German bridgehead within easy striking distance.

This proved fortunate for Guderian, because by midnight on May 13/14, the German bridgehead south of the river remained precarious as not a single tank had managed to get across. Working feverishly, German engineers managed to construct a 14.5-ton (16-tonne) pontoon bridge across the Meuse River by 2310 hours. This enabled the light tanks fielded by the 1st Panzer Division – Panzer I and II vehicles – to begin crossing into the bridgehead during the early hours of May 14. Luckily for Guderian, it was not until 0310 hours that General Grandsard, the French corps commander, managed to issue concrete orders for a counterattack, slated to commence at 0430 hours. Yet even this belated French riposte would involve just two weak battle groups, each with a tank battalion and an infantry regiment. One of these groups was to attack the German positions north of Chémery while the second assault went in at Bulson.

French Paralysis

By the morning of May 14, therefore, the lethargic French reaction, plus the first emerging signs of morale fragility, had prevented the French from seizing an excellent opportunity to throw Guderian's corps back across the Meuse River. If Grandsard's forces had managed to halt this critical German drive through the French center, the French would have been able to derail the entire German invasion. Above all else, however, Guderian's swift penetration of the Meuse obstacle greatly accentuated the profound sense of shock created within the French High Command by the news of the panicked flight of substantial French forces at Sedan. The speed and audacity of the German attacks had caused an increasing degree of paralysis within the French decision-making process. Late on the following day, May 15, for example, the seriousness of the military crisis now facing France hit Gamelin, who observed that for the first time his eyes had suddenly been opened. To Defense Minister Edouard Daladier Gamelin confided gloomily that Guderian's success meant the destruction of the French Army. That evening Colonel Minart, a liaison officer for the High Command, noted that an insipid paralysis was sweeping through the French headquarters at Vincennes. The growing psychological incapacity for timely decision-making was only exacerbated by the inadequate physical means of communications available to this headquarters: Vincennes lacked radios to keep in touch with French formations in the field, rendering it ill-equipped to cope with the pace of German operations.

By May 16, it was becoming clear that the French command system simply could not keep up with the speed of the German armored thrust in the center. By the time, for example, that Gamelin had issued the order to retreat to a line running along the Escaut River down to Omont, Reinhardt's panzers had already pushed beyond this line at Montcornet. Moreover, only now did the French High Command begin to realize that its assumption that the Germans would turn east to outflank the Maginot Line from the rear might be wrong. For during that day

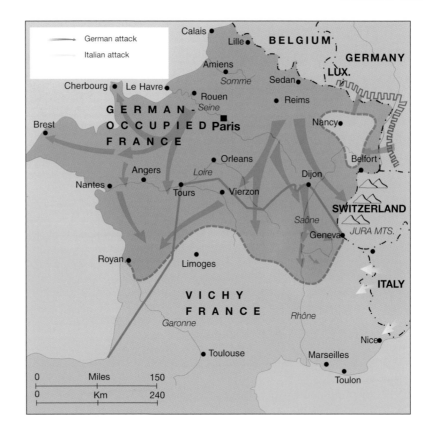

On June 5 the German Army commenced Operation Red, the second phase of their onslaught against France. Having rested and reorganized during the previous two days, the Germans unleashed their panzer and infantry divisions south across the River Somme. By now the German Army could field 120 divisions against the 65 French, and one British, divisions that Weygand could muster. Though popular perception views this phase of the campaign as a mere formality after the successful thrust to the coast, in reality the German attack against the French defenses along the Somme made little initial progress in the face of heavy resistance. During the week of June 5–12, defending French forces conducted a classic elastic defense that slowed the German push south toward Paris. By June 12, however, superior German combat power had broken the heart of French resistance. With the equivalent of just 27 divisions left intact in the field, Weygand was compelled to order a strategic withdrawal across the whole front. The solid purple line represents the demarcation line; the broken purple line the limit of German advance when the armistice was signed.

the German armor, through exhausting their supplies of gasoline, managed to push forward up to another 20 miles (32 km) west in the face of weakening French resistance and hesitant reactions at Vincennes. Guderian's forces linked up with Reinhardt's at Montcornet and both pushed on to Marle by night. To the north, Rommel's 7th Panzer Division pushed on 15 miles (24 km) to Solre-le-Cateau, this advance being slowed to an extent by Kluge's demands that Hoth's armor show greater caution than it had done previously. It was again noticeable that day that the increasingly disorganized and hard-pressed French center managed to undertake not a single substantial counterthrust against the German "panzer corridor."

By May 17, the eighth day of the campaign, the French center faced a truly critical situation. In the "panzer corridor" and the western end of the Gembloux Gap, nine panzer and 13 other German divisions now faced the disintegrating remnants of Blanchard's First and Corap's Ninth French Armies. The morale of many French soldiers had collapsed as the cumulative shock action and confusion imposed by the speed of the panzer divisions and the constant supporting aerial attacks took their toll. This collapse in morale was evident in the May 16–17 advance of Rommel's 7th Panzer Division to Landrecies on the Sambre–Oise Canal, during which it captured 10,000 prisoners and destroyed or captured 100 enemy tanks – all for the cost of just 41 casualties. Farther to the north, Reichenau's 13 infantry divisions pressed forward as the BEF and Belgian forces retreated in stages from the Dyle River to the Escaut River.

On May 19, a desperate Gamelin intervened directly in the conduct of operations by ordering a coordinated counterattack against the panzer corridor by British and Belgian forces from the north together with French units from the

A Rare Successful Integral Battle of Annihilation

Prussian/German military strategy in the 19th and 20th centuries displayed a fixation with the concept of the integral battle of annihilation (*Vernichtungsschlacht*). This military strategy was based, in part, on the Prussian/German High Command's interpretation – or rather, distortion – of Clausewitz's ideas on the climactic, decisive, individual battle, an event that was prominent during the Napoleonic period. This military strategy centers on the intent to defeat an opponent swiftly through one single, continuous offensive action. The 1870 Prussian attack on France, the 1914 German attack on the West (the Schlieffen plan), and the 1940 and 1941 German invasions of the West and the Soviet Union, respectively, all represented attempts by the Prussian/German militaries to achieve this military strategy. However, the strategy has often proved impossible to achieve against an evenly matched opponent, since the sustainability of offensive combat power has often proved inadequate in relation to the resilience of both fighting power and morale in the defensive. However, in the interwar period, new military technology – in the form of armored fighting vehicles, mechanization, and air power – increased the tempo, momentum, sustainability, and shock power of offensive action. After 1939, these advances made it possible for military forces to achieve this particular military strategy even against powerful opponents. Indeed, the most exceptional aspect of the stunning German success in the West in 1940 was that it represented a rare example of a successful integral battle of annihilation against an enemy of approximately equal combat power and effectiveness. Unfortunately, this success only fueled further German arrogance and led them to attempt a repeat of this strategy – on a scale magnified 12-fold – against the Soviet Union in 1941. The eventual German defeat at the hands of the Red Army in 1945 provided further evidence of just how difficult it was in the 20th century to achieve such a military strategy.

south. The never strong "Allied alliance," however, had further disintegrated under the strain of the unexpectedly successful German invasion, and this hampered the implementation of a synchronized, large-scale counterstroke. During the previous week, for example, General Gort, commander of the BEF, had received no direct orders whatsoever from his French superior, General Billotte, on how to conduct his command. It was these significant enemy weaknesses that the ruthless high-tempo advance undertaken by the panzer divisions so successfully exploited.

By June 12, the difficulties Weygand faced had worsened, since his forces now also had to defend southeastern France from the Italian attack initiated on June 10. Some four days later, a largely deserted Paris fell to Hitler's advancing troops. As nine German panzer divisions poured into the interior of France, the morale of French forces collapsed. By June 15 Britain had commenced withdrawing its forces from France through the ports of Cherbourg and Brest. At this late stage in the campaign, as the panzers advanced rapidly deeper into France, the Germans deployed a battery of a new type of armored fighting vehicle (AFV), the StuG III assault gun, an effective artillery weapon for infantry support (see text box page 103). As the German armor charged south, the by now disgraced French premier, Paul Reynaud, resigned and a new government was sworn in under Marshal Petain. During mid-June the demands from French politicians for an armistice reached a deafening clamor, while many senior commanders now desired to secure a quick peace settlement that guaranteed the honor of the French armed forces before the Germans overran the entire country. By the time the armistice was signed on June 22, German forces had advanced deep into France, reaching as far south as Bordeaux in the west, Clermont-Ferrand in the center, and Lyon in the east. In the process, the German advance south from Sedan had encircled the bulk of the French forces still holding the Maginot Line along the Franco-German border in Alsace-Lorraine.

The lessons learned in Poland the year before had been put to good use by the army in 1940, and, as the campaign in France would show, all arms were more proficient in battlefield skills. The campaign plan was quite sophisticated in terms of the operational art it displayed. For it constituted an excellent example of an operational-level campaign plan that combined effectively in time and space a coherent and synchronized series of tactical elements that produced the prospect of a rapid and decisive victory. The plan outflanked France's powerful Maginot Line defenses, while both the powerful northern deception thrust and the southern feint exploited existing French preconceptions and reinforced their strategic maldeployment. These combined tactical elements sucked the French to the north and south and allowed the Germans to concentrate their strength at the point of French weakness in the center. The plan also drove a wedge between the French forces that had moved into Belgium and those defending the Maginot Line. If a successful infiltration could be exploited ruthlessly toward the coast, such an advance threatened to split the defenders in half, allowing the enemy forces to be destroyed in detail.

Once the concentrated mass of seven panzer divisions had successfully penetrated through the Ardennes, these forces had to swiftly seize crossings over the Meuse River between Sedan and Namur. This river represented the last major obstacle to the interior of France, and if the panzers could bounce the French defenses along the river before the latter reinforced them, the plains of central France would be at the mercy of the rampaging advance of the German tanks. A swift crossing of the Meuse would enable the German Army to convert the operational potential achieved by their advance through the Ardennes into a decisive strategic penetration deep into the interior of France. The German High Command, however, had refused to set down during the planning phase what

Waffen-SS motorized infantry advance during the campaign in France. Once the Germans had broken through at Sedan, the speed of their advance kept the Allies off-balance. Doctrinally, the Allies were woefully ill-prepared to respond to German mobility. Guderian makes a pertinent point: "The French doctrine was the result of lessons the French had learned from the First World War, their experience of positional warfare, of the high value they attached to firepower, and of their underestimation of movement. These French strategic and tactical principles were the exact opposite of my own theories."

precise direction the advance would take once Sedan had fallen. The Germans faced at least three excellent axes over which to develop their attack: back east toward the northern rear of the Maginot Line, southwest toward Paris, or farther west toward the Channel coast. The High Command would delay such a decision until Sedan had fallen, in order to exploit the best tactical opportunity that had opened up and to receive the benefit of the judgment of the local commanders on the spot. This flexibility would pay great dividends.

The physical caliber of German troops far exceeded that of their Allied opponents. For example, the 12 infantry divisions of General Reichenau's Sixth Army pushed into central Belgium in what the French believed to be the main German attack. These physically very fit German infantrymen both conducted forced marches over long distances and fought hard tactical encounters with the enemy to advance west in a desperate race to reach the Dyle River before the French First Army Group reached it and consolidated its defenses.

Their morale was also much higher. At Sedan, at 1500 hours on May 13, the first German assault parties, which comprised pioneers and infantry, began to

During the engagement at Arras on May 21, the Germans found that none of their previously adequate 37mm Antitank Gun 35/36 (37mm Pak 35/36) weapons (seen here) could penetrate the 2.3-in. (60-mm) frontal armor of British Matilda II tanks, even though initially the brave SS gunners held their nerve and continued to engage the two approaching Matildas that had broken through even when they had reached point-blank range. Subsequent German inspection of a disabled Matilda some days later revealed that it had survived no fewer than 14 hits by rounds fired by the 37mm gun. Although this weapon had proved adequate against the lightly armored Polish tankettes during the 1939 campaign, experiences such as that at Arras in May 1940 led the Germans both to boost the rate of production of heavier antitank weapons, such as the 50mm Antitank Gun 38 (50mm Pak 38), of which a few preproduction examples served during the campaign, and to develop more rapidly the even heavier 75mm Antitank Gun 40 (75mm Pak 40).

cross the Meuse in inflatable boats. Even though these troops advanced under a hail of supporting fire, they nevertheless still encountered very fierce French defensive resistance. Despite this heavy enemy fire, the German assault infantry nevertheless managed to secure a bridgehead on the French bank, albeit in only three of the original six assault sectors. Once the Germans had secured these toeholds on the French bank, their engineers immediately began to construct ferries and pontoon bridges to transport the panzers across the river. By 1700 hours the Stuka attacks ceased in the Sedan area and moved farther west and south to interdict French reinforcements approaching the bridgehead from deeper within France. Some 90 minutes later the German spearhead, provided by the motorized infantry of the 1st Rifle Regiment, achieved a critical breakthrough of the French defensive line at Frénois. By 2200 hours these troops had captured Cheveuges, some 3.75 miles (5 km) southwest of Sedan. By 2230 hours, soldiers of the élite *Grossdeutschland* Regiment had successfully reached the dominant

A German 88mm Flak gun in action in France. During the Allied breakthrough at Arras, a battery each of 88mm Antiaircraft 18 (88mm Flak 18) and 105mm Light Field Howitzer 18 (105mm le HF 18) guns were used in the antitank role as part of a hastily thrown-together combined-arms defensive force at Wailly. The German antiaircraft and artillery gunners – egged on by Rommel, who ran from gun to gun shouting encouragement – in firing their pieces over open sights against the advancing British tanks at point-blank range, eventually won the day: the British attack petered out when these German efforts disabled the leading British Matilda tanks.

ground of the Marfée Heights. Finally, at 0330 hours on May 14, the Germans established defensive positions for the night along the Chehéry–Chaumont line, and awaited the anticipated French counterattack.

During Reinhardt's advance, as in other instances during the campaign, the successes achieved by the panzer divisions owed much to the evolving manner in which their armor and motorized infantry (subsequently termed panzergrenadiers) cooperated intimately on the tactical battlefield. During the Polish campaign, the few German halftracked armored personnel carriers (APCs) available had merely transported motorized infantry troops to the edge of the battlefield, where they debussed. In France, however, the well-trained motorized infantry often stayed in their APCs – now available in greater numbers – as these vehicles advanced alongside the armor in the face of what often constituted scarcely cohesive enemy resistance. The panzergrenadiers then provided intimate small arms fire support for the panzers from within their APCs, or while still embussed screened the flanks of advancing armored wedges, or even debussed on the battlefield to mop up disorganized enemy forces. Though this new tactical role inevitably brought somewhat higher casualties among the panzergrenadiers, it nevertheless augmented the combat power of the advancing panzer divisions, and contributed to the stunning success obtained in the West during 1940.

In late May, even nightfall did not prevent elements of Hoth's corps from exploiting the lack of cohesion now evident within the enemy forces facing them by continuing their attacks northwest throughout the hours of darkness. Back during the Polish campaign, the ordinary German soldier had demonstrated certain tactical frailties when it came to night-time operations, largely due to the modest time devoted to these skills during the otherwise rigorous German training programs undertaken prior to the invasion of Poland. During the winter of 1939–40, however, the German Army worked hard to improve the night-fighting skills of its soldiers through conducting extensive retraining courses.

The significantly improved effectiveness of the ordinary German soldier in such night-time scenarios was demonstrated on a number of occasions during the May 1940 invasion of the West. One notable example occurred during the night of May 20/21, when elements of Hoth's corps – notably Rommel's 7th Panzer Division – conducted a successful night-time crossing on the La Bassée Canal in the face of the heavy resistance offered by a battalion of the British Grenadier Guards. Once again, as Hans von Luck, a German officer who took part in the action, recalled, the forward momentum of the attacking troops in this difficult tactical situation was powerfully reinforced by the immediate presence of Rommel, who both exhorted his troops forward and personally directed artillery fire to support them. In addition, the assault was reinforced by the rudimentary and improvised supporting attacks undertaken by German aircraft, though German aerial night-fighting techniques still remained rather underdeveloped at this stage of the war. Clearly, the ability to conduct effective attacks at night increased the already high tempo of operations the German Army had achieved in the West and helped maximize the pressure its forces exerted on the increasingly disoriented Allied formations attempting to resist the German advance.

The Superiority of German Infantry

The decision to halt the panzers before Dunkirk was rendered unnecessary by the quality of the German infantry. The gravest threat to the German advance had passed by May 24, since follow-up infantry forces were rapidly filling out the vulnerable southern German flank established from the coast eastward along the Somme River back to Stonne near Sedan. Indeed, the success of the German armored drive to the coast owed much to the ability of the follow-up infantry not to fall too far behind. In an effort to keep up with the panzers and throw much-needed defensive screens across the exposed German flanks, the infantry had to march impressive distances each day: up to 35 miles (56 km) in some instances. In addition, German tactical reconnaissance aircraft contributed greatly to the successful screening missions undertaken by these follow-up infantry forces by forewarning the ground forces of impending enemy counterstrokes. The ordinary German soldier's ability to march such distances and then fight effectively, however, owed little to the aerial support provided and everything to the excellent physical resilience engendered in the ordinary soldier by the rigorous training regimen all recruits and soldiers underwent during basic training.

With these infantry forces now successfully managing to secure much of the exposed German southern flank, the threat posed by enemy countermoves had diminished somewhat. Thus, when British and French forces did manage to initiate two weak counterthrusts against the German positions along the Somme during May 23–26, when the 1st British Armored Division and what was left of de Gaulle's 3rd Armored Division attacked, these assaults made little headway. In fact, all Hitler's halt order "achieved" was to give the BEF precious time for its battered and disorganized forces to extemporize a shaky defensive perimeter around Dunkirk, into which the British and French could retreat. By then, unfortunately, what was left of the Belgian Army had reluctantly surrendered on May 28 on the orders of King Leopold. In the north, the overriding issue now was how the British and French forces could escape the impending annihilation as the jaws of the German encirclement closed around Dunkirk.

The StuG III Assault Gun

In the last days of Operation Red, the Germans deployed a solitary battery of a new type of AFV, the assault gun (*Sturmgeschütz*). This low-silhouetted, turretless four-man armored vehicle originated in the 1936 German Army requirement for an armored close infantry support artillery vehicle – a role which the panzers might have fulfilled had the Germans not decided to concentrate them as instruments of strategic breakthrough. The army received delivery of 30 preproduction StuG III Model A (Sdkfz 142) vehicles during the spring of 1940, which equipped five experimental assault gun batteries, one of which served in the last days of the French campaign. The StuG III Model A mounted the short-barreled 75mm gun fitted to the Panzer IV tank. The armament sat in a limited traverse mounting located in the front plate of the StuG III's fixed superstructure; the latter fitted directly on top of the standard Panzer III tank chassis. This design reduced the vehicle's height to just 6 ft 5 in. (1.95 m), which compared favorably with the 8.25-in. (2.5-m) tall Panzer III tank. In addition, the StuG III featured 2-in.

(50-mm) frontal armor and 1.7-in. (43-mm) plates on the sides – a better standard of protection than that possessed by the Panzer III or IV. In France, the assault gun battery employed demonstrated clearly to the German Army High Command that the StuG III was an effective infantry support vehicle, and this led to the commencement of full-scale production in July 1940. As the war progressed, the German Army relied increasingly on the later up-gunned and up-armored StuG III variants as substitutes for the always insufficient numbers of available panzers. As a cheaper and quicker-to-build AFV than a tank, the StuG III proved just the vehicle the over-stretched German war economy needed to produce from 1943 to offset the vast attrition suffered on all fronts.

As in Poland, the Luftwaffe's contribution to the campaign was essential to the army's success. As the ground forces commenced their attacks on the border defenses, massed formations of German bombers and fighter-bombers – mainly Dornier Do 17 and Heinkel He 111 bombers, Messerschmitt Bf 110 fighter-bombers, and Junkers Ju 87 Stuka dive-bombers – began attacking enemy air bases. These attacks proved particularly successful in Belgium and Holland, where dozens of aircraft were caught on the ground and destroyed, but inflicted less damage against the French Air Force. These aerial operations represented a classic attritional counter-air campaign designed to achieve local air superiority over the theater. Once this had been accomplished, the Germans could then employ their air power to facilitate the ground advance through undertaking the missions of aerial reconnaissance, battlefield air interdiction (BAI), and close air support (CAS).

To assist the speed of advance of Army Group B, the Germans inserted the paratroopers and air-landed troops of the 22nd (Airlanding) Infantry and 7th Airborne Divisions deep into Dutch territory, including some troops disguised as Dutch soldiers. The objectives of these forces were to seize several important bridges over the Maas, Waal, and Rhine rivers at Dordrecht, Gennep, Maastricht, Moerdijk, and Waalhaven. These actions were designed to enable General Schmidt's XXXIX Motorized Corps, with the 9th Panzer Division under command – the only German mechanized formation used in Holland – to advance swiftly toward The Hague. At Gennep, for example, a handful of superbly trained Brandenburg commandos disguised as Dutch policemen successfully seized the bridge with minimal losses, in an operation that aptly demonstrated how effectively élite covert forces employing classic *ruses de guerre*

could facilitate overall German success in the theater. To the immediate north of this airborne carpet, the infantry of General Küchler's Eighteenth Army pushed west toward the Zuider Zee and The Hague to support the advance of the 9th Panzer Division.

In addition, German air-landed forces attempted to capture the three principal Dutch airfields around The Hague and use them to enact a raid designed to seize Queen Wilhemina and her government. Although several of these operations failed, notably the attempt to capture the government, the other missions secured their objectives and successfully facilitated the subsequent advance of the invading ground troops. Once again, as in Poland, it would be effective German joint (interservice) and combined-arms cooperation that would go a long way to securing decisive success for the Wehrmacht in the 1940 Western campaign.

At Sedan, the Luftwaffe not only aided the initial crossing, it also fended off French attacks. By 0900 hours on May 14 the Germans had managed to transport the entire 1st Panzer Brigade across the Meuse River using a second, heavier, pontoon bridge for this formation's Panzer III and IV tanks. This achievement had been threatened that morning, however, when the Germans found their pontoon bridges under sustained enemy air attack; but the imminent arrival of Luftwaffe fighters and the concentration of 200 antiaircraft pieces around the pontoons helped restrict the damage these enemy aerial missions

The campaign in the West was won by the panzers, but victory would not have been possible without the support of the infantry, most of whom marched on foot. They secured the flanks of the "panzer corridor" and reduced pockets of enemy resistance. Man for man they were far better than their British and French opponents.

could inflict on the pontoons. By the time the two much-delayed French counterattacks commenced, large numbers of German tanks had reached the frontline infantry and assumed defensive positions. The French armor and infantry simply slammed themselves into the waiting German forces that now deployed armor, antitank, and light artillery assets to support the ground troops. Within 60 minutes these forces had smashed the attacking French units, which then withdrew 1.25 miles (2 km) to the south beyond Maisoncelle.

In the case of de Gaulle's counterattack, the ability of the highly trained and well-motivated soldiers within Guderian's panzer divisions to halt French ripostes owed much to the assistance rendered by the Luftwaffe. For as de Gaulle's armored columns crossed the plain of Laon to attack Guderian's forces in the flank, German tactical reconnaissance planes detected the French threat. Subsequently, German fighter-bombers repeatedly struck the enemy armor both to reduce their forward momentum and to inflict significant casualties on them. During the precious time bought by these aerial attacks, Guderian's forces rapidly improvised their own countermoves, which completed the task of halting de Gaulle's attempted riposte.

The Risks Inherent in "Blitzkrieg" – Arras

Enemy actions on May 21, 1940, were to prove how valid were the fears that haunted the German High Command over the vulnerability of the flanks of the armored corridor. During that day a British brigade group based around the 1st Army Tank Brigade counterattacked at Arras, spearheaded by 58 Matilda Mark I and 16 heavily armored and gunned – but slow – Matilda Mark II tanks. On its flank, the French also launched a supporting operation. This limited response represented the pitiful attempt to implement the large-scale attack originally ordered by Gamelin. Despite the modest forces committed, the British counterstroke nevertheless successfully pressed 3 miles (5 km) forward against the defense offered by the 7th Panzer and SS *Totenkopf* Divisions. Indeed, many of the Waffen-SS soldiers abandoned their antitank guns and ran as fast as they could toward the rear. Notwithstanding their "hard" training, the SS troops were horrfied to discover that their 37mm shells bounced off the hulls of the Allied tanks (an experience that was to be repeated against Soviet T-34 tanks on the Eastern Front). The men of the 7th Panzer Division fared no better, and it was only the presence of Rommel himself that steadied their nerves and saved the day (he was forced to run from gun to gun to prevent the crews from running). If the attack had been pressed with determination it may have caused serious problems for the advancing Germans.

While ultimately, the May 21 British and French counterstroke at Arras proved a failure, it profoundly shocked the German High Command, particularly Hitler, as fearful officers cast their military minds back to 1914, when the Allied "Miracle of the Marne" had halted the previously successful Schlieffen attack. Meanwhile, as the British counterstroke at Arras unfolded, Weygand flew over the panzer corridor to land at Calais. Here he attempted to arrange a coordinated attack from the north by elements of Billotte's First Army Group. Despite what was agreed that day, this plan was soon wrecked by the combination of Billotte being fatally wounded that night and the unrelenting German pressure, which prevented the earmarked forces from being able to deliver Weygand's proposed counterstrike. Ultimately, however, it was a case of too little, too late for the French and British armies.

Hitler's Balkan Interlude

The 1941 Balkan campaign was a stunning and speedy success for the Wehrmacht, but it interrupted the schedule for the invasion of the Soviet Union and left an unresolved partisan problem that would later tie down military resources.

The speed with which the hastily improvised April 1941 Axis invasion conquered Yugoslavia, Greece, and Crete demonstrated that the German Army had enhanced its combat performance in comparison with that delivered in Poland during September 1939. No doubt the valuable experience gained in the West during May–June 1940, and the confidence this victory imbued in the troops, helped the Wehrmacht's operations in the Balkans. The ability of commanders and staff officers to quickly produce improvised – yet still effective – planning in adverse conditions proved essential for the triumph obtained by the Wehrmacht. In addition, intimate German air-to-ground coordination proved highly valuable to compensate for the lack of artillery support experienced, as the gunners struggled to keep up with the mechanized spearheads in terrain as inhospitable as that encountered in the mountains of Greece and Yugoslavia.

Effective German all-arms cooperation, including the successful employment of specialist airborne, commando, and mountain forces, also went a long way to facilitate the German success, as did the impressive capabilities that German troops and vehicles demonstrated in covering terrain perceived by their enemies as virtually impassable. In addition, effective junior officer leadership, generally excellent troop training, the widespread physical resilience of ordinary soldiers, and the effective multi-role equipment available to them, all contributed significantly to the scale and speed of the spring 1941 Axis triumph in the Balkans.

During late 1940 and early 1941 Germany wished to see a stable Balkans that was either neutral or, preferably, pro-German. Hitler desired these conditions to ensure that events in the Balkans did not disrupt Germany's preparations for

April 26, 1941: elements of German Parachute Regiment 2 land along the Corinth Canal that straddles the narrow Corinthian isthmus to capture the only bridges that permitted a British withdrawal south into the Peleponnese. Utilizing the benefit of surprise, these forces captured their objectives and then exploited this success by securing the surrender of a numerically larger Anglo-Greek force.

Barbarossa, the planned invasion of the Soviet Union, slated to begin in late spring 1941. On October 28, 1940, however, the Italians – without German foreknowledge – invaded northwestern Greece from their colony of Albania. Mussolini feared that the Germans desired a sphere of influence in the Balkans at Italy's expense, and he believed that an easy Italian conquest of Greece would forestall such a situation and win for Italy a sliver of the martial glory that the Wehrmacht recently had attained for the Third Reich. After modest initial Italian successes, however, the Greek Army forced the Italians back onto Albanian soil, until by December the fighting had degenerated into stalemate.

This deadlock threatened to undermine the conducive conditions the Wehrmacht desired in the Balkans to ensure that its preparations for Barbarossa could progress. Hitler feared that Greece would secure a military alliance with Great Britain against the Italians, an agreement that the British could then fashion into an anti-German front to threaten the southern flank of the German concentration areas for Barbarossa. Even worse, from Greek air bases British long-range bombers could attack the Ploesti oilfields in Romania, from where the Wehrmacht obtained most of its fuel. Initially, Germany responded to Italy's difficulties by sending limited military aid to its Axis partner first in Albania and then in North Africa, where the arrival of Rommel's Africa Corps would assist the struggling Italian Army in its battle against the British (see Chapter 7).

During November 1940, Hitler decided to initiate decisive military action during the spring of 1941 to settle permanently the Balkan imbroglio before Barbarossa commenced. This action comprised nothing less than an intended German conquest of Greece, staged from Bulgarian soil. In early 1941, Hitler began the necessary diplomatic moves to bring Romania and Bulgaria into the Axis pact, a situation that placed the Yugoslav government, certainly not a staunch enemy of Berlin, in a difficult position. During February and March, German forces moved first onto Romanian and then Bulgarian soil. Bowing to the political wind, the Yugoslavs reluctantly discussed with Germany plans for a joint invasion of Greece, thereby intending to avoid a German violation of Yugoslav sovereignty as a stepping-stone for its attack on Greece.

The War Against Yugoslavia

These threatening Axis moves prompted Greece to reconsider its strategic options. In late 1940, Greece had rejected the deployment of British military forces on its soil to fight the Italians lest this move provoke a German invasion. In early 1941, however, as Greece surveyed the aggressive steps taken by the neighboring Axis nations, its government felt compelled to accept the British offer to deploy two divisions on Greek soil. This unwelcome development reinforced Hitler's resolve to invade Greece, though he did not manage to slot into place the final piece of his anti-Greek Axis jigsaw until March 25, when Yugoslavia joined the Axis Pact. Just two days later, however, Hitler's carefully crafted plans disintegrated when a pro-British regime seized power in Yugoslavia. This move caused the enraged Führer immediately to order a full-scale German invasion of both Greece and Yugoslavia – codenamed Operation Marita – to commence at the earliest possible.

After hasty and heavily improvised planning, the first German forces announced that they would be ready to attack Yugoslavia and Greece on Palm Sunday, April 6, 1941. Though on paper the Yugoslav Army was numerically strong – it fielded 28 divisions – much of this strength remained illusory. By

German halftrack, motorcycle and sIG 33 assault gun in the Balkans in April 1941. German vehicles performed well in the adverse mountainous terrain, and Yugoslav, Greek, and British troops were often surprised at the ability of German tanks to traverse "impassable" mountain tracks.

April 6, for instance, some Yugoslav Army formations had not managed to mobilize, and those that had lacked modern and effective equipment (they possessed no armor whatsoever). In addition, the Yugoslav Air Force deployed just 300 operational aircraft and thus could offer only modest assistance to the unfolding ground operations.

In strategic terms the defensive power of the Yugoslav Army was also fundamentally compromised by the fact that it faced hostile Axis powers – Italy (including Albania), the Austrian parts of the Reich, Romania, Hungary, and Bulgaria – on three sides. Though the Greek Army both enjoyed a stronger geostrategic position and possessed greater cohesion, with 21 divisions it remained smaller than the Yugoslav Army and was almost as poorly equipped. In addition, the inconclusive war with Hitler's Italian allies had already tied down some two-thirds of the Greek Army in the northwestern part of the country, leaving just seven formations – plus the equivalent of four Commonwealth divisions – to resist the German invasion.

During April 6–11, the Axis ground war against Yugoslavia commenced from three sides in a staggered series of blows. That these attacks did not commence simultaneously on April 6 owed much to the hastily improvised nature of the invasion – many formations simply remained unready to attack on that day. However, that the invasion actually commenced at all that day said much about the ability of German commanders and staff officers rapidly to develop improvised plans under adverse conditions. In the first 72 hours of the war Yugoslavia desperately looked to its allies – the Soviet Union and Turkey – for assistance, while at the same time avoiding tactical arrangements with the Greeks that might restrict the freedom of maneuver of its army. Neither Turkey nor the Soviets wished to get involved in a conflict against Europe's premier military

On April 11, the Italian Second Army attacked the Yugoslavian Seventh Army from Istria and thrust southeast. During the previous day the German XLIX Mountain Corps – part of Colonel-General Freiherr von Weichs' Second Army – attacked south from southern Austria toward Zagreb. Also on April 11, along the northeastern front formed by the Yugoslav–Hungarian border, the German XLVI Motorized Corps struck west toward Zagreb, the capital of Croatia. That same day the Hungarian government reversed its decision not to participate directly in the invasion – since the previous German attacks had secured stunning initial success – and launched the Hungarian Third Army into the fray. Also on April 11, along the Yugoslav–Romanian border, the German XLI Motorized Corps – led by the experienced General Reinhardt – attacked west toward the Yugoslavian capital Belgrade, just 56 miles (90 km) away.

machine, however, and so avoided criticizing the German invasion. Stalin, in particular, wished to avoid worsening his already delicate relations with Hitler, in the hope that the Führer would not invade the Soviet Union while Britain remained undefeated. Consequently, the Axis remained free to deal with Yugoslavia without the risk of foreign interference.

On April 7, along the borders of southeastern Yugoslavia, Colonel-General Ewald von Kleist's First Panzer Group had advanced from Bulgarian soil northwest toward Nis and Belgrade. During the previous day farther to the south, XL Panzer and XVIII Mountain Corps, part of the German Twelfth Army, had attacked southwest across Macedonia in southern Yugoslavia toward Albania. Finally, in southwestern Yugoslavia, the Italians attacked from northern Albania northward along the coast toward Dubrovnik. Against weak opposition the Italian advance went smoothly.

Yet for Kleist to continue his advance after April 9, he had to take considerable risks with his flanks. For the German mountain troops tasked with the protection of his exposed northern flank could only make slow progress across appalling terrain. To cover his exposed southern flank, Kleist – in addition to relying on extensive German aerial interdiction efforts – had to direct elements of the 5th Panzer Division southeast toward Pristina, the capital of the Serbian province of Kosovo. On April 11–12, in the face of the outflanking threat from the southeast posed by Kleist's rapid advance, the Yugoslav First and Six Armies pulled back south and west some 62 miles (100 km) from the Hungarian and Romanian borders to a much shorter line along the Danube River around

Belgrade. This withdrawal led the Germans to commence the attack mounted by their XLI Corps from Romania toward Belgrade, slated for April 12, a day early.

On April 11, on the Hungarian border, XLVI Motorized Corps pushed both west toward Zagreb in central Croatia and southeast. During the next day the corps drove northwest of Belgrade, which it captured on April 13. Meanwhile, on April 11 the Italian Second Army commenced its attack southeast from Istria toward Delnice in western Croatia, which fell the next day. After the capture of this town, the Germans allocated the Italian Army a zone of operations along the Dalmatian coast that German forces would avoid, so as to minimize the risk of friendly fire casualties in a rapidly changing battlefield situation.

On April 13, Kleist's armored forces occupied Belgrade without a fight after the defending Yugoslav units retreated southeast into the mountains. The Germans now concentrated on securing the key towns and main roads as quickly as possible, while leaving largely unmolested the isolated Yugoslavian Army remnants in their mountainous positions.

By April 17, the Germans had reached the Adriatic coast and linked up with the Italians, who in the meantime had thrust south along the coast from Istria in the north to link up with Italian forces advancing northward from Albania. On April 14, realizing that continued resistance was futile, Prime Minister General Simovic resigned and the Yugoslavs requested an armistice. On April 15, after German forces had captured the Yugoslav High Command, German Second Army Commander Colonel-General von Weichs accepted the armistice offer, which was duly signed on April 17 in Belgrade.

Notwithstanding this intractable partisan problem that would dog the Axis grip on the Balkans for the rest of the war, from the perspective of mid-April 1941 Hitler had successfully wreaked a terrible vengeance on Yugoslavia for the pro-British coup of late March 1941. More significantly, the Führer had effectively cleared up one part of his thorny Balkan problem without excessively delaying Barbarossa, the planned German invasion of the Soviet Union. In April 1941, the Axis conquest of Greece and Crete represented Hitler's solution to the other unresolved part of his Balkan imbroglio.

The War Against Greece

The German invasion of northeastern Greece, launched by Field Marshal Wilhelm List's Twelfth Army from Bulgarian soil, commenced on April 6 simultaneously with the offensive into southeastern Yugoslavia; indeed, these two efforts merely represented the twin facets of an integrated invasion plan. A few hours earlier, the Germans had informed the Greeks that the alleged anti-German "allied" front created in the Balkans by Greek acceptance of British forces on its soil had forced a German invasion. The note stressed, however, that Hitler's quarrel was not with Greece but with Great Britain; but to the Greek soldiers facing coordinated panzer and Stuka dive-bombing attacks that afternoon, these diplomatic niceties held no relevance whatsoever.

The German XVIII Mountain Corps attacked from southwestern Bulgaria due south toward Serrai in northeastern Greece against the defenses manned by the Greek East Macedonian Army. Simultaneously, other elements of XVIII Corps attacked from Petrich in southwestern Bulgaria westward into the southeastern tip of Yugoslavia. Subsequently these German forces swung through 90 degrees to drive due south into northern Greece, thus bypassing the western end of the powerful Metaxas defense line. In response to this German attempt to

Mountain Warfare

Given the truly inhospitable mountainous areas encountered by the German Army in many of its 1939–45 campaigns, it regularly had to rely on its elite mountain troops (*Gebirgsjäger*) to spearhead attacks mounted in the most difficult terrain. The Army High Command carefully selected these troops from the cream of the available pool of army recruits who possessed extensive experience of living in alpine conditions. The conditions the *Gebirgsjäger* encountered during the spring 1941 Axis invasion of Yugoslavia and Greece exemplify the particular tactical realities of mountain warfare. The German Army employed four mountain divisions in this campaign, and the experiences encountered by General Julius Ringel's 5th Division in its attacks against the Greek Metaxas Line defenses around the Rupel Pass during April 6–9 remain typical of the sort of war the *Gebirgsjäger* faced. For Ringel's division even to get to its initial concentration area high up in the inaccessible mountainous region of the Greek–Bulgarian border required superhuman efforts. Traveling by night where possible to maintain surprise, pack mules struggled to bring up the dismantled components of the division's lightweight 75mm Mountain Gun 36 (75mm GebG 36) artillery pieces. Yet even these pack animals could not make it up to the very highest positions that Ringel's experienced alpine troops occupied. Consequently, half of the personnel in each of the mountain rifle companies deployed in such locations had to be employed just to bring up the required food, ammunition, and blankets for the other soldiers in the unit, and this obviously limited the combat power that could be employed against the enemy. Despite bringing all their training and tactical skills to bear during three days of intense repeated attacks, these mountain troops struggled to dislodge the determined Greek defense of the Rupel Pass that skillfully utilized the advantages offered by the terrain. Not until the fourth day – April 9 – did Ringel's *Gebirgsjäger* manage to outflank the defenders and, exploiting the element of surprise, roll up the enemy blocking positions from the rear to capture the vital Rupel Pass. Once again, the determination, tactical flexibility, and physical resilience of these specialist German soldiers, reinforced by the effective weapons that they possessed, ultimately proved sufficient to seize this strategically vital position.

penetrate the Metaxas Line by frontal attack, on April 7 British bombers attacked German logistic bases in southwestern Bulgaria. If the Royal Air Force had continued these efforts, it might have undermined the German Army's desperate attempts to meet the onerous demands for supplies emanating from its rapidly advancing mechanized spearheads. Farther to the east, however, the two divisions of the German XXX Corps enjoyed swifter success against weaker resistance, though by April 9 the Greek forces that had retreated to the eastern wing of the Metaxas Line along the Nestos River successfully halted the westward advance of the corps.

Farther to the west, during April 10–11, XL Motorized Corps continued its threatening thrust south in Yugoslav Macedonia. Now the panzers reached the critical part of their mission: the drive south deep into Greek territory to threaten the relatively weak Anglo-Greek center. Consequently, by the evening of April 11, these forces had raced farther south to capture Florina, 13 miles (21 km) from the border. This dangerous advance made possible a future German thrust farther south toward Ioannina that would cut off the 14 Greek divisions, then locked in combat with the Italians in southern Albania, from their only routes of retreat across the Pindus mountains.

Around Vevi, however, on 12 April the British forces located along the western flank of the central sector held by the Anglo-Greek W-Force managed to stem the advance of the now-weakened XL Corps. One reason for this decline in German combat power was that on April 11, Hitler – against the wishes of the German Army High Command — had diverted westward certain units from XL Corps, including the elite SS Motorized Division *Leibstandarte*. The Führer wished these forces to link up with the Italian units attacking the Yugoslav Third Army from Eastern Albania, whereas it made better strategic sense to concentrate all available German units for the decisive thrust south through the weak Greek center.

On April 12, after the Greek East Macedonian Army had capitulated, the German XVIII Mountain Corps commenced a thrust west from Salonika toward

Edessa to link up with the southerly drive of XL Motorized Corps from the area around Vevi. At the same time, other elements of XVIII Mountain Corps – including the 2nd Panzer Division – advanced rapidly south along the eastern Greek coast toward the successive objectives of Katerini, Mount Olympus, Larissa, and finally the Thessalonian Plain. As this attack developed, XL Corps attacked south beyond Florina and Vevi to penetrate the powerful Anglo-Greek defenses established in the key center sector of the theater.

Between them, these two German corps hoped to encircle the four British divisions of W-Force north of the Aliakmon. In addition, by advancing southwest toward Ioannina, XL Corps hoped to cut the lines of retreat available to the Greek forces then still holding back the attacking Italian forces located in southern Albania. To forestall the encirclement of W-Force, and to allow the Greek Western Macedonian and Epirus Armies to retreat southward, during April 12–13 British Commonwealth and Greek troops pulled back 19 miles (30 km) to a new defensive front: the Second Aliakmon Line. This position covered a front some 114 miles (180 km) long from Mount Olympus on the east coast through Servia and the Aliakmon Valley to Lake Prespa on the Greek–Yugoslav–Albanian border.

To the British and Greek forces desperately striving to resist the Axis onslaught on Greece, the successful German advance through the Aliakmon Valley represented a significant strategic setback: the Greek Western Macedonian Army then still successfully holding back the Italian attacks in southeastern Albania now had no line of retreat. Given this disastrous situation in the west, the 14 virtually encircled divisions of the Western Macedonian Army accepted the inevitability of their demise on April 21, and hence surrendered to Field Marshal List's forces.

Back toward the east, XL Corps had managed to drive back the British contingent of W-Force south a further 80 miles (129 km) to Thermopylae by

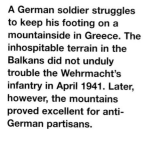

A German soldier struggles to keep his footing on a mountainside in Greece. The inhospitable terrain in the Balkans did not unduly trouble the Wehrmacht's infantry in April 1941. Later, however, the mountains proved excellent for anti-German partisans.

April 20. By this time, however, the British High Command had already begun intensive planning for a maritime evacuation of the British Expeditionary Force. Such a withdrawal was now imminently required because the Greek government had already commenced armistice negotiations with the Germans before its entire army collapsed. On April 23, Colonel-General Alfred Jodl, chief of staff of OKW, accepted the Greek capitulation. All the Wehrmacht needed to do now was to destroy those British Commonwealth forces that remained on Greek soil. During the night of April 23–24, while Commonwealth forces held the Germans along the Thermopylae defensive position, the British commenced Operation Demon, the naval evacuation of their forces from Greece.

Overall, by April 30, 1941, some 50,000 British and Commonwealth troops out of the 62,000 originally deployed had managed to escape across the Mediterranean Sea, mostly to the island of Crete. By then German units had pushed south to occupy the rest of Greece and had begun to cross the Aegean to establish their presence on the main Greek islands, a task they completed on May 3. Immediately after the campaign, the Germans transferred their units in Greece – apart from those earmarked for Operation Mercury, the invasion of Crete – to the east to participate in Barbarossa.

The Invasion of Crete

By May 3, 1941, therefore, Germany had conquered Yugoslavia and Greece and shored up the southern flank of the impending Axis Barbarossa invasion. By then, the only part of Greek territory that remained in Allied hands was Crete. By mid-May, the modest garrison on the island had been swelled by forces escaping from the Greek mainland to a significant force of 42,000 troops, including 11,000 Greek soldiers. The Allied possession of Crete posed a major threat to Axis operations. From there, British aircraft could interdict the naval convoys crossing the Mediterranean to resupply Rommel's forces in North Africa and could still undertake long-range missions to attack the Ploesti oilfields in Romania. In addition to these motives, any future German operations against Crete might also lead the Soviets and the British to conclude that German offensive activity during summer 1941 would occur in the Mediterranean, rather than in the east. Consequently, on April 25 Hitler in his Directive 28 ordered the Wehrmacht to invade Crete during mid-May in an attack designated Operation Mercury.

Though by mid-May the garrison on Crete was numerically stronger than the German forces earmarked for Mercury, their combat power was undermined by several factors. First, many of the British, Commonwealth, and Greek forces that had withdrawn from the mainland had only managed to transport a fraction of their equipment with them. Second, the RAF had taken heavy casualties on the mainland and was only able to offer minimal air cover to the ground forces. Consequently, the Germans enjoyed sustained aerial superiority throughout Mercury, and this hindered the support the Royal Navy could offer to the beleaguered island garrison. One British advantage, however, partially offset these weaknesses: foreknowledge. Through the "Ultra" intelligence obtained from decoding secret German Enigma transmissions, the garrison commander, Major-General Bernard Freyberg, had some idea of the nature and timing of the impending German assault. Knowing that air and sea landings were likely, he split his forces to defend both possible beach landing sectors as well as the main airfields.

During early May 1941 the Germans hastily improvised their Mercury plan, which envisaged exploiting aerial superiority by daringly employing airborne

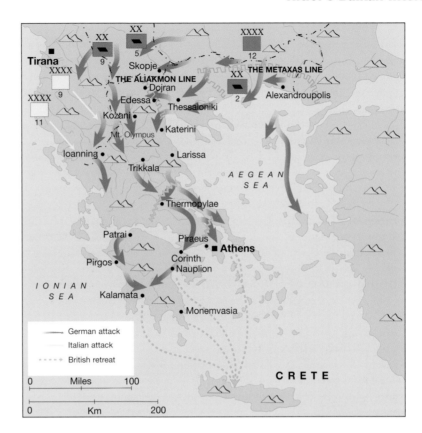

On April 6, 1941, the 10 divisions of the German Twelfth Army commenced their invasion of northeastern Greece and southeastern Yugoslavia. Elements of XL Motorized Corps attacked east from Kyustendil on the Bulgarian border in a pair of thrusts. Along the northern axis, German armor advanced rapidly through Yugoslav Macedonia to Skopje, some 60 miles (97 km) distant. XXX Corps attacked from southeastern Bulgaria toward the Greek town of Komotine. Subsequently, the German forces pushed southeast 44 miles (70 km) until they reached the Greek–Turkish border near Alexandroupolis. Simultaneously, other elements of XXX Corps advanced southwest to engage the eastern sector of the Metaxas Line defenses. To facilitate the German Army's attack on the Metaxas position, the Luftwaffe commenced effective massed bombing attacks on the line during April 6. Simultaneously, the 23 divisions of the Italian Ninth and Eleventh Armies commenced offensive operations against the 14 Greek divisions of the Epirus and Western Macedonian Armies deployed in southern Albania.

forces for the initial attack. Some 16,000 elite airborne troops – both paratroopers and glider-borne soldiers – of the 7th Parachute Division would land on Crete's three main airfields at Maleme, Retimo, and Heraklion, as well as near the capital, Canea. Once these forces had captured these landing strips, German aircraft would transport some 3,000 reinforcements from the 5th Mountain Division to these locations. Simultaneously, maritime convoys would carry a further 7,000 mountain soldiers to Crete for amphibious assault operations. To protect the airborne and amphibious landings, the Luftwaffe deployed 180 fighters and 430 bombers of all types.

During the week prior to the landings, German bombers relentlessly pounded the defenses on Crete to soften up enemy resistance. The assault began on May 20. By May 21, the Germans had secured most of Maleme airfield, though it remained under intense enemy fire. German reinforcements arrived in Ju 52 aircraft, though British fire shot down many before they could land. But that day General Kurt Student, Germany's parachute commander, urgently needed to get additional troops onto the island irrespective of the risks involved. Consequently, late on May 21 he decided to risk sending two naval convoys with mountain troops to Crete. Despite the threat posed by German air superiority, the Royal Navy nevertheless managed to intercept both convoys, destroying one and forcing the other to turn back. Student would have to get further reinforcements to Crete by air, whatever the casualties inflicted by enemy forces.

On May 23, General Freyberg concluded that his desperately overstretched forces could not hold their positions in western Crete as well as those in the rest of the island. Consequently, he ordered his forces at Maleme to withdraw to Canea. The battle-hardened troops of Group West immediately followed up the enemy withdrawal, and prepared themselves for an attack that would break through the British defenses at Canea and enable them to race east to rescue their encircled comrades at Retimo and Heraklion. By now the tide was turning away rapidly from Freyberg's gallant defenders. For due to the German aerial threat, the Royal Navy that day had to abandon its efforts north of Crete to intercept the naval convoys bringing reinforcements to the island.

Between May 28 and June 1, the Royal Navy evacuated 12,000 troops from Sfakia, while on May 29 a further 3,800 troops were evacuated from Heraklion. On June 1, the last British ship departed from Sfakia, and the troops that remained on the island – including most of the Greek forces – either surrendered or fled to the hills. Ironically, the most lasting impact of this operation was that it convinced Hitler that the German airborne arm could not again be risked in any future large-scale air assault (see text box page 124). The day of major German airborne operations was over.

The Influence of the Luftwaffe

As with other Blitzkrieg campaigns, the use of the Luftwaffe was crucial to the army's success in the Balkans. In Yugoslavia actual operations were carried out by VIII Air Corps under Lieutenant-General Wolfram von Richthofen. The Wehrmacht inaugurated their attack on Yugoslavia, at Hitler's personal insistence, with Operation Retribution, a terror bombing attack on Belgrade, the Yugoslav capital. Despite the Yugoslav declaration of April 4 that Belgrade was an "open city" free of military units, some 500 German aircraft pounded the city during April 6–7. These aerial attacks devastated large parts of the city and killed perhaps as many as 6,000 civilians. In addition to the propaganda benefits obtained from this demonstration of German aerial power, the operation also achieved the useful tactical mission of smashing the Yugoslav command and control facilities located in the city.

The advance of the 14th Panzer Division in Yugoslavia illustrates the importance of airpower to army operations. On the morning of April 10, split into two armored formations, the division broke out of the Drava bridgehead and advanced southeast toward Zagreb. Preceded by dive-bombers clearing the way, Luftwaffe reconnaissance aircraft reported back to the divisional command on the strength and location of enemy forces. The combination of aerial firepower, precise intelligence, and high mobility destroyed the enemy's cohesiveness, and the division was in Zagreb that evening, having covered 100 miles (160 km). In fact, so rapid was its advance that its radio communications with XLVI Corps were temporarily severed and reconnaissance aircraft had to be dispatched to ascertain its exact position.

In Greece, during the attempts to break the Second Aliakmon Line during April 15–16, the Luftwaffe provided intensive and effective tactical support. Clearly, in the Balkans during the spring of 1941 German ground-to-air cooperation proved somewhat more effective than it had been during the heavily improvised days of the fall 1939 Wehrmacht invasion of Poland.

Despite the inhospitable terrain encountered by German divisions in the Balkans, Wehrmacht motor vehicles and tanks exceeded all expectations. In addition, upgraded tanks gave the Germans a tactical advantage against their adversaries. In Yugoslavia, on April 7, Kleist's armor commenced its attack northwest toward Nis, after the advance of the XL Motorized Corps from Kyustendil to Stracin the previous day had secured Kleist's left (southern) flank. During April 8, First Panzer Group managed to continue its advance despite encountering stiff resistance from the Yugoslav Fifth Army south of Nis. In these often initially tough operations mounted against periodically effective Yugoslav resistance, Kleist's panzer divisions discovered that the still relatively modest numbers of potent new weapons they now fielded constituted a real tactical asset.

Such equipment included the 50mm Antitank Gun 38 (50mm Pak 38) and the Panzer III Model G, both of which the German Army employed widely for the first time in the 1941 Balkan campaign, after a tiny number of examples had been experimented with during the May 1940 invasion of the West. The Panzer III Model G was the first variant of this tank to mount the more powerful 50mm KwK L/42 gun in place of the 37mm KwK L/45 gun, which combat experience gained in France indicated possessed only a scarcely satisfactory penetrative capability. In addition, the German Army fielded several hundred of the newest version of the Panzer III tank, the Model H, previously unblooded in actual combat. These Model H tanks featured increased levels of armor protection, again an appropriate tactical lesson derived from the German Army's thorough study of the stunning success it achieved in the West during 1940.

On April 9, the deteriorating strategic situation forced the Yugoslav Fifth Army to withdraw northwest behind the Morava River, which allowed Kleist's

Panzer IIIs of the 2nd Panzer Division in Salonika in April 1941. The fast tempo and sheer daring of the German mechanized advance had created such a rapidly deteriorating situation that the Greek Army, like the French before it in May 1940, had struggled to react effectively to the unfolding invasion.

forces swiftly to secure Nis. During April 10, the First Panzer Group managed to cross the Morava River northeast of Krusevac and push on a further 25 miles (40 km) toward Kragujevac against declining resistance. This drive represented a critical move, because it threatened to undermine the viability of the forward Yugoslavian positions located in the south and east of the country.

The adverse terrain over which the panzer divisions had to advance in the Balkans increased significantly the rate at which these formations consumed

gasoline. To some extent, the employment of German transport planes to deliver supplies to airfields near the advancing armored spearheads ameliorated this situation; nevertheless, the Germans only managed to keep their panzer divisions moving through desperate improvisations. But given the modest resistance encountered in Yugoslavia, these ad hoc measures proved adequate – albeit only just – to sustain the German advance at a sufficiently high tempo that it rapidly unraveled the cohesion of the defending Yugoslav forces.

In Greece the panzers were similarly effective. During April 6, for example, the crack troops of the 2nd Panzer Division successfully advanced west an incredible 45 miles (74 km) to capture Strumica in southeastern Yugoslavia. The next day the division then swung south and crossed the Yugoslav–Greek border near Lake Doiran to outflank the western end of the Metaxas Line. To keep the division's vehicles going in the face of the attritional damage inflicted by the poor-quality roads, its workshop units had to work round the clock replacing or repairing damaged suspensions, tracks, and engines. Once again, the vital supporting "tail" units included in the well-balanced composition of the German armored divisions had proven crucial for the success achieved by the spearhead "teeth" arms in the Balkans.

By noon on April 8, the increasingly exhausted soldiers of the 2nd Panzer Division had notched up a potentially critical strategic success by swiftly advancing south to a point halfway from the key port of Salonika. If the panzers could capture the port, they could cut off the four divisions of the Greek East Macedonian Army deployed in northeastern Greece. Despite the desperate

Colonel Brauer (left), one of the German paratroop commanders on Crete, issues orders to one of his subordinates. During May 22, the Luftwaffe airlanded more mountain troops at Maleme, though again only at the expense of heavy casualties. At Retimo and Heraklion, the beleaguered German forces had managed – through sheer determination – to hold onto their positions despite repeated enemy counterattacks. Though the prospect of German success on Crete still hung in the balance, the military initiative on the island had clearly begun to tip in favor of Student's forces.

countermoves launched by the Greek 19th Division that day, a series of well-coordinated all-arms attacks enabled the 2nd Panzer Division nevertheless to race south and reach the outskirts of Salonika by the evening of April 8. Lacking any available shipping either to evacuate the cut-off Greek East Macedonian Army or resupply it with munitions, and in the absence of any reserves to stop the advance of the 2nd Panzer Division farther east beyond the Axios River toward Serrai, the surrounded Greek forces – some 60,000 troops – faced a hopeless situation. On April 11 they recognized the inevitable, and surrendered to the numerically inferior advancing German forces.

Junior Commanders

The Balkan campaign is full of examples of the great initiative shown by Wehrmacht junior commanders, often acting in contravention of orders from the High Command. In Yugoslavia, the Germans employed so-called *Feuerzauber* ("Fire Magic") probing attacks. Where the ground was unsuitable for motorized units – across the Austrian–Yugoslav border – special groups of assault troops were organized from cadre personnel and recently inducted trainees. Originally these units were to reinforce frontier guards and cover the assembly of Second Army forces. However, several junior commanders had other ideas. One group was Force *Palten*, under the command of Captain Palten, which on April 8, and against orders, attacked toward Maribor. Since the Yugoslavs had blown all the bridges, the Germans had to carry their kit on their backs. They encountered a number of enemy units, which they brushed aside by a series of flanking and frontal attacks. That evening Palten captured Maribor and took 100 prisoners, having lost one man killed and one wounded.

Similarly, on April 14, by continuing until its vehicles had emptied their fuel tanks, the German 16th Motorized Division managed to advance rapidly south from Mitrovica toward Sarajevo, the capital of Bosnia-Hercegovina, which fell the next day. Subsequently, after German transport aircraft had delivered fuel to the nearby airfield, the division linked up with the southeasterly thrust developed by the 14th Panzer Division from the Una River via Banja Luka. In these operations, German junior commanders – ignoring their own exhaustion as well as that of their men – seemed to relish the challenge of beating their peers in the race to reach distant objectives deep within Yugoslavian territory.

In Greece, despite possessing significant amounts of equipment that was less effective than that fielded by the best German Army units, the SS *Leibstandarte* Division nevertheless managed to accomplish a swift rate of advance during the invasion. This success owed much to the ideological beliefs held so fanatically by these physically superb and determined volunteer Nazi soldiers. Yet these "qualities" were also reinforced by the ruthless determination and discipline displayed by the division's junior commanders. One egregious example of this fanaticism involved the commander of the division's reconnaissance battalion, SS-*Sturmbannführer* Kurt "Panzer" Meyer. With scant regard to either his own safety or that of his troops, Meyer savagely drove forward an attack that had faltered in the face of intense enemy resistance by dropping a primed grenade behind the rearmost soldier in each section. Needless to say, Meyer's "leadership" successfully restored forward momentum to the German attack.

Not content with achieving a rapid defeat of the Greek Army, local German commanders ruthlessly attempted to annihilate the remaining British forces before they could evacuate. Consequently on April 26, to stop British forces from retreating south into the Peleponnese to embark from the ports of Nauplion and Kalamata, the Germans audaciously deployed glider-borne and paratroop forces deep into the enemy's rear. Through no fault of their own, however, these airborne forces failed to disrupt significantly the last phase of the British disembarkation; the operation commenced 24 hours too late, by which time significant numbers of British troops had already crossed to the southern side of the canal and closed on the evacuation ports.

On Crete, despite the battle being initially highly unfavorable to them, the surviving lightly armed German airborne troops managed to secure several small defensive positions; they stood no chance of pushing on to capture the airfields in the face of fierce enemy resistance. Small groups of isolated paratroopers were even attacked by Greek civilians armed with pitchforks and hunting rifles in a series of partisan incidents. In such conditions, the main task of the German troops was merely to survive. Yet both the initiative shown by NCOs in assuming the functions of their fallen officers and the resilience displayed by these crack paratroopers ensured that the isolated German positions held firm despite the disastrous way in which the invasion plan had unfolded.

Tactics

As in the West in 1940, German tactics in the Balkans proved superior to those employed by their opponents. Thus in Yugoslavia, in the few instances where Yugoslav forces did manage to establish obstacles to block the German advance, the engineers contained within Kleist's panzer divisions came to the fore. Often operating in mobile halftracked vehicles, the engineers – usually carefully deployed near the front of the armored columns and at intervals farther back – provided sterling service clearing the way for the other German vehicles.

The German divisions now contained veteran troops who could evaluate tactical situations and act accordingly. This meant they did not panic when they came under fire, but merely took cover and made plans to suit the situation at hand. This coolness under fire went a long way toward maintaining the momentum of the German advance. By the evening of April 12, for example, Kleist's armor had taken the high ground southeast of Belgrade while XLI Corps approached the city from the northeast. To capture a key bridge in this sector, a company of well-trained German mountain troops silently paddled across the treacherous waters of a fast-flowing river in inflatable boats. Once established on the far bank, the German soldiers bravely stormed the heavily armed Yugoslav bunkers that dominated the bridge and quickly captured the position by exploiting the surprise they had achieved. After removing the demolition charges that the defenders had fixed to the bridge, Kleist's armored columns crossed the bridge to continue the advance toward Belgrade. Once again, the combination of tactical audacity, speed of action, and well-coordinated operations had enabled the Germans to achieve rapid success even in difficult battlefield situations, plus a small degree of luck.

To help maintain the lightning pace of the German armored advance through Macedonia, Field Marshal List employed a detachment of Brandenburg commandos to capture key crossings over the Vardar River. With these secured, the panzer spearheads of XL Corps continued to race west through southern Kosovo to reach Italy's Albanian colony. As in the 1940 invasion of the West, the German Army effectively employed highly trained special forces to sustain the forward momentum of its mechanized vanguards.

The attack made on April 6 by the elite, specially trained troops of General Ringel's 5th Mountain Division, part of XVIII Mountain Corps, against the center of the Greek Metaxas Line defensive position near the Rupel Pass made only slow progress, despite intensive close air support. During the infantry attacks the division mounted that day against the powerful Greek fortifications, its lightweight 75mm Mountain Gun 36 (75mm GebG 36) pieces provided invaluable firepower support, while Stuka dive-bombers provided additional assistance from above. Under this supporting fire, the mountain rifle troops pushed toward the Greek bunkers, hugging the available terrain, before bravely

German paras on Crete. Through a daring air assault executed with ruthless determination the German Army successfully secured the island after 13 days of combat against a numerically stronger and determined force. Yet the triumph remained a hollow victory, given the immense price paid. Of the 23,000 invading troops, no fewer than 7,000 had been killed or wounded. In addition, the Luftwaffe lost 264 fighters and bombers, plus 118 Ju 52 transport aircraft.

engaging the enemy strongpoints with grenades and demolition charges. Such work was at close ranges and highly hazardous.

Yet despite the high tactical skills possessed by these select German troops, they still encountered bitter Greek resistance that even they struggled to overcome. Eventually, typically effective German tactical improvisation enabled these alpine troops during April 9 first to outflank the defenders and then to utilize surprise to capture the remaining Greek positions in the Rupel Pass. However, the mountain troops only ultimately secured this key tactical mission at very high cost in terms of casualties – some 2,300 killed and wounded in just four days of intense mountain combat. The appropriate doctrinal lesson the German Army drew from this, and other similar experiences encountered in the Balkans, was that combat in difficult mountain terrain against prepared enemy field defenses would always remain a tough mission, but that with perseverance, resourceful and tactically skilled assaulting alpine troops could still achieve victory over their opponents.

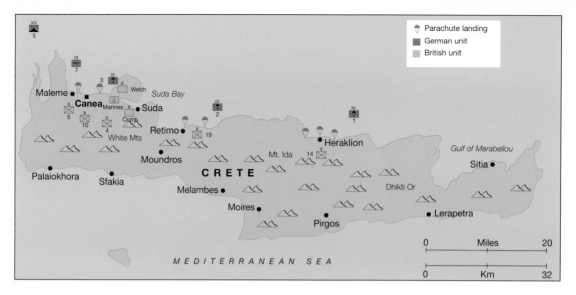

The German 72nd Infantry Division also took 48 hours to pierce the powerful Metaxas Line defenses and penetrate beyond a modest 19 miles (30 km) toward Serrai in the face of fierce Greek resistance. In these hard-fought engagements, the resilience instilled in German soldiers by both the realistic battle simulations undertaken in training and the prior experiences of combat gained during 1939–40 proved a real advantage. One infantryman recalled the collective shudder of terror that went through his section when the Greek defenders they faced fixed bayonets and charged in a counterattack. Despite their fear, however, the discipline of the German soldiers held, and they mowed down the charging enemy troops with intense MG 34 and small-arms fire before the enemy could reach them to engage in hand-to-hand combat.

To the east of Servia around Mount Olympus, however, the German XVIII Corps found a ground-based solution to unlock the staunch British defense it encountered. The German forces employed a combination of effective all-arms cooperation and the audacious use of physically robust soldiers over extremely inhospitable terrain to break the entrenched British positions. During April 15, elements of the 2nd Panzer Division, commanded by *Oberst* Hermann Balck, began to advance south from Katerini along the coastal road and railroad. Their objective was to cross the Pinios River and then seize Larissa, thus cutting the escape route south of the British forces in this sector. Meanwhile, to Balck's immediate right-hand flank, the specially trained troops of the 6th Mountain Division undertook the extremely arduous ascent of Mount Olympus to outflank the enemy defenses.

The tactical situation remained difficult since the rough terrain prevented Balck's armor from operating across country, while the road was heavily mined and covered by British defenses that had been established in some depth. Undeterred, Balck ordered the bulk of his infantry assets – a motorcycle company and a motorized infantry battalion – to abandon their vehicles and outflank the British defenses on foot in a daring night-time maneuver. This left only his engineer battalion to cooperate with the armored regiment in a night-time feint mounted to distract British attention. Pushing themselves to the limits of their endurance that night, the outflanking troops laboriously picked their way on foot through terrain so appalling that it was suitable only for specially trained

At 0720 hours on May 20, 1941, the first wave of the German airborne assault reached the northern coast of Crete. In the west, highly trained and well-motivated elite gliderborne assault troops landed at Maleme airfield, while others dropped at Heraklion. Simultaneously, 3,000 paratroopers of Group Center dropped to capture Canea. That afternoon, the second German airborne wave landed, with the remaining paratroopers of Group Center dropping on Retimo airfield, and those of Group East landing at Heraklion. The Germans, anticipating that these airborne assaults would meet only modest resistance, expected quickly to secure their objectives, so that follow-up forces could land and complete a rapid conquest of the island. However, resistance was heavier than expected, and the Germans began to take significant casualties.

mountain soldiers. At dawn, the utterly exhausted soldiers struck the surprised New Zealander defenders from the rear, while simultaneously Balck's mixed armored and engineer battle group assaulted from the front. Under the weight of these synchronized blows, the Commonwealth forces rapidly withdrew south, leaving behind much heavy equipment.

Through such audacious tactical improvisation the German attacks managed to break through the enemy defenses and capture the whole of the Aliakmon Valley by April 18. During these battles, the German Army again demonstrated the significant tactical value of equipment that, in addition to its principal battlefield function, could be used effectively in a variety of other tactical roles. The outstanding example of this flexibility was the 88mm Antiaircraft Gun 18 (88mm Flak 18), which during the Aliakmon battles underscored the reputation it had achieved in the West as a lethal weapon when used in an improvised antitank role. In one example of its effectiveness in this secondary role, one of the three 88mm guns employed by the SS *Leibstandarte* Division in Greece knocked out a British tank at the incredible range of 3.75 miles (6 km) to establish a new German distance record for tank destruction!

Exploiting Ethnic Divisions

During the Balkan campaign the Germans successfully exploited the region's ethnic divisions to aid their military campaign. The serious internal ethnic tensions that crippled the Yugoslav Army, for example, considerably weakened its combat power. Many ethnically Croatian Yugoslav Army units, for example, surrendered immediately to the invading German forces, whom they regarded in a favorable light. To reduce further the resistance encountered, several German Army propaganda companies, deployed alongside the advancing frontline troops, effectively exploited these tensions by promising to assuage the nationalistic aspirations of the repressed non-Serb minorities within Yugoslavia. A Croat air force officer handed over to the Germans a list of airfields where Yugoslav aircraft were located. Thus the Luftwaffe was able to destroy the enemy's airpower at the beginning of the campaign.

The early successes achieved in eastern Yugoslavia prompted the German High Command to bring forward the planned attack by XLIX Mountain Corps from southern Austria, originally slated for April 13. The assault commenced on April 10, even though some units were not yet ready for operations, and the corps nevertheless quickly advanced south. For in northwest Yugoslavia the Germans encountered, as expected, much lighter resistance thanks to the pro-German attitudes held by the Croatian elements within the Yugoslav Army. Many Croat soldiers, convinced by the promises contained in the pamphlets issued and the messages broadcast by German frontline propaganda units, surrendered immediately to the Wehrmacht. Similarly, other Croat units refused to obey orders to attack the German invaders or even engaged other, Serb-dominated, Yugoslav Army units (in Vinkovic Croat troops openly revolted against their Serb superiors). Through such tactical psychological operations the German Army in Yugoslavia reaped greater rewards than they did in any subsequent World War II campaign.

Given this unwelcome situation in northwestern Yugoslavia (that is, Croatia), the Yugoslav High Command realized that its forces could not defend this region against the Axis onslaught. Consequently, at noon on April 10, still-loyal Yugoslav units commenced a disciplined withdrawal southward some 124 miles (200 km) to the Una River. During the afternoon of April 10, therefore, as the

The Demise of Air Assault

During Germany's early Blitzkrieg campaigns, particularly that in France during May–June 1940, the German Army had extensively used air assaults by parachute and glider-borne troops to sustain the tempo and momentum of the advancing ground troops. The catastrophic losses that the German airborne forces suffered during their May 1941 air assault on Crete, however, convinced Hitler that such operations were now too costly to remain strategically justified. At a medal ceremony in mid-July 1941, Hitler informed General Student, commander of German airborne troops, that the experience of Crete had led him to conclude that now the day of the large-scale air assault was over. For such operations required surprise to succeed, the Führer declared, whereas by now all of Germany's enemies had anticipated that the Wehrmacht might use airborne landings against them. As a result of this decision, for the rest of the war Germany's airborne forces served almost exclusively as elite infantry forces employed for ground combat. This trend culminated in fall 1944, when the German Army in the West fielded the First Parachute Army in a defensive ground combat role. In objective terms, however, Hitler's July 1941 decision misrepresented the real lessons to be gleaned from the invasion of Crete. For under favorable circumstances – particularly when surprise had not been compromised – large-scale air assault could still deliver success, as the September 1944 Allied Market-Garden offensive showed, albeit often at a high price. However, the lack of airborne experience after spring 1941 eroded the German Army's airborne capabilities to such an extent that in December 1944 it could not even enact effectively the modest – regimental-sized – tactical air assault incorporated into the plan for the Ardennes counteroffensive.

Yugoslavian Army fell back, the German Second Army made swift advances to capture Zagreb by the evening. Immediately, the Croat nationalist leader, Ante Pavelic, announced the creation of a pro-German Croatian fascist state.

The German-led Axis invasion had conquered Yugoslavia quickly and with amazingly light casualties, and in the immediate aftermath of this triumph the victorious Axis powers promptly claimed the spoils of conquest and dismembered Yugoslavia. Yet in reality, this victory remained less complete than it appeared. For the Germans scarcely controlled many of the mountainous areas, where embryonic partisan forces soon began to emerge, largely from the Yugoslav military personnel that had evaded capture, but also from communist activists. As soon as the armistice came into effect, the Germans hastily withdrew most of their forces from Yugoslavia and redeployed them to the East to begin their final preparations for Barbarossa, now slated to commence at the earliest possibility. This haste to leave Yugoslav territory, however, prevented the Wehrmacht from crushing in its infancy the embryonic partisan movement then emerging in the mountains. For much of the rest of the war, five German divisions, plus substantial other Axis forces, would remain locked in a protracted and appallingly brutal antipartisan war that spanned large parts of conquered Yugoslavia.

The Question of Will

Adolf Hitler was always keen to stress to his generals the importance of will power to military success: that mental determination could overcome superior numerical and physical odds to achieve eventual victory. This eventually became the Führer's dogma, especially during the last two years of the war when his armies were being defeated on all fronts, and especially so in the Soviet Union. Though the question of will has been dismissed as being nothing more than Nazi racial hogwash and proof of Hitler's detachment from reality, in fact "will" could have a decisive military impact on the battlefield, and was certainly a factor in the German victory in the Balkans. A few examples will illustrate the point.

In Yugoslavia the bad weather made movement on the secondary routes – let alone cross-country – all but impossible, and this channeled Kleist's mechanized forces along the obvious axes of advance: the primary roads. In poor terrain scarcely conducive to the high-tempo mechanized operations at which the German Army had excelled in 1940, his panzer divisions ran real risks of being slowed to a crawl by an effective enemy defense based on the extensive employment of obstacles and blocking positions. The shock action imposed on the Yugoslav Army by the ferocity, audacity, and momentum of the initial German armored thrusts, however, ruthlessly exploited the underlying nationalistic frailties that existed within the defending forces. As a result, the Yugoslav Army quickly disintegrated, and this prevented its troops from effectively taking advantage of the terrain to slow the rapid Axis advance. By April 12, the morale of large sections of the Yugoslav Army had all but collapsed, with mutinies and mass desertions a common occurrence. Consequently the Axis forces continued to drive rapidly from all sides into the heart of the country.

By April 8, XL Corps had captured Shtip and Prilep, the latter 76 miles (122 km) from the Bulgarian border. During these advances it became clear to the German forces that the morale of the Macedonian elements within the Yugoslav Army had already disintegrated. Though this resulted largely from effective German propaganda, this collapse was reinforced by the shock action inflicted by the intensive close air support and interdiction attacks that German aircraft had undertaken on April 7 and 8. Such effective air support was possible because on the first day of the invasion German aircraft had undertaken concentrated attacks on Yugoslav and Greek airfields, which quickly gave the Germans aerial superiority. With the Luftwaffe largely free from the need for extensive missions to protect this air superiority against the initially weak, and now further weakened enemy air forces, it could concentrate on supporting the ground war with aerial reconnaissance, close air support, and interdiction operations.

Doggedness on Crete

Furthermore, it was surely will power that sustained the German paratroopers on Crete. Consider the facts. From the first minutes of the landings, it became clear that the Germans were not going to find it easy to capture the island. The defenders, having anticipated an imminent attack, poured devastating defensive fire into the slow-moving German gliders and the lumbering Ju 52 transport planes that carried the paratroopers. Moreover, once out of the remaining aircraft, the descending paratroopers met heavy fire as they floated down to earth. In several places, such as at Retimo, the Germans jumped into areas that they believed to contain only weak defenses, only to find themselves in powerful positions that poured a lethal stream of metal up at them. Many paratroopers were killed in the air before they reached the ground, while those who did manage to land safely often found themselves pinned down by enemy fire and unable to reach their weapons cannisters or establish contact with their commanders or regiments.

It looked to General Student that he might have to abandon the operation. Just one sector of the invasion seemed to offer any chance of success, for near Maleme elite troops of the Air Landing Assault Regiment had seized key terrain from which it might be possible to secure the airfield. Gambling everything, Student ordered that all efforts should be concentrated on capturing Maleme. The plan worked, and aircraft began to land on the airfield to bring in desperately needed reinforcements. Such a risky effort to snatch victory from the jaws of looming defeat through a determined act of superior will would subsequently typify German reactions to offensive operations that had gone badly awry, especially on the Eastern Front.

The North African War

The German Army was reluctantly drawn into North Africa. And although a combination of mechanized units and a bold commander gave it a string of victories, inadequate supply lines and growing Allied material superiority ultimately doomed Rommel's African Adventure.

German armored units on the advance during the Battle of Gazala in late May 1942. The German Army's 1941–43 war in North Africa was characterized by rapid mobile operations that involved a series of see-saw advances by both sides across the deserts and coastal plain of Libya and Egypt.

When considering the successes of the German Army in North Africa during World War II, one starting fact must be considered: before 1939, no one in the army imagined that it would be necessary to conduct land warfare outside of Europe. Thus no preparations of any kind had been made for any sort of desert campaigns, and it is staggering that when German troops reached the African theater in early 1941 they were entirely unprepared for their new missions. This makes the army's success in Africa all the more impressive, and is a testament to the overall caliber of German leadership, tactics, equipment, and flexibility.

Erwin Rommel commanded the *Deutsches Afrika Korps* (or DAK) – the German Africa Corps – during the early part of the North Africa campaign. This formation spearheaded the Axis drive in Africa but was merely one part of a larger, binational, Axis command variously known as Panzer Group Africa, Panzer Army Africa, and the German–Italian Panzer Army, which Rommel commanded for much of the campaign. It is worth remembering that the main body of Axis troops in North Africa throughout the campaign was Italian, not German.

Initially, just two German divisions, the 5th Light (which later became the 21st Panzer) and the 15th Panzer, formed the core of the Africa Corps. During 1941–42 the Germans augmented the force with the 90th and 164th Light Africa Divisions, the *Ramcke* Parachute Brigade, and the 999th Africa Brigade, a penal unit. In addition to these German formations, during particular stages of the campaign the Italian High Command attached various Italian units to reinforce Rommel's command. The last component of Rommel's success in this theater was the effective air support he received from the Luftwaffe. During the campaign the

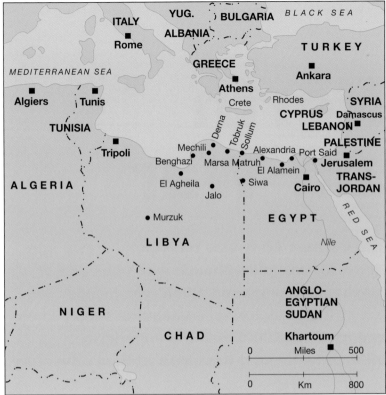

When Rommel arrived in Libya in February 1941, Italian forces had been pushed back to El Agheila. The initial German force, which comprised just the 5th Light Division, benefited from a redirection of many of the British Commonwealth forces deployed in eastern Libya away from that theater to defend mainland Greece. This redeployment left just inexperienced Commonwealth troops, partly equipped with captured Italian weapons, to defend the British front in Libya. Rommel, ever the audacious armored commander, ignored the advice of his superiors and seized the opportunity presented by this momentary British weakness by initiating an immediate offensive.

Air Commander Africa controlled various aircraft squadrons, detached from X Air Corps located in Italy. Rommel arrived in Libya on February 12, 1941, as commander of the Africa Corps. He was technically under Italian command, though he did have the right to refer to Berlin if he was unhappy concerning the way his command was being handled. From the beginning, though, he conducted things his way: disregarding German High Command orders that he should wait for his second panzer division to arrive in May before commencing offensive operations, Rommel attacked the British line on March 20, 1941, with just his 5th Light Division and some available Italian troops.

During late March and the first half of April, Rommel's offensive drove the British back east, forcing them to abandon Benghazi and leave behind an encircled garrison at Tobruk. He drove the British right out of the Libyan province of Cyrenaica and onto Egyptian soil, until the enemy managed to reestablish a cohesive front between Sollum and the Halfaya Pass. During the Axis advance, a concerned German High Command had ordered Rommel several times to halt, but the "Desert Fox" ignored these orders and continued to advance.

Having pushed the British forces right the way back to the Libyan–Egyptian border, the overstretched Axis supply lines now put their 164,000-strong forces in North Africa at a significant strategic and tactical disadvantage. Nevertheless, the Africa Corps blocked two subsequent attempts by the British to dislodge it from its new defensive positions along the Egyptian border. On May 15, 1941, in Operation Brevity, the British attacked the Axis positions at Sollum, the Halfaya Pass, and Capuzzo. After a successful initial British advance some 15 miles (24 km) west, Rommel counterattacked and recaptured all the ground his forces had just relinquished. In the subsequent Battleaxe offensive, initiated on

June 15, the British attempted to break the Axis line at Sollum and exploit this success with an advance all the way to Mechili, some 200 miles (322 km) farther west. Battleaxe, however, failed to drive back Axis forces. After tying down British momentum in the extensive German defenses, Rommel initiated armored counterattacks on June 16–17 that decisively defeated the British offensive and restored the original frontline.

When Rommel's initial offensive of March–April 1941 had pushed the British forces back out of Cyrenaica, an isolated Commonwealth garrison managed to hold onto the key port of Tobruk. With Rommel's panzer forces dispatched east to drive back the British into Egypt, the least mobile elements of the Africa Corps had to conduct forced marches to reach and surround the British perimeter around Tobruk. To accomplish marches of 20 miles (32 km) per day in terrible conditions of heat and desert terrain represented a tremendous achievement that again testified to the physical toughness that extensive training had engendered in the ordinary German soldier. Axis forces besieged the encircled Tobruk garrison for eight months from April 9 to December 7, 1941, but nevertheless failed to capture the town.

The first determined German assault on Tobruk commenced on April 30, 1941, but British counterattacks pushed the German forces back to their starting line. After this costly tactical setback, the German High Command vetoed any further attempts to take Tobruk by storm and instead ordered siege operations like those subsequently used against Leningrad during 1941–42.

Rommel on the Retreat: Operation Crusader

In November 1941, the British initiated their own offensive commanded by General Claude Auchinleck, codenamed Operation Crusader, that caught Rommel's overextended command in an unfavorable strategic and tactical situation. The 5th Light Division remained just as weak in armor as it had during Battleaxe, despite the German High Command renaming it the 21st Panzer Division. Furthermore, while Rommel had recently created another division, called initially the *Afrika* (Special Employment) Division, and subsequently the 90th Light Africa Division, this remained an improvised and unmotorized unit that nonetheless performed well despite its modest equipment base. To counter the British air force of 700 aircraft Rommel could call on the support of just 120 German aircraft in addition to 200 Italian aircraft.

The British offensive commenced on November 18, 1941. While the British XIII Corps engaged the main Axis defenses, XXX Corps successfully swept around the southern end of the Axis line in an attempt to meet and engage the bulk of Rommel's armor. By the end of the next day XXX Corps had advanced west and northwest 60 miles (96 km) to threaten Bir el Gubi and Sidi Rezegh respectively, the latter just 20 miles (32 km) away from the encircled Commonwealth garrison at Tobruk. On occasion, even Rommel's 105mm Light Field Howitzer 18 (105mm le FH 18) artillery pieces directly engaged advancing British tanks over open sights in a desperate attempt to stem the British advance. By November 19, however, the British forces had become jumbled and "untidy," and this situation presented Rommel with a fleeting opportunity, which he grasped eagerly.

On November 24, 1941, he gathered together a scratch force from the 21st Panzer Division and, in a "dash for the frontier wire," boldly raced east over the Egyptian frontier to cut the lines of communications of the British forces now deployed many miles behind him to the west and northwest. But held up at the

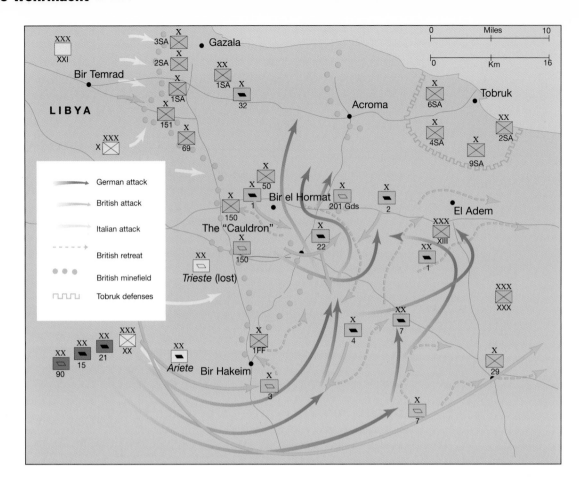

frontier wire, Rommel's thrust lost its momentum as his armor ran short of fuel, and even his physically resilient soldiers collapsed in exhaustion. To make matters worse, during November 27–28 the New Zealand Division managed to strike rapidly west along the coast from Bardia toward Tobruk, threatening Rommel's lines of supply. The new development forced the Desert Fox to abort his armored raid and bring back this force so as to halt the dangerous advance by the New Zealanders.

This failure forced Rommel's units back onto the defensive against repeated attacks by numerically superior Commonwealth forces. Consequently, by early December the Africa Corps's relatively successful attempts to halt the Crusader offensive had left it decimated – it fielded just 60 operational tanks. Rommel had no choice but to order a strategic retreat west on December 7. As the German and Italian forces moved west through Cyrenaica, the following Allied advance relieved the encircled garrison at Tobruk after 242 days of being cut off.

By December 26, 1941, the Axis forces had managed successfully to retreat 151 miles (243 km) to assume new defensive positions along the western border of Cyrenaica at El Agheila, without losing their cohesion in the process. It was now the British forces – rather than Rommel's – who were at the end of overextended lines of supply. At this critical moment Rommel received, from a resupply convoy that had made it across the Mediterranean, a delivery of 54 precious new tanks. Thus reinforced, Rommel planned once again to attack the overstretched British forces that faced him before they managed to establish a firm logistic network to support their defenses. Initiated on January 21, 1942,

The Battle of Gazala, May 26–June 11, 1942. Given substantial British quantitative superiorities and partial qualitative advantages, together with the supposed advantage of being on the defensive, the British in theory ought to have defeated the Axis forces during battle. That they did not says much about the thorough training, excellent motivation, and effective tactics of Germany's Africa Corps, as well as widespread competence demonstrated by the Italian forces deployed in North Africa.

Antitank Screens

In North Africa the Germans used their halftracked-towed antitank guns as mobile, integrated defensive "screens" linked into an in-depth defensive position, rather than static points of defense. These screens fielded 37mm and 50mm Pak antitank guns – plus occasionally a tiny number of the newer 75mm Antiaircraft Gun 40 (75mm Pak 40) – together with German Luftwaffe-operated 88mm Flak 18/36/37 antiaircraft guns employed in an antiarmor role. Behind the screen the Germans held their panzer forces, which would maneuver around the screen in a local counterattack role. Occasionally the armor moved in front of the carefully concealed screen to lure unsuspecting British tanks into the killing zone of the Pak weapons. Given the fluid nature of the battles in North Africa, maintaining the mobility of German antitank guns remained essential, which is where the Pak-towing halftracks such as the Sdkfz 10 proved their tactical worth. In these battles, Rommel never had sufficient numbers of 88mm Flak guns, but even just a few of these weapons could prove devastating. The gun could penetrate 6.3. in. (160 mm) of frontal armor tank at ranges of 6,564 ft (2,000 m), enough to penetrate any British tank, including the heavy Matilda. During Operation Battleaxe, for example, only one Matilda out of 13 returned from the attack on Halfaya Pass (aptly nicknamed "Hellfire Pass" by British troops), which the Africa Corps defended with just four 88mm Flak guns. Throughout the North African campaign, the Germans combined effectively – through "leapfrogging" – their antitank guns with their armor to exert even greater influence on the battlefield. In the early stages of the North Africa campaign, for example, the principal cause of the heavy British tank losses was the way in which the small, portable German 50mm Pak 38 antitank guns were pushed ahead of the panzers in an offensive screen. Located in small hollows in the desert, these guns engaged British armor which assumed that the fire was coming from the more distant (and more visible) German tanks. The British then attempted, with little success, to engage the panzers at great distance, and consequently British morale fell as the tank crews assumed their equipment was deficient compared to that of the Germans.

Rommel's devastating 22-week offensive took the Germans to their farthest advance east during the entire North African campaign. By July 1942, exhausted Axis troops reached the railway station of El Alamein. They were just 60 miles (96 km) from Alexandria in Egypt.

Rommel's five-and-a-half-month-long offensive to El Alamein developed in two distinct stages. First, between January 21 and February 6, 1942, his forces advanced to the Eighth Army's powerful defensive line at Gazala–Bir Hakeim. Then, after a 15-week lull during which both sides steadily built up their forces, Rommel commenced his assault on the Gazala Line on May 26, 1942. By June 11, after 17 days of hard-fought operations, Rommel's recently renamed Panzer Army Africa finally overcame enemy opposition along the Gazala–Bir Hakeim Line. If Rommel could breach the Gazala Line, Hitler now began to consider, Panzer Army Africa might even be able to push through the Middle East to link up with a successful German advance from the southern Soviet Union through the Caucasus. Unfortunately for Rommel, Hitler's growing ambitions for Panzer Army Africa were not matched by a greater willingness to reinforce this command. Consequently, the Desert Fox now had to pursue more ambitious objectives with the same modest forces previously available to him.

On June 7, 1942, the Africa Corps ruthlessly exploited his success on the battlefield by swinging northeast toward Tobruk to cut the British lines of communication. Panzer Army Africa had broken the Gazala Line. On June 13, the Axis forces once again encircled the port of Tobruk, but this time experienced little trouble penetrating the Commonwealth defenses and soon accepted the surrender of over 30,000 enemy troops, plus a huge haul of Allied stores and motor vehicles. The German willingness to improvise by utilizing a motley collection of captured equipment went a long way to sustain Rommel's advance toward El Alamein.

As Rommel pushed up to the El Alamein position during late June 1942, he remained determined to maintain the momentum of his advance despite his

dwindling combat power. His forces could now muster just 44 German and 14 Italian tanks, and his lines of supply had become grossly overextended. But despite this, the Axis remained confident that their enemy was all but beaten in North Africa. By the evening of June 30, the Panzer Army Africa had advanced to a point just 60 miles (96 km) from Alexandria, but at this juncture the Axis advance ground to a halt due to both their own logistic collapse and mounting enemy resistance in the First Battle of El Alamein.

The Battle of Alam Halfa

As Rommel planned for a renewed attack on the El Alamein position during the fall of 1942, large amounts of new American equipment poured into Egypt to reinforce the British forces. In comparison, during August 1942, Rommel received the *Ramcke* Parachute Brigade and an Italian division as reinforcements. These significant forces in no way matched the scale of British reinforcements in the same month. In addition, the geography of the El Alamein position exacerbated the numerical disadvantage experienced by Rommel's command. For the presence of the expansive Quattara Depression to the south of the British El Alamein defense line prevented Rommel from employing his favorite tactic: an outflanking movement through the open desert.

Rommel commenced his attack at Alam Halfa on August 30, 1942. The new commander of the British Eighth Army, Bernard Montgomery, had built upon the foundations laid by Auchinleck to establish a strong position around Alam Halfa most noticeable for its deep minefield system. During the period September 3–6, the British troops had the gratifying sight of seeing the Germans, at last, beaten and in retreat back to their own starting positions. The British had won the battle by a purely defensive action and made no attempt to follow up the retreating Axis forces.

In the aftermath of Alam Halfa, Montgomery carefully prepared for his first major offensive: the Second (October 1942) Battle of Alamein. On September

Rommel's audacious generalship in North Africa was characterized by his presence near the front in "Griffin," his Sdkfz 250/3 command vehicle based on the standard German halftracked armored personnel carrier. This presence enabled Rommel to respond swiftly to the rapidly developing battlefield situation and contributed to the success achieved by the Africa Corps. When not in "Griffin," Rommel regularly flew over the battlefield – often at some risk – to obtain up-to-date information on developments across the wider battlefield.

23, 1942, a sick Rommel flew home for medical treatment. General Georg Stumme arrived from the Eastern Front to act as deputy commander of the Panzer Army Africa in his absence, while General von Thoma took over the subordinate command of the Africa Corps. When the British attack came at El Alamein, it proved unstoppable.

Rommel's "Great Retreat"

The surviving German troops packed themselves into whatever transport was left available and retreated west in a staged series of disciplined and well-handled withdrawals that avoided the general collapse that many British commanders anticipated. During the first half of November 1942, the battered remnants of the Panzer Army Africa retreated west some 700 miles (1,120 km) through Cyrenaica to Mersa el Brega, where Italian forces under Marshal Ettore Bastico were constructing a thin defensive line.

Rommel's command, however, remained too weak to hold this fragile line as the Allies approached their positions on December 11, 1942. Consequently, over the next two weeks Panzer Army Africa continued its retreat west a further 290 miles (467 km) through the Libyan province of Tripolitania. On December 23, 1942, the Germans established themselves in the flimsy defensive positions just begun at Buerat. Here, on January 18, 1943, Montgomery's forces strove to outflank Rommel's weak defenses to the south. But before the British accomplished this maneuver, the Panzer Army Africa again retreated, this time a further 290 miles (467 km) west, abandoning Tripoli in the process. On January 26, 1943, the Axis forces established themselves along the more easily defensible line of the old French Mareth Line frontier fortifications on the Libyan–Tunisian border.

Meanwhile, on November 8, 1942, as the Second Battle of El Alamein raged, Anglo-American forces had staged Operation Torch, a series of amphibious landings in Vichy-controlled Morocco and Algeria. Once the Torch landings had been undertaken, the Allies hoped that these forces would drive rapidly east into the rugged terrain of western Tunisia to attack the rear of Rommel's forces as they retreated west though Libya to the Mareth Line. Both impressively rapid German improvisation – which included rushing reinforcements from Sicily by sea and air – and rather sluggish exploitation by the British First Army enabled the German Army by late November to establish a shaky defensive line facing west against the approaching Anglo-American forces.

By mid-December 1942, thanks in part to the use of the new Tiger I tank, Axis forces had successfully consolidated the defensive positions held in Tunisia by the recently formed Fifth Panzer Army. This achievement also owed much to the personal efforts of commanders to motivate exhausted and dispirited troops. At Terbourda in Tunisia on November 30, for example, Lieutenant-General Wolfgang Fischer personally led several platoon attacks by the battle-weary troops of his 10th Panzer Division. Through measures such as this, by mid-December the Fifth Panzer Army had consolidated an improvised frontline that ran from Sedjenane through Bou Arada, Kasserine, and Gafsa, where it joined the front held by Rommel's former Panzer Army Africa, now redesignated the German–Italian Panzer Army.

In western Tunisia, Colonel-General Hans-Jürgen von Arnim's hastily improvised Fifth Panzer Army controlled, by early January 1943, the equivalent of one Italian and three German divisions to resist the drive east of the Anglo-American troops of General Anderson's British First Army. The German–Italian

Panzer Army, now under the command of the Italian General Giovanni Messe, held the southeastern front along the Mareth Line against the attacks launched by Montgomery's seasoned Eighth Army.

Encouraged by the success of these minor ripostes, the Germans now developed more ambitious counteroffensive plans that would deliver an unsettling blow to stem the tightening Allied grip on western Tunisia. With the Allies now operating on two geographically separate fronts, the German Army hoped to exploit the advantage it possessed by operating on interior lines of communication. Being concentrated between two separate ("exterior") Allied forces, the "interior" Germans could concentrate their combat power at a single point more quickly than the separate Allied commands could react.

Consequently, during February 14–22, 1943, elements of both the Fifth and the German–Italian Panzer Armies coordinated a savage counterassault against the raw American troops deployed in the Kasserine Pass area of western Tunisia. The attack successfully advanced some 60 miles (96 km) in the face of collapsing enemy cohesion – some American units broke in panic. The victory at Kasserine did little more than delay the inevitable Allied victory in North Africa, however.

After Kasserine, Rommel initiated an attack during March 6–7, 1943, at Medinine against Montgomery's forces that faced him on the Mareth Line. He concentrated three panzer divisions with 160 tanks that were supported by some 200 guns and 10,000 infantry. Yet Montgomery, due to his foreknowledge of the attack ("Ultra" intercepts had provided the British commander with vital intelligence), had managed to assemble a force of 400 tanks, 350 artillery pieces, and 470 antitank guns to halt Rommel. The weight of Allied numbers soon defeated Rommel's thrust and inflicted heavy casualties on Axis forces. Medinine proved to be Rommel's last battle in North Africa as Hitler recalled him on sick leave back to the Reich, with Arnim replacing him as army group commander.

Rommel's costly attack at Medinine on March 6–7, 1943, weakened the Axis ability to withstand the renewed British attacks in late March and early April 1943 that ruptured the Mareth Line. By mid-April, the combined Anglo-

A German 88mm Flak gun in North Africa. Throughout the desert war the Germans expertly used a combination of tanks and antitank guns to achieve results. In the desert it was soon discovered that the unimpeded views favored long-range weapons such as the "88" since the enemy could be detected at great distances. Whenever possible, vehicles were dug in to lessen the effects of shell and bomb splinters. In addition, to combat the dangers of enemy air attacks German soldiers were instructed to dig foxholes for personal protection.

The Second Battle of El Alamein, October 23–November 2, 1942. Montgomery's plan of attack involved a diversionary assault in the south by XIII Corps, while farther to the north XXX Corps launched the main British break-in thrust to open up two corridors in the enemy minefields through which the armor of XXX Corps would advance. During the last week of October, the sophisticated Axis minefields successfully slowed the attacks spearheaded by the armor of XXX Corps to some extent, while local panzer counterattacks effectively blunted some British armored penetrations. It was creditable that the exhausted and rapidly weakening units of the Africa Corps held on as long as they did against the repeated and determined attacks undertaken by the numerically superior forces of the Eighth Army. By November 2, Montgomery concluded that his enemy was on the point of collapse and consequently initiated Operation Supercharge. This was his final breakthrough attack launched toward the Rahman Track north of Ruweisat Ridge. During the night of November 3–4, Rommel realized that his forces could hold the El Alamein position no longer. Consequently, he ordered the Panzer Army Africa to conduct a strategic withdrawal west, despite Hitler's recent order to stand and fight to the last man along the Alamein position. The brutally hard-fought Second Battle of El Alamein, in which the Axis and Allies respectively incurred 51,000 and 14,000 casualties, proved to be the decisive turning point of the war in North Africa.

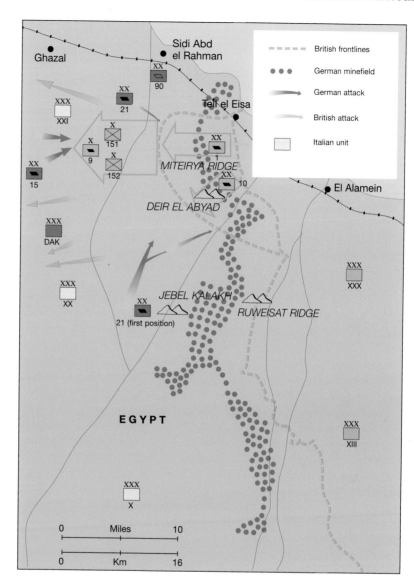

American assaults from the west and Montgomery's advance from the south forced the Axis into a small perimeter around Tunis and Bizerta based on the last ring of hills before the open coastal plain. Axis soldiers continued to resist bravely, despite the obviously unfavorable circumstances. Hitler hoped that the resilient troops of Army Group Africa could hold their precarious bridgehead in Tunisia for a few more months to tie down Allied forces. But on May 7, 1943, the Allies captured the key ports of Bizerte and Tunis, and just five days later, on May 12, the war in North Africa was over: 275,000 Germans and Italians soldiers went into the POW stockades.

The Impact of Armor in North Africa

In North Africa the tank was the catalyst of victory. The panzers were the backbone of the army – everything depended on the tank; the other units merely supported it. For both sides, therefore, the armored struggle was of paramount importance. The myth of the Africa Corps is that Rommel had more tanks than

Italian Army Combat Performance

During the North African campaign, both the Germans and British denigrated the fighting capabilities of Italian troops. After the war, the Anglo-German accounts of the campaign developed the idea of the Italians as a "nonmartial" race, in a caricature based on the alleged "Latin" temperament. The Italians supplied the bulk of the Axis troops fighting in North Africa, and too often the German Army unfairly ridiculed Italian military effectiveness either due to its own arrogance or to conceal its own mistakes and failures. In reality, a significant number of Italian units fought skillfully in North Africa, and many "German" victories were the result of Italian skill-at-arms and a combined Axis effort. The British created something of a myth around Rommel, since they preferred to justify their defeats with the presence in the enemy camp of an exceptional general, rather than recognize the superior qualities of the combatants, whether Italian or German. That certain Italian formations fought as effectively as they did remained an impressive feat considering that on the home front Italy's population had little stomach for their state's participation in the war.

the British, and that they were better armed and armored. The truth is rather different. Regarding the numbers issue, the facts are that during Operation Crusader in November 1941, both the number of British Commonwealth formations that faced Rommel and the equipment levels they deployed had risen markedly. Furthermore, the relative German weakness in armor was even more noticeable at the start of Crusader than previously. While the British deployed over 700 tanks in mid-November 1941, Rommel's German units possessed just 174 tanks, with an additional 146 operational Italian vehicles. Moreover, while the British possessed a further 500 tanks in reserve, Rommel's Africa Corps had no armored reserve whatsoever.

At Gazala in May 1942 the British – now receiving large amounts of equipment from the United States after its December 1941 entry into the war – had available 850 tanks with 420 more in reserve, while the Axis could deploy just 560 tanks, including 230 largely obsolete Italian tanks and 50 ineffective German Panzer II light tanks. At Second Alamein in October 1942, the Eighth Army had 1,029 tanks available for the offensive, including 252 of the new M4 Sherman, which outclassed even the Panzer III Model J. In contrast, the Germans fielded just 211 (173 Panzer III and 38 Panzer IV) tanks, plus 278 largely obsolete Italian tanks. By November 2, Montgomery's attacks had reduced Rommel's two key formations – the 15th and 21st Panzer Divisions – to just 30 operational tanks and 2,500 combat-fit soldiers between them. But at this stage of the offensive, these battered panzer battle groups faced a British armored force of 600 tanks: odds of 20 to 1.

In terms of the quality of equipment, again Rommel's forces were often at a disadvantage. At Gazala, for example, British numerical superiority was reinforced by qualitative advantage as well. Most German medium tanks – the Panzer III vehicles – were equipped with the short 50mm KwK L/42 gun, whose penetration capabilities remained inferior to that of the British six-pounder. In terms of armor protection, the German tanks were, on the whole, not superior to the newer British Cruiser tanks. It was true that the Germans had available for this offensive the effective new Panzer III Model J tank (the Mark III Special in British parlance). With its potent long-barreled 50mm KwK 39 L/60 gun and 1.96-in. (50-mm) thick armor, this vehicle outclassed any British tank in the theater and even enjoyed parity with the new British M3 Grant tank (an American tank that was modified by the British) that arrived during May 1942. But by the middle of that month, however, only 19 Mark III Specials had reached the front with a further 19 being off-loaded at Tripoli. This small reinforcement was outweighed, however, by the arrival of 400 new American-supplied Grant tanks for the British forces, which delivered a penetration capacity superior to that of the Panzer III Model J.

With regard to armor, the British Matilda, Valentine, and Crusader had better armor protection, as did the American Stuart. The only real qualitative tank advantage the Germans enjoyed came toward the end of the campaign, when they received Mk IV and Tiger tanks.

Reinforcements received in November 1942 not only included mortar rocket projector (*Nebelwerfer*) units, but also the Heavy Tank Battalion 501, equipped with 45 new Tiger I heavy tanks with their lethal 88mm guns and heavy armor protection. Tactically, the Germans usually employed the small number of Tigers available in Tunisia to form the center and center-rear of modestly sized armored wedges, while around them were deployed the lighter and more mobile Panzer III and IV tanks. Though the Tiger proved an impressive tank-killer in Tunisia that accounted for dozens of Allied AFVs, German commanders soon discovered that the great weight and thus limited mobility of the Tiger, together with its high rate of fuel consumption, restricted the tactical utility of the vehicle. In addition, its engine was too weak and sensitive for desert operations. The engine of the Panzer IV, on the other hand, proved very efficient and needed an overhaul only every 9,375 miles (15,000 km). But for the defensive and limited counteroffensive actions undertaken by the German Army in Tunisia during early 1943, the Tiger proved an ideal weapon that significantly bolstered Axis defensive resilience in the face of Allied numerical superiority.

Antitank Weapons

The Africa Corps did enjoy a qualitative superiority over the Allies when it came to antitank weapons, though mainly because they used a Flak gun in the antitank role. During the British offensives Brevity and Battleaxe in May and June 1941, for example, the standard German 37mm Antitank Gun 35/36 (37mm Pak 35/36) proved ineffective against the heavier British tanks; even the newer 50mm Antitank Gun 38 (50mm Pak 38) remained inadequate against the heavy British Matilda tank except at close range. It was here that the German 88mm Antiaircraft G 18 (88mm Flak 18) and its modified versions, the 88mm Flak 36 and 37, proved their tactical worth deployed in a ground role. The 88mm gun proved capable of penetrating even the British Matilda tank's 3-in. (77-mm) frontal armor at ranges of up to 6,564 ft (2,000 m). The antitank capabilities of the dual-capability 88mm Flak gun, along with the tactical skill and professionalism of the German troops, made up for the fact that during Brevity and Battleaxe Rommel's forces fought at a serious disadvantage in terms of armor (German commanders were always at a loss to explain why the British did not use their 3.7in. antiaircraft guns in the antitank role).

At the Battle of Gazala, it was the few 88mm Flak guns that Rommel possessed that remained largely responsible for the high enemy tank casualty rates. The recent replacement of the British antitank gun arsenal with the 57mm six-pounder gun, which was superior to the German 50mm Pak 38 antitank piece, however, gave the Allies a tactical edge in the antiarmor struggle that went some way to offset the antitank killing power of the 88mm Flak gun. This development – coupled with the frontal invulnerability of the British Matilda II to the 50mm Pak 40 antitank gun – led Hitler in May 1942 to rush a new mobile antitank vehicle to the theater. The Tank-Hunter 38(t) Marten III (Panzerjäger 38(t) Marder III) mounted the potent ex-Soviet 76.2mm Pak 36(r) antitank gun

in an open three-sided shield on top of the chassis of the obsolescent Panzer 38(t) tank. During the Battle of Gazala, the Marder III provided Rommel's infantry with desperately needed mobile killing power to augment that provided by the small numbers of 88mm Flak guns available. The vehicle demonstrated the lethality of its 76.2mm gun by knocking out several dozen British tanks. Indeed, so impressed were Commonwealth troops that they assumed the Germans had simply mounted their potent 88mm Flak guns on fully tracked chassis.

Rommel

No discussion of the German Army's performance in North Africa can exclude an analysis of Erwin Rommel, the "Desert Fox." The war in North Africa made his reputation. On February 12, 1941, Hitler dispatched Rommel by air to Tripoli in response to the major defeat that the Italian units had just suffered at the hands of British and Commonwealth forces. The new commander had with him just a small mobile force to stiffen Italian resolve and to assist them in reversing the possibility of total defeat at the hands of the British-led forces advancing from Egypt. Hitler did not, however, envisage the Africa Corps making spectacular successes, lest the need to protect these accomplishments from British ripostes led to the diversion of precious German reserves away from the impending Barbarossa invasion of the Soviet Union to the North Africa theater.

For his first battle in early 1941, Rommel used mobility and ruse to magnify his slender strength, and this helped win the psychological battle with the British. The Germans even deployed lines of trucks to create dust clouds to give the impression of greater strength, and by such a ploy surrounded and captured the commander and a brigade of the British 2nd Armored Division at Mechili. As in the Western campaign during 1940, here the German Army effectively employed

German motorized infantry during Rommel's offensive in early 1942. By late 1941, the defending Germans had been able to inflict high casualties on the British by utilizing their superior tactical mobility to deliver audacious counterstrokes with limited resources at unexpected places.

British troops in Tunisia in March 1943. By this time the Germans had taken delivery of a completely new and improved version of the famous 88mm antiaircraft gun, the Flak 41, which boosted German antiarmor capabilities. The 88mm Antiaircraft Gun 41 (88mm Flak 41) outperformed the Flak 18 by 20 percent in terms of muzzle velocity and by 30 percent in vertical range. Thankfully for Allied ground troops and unfortunately for the German Army, after the Tunisian campaign Hitler subsequently allocated all available Flak 41 weapons – their numbers peaked at only 318 in January 1945 – to the defense of the Reich against Allied strategic bombing.

standard *ruses de guerre* as a force multiplier to maximize their battlefield impact on the enemy facing them.

Rommel's maverick qualities did little to endear him to the German General Staff, and it was often only Hitler's patronage that saved him from the wrath of a High Command eager to punish a subordinate who ignored orders. But audacity had its rewards: what remains remarkable about Rommel's success during the Battle of Gazala, for example, was that Panzer Army Africa remained outnumbered in all key areas. The Germans, in addition, had almost no reserves. This meant that for the battle, the Germans, the attacking side, remained outnumbered three to one in terms of effective armor. The British also outnumbered the Germans three to two in artillery. However, the German advantage of being able to concentrate their guns – mainly 105mm Light Field Howitzer 18 (105mm le FH 18) pieces – rather than distribute them among all their divisions like the British, partially offset this numerical disadvantage. Finally, in terms of air support, both sides were more evenly matched, with roughly 430 British and 350 Axis operational aircraft.

During the First Battle of El Alamein on July 2–4, 1942, Rommel failed in his bid to break the British lines. However, the British were so afraid that he might succeed that British diplomats in Cairo burned their secret papers, the British fleet left the port of Alexandria, and civilians grabbed whatever transport was available to take them east to Palestine. But the German units remained too tired and depleted after their marathon advance to secure victory. This defeat suggests that Rommel's generalship had its limitations in that he remained willing to fight battles with inadequate forces at the end of overextended supply lines that more cautious commanders would have avoided.

At Alam Halfa, Rommel's plan employed his well-tried gambit of launching a feint in the north, while swinging through the southern axis to then turn north to the Alam Halfa Ridge, thus cutting the British lines of supply. Though the

Quattara Depression restricted the freedom of movement available to the panzers, by September 2 the Africa Corps had nevertheless managed to advance east 20 miles (32 km) to reach the Alam Halfa Ridge. Here, however, fierce enemy resistance, deep minefields, and the battering inflicted from the skies during daylight by British air power, as well as Axis fuel shortages, all combined to halt Rommel's determined thrust. He often ignored logistical problems, believing that audacity and aggressiveness could offset them. However, in a campaign that was increasingly dominated by such considerations, this was a major misconception.

Desert Tactics

The Africa Corps often effectively employed standard German Army offensive and defensive tactics, most notably the use of antitank screens to destroy enemy armor, thus giving the panzers freedom both to outflank enemy armor and to destroy enemy infantry and operational cohesion. In the North African campaign, Rommel's Africa Corps put up a tremendous fight against overwhelming odds, and through their professionalism and boldness achieved remarkable battlefield successes. That Rommel's force failed to conquer Egypt was partly down to the field marshal's often overambitious plans given the limited resources at his disposal, and the incessant problems of logistics (see below). Interestingly, the Germans did not acclimatize their troops to desert warfare, as it was felt that this would waste part of their first year in theater – a period in which they were at their maximum physical efficiency.

German antitank traps, along with daring mobile countermaneuvers, outwitted the infantry-minded assaults of the British (from early 1942, all German infantry units were assigned antitank guns, though the aim of equipping each battalion with 18 76.2mm guns was never achieved). The Germans proved particularly adept at using the open desert flank in the south to turn the British position and attack the enemy rear. During Brevity and Battleaxe, for example, the Germans showed how effectively a flexible, aggressive defense that employed mobile antitank screens in conjunction with armored counterattacks could blunt a numerically superior attack.

On occasions, though, Rommel's lack of tanks made exploitation difficult. On November 20–22, 1941, for example, he used his antitank guns aggressively to pin down the British armored attacks while he concentrated his panzer forces at Sidi Azeiz for a daring counterthrust. Then he struck southwest toward Gabr Saleh to engage the enemy armored forces in the rear, before turning northwest to smash the British spearheads that threatened Sidi Rezegh. That the Axis forces could field so few tanks, however, proved a severe handicap to Rommel's conduct of these mobile counterattack operations. For any tactical successes the Africa Corps obtained during its defense against Operation Crusader could only be achieved at the expense of heavy tank losses in the face of brave British antiarmor actions, such as the destruction experienced around Sidi Rezegh on November 23, dubbed "Sunday of the Dead." Such heavy AFV losses made it difficult for the modest panzer forces that remained subsequently to exploit the tactical successes already achieved.

The unwillingness of the German High Command to send extra troops to North Africa to aid Rommel, principally because of the vast numbers of troops the Eastern Front now consumed, forced Rommel's units to adopt the remarkably successful extemporized tactics that went so far to create the legend of the Africa Corps. What were these tactics? Several examples from the desert war will

The North African War

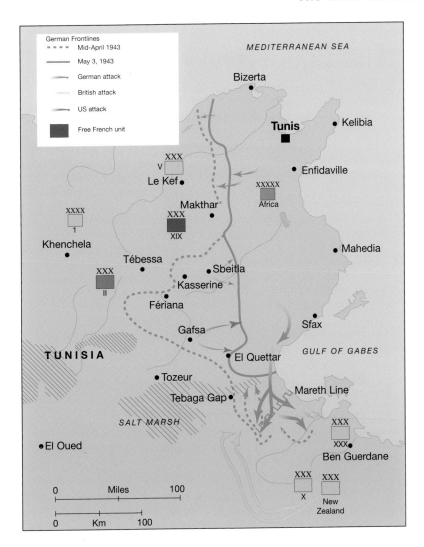

The situation during the final phase of the North African campaign. The Germans were faced by opponents who had a marked superiority in air power, manpower, and equipment. Final defeat could only be averted, not prevented.

illustrate the effectiveness of German tactics, especially the use of all-arms formations, and the potency of the constituent parts of a panzer division.

In January 1942, during Rommel's offensive, Battle Group *Marcks*, commanded by *Oberstleutnant* Werner Marcks, was created by amalgamating units drawn from the 155th Regiment, 21st Panzer Division, 90th Light Division, and the Italian Armored Division *Ariete*. It was detailed to act as the spearhead of Rommel's offensive. The formation adopted for the advance was armored cars in the lead (the Germans relied heavily on battlefield intelligence and were always willing to fight for information – the reconnaissance units in the panzer divisions relied on audacity and speed, plus superior training, to collect intelligence), followed by tanks, then lorries containing infantry and halftracks towing Flak guns and artillery. On each flank were motorcycles from the panzer division's reconnaissance unit.

On January 21 the battle group ran into British tanks and antitank guns. Marcks quickly deployed his artillery, which opened fire, and then the tanks closed with each other and began to exchange fire. The motorcyclists of the reconnaissance unit were then sent forward. Dismounting, they advanced under cover of mortar and machine-gun fire and radioed back the positions of the

The Tiger I Heavy Tank

The introduction of Panzer VI Model E Tiger I heavy tanks into the North African theater during December 1942 helped the Axis restabilize the strategic situation following the twin disasters of Operation Torch and Rommel's "Great Retreat" after the Second Battle of El Alamein. The Tiger I heavy tank was a squat and angular 55-ton (56-tonne) vehicle that mounted the lethal 88mm KwK 43 L/56 gun. It possessed impressive levels of protection, with frontal armor some 3.9 in. (100 mm) thick, plus 3.1-in. (80-mm) plates on its sides and rear. Apart from the earliest vehicles, the Tiger was powered by a 700-bhp Maybach HL 230 engine that delivered a satisfactory top road speed of 23.5 mph (38 km/h) but only a modest 12.5 mph (20 km/h) off road. Since the Tiger was too large to be transported on the standard German railroad flat-car, the manufacturers, Henschel, developed a novel two-track system for the vehicle. In battle the Tiger utilized wide 28.5-in. (725-mm) combat tracks, but when being moved by rail these were replaced with narrower transportation tracks. The Tiger made its operational debut during August 1942 on the Eastern Front, but fought many of its earliest actions in North Africa during early 1943. Though the Tiger both mounted an extremely potent gun and was heavily armored, its combat effectiveness was undermined somewhat by persistent mechanical unreliability and its limited mobility. Nevertheless, when employed in the defensive battles that dominated the German Army's experiences from 1943 onward, the Tiger proved a formidable tank-killer that bolstered German defensive resistance against superior Allied numbers. Unfortunately for the German Army, there always remained too few Tigers available – only 1,354 were produced – to restore the steadily deteriorating strategic situation during the second half of the war.

enemy antitank guns. Marcks pushed forward his Flak guns, which opened up a devastating fire on the British antitank guns and tanks. When Marcks judged enough enemy tanks and antitank guns had been destroyed, he ordered his panzers and halftracks to advance through the breach, supported by his artillery and Flak guns. What was left of the British force retired, leaving Marcks master of the field. His artillery and Flak guns were limbered up and followed the rest of the battle group. When, later, the battle group was attacked by British infantry, the latter were driven to ground by machine-gun fire and then smothered by 88mm airburst shells.

During the early part of the desert war, the Germans had a range advantage over the British that proved telling in many engagements. Panzer units were usually made up of Mark IIIs and IVs. The Panzer III was armed with the 50mm gun, but the IV mounted a 75mm gun that could fire HE up to a range of 9,000 ft (2,743 m). During Battleaxe, the panzers of the 5th Light Division engaged the 7th Armored Division. At a range of 9,000 ft (2,743 m) the panzers opened fire. The British tanks, armed with two-pounders, were untouched, but the crews and guns of the supporting 25-pounders were annihilated. Thus on June 16, 1941, a squadron of 40 panzers attacked a line of 10 British Cruisers supported by a troop of 25-pounders. As the panzers advanced, the 25-pounders were knocked out one by one before the British tanks could reply.

Battle groups were also used effectively for defense. On June 6, 1942, during the Battle of Gazala, Battle Group *Wolz* was formed from elements of the 33rd Reconnaissance Battalion, 33rd Antitank Battalion, and 2nd Battalion of the 25th Flak Regiment. During an attack by British tanks in the Knightsbridge area, the battle group's 88mm Flak guns were deployed in line to halt the enemy armor. This they did effectively, destroying 50 British tanks.

At Gazala, Rommel employed his favorite stratagem of launching the northern corps of the Panzer Army Africa in a feint attack along the direct route to Tobruk, while the Africa Corps wheeled around the south of the southernmost enemy defensive "box," at Bir Hakeim, to attack the other "boxes" from the rear. The 1st Free French Brigade, however, undertook an heroic 10-day stand at the Bir Hakeim box, an action that disrupted Rommel's unfolding offensive. During

May 28–31, the Africa Corps successfully crushed the British 150th Brigade Box in the "Cauldron," which allowed it to open up direct supply lines to its spearhead units. Subsequently, on June 5–6 the Africa Corps fought off the expected – and by now belated – British armored counterthrust launched from the east, and inflicted heavy casualties on these forces. But the Axis armor only accomplished this key success at a very high price in casualties. For the new Grant tanks deployed by the British at Gazala brought effective fire to bear against the panzers and consequently inflicted heavy casualties on Rommel's armor (the range advantage mentioned above had been neutralized). But the Desert Fox persevered with his armored operations, and by the evening of June 6 the Africa Corps had seized the initiative at Gazala. The battle stands as a perfect example of what can be achieved by a combination of effective tactics, combined-arms units, and an audacious commander.

Triumph of the Tigers

During the campaign in Tunisia, German defeat was inevitable. However, the Africa Corps still displayed a mastery of battlefield tactics. In February 1943, for example, German resistance in Tunisia was bolstered by Arnim's adoption of a limited counteroffensive posture despite the unfavorable balance of forces at the front. In one such limited riposte, along the road to Pont du Fahs, the Tigers of the 501st Battalion demonstrated once again their resilience to British antiarmor equipment. That day a German armored wedge of 16 Panzer III and IV tanks, led by two Tigers, ran into a British antitank ambush. A dozen six-pounder antitank guns engaged the Tigers at point-blank range, and after hitting the lead vehicle nine times managed to knock it out with the tenth hit, which penetrated the side armor. Subsequent Allied tests on the wreck revealed that the British six-pounder gun could not penetrate the Tiger's frontal armor at even suicidally close range!

During the Kasserine operation, notably at Djebel Chambi on the night February 19/20, German soldiers successfully attacked American defensive positions or infiltrated past them during effectively conducted night-time operations. Once again, these successes testified to how far the German Army had improved its night-fighting training after the weaknesses exposed during the 1939 Polish campaign. However, after this initial success, British and American reserves quickly plugged the gap, and the Germans remained too weak to exploit their success. Though the Axis had inflicted 10,000 casualties on the Allies at the expense of just 2,000 of their own troops, it would be the latter who could replace these losses far more easily than Rommel.

As well as superior tactics, better training, and the utmost faith in their equipment, the Germans in North Africa enjoyed another advantage over their adversaries, as the military historian Barrie Pitt notes: "British reinforcements came out in complete formations – preferably as divisions but, as had happened in Crusader, at times in brigades – and these went into action as such. ... But Rommel's reinforcements arrived as individual soldiers and were fed piecemeal into understrength formations – and when they went into action they were accompanied, and most often led, by men who had just come out of it ... a core of battle-hardened veterans who could not only shrug off the discomforts of desert fighting with accustomed ease, but also recognize danger immediately it appeared, ignore empty sound and irrelevant fury in concentration on the purpose in hand – and teach the newcomers to do the same." Pitt might also have mentioned the frequent exercises that were held, particularly between July and November 1941, to improve the standard of training. Emphasis was placed on combined infantry–artillery–tank, and artillery–tank–air forces actions. A high standard of training in the use and care of weapons, equipment, and vehicles was also maintained by the Germans. All weapons, for example, were cleaned very carefully, but afterward were only lightly oiled; otherwise, dust would eat its way into the metal surfaces.

Ultimately, however, external factors critically hampered the German effort in North Africa. First, successful enemy attacks on the Axis supply lines across the Mediterranean starved Rommel of the resources he needed for operational effectiveness. In this war dominated by logistics, the British use of "Ultra" intelligence proved especially useful as it gave them foreknowledge of times and routes of Axis supply convoys. Second, the effectiveness of the Italian forces fighting with the Germans remained mixed. Third, the need to combine varying Italian and German strategies weakened Rommel's position. Fourth, the main Axis port of Tripoli remained inadequate for the scale of supplies required. Fifth, because Hitler never saw the North African theater as anything more than a holding campaign, Rommel was never given the necessary support from Berlin to achieve a strategic victory, capture Cairo, and – possibly – alter the outcome of the war. And ultimately, after Second Alamein in October–November 1942, increasing British numerical superiority gave them such a large battlefield advantage that no degree of German tactical excellence could offset this unfavorable battlefield reality.

Even once across the Mediterranean, Axis supplies still had to travel many hundreds of miles by road to reach the frontline troops. Simply getting the supplies to the front along North Africa's limited road network used up much of

German tanks are unloaded at Tripoli. Given that in North Africa both sides fought in a hostile climate over wide geographical areas at the end of long and vulnerable lines of supply, logistics dominated the outcome of operations. The German supply lines proved particularly vulnerable since they stretched across the Mediterranean Sea from Italy to the ports of Benghazi, Tripoli, and Tobruk, as well as – from late 1942 – the ports of Tunisia. As the Allies won the war of interdiction against these lines of communication they could starve their opponent of matériel and supplies.

the precious fuel needed for the frontline motorized units, while Royal Air Force attacks destroyed many vehicles as they traveled across the open desert. The island of Malta, which sat astride the route from Italy to Africa, soon became the fulcrum for German efforts to keep open their supply lines. The Axis subjected the island to a long and ultimately unsuccessful siege spearheaded by aerial bombing. Had they carried out their plan to capture Malta by air assault, and had Hitler allocated greater resources to the war in the Mediterranean and North Africa, Rommel might have been able to capture the Middle East. An Axis supply convoy getting through to North Africa could make all the difference. The arrival of six ships in January 1942 with new tanks enabled Rommel to launch his assault that eventually reached El Alamein. Conversely, the loss of two Italian ships with 3,995 tons (4,400 tonnes) of fuel during the Second Battle of El Alamein proved critical as Rommel's forces were already seriously short of fuel. Like Rommel, Stumme soon began to complain bitterly about the shortage of supplies, especially fuel for the tanks and lorries. On October 19, 1942, four days before the British offensive, Stumme reported that his forces had sufficient fuel for just 11 days of operations at current consumption levels, enough ammunition for only nine days' fighting, and bread rations for just 21 days. Tires and spare parts for vehicles were badly wanting, reinforcements were low, malnourishment was common, and the sick rate increasingly high.

On October 23, 1942, Montgomery's Eighth Army struck with an incredibly intense artillery bombardment by 1,000 guns – the largest yet seen in North Africa – augmented by aerial attacks. Under this truly awesome hail of firepower, Montgomery initiated a large-scale armored and infantry assault into the deep German defenses. The British and Commonwealth forces amounted to 194,000, while Rommel's command fielded 104,000 troops. In the air, 530 serviceable aircraft supported Montgomery's offensive, while Rommel could call upon just 340 aircraft to assist his ground defense.

Logistics – the Achilles' Heel

The shortage of Axis men and equipment prevented him from decisively halting Montgomery's determined thrusts. Rommel rushed back from his convalescence in Germany to deal with the crisis. On October 28, having moved the 21st Panzer and the Italian *Ariete* Divisions to the north, Rommel employed them for a counterattack against the threatening Australian thrust along the coast, part of Montgomery's "crumbling" attacks. By now Rommel was acutely aware that his countermeasures had to succeed, since Panzer Army Africa lacked the transport or fuel to extricate all its troops once its defensive line broke. If he failed to halt Montgomery, the whole of his army could be wiped out in the subsequent British exploitation operations. As the Axis forces lacked the mobility to continue holding Montgomery's attacks, Rommel had no choice but to flee west and abandon the whole of Libya.

During early 1943, the Germans and Italians both undertook valiant efforts to keep the already understrength Axis forces in Tunisia supplied with gasoline, ammunition, and food. During January–February 1943, for example, the Germans instituted an airlift to deliver a small but steady steam of reinforcements and supplies. In the face of determined Allied aerial and maritime interdiction campaigns designed to cut off Axis forces in Tunisia, some 200 two-engined Ju 52 transports, together with 15 huge six-engined Me 323 aircraft, repeatedly flew dangerous resupply missions to Tunisia. This airlift lasted until April 1943, when escalating Allied air attacks made all Axis attempts to supply Army Group Africa in Tunisia by either air or sea virtually impossible.

The Eastern Front 1941–42

Hitler's June 1941 invasion of the Soviet Union – Operation Barbarossa – was a titanic clash of arms. Instead of the swift destruction of the Bolshevik state, however, Barbarossa locked the German Army into a vast and brutal attritional war on the Eastern Front.

All things considered, the 208-division German Army that commenced Barbarossa on June 22, 1941, was only marginally more powerful than its smaller predecessor of May 1940. By June 1941, the German Army had introduced small numbers of effective new weapons such as the 50mm Antitank Gun 38 (50mm Pak 38). It had also enhanced its standards of junior officer and troop training. The improvements in troop equipment, training, and motivation, however, were offset by manpower and equipment shortages, and by the inability to increase the numbers of tanks, artillery, and antitank guns available at the front. These deficiencies would prove important given that in summer 1941 a Wehrmacht marginally more powerful than ever before would engage a far stronger enemy force than any it had hitherto encountered. However, numbers were only half the story. The German Army began the invasion of the Soviet Union having experienced nearly two years of unbroken victories. Morale was at its height – the Wehrmacht believed it could defeat the Red Army with ease.

The final Barbarossa plan envisaged a three-pronged onslaught undertaken by three army group commands. Along the northern axis, Field Marshal Ritter Wilhelm von Leeb's Army Group North was to capture Leningrad, link up with the cobelligerent Finnish forces pushing south from Karelia, and then push on to capture Archangel on the White Sea. Five additional German divisions were to advance from northern Norway to assist the Finnish drive through northern Karelia to capture the port of Murmansk. In the central sector, Field Marshal Fedor von Bock's Army Group Center was to advance through Belorussia along the direct route via Smolensk to Moscow, and thence through Gorky and Kazan to the Ural mountains. Army Group Center remained physically separated from

German infantry during the first few days of Barbarossa. The physically robust soldiers within the horse-drawn infantry divisions desperately attempted, through forced marches, to keep up with the armor. In the five weeks to July 28, for example, the men of one of Leeb's formations – the 12th Infantry Division – marched 560 miles (900 km) at an average rate of 15 miles (24 km) per day!

the southern sector of the theater, where Field Marshal Gerd von Rundstedt's Army Group South deployed, by the extensive Pripet Marshes. The latter formation contained Romanian, Hungarian, and Slovakian forces. Army Group South was to advance through the Ukraine – via Kiev and Kharkov – to Rostov on the Sea of Azov, and thence thrust southeast into the oil-rich Caucasus and east through Kazakhstan to the southern Urals around Orsk.

The objectives of Barbarossa remained a confused mixture of contradictory aims. The plan included economic objects such as the agriculture of the Ukraine, the industry of the Don basin, and the oil of the Caucasus; it targeted the population centers that doubled as key communications nodes, such as Moscow, Kiev, and Kharkov; and it also aimed for maritime centers such as Leningrad, Rostov, and Sevastopol, whose capture would protect the flanks of the Axis advance. The pursuit of so many different targets left the Axis invasion forces without a clear overriding objective toward which their main effort could be directed.

The most fundamental feature of Barbarossa was its immense scale. The initial start line, excluding the Finnish sector, stretched 910 miles (1,464 km) from the Baltic Sea to Romania's Black Sea coast. Army Group North had to advance 490 miles (788 km) to reach Leningrad, while Army Group Center's intermediate objective – Moscow – lay 615 miles (990 km) distant. Army Group South needed to push 876 miles (1,410 km) to reach Stalingrad, and 1,500 miles (2,415 km) to reach the southern Urals.

Order of Battle

Colonel-General Hoepner's Fourth Panzer Group spearheaded the Army Group North with the six mechanized divisions of XLI and LVI Motorized Corps. Two panzer groups – Colonel-General Heinz Guderian's Second and Colonel-General Hoth's Third – led the attack launched by Army Group Center. Guderian's command deployed XXIV, XLVI, and XLVII Motorized Corps with a total of nine mobile divisions, while the Third Panzer Group comprised the seven divisions of XXXIX and LVII Motorized Corps. Last, Colonel-General Ewald von Kleist's First Panzer Group spearheaded the advance of Army Group South with the nine mechanized divisions of III, XIV, and XLVIII Motorized Corps. In addition to these formations, the bulk of the three army groups comprised infantry armies designed to follow up the armor, occupy ground, and mop up. In the Finnish sector, Marshal Mannerheim deployed a Finnish army of 18 divisions. Army Group North deployed the 21 infantry divisions of Sixteenth and Eighteenth Armies, Army Group Center fielded the Fourth and Ninth Armies, with 15 and 17 divisions respectively, while Army Group South fielded three German armies – Sixth, Eleventh, and Seventeenth – with 32 divisions, plus the 14 divisions of the Third and Fourth Romanian Armies. The Second Army was in reserve.

The German campaign in the East in 1941 can be divided into four distinct phases. First, the early phase of Barbarossa between June 22 and July 19. During this period the fast-moving panzer spearheads trapped hundreds of thousands of Red Army troops in giant pockets, such as at Minsk and Smolensk, and totally defeated the Red Army in Belorussia. The second phase, between July 20 and August 21, witnessed Hitler, in Directive No. 33, reinforcing the flanks and diverting panzer forces away from the central Moscow axis. Thus Guderian's Second Panzer Group was sent south to reinforce Army Group South, while Hoth's Third Panzer Group was sent north to bolster the attack on Leningrad. The third phase, from August 22 to September 26, saw the reduction of the Kiev

The first German plan (August 1940) for the invasion of the Soviet Union envisaged a drive through Belorussia toward Smolensk, with a twin drive on Kiev. The Baltic and Black Sea flanks were regarded as mere masking operations.

The OKH variant of December 5, 1940, turned the original twin thrusts into three. The drive against Leningrad was strengthened.

Führer Directive 21 (Case Barbarossa) of December 18, 1940, which set the invasion's objective as the destruction of the bulk of the Red Army located in the western areas of the Soviet Union. The Germans sought to destroy the Red Army in the 250-mile (400-km) border region up to the Dnieper and Dvina rivers. Once the German Army had achieved this task, it was to push on toward the Ural mountains.

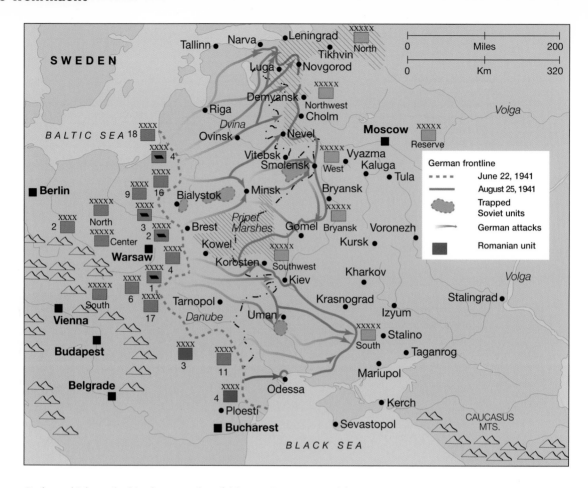

Pocket, which resulted in the surrender of 665,000 Soviet troops. This victory, a 20th-century Cannae, was probably the German Army's greatest triumph in World War II. The fourth phase lasted from October until early December 1941. During this period Hitler changed plans again and ordered an attack on Moscow. Codenamed Typhoon, it began on the last day of September. However, German armored and infantry divisions had been reduced to 50 percent effectiveness due to attrition, and the two-month delay meant another factor entered the equation – mud. The rains turned the poor roads into mud baths which slowed the advance, then stopped it altogether. The start of the intensely cold Russian winter in November allowed the resumption of the advance, but by this time the German Army was at the limit of its endurance. Typhoon was halted in early December, signalling the failure of Barbarossa and the beginning of the German Army's ordeal in Russia.

In the early hours of June 22, 1941, 161 Axis divisions commenced their attack on the Soviet Union. Once through the Soviet border defenses, during the first week of Barbarossa, German armored formations headed deep into the enemy's rear areas, where they soon overran the logistic supplies that the Red Army had stockpiled well forward. To facilitate this advance, the German Army again deployed special forces – particularly Russian-speaking Brandenburg Commandos in captured enemy vehicles and uniforms (these having been acquired by the Finns during the 1939–40 Winter War). These units operated covertly deep behind the Soviet lines to seize key bridges and to cut

During the first 10 days of the campaign, the German mechanized spearheads raced through the western borders of the Soviet Union. On July 1, for example, the mobile divisions of Army Group North crossed the Dvina River in Estonia, having advanced 200 miles (321 km) at a rate of 20 miles (32 km) per day. Unfortunately, Leeb's dual mission of advancing on Leningrad and protecting the northern flank of Army Group Center forced him to split the already weak Fourth Panzer Group. Subsequently, Reinhardt's XLI Motorized Corps advanced directly toward Leningrad, while Manstein's LVI Panzer Corps took the more southerly and easterly route via Novgorod.

Hitler's Directive 33 of July 19 shifted the German main effort south away from Moscow toward the Ukraine. Here, after mid-August, the Germans planned to enact another great double envelopment through the cooperation of Kleist's First Panzer Group from Army Group South with Guderian's Second Panzer Group from Army Group Center. Back in mid-July, Kleist's armor had commenced its preparatory operations with a thrust southeast toward the River Dnieper to turn the southern flank of a mass of immobile enemy infantry west of Kiev. Elements of Kleist's formation also thrust south to link up on August 3 with the Seventeenth Army to create an ancillary encirclement of 200,000 Soviet infantrymen at Uman. Meanwhile, Kleist's forces continued to thrust rapidly east until on August 12 they captured Kremenchug on the Dnieper River, 110 miles (177 km) behind the main north–south Soviet defensive line between Gomel and Kiev. If Kleist's panzers could push north to meet the intended thrust south by Guderian's armor, the ensuing encirclement would engulf five Soviet armies. They could, and the trap closed on 665,000 Red Army soldiers in the Kiev Pocket.

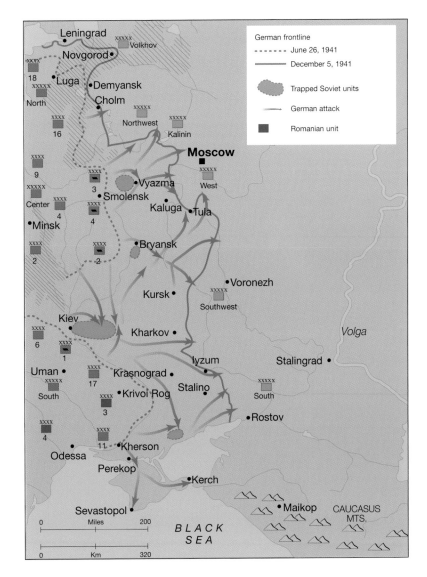

communication cables to paralyze enemy command and control – a particularly crucial task given the centrally initiated command ethos on which the Soviet military operated. Indeed, during those first hours of the war the Soviet High Command lost touch with the reality at the front – for example, by ordering armies to counterattack that had already been destroyed by the Axis onslaught!

Soon after the opening of the offensive the Germans created vast pockets of trapped Red Army armies – at Bialystok, Minsk, Smolensk, and Kiev – while the panzers raced ahead toward their objectives. In the north, for example, Hoepner's armor had covered 365 miles (587 km) in just 24 days, at an average rate of 15 miles (24 km) per day. At that tempo, the panzers would be in Leningrad within four days.

While the Germans cleared up the Ukraine during August–September 1941, along the northern axis the crack troops of the Fourth Panzer Group continued to push northeast toward Leningrad. By September 7 they had reached Lake Lagoda, cutting the last land route from the city to the rest of the Soviet Union. On the next day Hitler issued new orders for the continuation of the campaign, instructing that

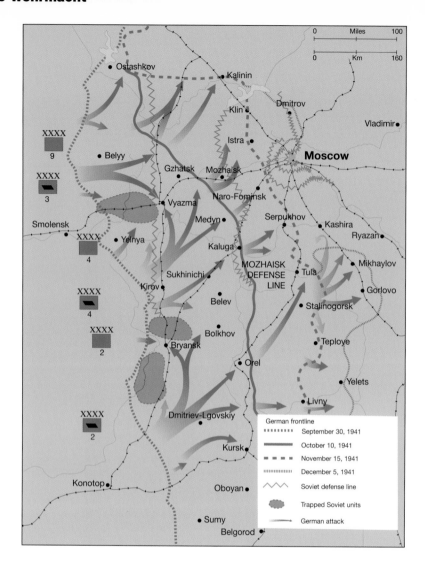

Operation Typhoon, the attack on Moscow. During the first week of October 1941, amid good weather, the initial phase of Typhoon unfolded promisingly for the Germans. However, they still encountered fanatical enemy resistance. Unfortunately, as the Germans strove to complete their encirclements from October 8 onward, the belated autumn rains arrived with a vengeance. By October 15 the torrential rain had turned the few roads and tracks in the region into impassable bogs which slowed the German drive toward Moscow to a crawl. It took truly heroic efforts by exhausted and soaked troops – repeatedly digging out or hauling out bogged-down tanks from the feet-deep mud – just to permit the panzer divisions to advance five-eighths of a mile (one kilometer) per day. These conditions prevented the Germans from exploiting their incredible successes at Bryansk and Vyazma with a rapid armored push against Moscow.

the promising thrust in the Ukraine be expanded into a drive on Kharkov and the Crimea. At the same time, he insisted that Army Group North continue its operations against Leningrad, although the city would now be starved into submission rather than stormed to free up armor for the Moscow axis.

If these two missions were not more than enough for the German Army to manage, Hitler's September 8 instructions insisted that Army Group Center simultaneously resume its critical attack on Moscow. To implement the Führer's orders, the Second Panzer Group redeployed during late September from the Ukraine back to the positions it had held around Smolensk in late July. In addition, elements of Hoth's Third Panzer Group also returned to the Smolensk area from the north during the same period, while elements of Hoepner's Fourth Panzer Group also moved down from Leningrad to join the thrust toward Moscow. On September 30, 1941, the 78 divisions of the Army Group Center, now spearheaded by the bulk of three panzer groups with 1,350 tanks, commenced Operation Typhoon against Moscow.

Heavy rains slowed the German advance to a crawl as the ground was turned into a sea of mud, and provided the Red Army with a desperately needed 14-day

German Logistic Difficulties

The unprecedented scope of Barbarossa presented enormous logistical problems for the German Army. Though the Wehrmacht made strenuous efforts to increase its logistic capabilities prior to June 1941, the overconfidence that permeated German planning led to overly-optimistic logistical calculations. Even during the planning phase the German Army realized that it could not sustain itself beyond Smolensk against a cohesive Red Army, and hence set as its objective the destruction of the Red Army west of Smolensk. Contrary to popular belief, the 1941 German Army was not a motorized force. Outside its small number of elite mechanized divisions, the bulk of the army comprised infantry divisions equipped with horse-drawn vehicles; some 625,000 German Army horses invaded the Soviet Union in 1941. As the invasion progressed, the army also confiscated many hundreds of sturdy local wagons to augment divisional mobility. The main logistical basis of the German invasion, however, was the large transport park of 6,500 vehicles deployed for each of the three army groups for the purpose of strategic resupply. Although 19,500 vehicles sounds an impressive figure, it was simply inadequate for the vast scale of Barbarossa. The inadequacy was compounded by the fact that this figure comprised 1,800 different types of vehicles confiscated from military and civilian use from across Axis-occupied Europe. This diversity made acquiring the necessary spare parts an impossible undertaking.

In addition, other problems dogged German resupply efforts in 1941. The Soviet road system was sparse, and even the few good roads broke up under the incessant German traffic and the inclement weather. The Germans also planned to use Soviet railroads to resupply their troops, but as these were on a wider gauge than the European lines, engineers had to regauge every mile of track before German locomotives could operate along them. These difficulties led, in mid-July, to Leeb being able to resupply the Fourth Panzer Group only by stopping supplies to the follow-up infantry armies. Similarly, the advance of Army Group Center was halted first at Smolensk during August and again in late October during Operation Typhoon because the logistic system could not cope. As subsequent events showed, the German Army would continue to neglect the logistical dimension of war, instead relying on its impressive tactical skills to offset any deficiencies. Given the scale of tactical victories that the German Army achieved in Barbarossa, it remains a moot point as to whether a firmer logistical basis might have enabled the Germans to achieve that elusive destruction of the Red Army in 1941. In all probability, however, whatever logistic system the Germans established during 1941, it was likely to be inadequate given both the sheer scale of Axis objectives and the continuing fierce resistance offered by the Soviets.

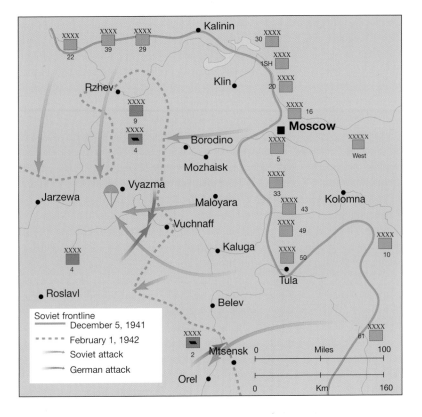

On December 6, 1941, the Soviets committed the 30 divisions they had carefully husbanded behind the lines around Moscow to a strategic counteroffensive designed to destroy the battered, weary, and frozen soldiers of Army Group Center. Paratroopers were also landed behind German lines. Army Group Center was fighting for its very existence.

breathing space hastily to improvise a makeshift defensive position – the Mozhaisk Line – in front of Moscow by throwing into the line any forces that had completed their mobilization. During the attacks on the Mozhaisk Line, the motorized infantry repeatedly encountered determined Soviet flanking ripostes that employed heavy armor. Virtually every time the motorized infantry that operated in poorly protected armored personnel carriers (APCs) encountered these ferocious Soviet responses, they suffered severe casualties. The disturbing experiences encountered at Mozhaisk led the Germans during 1942–43 to modify their motorized infantry tactics to the less lethal mission of reconnaissance, and to introduce in 1944 the Sdkfz 251/22 APC that mounted the potent 75mm Antitank Gun 40 (75mm Pak 40) to engage enemy armor at safer distances.

Bock temporarily halted Typhoon on October 25 so that his forces could reorganize and resupply themselves in preparation for a renewed thrust on Moscow. The German inability to sustain their main effort for more than 26 days ought to have made it clear to the High Command that by now the chances of their forces fulfilling the ambitious objectives of Barbarossa remained extremely remote. Yet this reality did not divert Hitler from mounting one last-gasp offensive effort to reach Moscow, win the war, and thus snatch – through the exercise of sheer will – decisive victory from the jaws of imminent defeat.

As these events unfolded, Army Group South in the Ukraine, having mopped up the Kiev Pocket, recommenced its advance east. Despite the arrival of the fall rains that slowed Kleist's tanks, the determined attacks mounted by the exhausted, yet still reasonably well-motivated, German infantrymen nevertheless managed to capture the city on October 24.

Resumption of the Advance

On the night of November 5–6, the first severe frosts of the approaching Soviet winter hardened the muddy morass on the ground, making it feasible for the Germans to renew Typhoon. However, Soviet forces opposing Army Group Center had swelled to 84 divisions with 1.2 million troops and 850 tanks. Moreover, during mid-November, after Stalin had learned from Soviet spies that Japan did not intend to attack eastern Siberia, the Soviets hastily redeployed another 100,000 Asiatic troops to the Moscow front.

On November 15 Army Group Center recommenced its drive on Moscow, but progress remained slow in the face of determined Soviet resistance, the terribly cold weather, and serious logistic problems. Even to keep the panzer divisions moving at a crawl, German troops had ruthlessly to confiscate from the local population all available pairs of snow shoes, every sledge, and all the hardy Russian ponies left alive. In the southern thrust, moreover, the fanatically stubborn Soviet resistance at Tula, despite being all but surrounded, prevented the Germans opening up the railroad to that town as a vital lifeline to bring in desperately needed supplies for the frontline troops.

By December 1 the rapidly dwindling German armored spearheads of the northern thrust had nevertheless crawled forward to within 12 miles (19 km) of Moscow. But by now many of the panzer divisions could field less than 10 serviceable tanks, and despite the best efforts of the German Army, by 4 December it was clear to all that the combination of massed Soviet artillery fire and resistance had destroyed the offensive power of Typhoon. On December 5, Hitler bowed to the inevitable, called off the German offensive, and permitted Bock's forces to go over to the defensive. To make matters worse, as these events

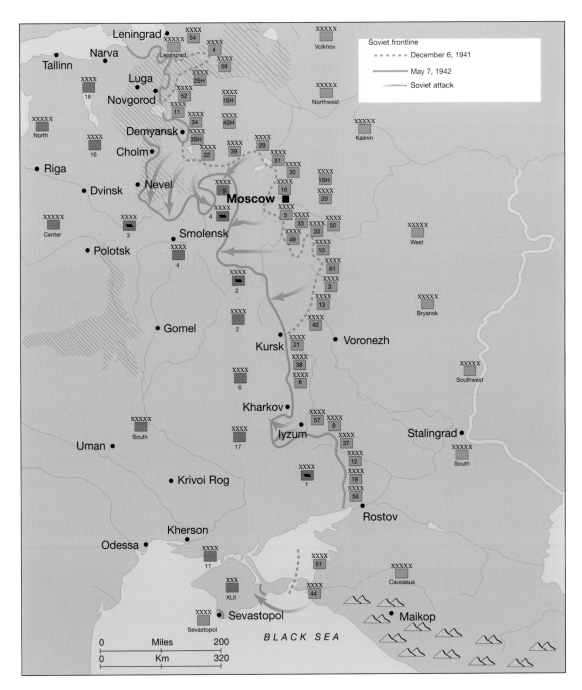

Soviet offensive operations between December 6, 1941, and May 7, 1942. Though many were conducted by understrength and poorly equipped and led Soviet armies, they did demonstrate to the Germans that Barbarossa had not destroyed the Red Army – far from it.

unfolded at Moscow, Army Group South's successful drive through the eastern Ukraine also turned into defeat. By November 28, Soviet forces had evicted German forces from Rostov. The Germans were now on the defensive in the East.

The end of Typhoon saw the beginning of a Soviet counteroffensive all along the Eastern Front (see map above). German forces were driven from the gates of Moscow, and for a while it appeared that the Wehrmacht would be defeated. However, Hitler ordered a "stand-fast" policy, and so the freezing and ill-equipped troops at the front held. By improvising strongpoints they were able to withstand the Soviet attacks and save the Eastern Front.

One reason for Hitler refusing to yield ground to the Red Army was that to him Barbarossa was an ideological struggle, and many of his decisions, which affected the army's conduct of the war, must be seen in an ideological context. Hitler's political treatise, *Mein Kampf*, should have left any reader with little doubt as to his future ambitions. Hitler viewed the Soviet Union as an internationalist, anticapitalist, Slavic/Asiatic and Jewish-dominated Bolshevik regime that posed a fundamental ideological threat to the existence of the expansionist Nazi state that formed the home of the Aryan German people. Put simply, the Thousand Year Nazi Reich could not flourish as long as the Bolshevik regime existed. In addition to this ideological antithesis, Hitler held designs on Soviet territory to provide "Living Space" in the East. Germany had lost the 1914–18 war, Hitler believed, because its geostrategic position in central Europe had enabled the Allies to cut off the food and raw materials Germany needed to obtain from foreign imports to continue her war effort. For the Thousand Year Reich to flourish, Hitler required an economic self-sufficiency that could be achieved only by acquiring the vast agricultural and economic assets of the western Soviet Union.

In August 1939, Hitler and Stalin had signed a non-aggression treaty, the Molotov–Ribbentrop Pact. The pact did not, however, alter the underlying tension that existed between the two countries. Rather, the treaty was simply a temporary piece of cynical expediency by both leaders. In the pact the two agreed jointly to invade and then divide Poland, while Stalin also guaranteed to send large grain exports to Germany until mid-June 1941 – note that date! Thus, Hitler obtained a free hand from a quiescent Stalin to deal with the West in 1940 without fear of the traditional German strategic specter of a two-front war. The period also gave Stalin time to prepare for a war he was certain would come.

Well-wrapped Soviet soldiers march past the frozen corpses of German troops during the Red Army counteroffensive outside Moscow in December 1941. The Germans had great difficulty in halting this offensive, fighting as they were at the end of overextended and vulnerable supply lines.

Recognizing the immense physical and mental demands that Barbarossa would place on the ordinary German soldier, the High Command for the first time systematically inculcated its troops with the Nazi "world view." Junior commanders and the euphemistically termed "welfare officers" devoted many hours in both seminars and informal discussions to instilling Nazi values in their soldiers in order to condition them with "eastern hardness" in preparation for the appallingly brutal campaign Hitler intended to unleash. To reinforce this process,

A German artillery column on the retreat following the failure of Typhoon. That the German Army survived the winter of 1941–42 owed much to the improvisational skills and determination of ordinary German soldiers. The troops, such as those of the 18th Panzer Division, soon fashioned fur boots and hats for themselves from captured animals, quickly confiscated felt ones from the local populations, or even lined each layer of their clothing with newspaper or straw. The Wehrmacht held – just.

an incessant barrage of propaganda incited the troops to behave in a bestial fashion against the "sub-human" Slavic enemy.

Once Barbarossa was under way, ideology played a part in the campaign on many levels. The most obvious feature of the first 10 days of the invasion was that it seemed to confirm the German view of the Red Army and its soldiers. This attitude was epitomized by Hitler's comment on June 22 that "all we have to do is kick down the door and the whole crumbling structure will collapse." The incredible victories the Wehrmacht already had achieved during 1939–41, and the permeation of every aspect of Barbarossa with ideological elements, with hindsight fostered overconfidence. Indeed, as many Germans perceived Barbarossa to be an ideological war essential to the survival of the Reich, few officers wished to appear defeatist in a struggle that nobody could contemplate as anything other than a success. This ideological prism led the Wehrmacht to underestimate vastly the determination of the alleged racially inferior Soviets to resist the Axis onslaught in a conflict whose outcome would be determined principally by the greater application of will power. This latter misperception was

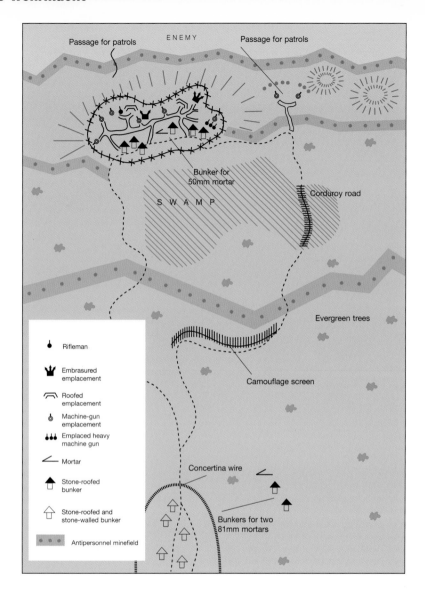

Passage for patrols
ENEMY
Passage for patrols

Bunker for
50mm mortar

S W A M P

Corduroy road

Evergreen trees

Camouflage screen

Rifleman

Embrasured
emplacement

Roofed
emplacement

Machine-gun
emplacement

Emplaced heavy
machine gun

Mortar

Stone-roofed
bunker

Stone-roofed and
stone-walled bunker

Antipersonnel minefield

Concertina wire

Bunkers for two
81mm mortars

Diagrammatic representation of an improvised German strongpoint on the Eastern Front at the end of 1941. To keep fighting in subzero temperatures, the ever resourceful German soldiers soon learned to defrost their rifles and infantry support guns by rubbing gasoline on them, or to prevent them freezing by keeping fires going near them 24 hours a day. Some infantrymen even constructed snow-shoe type mountings that fitted on the feet of the bipod for their vital firepower asset – the MG 34 machine gun – to ensure that the weapon did not sink into the deep snow.

reinforced by the Germans' overestimation of the damage the purges had inflicted on the Red Army. The success achieved against the Red Army by the weak Finnish Army in the 1939–40 war reinforced this overestimation, but at the same time the Germans ignored the contrary evidence provided by the stunning 1939 Soviet success over the Japanese at Khalkin Gol.

To the German leadership, the Axis invasion of the East was to be a ideologically driven war of racial annihilation (*Vernichtungskrieg*), which from its earliest conception they intended to prosecute with unprecedented barbarism. The Germans insinuated that, given the Soviet failure to sign the Geneva Convention, their enemy would employ appalling "Asiatic" standards of warfare, and used this pretext to justify their own preparations for the brutal war that they had always intended to unleash. The pre-existing widespread hatred of Bolshevism among German troops, and the High Command's systematic inculcation of soldiers with the Nazi "world view" during the winter of 1940–41, meant that in 1941 the German Army in the East was more Nazified than in

The Paradox of "Cauldron Battle"

During Barbarossa, the German Blitzkrieg operational technique utilized the concept of "Cauldron Battle," where armored spearheads carried out a series of deep double envelopments to surround and then destroy large elements of the Soviet order of battle. The German concept of operations was what would now be doctrinally termed maneuver warfare, in that it aimed to achieve swift victory through destroying the cohesion of Soviet forces. However, the methods through which the Germans hoped to achieve this neutralization of Soviet cohesion – through a series of encirclements – represented a method based on elements of attritional fighting. Above all else, given the lessons of Napoleon's disastrous 1812 invasion, Barbarossa strove to destroy the Red Army in the Soviet border regions. As the German Army High Command realized it could not sustain itself logistically beyond Smolensk against a still cohesive enemy, the Wehrmacht would have to destroy their opponent before Smolensk was reached. To this end, Hitler ordered the panzer spearheads to stop and seal off the pockets that their envelopments had created to prevent the Red Army escaping to fight again deeper within Soviet territory. This was necessary because the bulk of the German Army comprised nonmotorized infantry divisions that simply could not keep up with the armor. In addition, the infantry lacked mobile direct fire assets because virtually all the armor had been concentrated in the mechanized formations; the infantry thus needed the intimate cooperation of the panzer divisions to help reduce the pockets.

In retrospect, the German Army's force structure remained inappropriate for the scale of its mission in the East. The need for the panzers to stop and seal the pockets prevented them from continuing their advance deeper into the Soviet Union. German maneuver warfare, therefore, ultimately lost momentum, and this gave the enemy time to recover from the shock action and confusion that the German advance up to that point had already inflicted on them. Blitzkrieg had been caught in an intractable dilemma created by the scale of the objective and the inadequacy of German force structure for such an ambitious task – a dilemma few of the German High Command even seemed to have realized.

previous campaigns. This change was manifested in the willingness the troops displayed during Barbarossa to implement the brutality integral to the genocidal racial war Hitler unleashed in June 1941.

For Barbarossa was intended to secure the future of the Reich not just by occupying the Soviet Union but by destroying the alleged disease of Bolshevism. The Political Commissars were the agents of the Communist Party that served with Soviet military units to ensure political loyalty to the Party. Hitler's June 1941 Commissar Order instructed German troops summarily to execute all Commissars. Moreover, the Germans orchestrated appalling occupation policies for the East. As the occupied territories were designed to provide the "Living Space" that the Reich required, the conquerors had to depopulate the agricultural regions so that ethnic German families could move out and take over the farms. Through expelling Soviet families into the depths of the winter, through starvation rations, and through mistreatment and the disease that went with these conditions, the Axis occupation would reduce the indigenous Slavic agricultural population – skilled Soviet urban labor, though, would be preserved for employment as slave workers. On July 16, 1941, Hitler stated that "the order of the day" in the Axis-occupied East would be "first, conquer, second, rule, and third, exploit."

Even when Barbarossa began to falter, the frenzy of the ideological crusade continued unabated. In late October 1941, for example, Army Group South extended its propaganda efforts with the frontline soldiers. Additional film vans arrived in the forward areas so that the troops, during rare periods of rest out of the line, could watch heavily biased propaganda movies that extolled Germany's duty to "protect" European civilization from the Jewish–Bolshevik dominated Slavic "sub-humans." Furthermore, despite the desperate demands for munitions and gasoline, the army group also devoted significant supply assets to carrying forward to the front the heavily skewed biweekly army newsletters and pamphlets, such as *Information for the Troops*. Last, they allocated resources to

establish divisional library vans equipped with vitriolic German nationalistic, anti-Semitic, and anti-Slavic literature.

Ideology may have stiffened resolve, but it was the professionalism, aggressiveness, and elan of the panzer divisions that were largely responsible for the success of the German Army during the early weeks of Barbarossa. To implement Hitler's intent to destroy the Soviets during the summer of 1941, the army had to reorganize its force structure. In mid-June 1940, it concluded that its hasty spring 1940 expansion to 153 divisions had actually undermined its cohesion, and so demobilized to a smaller, yet more powerful, 141-division Order of Battle. However, Hitler's decision to launch Barbarossa undermined this process of consolidation as in fall 1940 the Führer ordered the doubling of the existing panzer arm to 20 divisions. This mechanized force represented the minimum required to undertake the deep strategic penetrations necessary to conquer a country as large as the Soviet Union.

During the winter of 1940–41, however, German tank production remained modest. Moreover, in late 1940 Hitler redirected resource-allocation priority away from the army in favor of the air force and navy. Consequently, the doubling of the army's panzer arm could be achieved only by halving the tank strength in each division. Thus by spring 1941, instead of 10 panzer divisions that each fielded roughly 320 tanks, the German Army now deployed 20 such formations, 11 of which fielded fewer than 200 tanks each. In addition, Hitler ordered the total number of German divisions to be raised by 50 percent from 141 to 208 by the spring of 1941. However, as in previous campaigns, this expansion taxed severely German manpower and equipment capabilities.

A 50mm Antitank Gun 38 (50mm Pak 38) in action during Barbarossa. It could penetrate 2.4 in. (60 mm) of vertical armor at 1641 ft (500 m) range, sufficient to penetrate the T-34, but not the KV heavy tanks. As for the 37mm, the Germans also developed a tungsten-carbide round for the Pak 38 that further increased its penetration capability. German troops soon came to clamor for the 50mm gun as the only realistic way of stopping Soviet counterattacks spearheaded by T-34 tanks.

Consequently, many of these divisions failed to reach specified levels of equipment, even though they utilized large amounts of captured weapons, including a motley collection of hundreds of different motor vehicles acquired from nine different nations.

Four panzer groups (subsequently retitled panzer armies in late 1941) spearheaded the invasion. Typically, a panzer group comprised two or three motorized corps. In total, these four spearhead German formations deployed 17 armored divisions with 3,584 tanks, 11 motorized divisions, and one cavalry division, to make a total of 29 German mechanized divisions. The 17 spearhead armored divisions, together with three independent battalions, fielded a total of 160 Panzer I, 831 Panzer II, 187 Panzer 35(t), 772 Panzer 38(t), 965 Panzer III, 439 Panzer IV, and 230 command tanks – a total strength of 3,584 vehicles. In addition to the armor concentrated as a strategic instrument within the panzer divisions, the 126 infantry divisions of the German second echelon and strategic reserve had available between them just 250 StuG III assault guns to provide mobile direct fire support. This gave the Germans a total spearhead AFV strength of 3,834, while the Romanian Army also deployed a further 227 tanks. In addition to these 4,061 AFVs, the Germans held back 350 tanks in reserve, thus producing a total Axis AFV force of 4,411 vehicles.

Panzergrenadier Tactics

One reason for the success of the panzer groups in Russia was the more aggressive combat roles that the motorized infantry (panzergrenadiers) included within the panzer divisions undertook during these first weeks of Barbarossa. In Poland in 1939, the few motorized infantry battalions within the armored divisions equipped with halftracked APCs had simply de-bussed their soldiers on the edge of the tactical battlefield so that they could support the armor on foot. By the 1940 Western campaign, APC-mounted motorized infantry had assumed more ambitious tactical roles, providing intimate support to the armor while in their vehicles. During Barbarossa, the excellently trained motorized infantry troops undertook yet more ambitious combat functions. Often, the APCs advanced on the flanks of armored wedges to screen them from Soviet flanking countermoves. Alternatively, the APC-mounted panzergrenadiers advanced within the panzer division armored wedge to provide intimate small-arms and machine-gun fire support for the tanks. This timely and effective cooperation frequently enacted between the tanks and the APC-mounted troops, when combined with devastating close air support, went a long way to account for the tremendous successes achieved against an ill-prepared enemy in the first months of Barbarossa.

The Second and Third Panzer Groups achieved stunning advances during Barbarossa. By July 20 these forces had pushed on another 180 miles (290 km) toward Moscow, to all but encircle another 300,000 Soviet troops at Smolensk. During these engagements, the Luftwaffe provided sterling support for the panzer spearheads. Sustained aerial interdiction missions destroyed the west–east routes of communications behind the Smolensk front, thus preventing the less mobile Soviet forces, already outflanked by the panzers, from withdrawing east out of the jaws of the German encirclement. Again, the successes achieved on the ground owed much to effective joint (ground-to-air) cooperation. Consequently, during these first four weeks, the Germans successfully advanced 355 miles (571 km) – nearly two-thirds of the distance to Moscow – at an average rate of 12 miles (19 km) per day. If the German armor had managed to maintain this momentum, it would have reached the Kremlin in just 21 days – on 11 August. Indeed, to the field commanders of Army Group Center it seemed inevitable that one further armored push toward the capital would successfully capture the city.

The impressive combat performance displayed by the German armored spearheads in the Ukraine during August–September 1941 owed much to the fact that these formations fielded the cream of German soldiers. The panzer arm only accepted into its ranks as trainee tank crews recruits who had excelled during basic (infantry) training. These trainees then underwent extensive specialized training at a panzer training school where they received instruction, training, and practical exercises on ballistics, tank gunnery, vehicle maintenance, and combat tactics. Typically, this instruction was delivered by some of the army's most proficient and experienced tank officers, brought back from the frontline for periods to train new recruits despite the desperate need for every single available experienced commander to fight at the front, especially in Russia. Right through until 1944, when shortages forced a curtailing of such training, the trainee tank crews also undertook extensive and rigorous field firing exercises. The combination of these elements – aided by excellent optical equipment – consistently produced excellent standards of tank gunnery, at least until 1944. A further reason for the effectiveness of the panzer divisions was that, in addition to the above, their tank crews also received at these schools extensive instruction on interarm cooperation – such as intimate battlefield cooperation with motorized infantry and armored artillery units – as well as the practicalities of joint (ground-to-air) tactics.

The Role of the Luftwaffe during Barbarossa

Aerial superiority was crucial to the success of the German attack, and as in Poland and the West in 1939–40, the Luftwaffe gave sterling support to the army. During the first 48 hours of Barbarossa the Luftwaffe committed its 2,150 available first-line aircraft to a concentrated counter-air campaign to secure aerial superiority over the theater. Aided by total surprise, massed German aerial formations attacked the rows of enemy planes sitting on the runways of the western Soviet Union. In these first 48 hours alone, the Luftwaffe succeeded in destroying 2,200 Soviet aircraft, at a rate of one "kill" every 80 seconds! This initial success enabled the Germans to achieve a good measure of air superiority, at least in several sectors of the vast theater for selected periods of time. Having accomplished this, on June 24 the air force shifted its focus to missions in support of the four advancing panzer groups: mainly interdiction behind the enemy frontline and close air support for the contact battle. Interdiction efforts concentrated both on preventing Soviet reserves from redeploying to the front to seal off key battle zones from reinforcement, and on preventing surrounded enemy forces from breaking out, or outflanked ones from withdrawing east to avoid encirclement. Through such actions the Luftwaffe helped the panzer groups both successfully to accomplish large encirclements during Barbarossa and then to digest the resulting pockets in timely fashion.

The Luftwaffe also provided valuable close air support, often substituting for the dearth of artillery firepower available at the front as the usually horse-drawn German guns struggled to keep up with the rapidly advancing panzer units. Measures introduced early in 1941, and expanded during the rest of the year, meant that during Barbarossa the mechanics of German air-to-ground cooperation were more sophisticated than previously. During 1940–41, the number of air signals liaison detachments were raised so that most of the 40 German corps committed to

Barbarossa, plus some select panzer divisions, possessed one. Equipped with armored cars and occasionally with tanks that mounted powerful signal devices, these detachments advanced with the spearhead panzer groups and reported back conditions at the front and the current position of the troops. Requests for close air support, however, still passed from army corps headquarters back through the army to the relevant air commands and thence to air assets earmarked for such tasks.

Increasingly during Barbarossa, to aid the fighter-bombers in their provision of close air support, forward observation officers in armored vehicles also began to relay targeting information by radio to the aircraft, although they could not call in this support themselves. Through these measures, Luftwaffe provision of close air support for the advancing ground troops clearly had improved in a technical sense compared with previous campaigns. However, the vast size of the theater, the difficulties the tactical air squadrons experienced in keeping up with the rampaging panzers while operating from improvised forward grass airstrips, the often appalling weather, and heavy attrition rates all meant that effective air-to-ground cooperation was a sporadic phenomenon rather than a constant one. Nevertheless, such effective aerial support could be devastatingly effective against enemy forces. Moreover, to spearhead panzergrenadiers and tank crews already pushed to the limits of their physical endurance, such highly visible support from the air proved a real boost for their fighting spirit.

To utilize fully the combat power and high morale of an army and air force that had both experienced a string of unbroken victories over a two-year period, the December 1940 Barbarossa plan ordered the German Army to undertake bold and rapid operations that involved deep strategic penetrations by armored spearheads. Four panzer groups would conduct a series of double envelopments

Soviet aircraft destroyed on the ground on the first day of Barbarossa. German surprise was total. Initial German armored assaults achieved overwhelming tactical, operational, and strategic surprise, benefiting from Stalin's refusal to believe British warnings that an invasion was imminent. In addition, during the first morning of the invasion, he ordered that Soviet border units were only to fight back if it were clear that they were facing a major Axis invasion, but not to respond if they faced only minor military provocation!

The Need for New Panzers

On June 23–24, 1941, the second and third days of Barbarossa, elements of both Hoepner's Fourth Panzer Group in Lithuania and Kleist's First Panzer Group near the Bug River experienced their first encounter with the new Soviet KV-1 heavy tank. To the German troops' dismay, at ranges as low as 2,700 ft (820 m), even the rounds fired by the 50mm KwK L/42 gun mounted in their most modern Panzer III tanks simply bounced off the front of these Soviet heavy tanks. Subsequently, on July 4 a counterattack led by the new Soviet T-34 tank threw back the spearhead of the Second Panzer Group. Similarly, on October 4, 1941, at Mtsensk, near Orel, the 4th Panzer Division encountered a determined riposte led by 51 Soviet T-34 and KV-1 tanks. This surprise Soviet response destroyed 10 Panzer III tanks (seen

below) and drove back the German armor across the Lisiza River. These unsettling battlefield experiences demonstrated both the superiority of these Soviet tanks to any tank the Germans could deploy and their virtual invulnerability to German antitank rounds.

In response to these disturbing experiences the German High Command urgently began to introduce the longer 50mm KwK L/60 gun into the latest Panzer III tanks and to increase the vehicles' armor protection. But above all, they also led the Germans to begin development of the new long-barreled 75mm-gunned Panzer V Panther medium tank and the 88mm-equipped Panzer VI Tiger I heavy tank, which would exert a major influence on the battlefields of Europe from 1943 on.

that would encircle and destroy large parts of the Red Army in "cauldron battles" (see page 159). In addition, Barbarossa emphasized the need for these armored groups to prevent the withdrawal of battleworthy Soviet forces (including those trapped in the pockets) deeper into the Soviet interior, where any invader would struggle logistically to defeat them. These four panzer groups would enact the operational technique of "cauldron battle" by advancing rapidly on converging axes to form vast pincer movements (double envelopments) that would encircle and destroy large portions of the Red Army. Once the well-trained troops of the elite panzer divisions had formed these encirclements, some would remain to seal the pocket to prevent the surrounded Red Army forces from breaking out and withdrawing deeper into the Soviet interior. Meanwhile, the rest of the armored divisions would continue the momentum of the German advance deep into the Soviet rear areas to destroy enemy cohesion.

As the relatively few Axis mechanized formations pushed forward, the bulk of the invading force, some 126 infantry divisions – with 625,000 horses – would march forward trying desperately not to fall too far behind the panzer spearheads. In addition to occupying ground and mopping up, these infantry formations would help the four panzer groups to reduce the Soviet pockets. Together these actions were conceived as parts of a single, continuous, offensive effort that would win the war in a matter of months. The key question remained, however, as to whether the German Army could maintain its advance in a country of this size against an enemy as powerful as the Soviets if the latter's cohesion did not swiftly collapse. The first few weeks indicated that it could.

On August 26, Kleist unleashed his panzer divisions of the First Panzer Group across the Dnieper to race north toward Guderian's panzers as the latter pushed south. As the two approached one another the vast anticipated German encirclement of the Soviet forces west of Kiev began to materialize. Guderian's Second Panzer Group only managed to commence its drive south on August 22, four weeks after Kleist's armor had recommenced its drive in the south. This delay had resulted from the attempted insubordination of the German commanders who wished to head for Moscow, the dreadful German logistic situation, and the fierce Soviet counterattacks at Yelnya. On August 22, Guderian's crack panzer divisions thrust south deep into the rear of the Soviet armies deployed in front of Kiev. After a 26-day fighting advance southward, and despite the terrible conditions of dust and heat, the rapidly moving troops of the Second Panzer Group reached Lokhvitsa, 248 miles (399 km) south of Roslavl and 117 miles (188 km) behind the Soviet frontline. At Lokhvitsa on September 15, the Second Panzer Group joined up with Kleist's armored units to create a vast pocket around Kiev that held 665,000 Soviet troops. Stalin's insistence that Kiev not be abandoned at any price prevented the outflanked Soviet forces from withdrawing to escape the looming German pincers.

By mid-September, therefore, Guderian's and Kleist's armor had encircled 665,000 Soviet troops in the Kiev and Uman Pockets and inflicted a further 300,000 combat casualties. Although it would take them another two weeks to digest the vast Kiev encirclement, by this point the Germans had decimated the Soviet positions in the Ukraine. Now the routes east toward the rich agriculture and industry of the eastern Ukraine lay open to the advancing panzers. All that barred their way were the disorganized remnants of the Soviet Southwestern Front, the hastily mobilized cadets from the training schools beyond the Dnieper, and the capability of the German logistic system to sustain the continued advance. Once again, the Red Army had proved incapable of responding effectively to the high tempo and momentum achieved by the elite German mechanized formations.

The Input of Stalin and Hitler

It must be mentioned at this point that Stalin often aided German encirclements. During Typhoon, for example, although the Red Army, recognizing Moscow as its center of gravity, had concentrated powerful forces in front of its capital, Stalin continued his twin policies of static, linear defense and a prohibition on withdrawals that had led to the disaster of the Kiev Pocket. Such policies invited the panzer divisions, with their superior operational mobility, to outflank and encircle these fixed Soviet formations. In the first 12 days of Typhoon, rapidly moving German armored formations outmaneuvered the static Soviet defenses in front of Bryansk and Vyazma to create two pockets that contained 660,000 Soviet troops. During this period, as air ace Hans Ulrich Rudel recollected, the air force again took advantage of the favorable weather to undertake extensive close air support attacks by Stuka and Henschel Hs 123 aircraft. Such support, for example, facilitated the successful attacks launched by the SS *Das Reich* Motorized Division at Pokrov on October 8. Though again it would take Army Group Center another 11 days to digest these two vast encirclements, by October 13 German forces had already broken into the heart of the Soviet defensive system in front of Moscow: the road to the Kremlin lay open.

What of the German Führer? Overall, there is no doubt that the interference of Hitler reduced the army's ability to defeat the Red Army in 1941, aided and abetted by the High Command. The latter, fearful of the large enemy forces trapped in the pockets behind the front, overruled its field commanders' advice to keep the armor advancing; instead it ordered the panzer divisions to stop and mop up the Smolensk Pocket until the marching infantry divisions could reach the area, and only then resume their advance toward Moscow. Consequently, German momentum toward the Soviet capital faltered just at the moment when Army Group Center had broken the Soviet forces that protected Moscow. However, it remains far from clear that Guderian's and Hoth's armor could have continued their advance even if Hitler had permitted this. Even in mid-July, such an advance was scarcely sustainable in logistical terms, and both formations desperately required an operational pause to repair their battered vehicle fleets. None of Hoth's panzer

divisions, for example, could field more than half of their authorized establishment of armored vehicles, while the remaining crews – despite their excellent training and physical resilience – were at the limits of their endurance.

Hitler's decisions were even more disastrous. Concerned about the counterattack threat posed to the southern flank of Army Group Center by the still-cohesive Soviet forces deployed in the Ukraine, the Führer ordered his forces to defeat the Red Army in the Ukraine before Army Group Center resumed its advance on Moscow. Stemming from this fear of Soviet counterattack, Hitler's Directive 33 instructed the Second Panzer Group of Army Group Center to divert its advance south behind the Soviet defenses in the Ukraine, where it would link up with the eastward advance of the First Panzer Group from Army Group South. In addition, Hitler ordered Army Group Center's remaining armor – Third Panzer Group – to turn north to help the German advance on Leningrad. Last, Hitler instructed Army Group Center to continue its critical mission, the advance on Moscow, but using only its remaining, relatively immobile two infantry armies. In retrospect, Hitler's Directive 33 was an enormous strategic

German panzers and Sdkfz halftracks in Russia. By the tenth day of the campaign, the spearhead armor of Army Group Center had crossed the Beresina River in Belorussia, having advanced 249 miles (400 km) into Soviet territory. Already Guderian's and Hoth's panzer groups had created two successful encirclements of Soviet forces: at Bialystok and Minsk.

mistake. During late July and early August, the Soviets could deploy only weak forces in front of Moscow after the catastrophic losses suffered in the Minsk and Smolensk Pockets. In these circumstances, a renewed German armored thrust might well have captured Moscow before the Soviets could reinforce it with newly mobilized reserves. However, any thrust undertaken by Bock's two infantry armies alone was likely to be so slow that it would fail to capture Moscow before the Red Army recovered its cohesion. The folly of Directive 33 was clear to many field commanders in the East, as well as some in the High Command – some brave officers criticized this decision and attempted to evade diverting the armor in the hope that Hitler might change his mind.

As it was, battlefield events prevented Army Group Center from completing the redeployment of its two panzer groups for these new northward and southward thrusts until August 21. For one whole month, the Second and Third Panzer Groups had not advanced a single mile closer to Moscow, then 255 miles (410 km) away; yet in the first month of the war these formations had advanced no less than 355 miles (571 km) toward the Soviet capital.

Conclusions

The most startling aspect of Barbarossa was that the Axis forces, despite achieving some of the most spectacular tactical victories in the history of warfare, failed to achieve a decisive strategic defeat over the Soviets. During the 166-day period between June and December 1941, the Germans advanced up to 802 miles (1,290 km) on a 995-mile (1600-km) front and inflicted 4.3 million casualties on the Red Army, destroying the entire Soviet ground forces in the western Soviet Union 1.3 times over! Yet despite these achievements, in mid-December 1941 the German Army faced a Red Army more powerful than it had been when Barbarossa commenced on June 21, 1941. This unpleasant reality was exacerbated by the fact that these German victories had only been achieved at painful – and often irreplaceable – cost. By December 5, 1941, for example, the German Army had lost 87 percent (or 3,370) of the original 3,854 AFVs committed on June 22, and 26 percent (780,000) of the 3.05 million troops committed. With replacements amounting to just 663 AFVs and 410,000 troops, by early December the German Army was 2,707 AFVs and 340,000 soldiers short of its strength at the start of Barbarossa.

A key reason for the German inability to replace the losses suffered during Barbarossa was Hitler's spring 1941 decision to scale back significantly armaments production for the ground forces, especially light howitzers and mortars. During the winter of 1941–42, the badly weakened German Army in the East found itself – despite all the vast tactical successes it had achieved – facing a more powerful enemy than ever before that was ruthlessly determined to drive the brutal Axis forces off Soviet soil. In addition, Hitler was making exorbitant demands on the already shaken troops, as Guderian noted: "We had suffered a grievous defeat in the failure to reach the capital which was to be seriously aggravated during the next few weeks thanks to the rigidity of our supreme commander [Hitler]: despite all our reports, these men far away in East Prussia could form no true concept of the real conditions of the winter war in which their soldiers were engaged."

The Soviet counteroffensive had been checked by dogged defense by March 1942. The subsequent spring thaws and ensuing mud halted all movement, though by this time the Soviets had outrun their supply lines. This stalemate on the Eastern Front would last until May 1942.

The Eastern Front 1942

The German summer offensive in the Soviet Union, codenamed Operation Blue, ended in utter defeat at Stalingrad. Once again, the Wehrmacht lost tens of thousands of men and hundreds of armored fighting vehicles – losses it could ill-afford on the Eastern Front.

A German soldier during street fighting in Stalingrad. By tying themselves to a protracted attritional urban battle in the city, the Germans not only played to their enemy's strengths but also failed to utilize effectively the superior operational mobility possessed by their well-trained and tactically flexible panzer divisions.

The Germans never recovered from the horrendous losses of the 1941 campaign. By April 1942 the army had lost one-third of the troops, 40 percent of the antitank guns, half the horses, and 79 percent of the armor that had began the campaign. Massive vehicle losses had significantly reduced mobility, while munitions stocks had fallen to one-third of June 1941 levels. New production and replacements could not offset losses, and as a result infantry, officer, and equipment strengths plummeted. Moreover, limitations imposed by terrain and weather, by shortages in troops, equipment, and supplies, as well as by Hitler's hold-fast orders, prevented the Germans during the winter of 1941–42 from conducting the elastic defense in depth proscribed by established doctrine. Instead, the adaptable Germans swiftly adopted expedient, improvised defensive techniques dictated by the circumstances that faced them. The Red Army launched heavy, if unsophisticated, ill-coordinated, and dispersed frontal assaults all along the central sector of the front to drive the Germans back from Moscow and gain some operational room for maneuver. This counteroffensive embroiled the depleted and exhausted panzer divisions that had spearheaded the German advance on the Soviet capital in heavy defensive fighting, for which they were ill-suited.

Initially slow to predict the counteroffensive or to discern its magnitude, German racial prejudice ensured that local commanders also underestimated their own weaknesses, as well as Soviet powers of endurance. Short on troops, weapons, and supplies, as well as inexperienced at defense, the initially overconfident Germans merely conducted half-measures. Not surprisingly, such moves, including piecemeal local retrograde movements and small-scale unit rotations, failed to stem the Soviet tide.

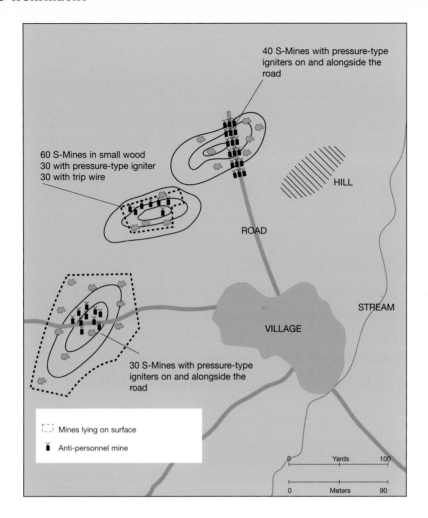

40 S-Mines with pressure-type igniters on and alongside the road

60 S-Mines in small wood
30 with pressure-type igniter
30 with trip wire

HILL

ROAD

STREAM

VILLAGE

30 S-Mines with pressure-type igniters on and alongside the road

⌐ ̣ ⌐ Mines lying on surface

🯁 Anti-personnel mine

0   Yards   100

0   Meters   90

Typical German mine arrangement as part of a defense sited around a village on the Eastern Front. The mines were designed to funnel attacking Red Army infantry into areas that were covered by German machine-gun teams.

The adaptable German Army responded to the Soviet December 1941 counteroffensive by altering its strategy and by modifying its doctrinal defensive tactics. It faced two strategic options: a general withdrawal to a shorter, more defensible, winter line (which the generals wanted); or to stand fast and weather the Soviet onslaught, the option Hitler chose on December 16. A strategic withdrawal in midwinter with only limited mobility would have cost the Germans their heavy weapons and might well have turned into a rout, as had Napoleon's retreat in 1812. In addition, the Führer wished to maintain a front close to Moscow so that he could attack and capture the capital later in 1942. He ordered German troops to hold all along the front and to defend unflinchingly "hedgehog" positions built around the fortified village strongpoints into which the beleaguered German forces had retired during December. By the end of the month most of the central sector of the front comprised hedgehog defenses that the Germans fortified as best they could, but combat readily exposed the stark reality that doctrine, equipment, and training remained inadequate for winter defensive warfare. Nonetheless, the German hold-fast policy, aided by the tactical adaptability and determination of the troops, the winter weather, and the offensive limitations of the enemy, ultimately halted the Soviet offensive during early 1942.

That such expediency halted the Soviet steamroller, however, was almost as much due to Soviet inexperience at conducting offensive operations as it was to the defensive qualities of hedgehog positions or the steadfastness of German troops. While holding fast did ultimately prevent the German front from collapsing, it cost the German Army heavily. Ill-prepared for winter warfare, the Germans suffered 228,000 frostbite casualties alone during the winter of 1941–42. In addition, the Soviets successfully encircled and crushed a number of hedgehog positions in the same period. Soviet armor posed a particular danger as the T-34 medium tank demonstrated excellent winter mobility, whereas such terrible conditions rendered many of the normally reliable German weapons – including the essential MG 34 machine gun – unreliable or ineffective.

During January 1942, however, the resourceful German defenders quickly improved their defensive and winter warfare capabilities as well as the strength of their hedgehogs. The German units achieved this rapid adaptation in part through individual trial and error, but also through rapid dissemination of perceptive after-action reports. German troops quickly recognized that village strongpoints had major limitations: the massed defenders were vulnerable to Soviet artillery fire and their defenses lacked depth. In particular, hedgehog defenses conceded control of the ground between these positions to the enemy, who regularly infiltrated the lines seeking to isolate and eliminate individual hedgehog locations. Thus, from late January 1942, German troops gradually extended hedgehog defenses beyond village perimeters to improve security, enhance observation, and to reduce the gaps in the front through which Soviet forces infiltrated.

Combat experience during January 1942, in addition, quickly showed that vigorous, immediate counterattacks that employed massed firepower were necessary to repel Soviet incursions. Given the severe logistic shortages at the front, local German commanders had to learn quickly to husband artillery stocks during less dire tactical situations, to permit effective massed fire that would stop critically threatening enemy attacks. These defensive experiences led the German Army during 1942 to develop for the first time command mechanisms for coordinating massed defensive fire from all available heavy weapons. Though the strongpoint defense system did not conform exactly to existing German doctrine – which stressed an elastic defensive posture – its emphasis on depth, firepower, and rapid counterattack demonstrated that it was firmly rooted in traditional German defensive practices. By maintaining an active and aggressive defense, German hedgehogs, despite their expedient nature, often survived against great odds. At Sukhininci, for example, a single isolated German regiment from the 216th Infantry Division held off two Soviet rifle divisions for over a month until relieved.

Defensive-Offensive Operations

Thus, despite overextension, exhaustion, and unpreparedness for winter warfare, the Germans had improvised a strongpoint defense system that weathered the Soviet onslaught. During the spring of 1942, after the Soviet offensive had spent itself, the German Army urgently studied and rapidly disseminated appropriate lessons that had been learned from the winter crisis. The result was substantial and rapid revision of German doctrine, training, and defensive practices in the light of these experiences. Frontline formations compiled comprehensive after-action reports that detailed flaws in German equipment, organization, and training, as well as suggested solutions to these weaknesses. The German success, though, also apparently vindicated Hitler's hold-fast orders. Furthermore, it reinforced his mistaken belief – epitomized by the heroic resistance offered by the SS *Totenkopf* Division in the Demyansk Pocket in northern Russia – that the iron

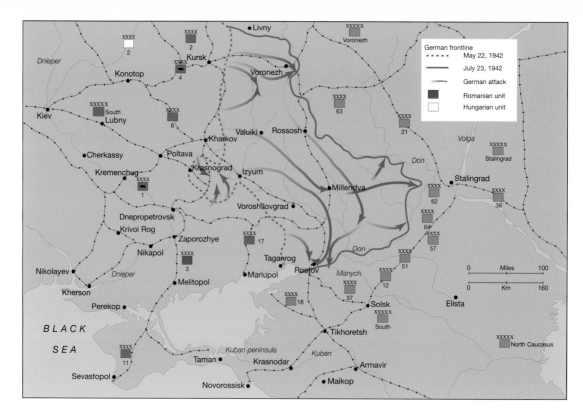

will of a racially superior military could always triumph over a more powerful enemy, irrespective of disparities in strength, firepower, and supplies. Armed with these false notions, Hitler thereafter routinely ordered German troops to hold fast against overwhelming odds, which, despite the heroism often displayed by the troops, frequently only aggravated losses and hastened disaster.

The German technique of the defensive-offensive, when well executed by highly trained and determined forces, had proven both very effective and economical against a Red Army High Command (the STAVKA) that during 1942 was still struggling to master the art of offensive operations. As an extension of its winter 1941–42 counteroffensive, on May 12, 1942, the Red Army launched a two-pronged offensive in the south that aimed to retake Kharkov. In the northern pincer, the Twenty-Eighth Army attacked from Volchansk southwest toward Kharkov, while along the southern axis, the Sixth Army attacked from the Izyum–Barvenkovo salient to strike both due west toward Krasnograd and north toward Kharkov. Subsequently, this operation became known as the Second Battle of Kharkov. The Soviet decision to attack reflected their own detection of German preparations to resume the offensive in a limited operation slated to commence on May 18 that aimed to secure easier jumping-off points for the intended German summer offensive by eliminating the Barvenkovo salient. On May 12 the Soviet Southwestern Front attacked the positions held by Army Group South. Some 46 Soviet rifle divisions and 19 motorized brigades slammed into the sectors held by XVII, LI, and VIII Corps plus VI Romanian Corps. While the desperate defensive actions undertaken by the determined Axis infantry divisions managed to prevent a significant Soviet breakthrough on the northern axis, they failed to halt the southern Soviet thrust. Consequently, by May 15 the Red Army spearheads in the south had managed to advance 57 miles (92 km) west, forcing the Germans to abandon Krasnograd.

During June 28–31, the troops of Fourth Panzer and Second Armies (Army Group South) smashed through the Soviet defenses east of Kursk, and pushed rapidly toward the Don River, enacting several small encirclements as they advanced. To support these ground attacks, the air force – enjoying the benefits of temporary local air superiority – undertook concentrated close air support and interdiction efforts. The latter missions, targeted mainly against Soviet night-time railroad movements, sought to prevent the enemy redeploying reserves to block the advance of Hoth's panzers. By July 6 the crack troops of Fourth Panzer Army had swiftly advanced 85 miles (136 km) to reach Voronezh. It would take until July 23 to overcome the last pockets of Soviet resistance within this key city.

The Red Army secured these initial successes during May 12–15, even though Army Group South had discerned enemy intentions through the increase of Soviet tactical reconnaissance in the area. While the Soviets pushed deeper into the German lines, Army Group South coolly redeployed armored reserves to the northern and southern flanks of the Barvenkovo salient in order to launch a daring counterstrike. Even though Soviet intelligence had discerned the build-up of German forces on either flank, Stalin nevertheless insisted that the Red Army continue its advance. On May 17, Army Group South initiated its counteroffensive – codenamed Operation Fredericus – that hit the overextended Soviet forces on both flanks. The well-trained troops of the German Sixth Army attacked from the north and drove south toward the bridges across the River Donets south of Balakleya. Simultaneously, the crack mobile troops of Kleist's First Panzer Army drove north from the Barvenkovo area to link up with the German northern pincer. Other elements of the Sixth Army also struck due east toward Kupyansk on the River Oskel.

On May 22, after six days of well-executed, high-tempo attacks backed by intensive aerial strikes, the two Axis pincers successfully linked up some 20 miles (32 km) south of Balakleya, surrounding 280,000 Soviet soldiers of the Sixth, Ninth, and Fifty-Seventh Armies. While sizable German forces dealt with the encircled Soviet forces, other mobile formations ruthlessly exploited this success with a rapid advance east across the River Donets to the line of the Oskel River. By May 30, 1942, when the last encircled Red Army troops surrendered, Fredericus had netted 239,000 prisoners, inflicted an estimated 1,250 tank losses, and secured a tidy front along the Donets–Oskel line from which the intended German summer offensive could commence.

Operation Blue

Hitler, now in direct command of the German armies, decided that his forces would stand on the defensive in the center and north while in the south they would attack to capture the oil of the Caucasus. However, he was unsure whether the army should capture Stalingrad on the Volga to prevent the movement of oil north or drive into the Caucasus to capture the oil. This indecision would continue throughout the campaign. In fact, the campaign, codenamed Operation Blue, represented Germany's last chance of defeating the Red Army. The High Command recognized that in the spring of 1942 the German Army simply remained too weak for a general offensive. By mid-June 1942, fresh German reinforcements had only brought the army in the East to a strength of 3.13 million troops, just 80,000 more than at the start of Barbarossa. But having lost some of its best personnel and equipment during the 1941 campaign the summer 1942 German Army was qualitatively weaker than in June 1941. Thus the Germans attempted to destroy the Soviet Union's capacity to continue this war of industrial production by seizing its oil resources.

Army Group South commenced Blue on June 28, 1942. An assault force of 68 divisions with 1.4 million troops and 1,495 armored fighting vehicles (AFVs), supported by the Fourth Air Fleet with 1,550 of the 2,950 first-line aircraft available in the East, headed southeast toward the Caucasus.

On July 9, 1942, Hitler ordered that Army Group South split into two separate commands – Field Marshal von List's Army Group A and Bock's Army Group B. Hitler now envisaged that the latter, once it had cleared the Don basin, would advance east to capture Stalingrad, while Army Group A pushed deeper into the Caucasus beyond the Maikop oilfields. Army Group B commenced the

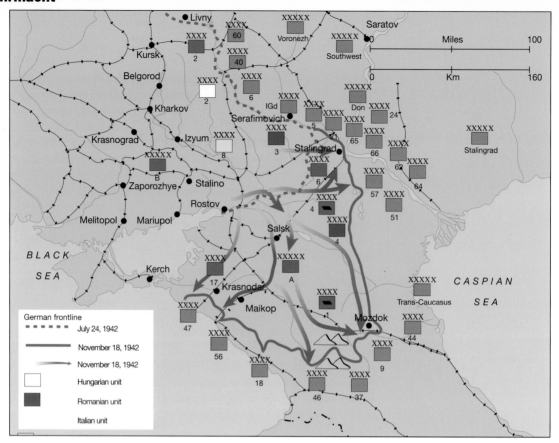

second phase of Blue when the Fourth Panzer Army – now deployed south of Voronezh – thrust southeast along the western bank of the Don to link up with the eastward advance of Paulus's Sixth Army that had commenced back on June 30.

Simultaneously, farther to the south, the three armies of the previously unengaged Army Group A – Kleist's First Panzer, Ruoff's Seventeenth, and Dumitrescu's Third Romanian – commenced their attack. Striking from the Izyum–Taganrog sector, their 22 divisions rapidly advanced east and southeast toward Rostov and the Don estuary to link up with the Fourth Panzer Army.

By August 11, the elite mobile troops of the First Panzer Army had swiftly advanced to the Caucasus mountains around Cherkessk. Meanwhile, to the northwest, LII Corps advanced through the sparsely populated and parched Kalmuk Steppe to capture Elitsa, 224 miles (360 km) east-southeast of Rostov, on August 12.

Throughout the Caucasus, however, the Axis advance now faltered in the face of rapidly stiffening Soviet resistance, dwindling supplies, disease, and severe manpower shortages – each division was on average 4,000 troops below strength. Hitler, who had by now lost interest in the Caucasus, handed control of Army Group A over to Kleist, so that he could immerse himself in the imminently anticipated Axis capture of Stalingrad. With Kleist's command now on the defensive, it was clear that not only would the overstretched Axis forces fail to reach the key Baku oilfields, but that they would struggle even to hold their greatly extended front in such inhospitable terrain.

During September 1942, around the city that bore Stalin's name, 20 Axis divisions fought their way forward literally yard by yard through the ruined streets against grim Soviet resistance in an attempt to reach the Volga and capture

During the last week of August 1942, the German advance into the Caucasus slowed to a crawl, hampered by the grossly overextended lines of supply, the dearth of hardy pack ponies, the difficult mountainous terrain, and Hitler's diversion of sizable forces – notably air assets – to Stalingrad. Meanwhile, the Soviets traded space for time.

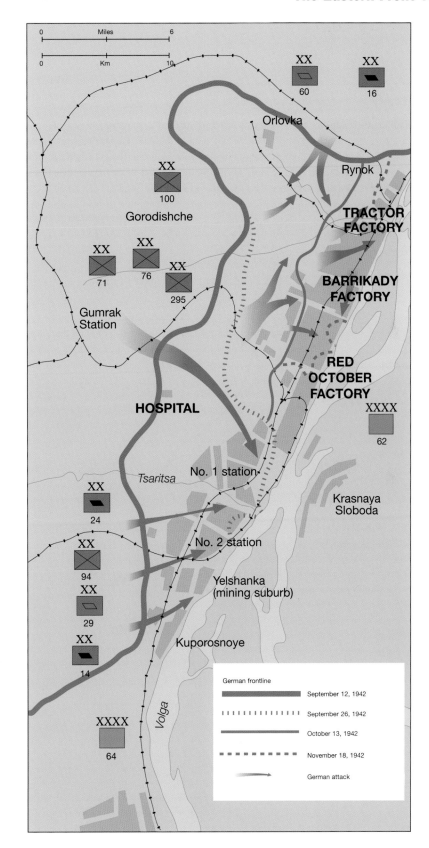

Stalingrad, September 12–November 18, 1942. By September 26, German infantry – using flamethrowers, grenades, satchel charges, and even entrenching tools – had managed to fight their way forward room by room in bitter hand-to-hand fighting until they reached the Volga River in the south of the city. After another two weeks' bitter combat the Germans had forced the Soviets back into a bridgehead west of the Volga River just 2.5 miles (5 km) deep and 15 miles (24 km) long. After another five weeks of brutal urban battle, by November 18, the Axis forces had driven the Soviets back until all the latter held of the city was a tiny enclave just 1.25 miles (2 km) deep by eight miles (12 km) long. Now, the Germans believed, Stalingrad would fall in a matter of days.

the city. Hitler's fixation with the psychological triumph of capturing Stalingrad now distorted the entire conception of Blue, sucking Axis forces into a limited geographical space, while in the Caucasus a few greatly overstretched formations operated over vast areas.

Unknown to the Axis, however, one reason why they had been able to continue their crawling advance was that the Soviets had only fed into Stalingrad just enough troops to prevent the Axis from capturing the city but not enough to stop them advancing. For Soviet strategy cunningly planned to draw in, fix, and then denude the Axis forces locked in this bitter battle, while the Red Army husbanded their reserves for a surprise riposte against the exposed flanks of Paulus's Sixth Army.

It appeared to the German High Command, therefore, that by mid-November their summer offensive had achieved a great deal. But the territorial gains accomplished by Blue did not equate to any worthwhile strategic achievement; if anything, they undermined rather than strengthened the Axis strategic position in the East. These gains captured relatively few useful economic assets, brought exhausted Axis troops into scarcely defensible inhospitable terrain, and stretched even further an already badly overstretched Wehrmacht. Crucially, these overextended forces now faced a still-cohesive Red Army in the south that had preserved much of its combat strength by withdrawing in the face of the Axis advance. Moreover, as the Axis advances at Stalingrad and in the Caucasus stalled during November, the Soviets – unknown to the Germans – finalized their surprise

On November 19, 1942, the Red Army initiated a counteroffensive – codenamed Uranus – that caught the Axis forces by surprise. Powerful Soviet forces hit and quickly penetrated the weak positions held by the Romanians. On November 23, the converging Soviet pincers met up to form a shallow encirclement that netted German forces at Stalingrad. In five days the Soviets had inflicted the greatest operational setback that the Wehrmacht had experienced to date during World War II.

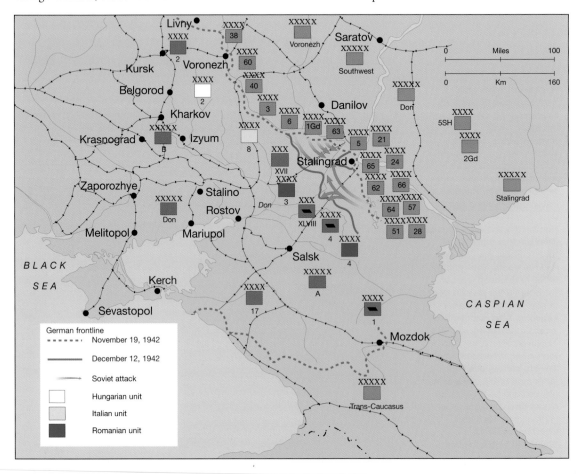

Concepts of War: The Leningrad Siege and War as a Clash of Wills

German military operations in the East remained dominated by the notion, based on a distorted interpretation of Clausewitz's military thought, that war overwhelmingly constituted a clash of moral forces. While this concept did – and still does – shed considerable light on military operations, during World War II the impact of Nazi ideology further distorted German understanding of the concept. Given the Nazis' supreme belief in the superior racial will of the Aryan Germans, most German commanders believed that the will of the "semiliterate" Slavic Soviets would not be able to resist the onslaught of the technologically advanced Wehrmacht. Consequently, Barbarossa would prove a short and decisive campaign. The appallingly brutal, 900-day German siege of Leningrad, however, proved how wrong was the German appreciation of the enemy facing them. The siege demonstrated how much suffering the Soviets could endure in their desperate struggle to resist the Axis onslaught. Despite being caught in a German encirclement that sought to starve the city's population to death, the Soviets mobilized most of the city's civilian population – men, women, and children – to help resist the German pressure. For nearly three years this population endured tremendous privations – especially starvation and disease – yet their will to resist did not break. The epic resistance the Soviets displayed at Leningrad proved that it was not the supposedly "racially superior" Aryan Germans who possessed the greater will to survive in the East. The faulty German perception about this balance of wills did little to facilitate the German Army's attempts to stem the resurgent Soviet forces after 1942. The ultimate consequences of this German misperception was the triumphant drive of Soviet armor through the ruins of Berlin in spring 1945.

counteroffensive against the Axis forces locked in combat around Stalingrad.

The Red Army launched its counteroffensive, codenamed Uranus, on November 19. The German relief operation – Winter Tempest – stalled on the Myshkova River in the face of Soviet resistance (see below). Moreover, three days previously the Soviets had launched their powerful Little Saturn offensive against Army Group Don's northern sector. By December 19, the Soviets had penetrated deep into the Axis rear and now threatened to turn the northern flank of the exposed Fourth Panzer Army locked in its Winter Tempest thrust along the Myshkova.

The Führer badly overestimated the Sixth Army's remaining ability to hold

German troops in Stalingrad. Wehrmacht defeat did not constitute – as popular opinion believes – the decisive turning point in the East, a description that fits the July 1943 Kursk offensive far better. Nevertheless, the disaster at Stalingrad represented the gravest setback the German Army had yet experienced in World War II: yet early in 1943 it faced even greater dangers.

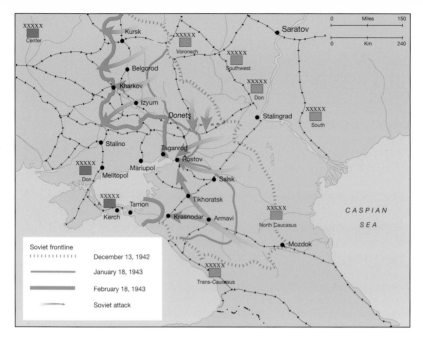

Soviet frontline
|||||||||||| December 13, 1942
———— January 18, 1943
———— February 18, 1943
→ Soviet attack

During late December 1942, after Little Saturn had broken through the Axis positions on the Don, Soviet armor pushed rapidly southwest toward Rostov to cut off the German forces in the Caucasus. During the first half of January 1943, Manstein's hard-pressed forces conducted a skillful delaying defense north of the Donets River to buy sufficient time to allow the First Panzer Army to retreat from the Caucasus behind the Don estuary before Rostov fell. These operations involved a series of desperate blocking and delaying actions carried out by both infantry and panzer forces, together with a number of boldly conducted local armored flanking counterthrusts. In a few of these defensive battles, the desperate defenders of the Fourth Panzer Army welcomed the arrival of a new firepower asset, a heavier version of the rocket launcher already in service. If Army Group Don failed to stem the Soviet advance to Rostov, however, the German Army faced a situation potentially far worse than that at Stalingrad. For in Manstein's hands rested the fate of the 900,000 troops fielded by Army Groups A and Don.

on, and so forbade any breakout that would mean relinquishing the German hold on large parts of Stalin's City. By December 24, anyway, it may already have been too late for the Sixth Army. For by then – even if it had been allowed to break out – it only possessed sufficient fuel to move its armor 20 miles (32 km), leaving them grounded some 15 miles (24 km) short of Hoth's forces on the Myshkova.

Back in November 1942, STAVKA had conceived Operation Saturn as the second phase of a series of coordinated offensives, inaugurated by Uranus, that would destroy the entire German position in the south. On December 16, 1942, in Little Saturn, a less ambitious version of the original Saturn plan, the Red Army attacked across the Don River to strike the weak Italian Eighth Army plus elements of Army Detachment *Hollidt*. The offensive aimed to drive 240 miles (386 km) southwest to Rostov in order to encircle the entire German Army Group A then deployed in the Caucasus. During December 20–24, in the face of the powerful outflanking threat posed by Little Saturn, LVII Corps took major risks in holding its positions on the Myshkova so that the Sixth Army could attempt its breakout. On Christmas Day 1942, however, Manstein (leading Army Group Don) bowed to necessity and withdrew Hoth's command back west of the Don in the face of heavy enemy attacks, in the process dooming the Sixth Army to annihilation.

In such dire circumstances, German junior commanders on the Eastern Front now resorted to exercising even stricter discipline on their exhausted troops to bolster their defensive resilience. When soldiers in Hollidt's command, for example, were found in the rear areas without good cause, they received – after courts martial – lengthy terms in prison, and in at least nine cases, the death sentence. While the First Panzer Army retreated north from the Caucasus back to Rostov in early January 1943, the Seventeenth Army now withdrew into the Kuban peninsula, which Hitler ordered to be held as a springboard for a future offensive back into the Caucasus.

On January 15, 1943, the 17 divisions of the Voronezh Front struck the defenses manned by the Second Hungarian Army, and successfully recaptured the key town of Voronezh by January 26. The successes achieved during the previous

When the Soviet offensive was launched on November 19, the German reaction was sluggish. By the fifth day of the Soviet attack the ring had been closed around the German Sixth Army at Stalingrad.

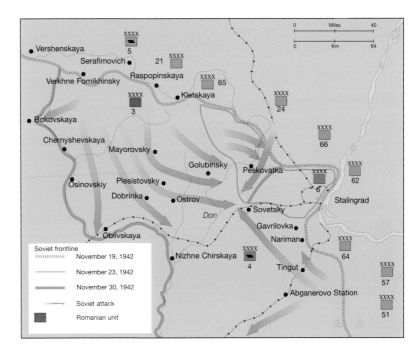

two months now led a confident STAVKA to increase the scope of its offensives. Consequently, on January 29 and February 2, 1943, respectively, Soviet forces initiated Operations Star and Gallop, in which the Voronezh and Southwestern Fronts strove to capture Belgorod, Kursk, and Kharkov, as well as drive southwest to the Sea of Azov to encircle the 650,000 troops of the First and Fourth Panzer Armies, plus Army Detachment *Hollidt*, in the Voroshilov–Mius River area. The successful Soviet encirclement of the 200,000 troops of Paulus's Sixth Army at Stalingrad presented the Germans with the problem of a synchronized relief

Unable to hold the perimeter due to lack of manpower and shortages of ammunition, German forces were steadily pushed into an ever-decreasing pocket. Hitler, as ever, issued orders that the men of the Sixth Army were to fight to the last man.

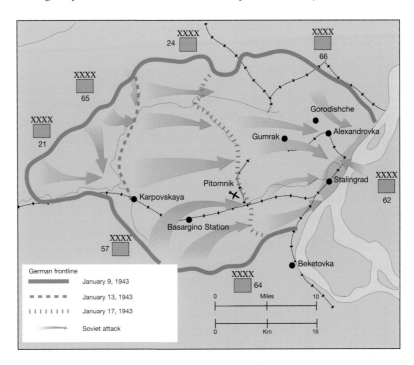

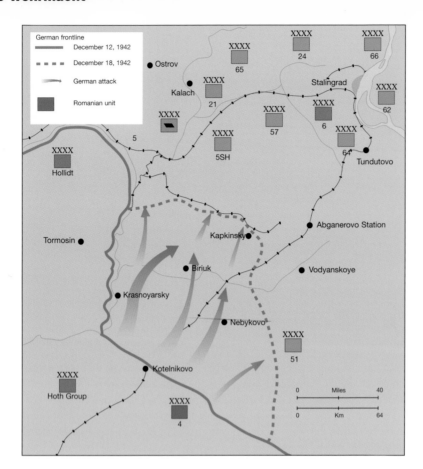

Operation Winter Tempest, the failed German attempt to rescue the trapped Sixth Army at Stalingrad.

operation. While the troops trapped within the pocket attempted to break out toward the main German lines, the relief force would attack toward the pocket to link up with the escaping forces.

The Sixth Army needed to break out swiftly before the Red Army consolidated its envelopment around Stalingrad if it were to stand any reasonable chance of escape. But Hitler ordered that the Sixth Army hold the city at all costs by forming a defensive hedgehog while troops outside the pocket along the Chir River prepared themselves for a relief operation to break back into Stalingrad. Such an operation, the Führer envisaged, would not only restore a land link to Paulus's command and allow it to hold onto large parts of Stalingrad, but also permit it to capture the remaining parts of the city. Sadly for Paulus's well-trained and as yet still determined soldiers, Hitler remained woefully ignorant of the true conditions that the German Army now faced in the East.

During August 23–27, 1942, after the Soviet link-up, the Germans reacted swiftly, enacting desperate measures to reestablish a coherent frontline west of Stalingrad along the Chir and Don rivers. Driven on by energetic junior commanders, German rear echelon troops joined up with new reinforcements in improvised, yet still cohesive, battle groups that soon established a thin screen along these two rivers to prevent further enemy advances. Next, German thoughts turned to a relief operation to rescue Paulus's trapped forces. The first step toward this was to rearrange the command set-up, since Army Group B now commanded five widely dispersed armies, more than it effectively could manage. In late November, therefore, the High Command instructed Manstein to use his

Eleventh Army headquarters to create the staff for the newly constituted Army Group Don, which would assume control of the Fourth Panzer and Third Romanian Armies, the improvised Army Detachment *Hollidt*, plus Paulus's encircled command at Stalingrad.

The new commander correctly concluded that the Sixth Army's only chance of escape lay in an immediate breakout, but Hitler had forbidden this. As Manstein prepared to launch his relief operation, he recognized that time remained critical since, due to the air force's inability to deliver even half of Paulus's daily resupply demands, every day the Sixth Army grew weaker. This resupply task was an enormous one given the paucity of the German transport fleet, but both bad weather and Soviet actions exacerbated the situation. The Soviets, anticipating the German aerial resupply efforts, massed antiaircraft and fighter defenses in the area which accounted for a staggering 488 German transport planes – one-third of the total committed. Whatever the cause of this failure – its inherent impossibility, despite Göring's rash promises; the bad weather; or enemy reactions – it led to a steady decline in the Sixth Army's combat power.

Operation Winter Tempest

Army Group Don, however, proved unable to initiate Operation Winter Tempest, its counterattack designed to reach Paulus, until December 12, 1943. The plan envisaged that XLVIII and LVII Panzer Corps – as the former motorized corps of 1941 were now designated – would launch simultaneous twin thrusts toward Stalingrad. The battle-experienced troops of LVII Corps, with their flanks covered by two Romanian corps also from Hoth's Fourth Panzer Army, were to strike north-northeast from Kotelnikovo east of the Don across 90 miles (143 km) of enemy territory to the southwestern corner of Paulus's perimeter at Marinovka. Some 50 miles (80 km) farther north, the crack troops of XLVIII Corps, part of Army Detachment *Hollidt*, was to attack from the Don–Chir confluence near Nizhne Chirskaya, force a crossing, and drive 38 miles (62 km) to Paulus's perimeter to link up with LVII Corps. Unfortunately for Sixth Army, both fierce Soviet pressure and the dearth of reinforcements available for Winter Tempest hampered the relief effort from its start. Heavy Soviet attacks along the Chir River prevented XLVIII Corps from even participating in the offensive, leaving just LVII Corps to spearhead the operation.

Given the increasing number of successful encirclements that the Red Army accomplished after late 1942, the Germans regularly needed to attempt such operations to rescue forces trapped in pockets. Some such operations in the East achieved much success, such as that at Kamenets Podolsk in the spring of 1944, while others such as that at Cherkassy in February 1944 only accomplished partial success. At Stalingrad, however, during December 20–24, 1942, a desperate Manstein finally convinced Hitler to allow Paulus's forces to break out to link up with Manstein's own faltering relief operation. But Hitler's simultaneous insistence that Paulus not yield his grip on Stalingrad, together with lack of fuel, doomed the operation before it even could took place. This sealed the fate of the encircled Sixth Army in the ruins of the city that bore Stalin's name.

By February 8, 1943, fast-moving Soviet mechanized spearheads had captured Kursk and had begun to encircle the city of Kharkov, the industrial and political center of the Ukraine. In these bitter German defensive battles, hard-pressed panzer commanders undertook ever more strenuous efforts to recover damaged tanks from the battlefield before enemy pressure forced the surrender of the ground to the Soviets. To aid them in these efforts, German armored units received during late 1942 and early 1943 additional recovery vehicles converted from the chassis of obsolete tanks like the Panzer 38(t). As German AFV production could never keep pace with the vast losses incurred in the east, the few damaged tanks recovered from the battlefield in early 1943 went a long way to augment the German Army's dwindling defensive capabilities.

However, Soviet armor reached Pavlograd, 102 miles (164 km) southwest of the Donets, and captured nearby the vital railway junction at Sinelnikovo to cut both of the direct rail lines that supported the German front on the Mius River. In these circumstances, the large Axis forces on the Mius would soon lose their remaining combat power due to lack of supplies. Farther east, Popov's armor (Fifth Shock Army) also reached Krasnoarmeyskoye, just 98 miles (158 km) short of their objective, the Azov coast, where they would achieve the encirclement of much of Manstein's Army Group Don. By February 17, 1943, therefore, it looked as if the entire Axis southern sector of the east was close to collapse. That it did not is testimony to the quality of Wehrmacht personnel, tactics, and equipment.

Averting Disaster

On February 11, 1943, Hitler ordered Army Detachment *Lanz* to hold the all-but encircled city of Kharkov at any costs, thus setting the stage for the Third Battle of Kharkov. Lanz allocated the defense of the city to the recently formed SS Panzer Corps, which then controlled the elite, determined, and battle-hardened troops of the SS Mechanized (Panzergrenadier) Divisions *Leibstandarte Adolf Hitler* and *Das Reich*. These now well-equipped formations had only recently completed their conversion from motorized to mechanized divisions in Nazi-occupied France. Led by *SS-Obergruppenführer* Paul Hausser, the corps had only just arrived in the East, however, and had not yet acclimatized to combat conditions in the theater.

Hitler's order to hold Kharkov – motivated by prestige rather than operational necessity – represented another major strategic mistake. At that moment, rather than hold Kharkov, the beleaguered German forces in the Ukraine desperately needed – through skillful, aggressive counterthrusts – to halt the Soviet armored spearheads then racing beyond the Donets toward Dnepropetrovsk and Pavlograd. If Hausser obeyed Hitler's instructions, however, this would not only lead to the destruction of his powerful corps, but also contribute nothing to restabilizing the dire Axis strategic position in the south. Yet the Führer remained confident that his loyal Waffen-SS would obey his order and defend Kharkov to the last man. Fortunately for the Germans, Hausser possessed the courage required to disobey Hitler so as to save his potent command – a key instrument in any German attempt to restabilize the front – from an inevitable destruction that served no useful strategic purpose.

By February 15, 1943, the Soviets had all but encircled Hausser's corps in Kharkov, save for a tenuous one-and-a-quarter-mile (two-kilometer) wide corridor back to the German main line. That night, after Hitler and Lanz again rejected his requests to withdraw, Hausser nevertheless ordered his crack troops to begin a bitter fighting withdrawal from the ruins of the city. As soon as Lanz heard of this move, he ordered Hausser to stop his withdrawal, but the SS general simply continued his escape bid; he was not prepared to allow a repeat of Stalingrad to engulf his seasoned troops. In these desperate rearguard actions, the well-equipped SS panzergrenadier sections found that their new squad firepower asset, the MG 42 machine gun, was an even more potent defensive weapon than its predecessor, the MG 34, which bolstered significantly their defensive resilience. Indeed, the MG 42 was one of the most effective machine guns ever designed. Economical to produce, highly reliable, and easy to maintain, it delivered a staggering rate of fire of 1,500 rpm, and an overheating barrel could easily be switched in order to maintain sustained fire. Special devices attached to the gun enabled the troops to aim and fire the weapon from the cover of a trench or foxhole without exposing themselves to enemy fire. The attacking Soviet soldiers at Kharkov, as well as elsewhere in the East – like those of Germany's other enemies too – soon came to fear the staccato sound of this awesome infantry firepower asset manned, in many cases, by determined and well-trained German soldiers.

When Hitler, at his headquarters in East Prussia, learned of Hausser's disobedience, he flew into a towering rage. But even as the furious Führer contemplated Hausser's punishment, the tactical sense of the SS general's actions began to dawn on him, and this instead led him – given that he needed a scapegoat for Hausser's disobedience – quite unjustifiably to sack Lanz a few days

A wounded German officer is loaded onto an ambulance having been airlifted out of the Stalingrad Pocket. He was one of the lucky ones. During February 1–3, 1943, the remaining 91,000 Axis troops of the Sixth Army – the remnants of 22 divisions – entered captivity. The Soviets forced-marched the prisoners through the winter to the infernal labor camps, from where during the 1950s just 5,000 emerged alive.

later. For even the Führer had to admit that Hausser's disobedience had saved two desperately needed elite German mobile divisions from destruction, while the determined delaying resistance the SS corps had offered at Kharkov had bought sufficient time to enable other German units to retreat west and reestablish a fragile defensive crust west of the city.

For here at Kharkov, as on many other occasions in the East, the German Army's skill at rapid and flexible improvisation helped avert a wider crisis. Energetic local commanders, often exercising their own initiative in confused and dislocated

Friedrich Paulus, the defender of Stalingrad. During January 1943, the Soviets drove back his emaciated troops – they had already eaten most of their horses – who by now were also chronically short of fuel and munitions. At the end of the month Hitler made Paulus a field marshal, a dubious "promotion" that sent the doomed commander a clear Führer order. For no Prussian or German field marshal had ever surrendered alive before, and thus it was clear that Hitler expected Paulus to uphold this tradition! By February 1, however, the starving, frozen, and demoralized soldiers of the abandoned Sixth Army could resist no longer, and so Paulus surrendered both his command and – in defiance of a Führer that had failed to save his encircled troops – himself to the Soviet authorities.

command conditions, took immediate steps to restabilize the front west of the city. Again, the army benefited from the training the ordinary German soldier received in carrying out the job of his superiors. When junior leaders fell in battle, for example, their subordinates often swiftly and effectively assumed the former's responsibilities, ensuring that high officer and noncommissioned officer (NCO) casualties did not wreck the cohesion of the remaining troops. Along this fragile front forming to the west of Kharkov, these junior leaders dispatched troops to intercept many small groups of retreating soldiers from all branches of the army, with some in a barely cohesive state, and swiftly welded them into improvised battle groups to hold the new line. The impressive ability of motley collections of panzergrenadiers, cooks, infantry-men, and clerks to "knit" rapidly into cohesive units owed much to the common doctrine and basic training experienced by every soldier, as well as the extensive all-arms training each had undertaken. No doubt, the increasing presence of military police behind the line, combing the rear areas for those seeking to evade combat, stiffened the readiness of the troops to stay in line and resist the "sub-human" enemy.

Despite Hausser's extrication of his ideologically driven SS troops from a repeat of Stalingrad, the Axis position in the Ukraine nevertheless deteriorated rapidly in the days that followed the fall of Kharkov. For Stalin believed that Hitler's fanatically loyal Waffen-SS soldiers would only abandon the Soviet Union's fourth largest city if the Führer himself had ordered the Germans to conduct a general strategic withdrawal behind the Dnieper River. This misinterpretation led an emboldened STAVKA to conclude that now was the correct moment to enlarge their offensive into one that would destroy the entire Axis front in the Ukraine. Consequently, STAVKA ordered the Sixth Army to advance to the Dnieper between Dnepropetrovsk and Zaporozhye to establish a bridgehead, while General Popov's Mobile Group pushed rapidly south toward Krasnoarmeyskoye and beyond that to Mariupol on the Sea of Azov coast, so as to encircle all the Axis forces on the Mius River line.

But Manstein was merely biding his time, and once the advancing Soviet divisions had reached the end of their logistical lines, he launched a devastating counterattack with his SS panzer corps. The result was 50,000 Soviet dead, a further 20,000 taken prisoner, and the Soviet offensive stopped in its tracks.

Unfortunately for the German Army, neither Hitler nor the High Command in their subsequent strategic planning in the East seemed to heed the key lesson, learned at Second and Third Kharkovs, that a skillfully executed, elastic defensive-offensive could be an extremely potent operational technique.

After-action reports starkly illuminated the inadequacy of German antitank doctrine and equipment and demonstrated the difficulty troops faced destroying Soviet heavy armor. Even the most effective existing German antitank gun, the 50mm Pak 38, could only destroy the heavy Soviet KV-1 tank at extremely short range. Consequently, troops soon learned to deploy their 50mm guns in reverse slope (defilade) positions and to engage enemy armor from the flanks or rear where they were most vulnerable. Though the German 88mm heavy antiaircraft gun could

Wrecked German vehicles outside Stalingrad. During the three-month period from November 19, 1942, to February, 19, 1943, the hard-pressed German Army in the East had experienced a strategic crisis of unprecedented dimensions. The elite, superbly trained German panzer arm, in particular, had suffered crippling losses, first in Blue and then in its frantic attempts to stem the various Soviet counterattacks described above. Indeed, by late January 1943, the German Army's total tank strength had declined to an all-time low of just 502 operational tanks.

destroy any Soviet tank at long range, the gun's short supply, its vulnerability due to its high silhouette, and air force control of antiaircraft artillery ensured that insufficient numbers of these guns were available in the East for infantry support. As during Barbarossa, combat necessity often compelled German artillery to engage Soviet armor that had broken through the front over open sites, which inevitably brought heavy losses. Otherwise German infantry and engineers had to engage Soviet armor at close range with mines (like the Teller mine 35), grenades, and satchel charges, all of which required iron nerves and discipline, which was often beyond the capabilities of exhausted, hungry, ill-supplied, and demoralized troops. As a result, after-action reports clamored for greater antitank capability.

Heavier Panzers

During 1942, therefore, Hitler accelerated development of new heavier tanks – the Panzer VI Tiger I and Panzer V Panther – and rushed them into service in summer 1942 and spring 1943, respectively. In the meantime, factories retrofitted Panzer III and IV tanks with heavier cannon and additional appliqué armor, developed more potent models of these tank types, increased their production of cheap-to-construct StuG III assault guns, and mounted heavy cannon on tank chassis to produce light tank-destroyers such as the Marten III. Though improvised designs that sacrificed armor protection and cross-country performance for maximum firepower, the Marten series tank-destroyers proved effective interim mobile antitank weapons and a valuable stopgap until purpose-built vehicles entered service during 1944. Simultaneously, German infantry and engineers underwent extensive conditioning for close-combat tank destruction, accompanied by a revised antitank warfare manual.

Efforts were also made to strengthen the panzer divisions at the front. On average, the panzer divisions that commenced Blue fielded just 126 tanks each – 40 percent fewer than in Barbarossa. To offset this, however, a tiny proportion of these AFVs – just 133 in fact – were the latest Panzer IV Model F2 vehicles that mounted the potent long-barreled 75mm KwK 40 L/48 cannon and featured frontal armor increased to 1.96-in. (50-mm) thickness. The powerful gun of the F2 delivered a muzzle velocity of 2,430 fps (740 m/s) and could penetrate 3.5 in. (89 mm) of well-sloped armor at the typical combat range of 3,282 ft (1000 m), sufficient to punch through even the frontal armor of the T-34. What the Germans desperately needed, though, was larger numbers of the Panzer IV Model F2 to neutralize the impact the T-34 then exerted on the tactical battlefield.

The infantry was reinforced with an offensive indirect fire-support weapon. The 150mm Rocket Launcher 41 (150mm Nebelwerfer 41) was a six-barreled launcher mounted on a modified 37mm Pak gun carriage. The relatively mobile weapon – it weighed just 1,695 lb (770 kg) when fully loaded – could fire a full salvo of six rockets to a maximum range of 4.3 miles (6.9 km). At Voronezh, the 52nd Rocket Launcher Regiment provided devastatingly effective fire support for the attacking infantry. One German infantryman recalled that the rockets made a terrible noise as they thundered across the dawn sky, leaving reddish streaks behind them. The barrage proved so effective that several Soviet soldiers, driven half-mad by the terror induced by the noise and unbearable concussive effect, simply ran forward toward the German lines to be mowed down. Within a matter of minutes, the infantry captured the Soviet position in the face of negligible resistance, then, aided by the fire support provided by the rockets, went on to capture the city. Sadly for the German infantry, the Rocket Launcher 41

German Siege Warfare

During late spring 1942, Colonel-General Manstein's Eleventh Army prepared to storm the powerful Soviet defenses around Sevastopol, following a siege that commenced in late 1941. To facilitate the siege and subsequent attack, the Germans allocated their largest-caliber super-heavy artillery around the port. These pieces included the 420mm Gamma Mortar, the ex-Czech 420mm Howitzer – 420mm H(t) – and the incredible 800mm Railway Gun – 800mm K(E) – "Gustav." The latter, manned by a crew of 1,500 and weighing 1,329 tons (1,350 tonnes), remains the largest artillery piece ever constructed. Once assembled and deployed along a specially built double railroad track, a process that alone took four weeks, the "Gustav" could fire one 15,620-lb (7,100-kg) standard round every 15 minutes to a range of 29 miles (47 km), and much farther when employing specialized long-range ammunition.

On June 2, 1942, a coordinated air force and super-heavy artillery bombardment commenced to soften up the Soviet defenses prior to the main ground attack, which started on June 7. By June 30, after protracted and intense combat, the German infantry and assault engineers – continuously backed by heavy aerial and artillery support – had fought their way into the last of the formidable Soviet fortresses around the city. Over the four-week struggle, the 400 available aircraft flew a total of 23,000 interdiction and tactical support sorties, with some resilient pilots undertaking as many as eight missions each day. Once again, German success at Sevastopol owed much to effective all-arms and interservice cooperation, as well as to the bravery of assault engineers repeatedly engaging Soviet bunkers at close range with demolition charges, grenades, and Flamethrower 41 (FlaW 41) devices.

In total, the huge "Gustav" gun fired 300 rounds during this battle, and played a prominent role in cracking the strongest Soviet defenses, the Maxim Gorky fort, which was protected by 13.2 ft (4 m) of steel-reinforced concrete. Its most spectacular achievement, however, was to destroy a Soviet ammunition magazine located 99 ft (30 m) below the bottom of the shallow waters of Severnaya Bay! Whatever its undoubted tactical value in such siege operations, "Gustav" cost vast amounts of labor, material, and money to develop. Like the "Mouse" super-heavy tank project, the 800mm gun reflected the most dreadful waste of effort associated with the German High Command's absurd fixation with what can only be termed impracticable "military gigantism."

remained a relatively scarce weapon, and there were never enough to meet the clamor for them among the frontline troops.

In addition, the 210mm Rocket Launcher 42 (210mm Nebelwerfer 42) could fire a full salvo of five 247-lb (112-kg) rounds in eight seconds, and repeat this three times in five minutes. With a greater range of 4.9 miles (7.8 km), this relatively mobile, yet still rare, weapon provided the luckiest of hard-pressed German infantry in southern Russia with a potent fire-support asset to break up and delay the repeated waves of Soviet attacks in late 1942.

Of course, the quality of the troops using the weapons was often more important than the hardware. On November 25 and 26, 1942, for example, Marshal Georgi Zhukov respectively commenced Operations Mars and Jupiter. In the latter, however, the Soviets failed even to achieve a breakthrough despite repeated attempts that incurred very heavy casualties in the face of a skillful and tenacious German defense. Here, German troops improvised an effective antitank defense using whatever weapons were at hand – infantry tank-hunting teams, 50mm Pak 38 guns, 88mm antiaircraft pieces, Marten III self-propelled guns, and field artillery firing over open sights, in combination with aggressive local counterattacks, to defeat the Soviet thrust. In the west of the Rzhev salient, Soviet forces broke through the German defenses around Belyi and exploited southeast. The Germans reacted swiftly and effectively, however, rapidly redeploying local reserves for an aggressive counterthrust. Well coordinated, high-tempo German all-arms actions soon halted the Soviet penetrations north of Belyi. Then, audaciously exploiting fleeting tactical opportunities, German mechanized forces maneuvered swiftly to outflank, encircle, and then destroy two entire Soviet corps south of the town.

While the bravely led and well-trained remaining troops retained a good measure of their former effectiveness, the dearth of operational equipment hampered the combat power of Germany's crack panzer forces on the Eastern Front in 1942. In all probability, only a series of daringly executed high-tempo armored counterthrusts, combined with appropriate adjustments to the more static areas of the front, could save the tottering Axis position in the Ukraine. But both Hitler's rejection of tactical withdrawals and the meager equipment levels available to the battered but still cohesive panzer divisions made this type of elastic response very difficult to implement effectively.

Soviet troops attack during the operations against Stalingrad in December 1942. In general, poor leadership, faulty doctrine, poor coordination, and unsubtle frontal attacks by raw, depleted, hastily trained and poorly equipped troops, hampered Red Army operations, as did shortages in artillery and munitions, inadequate communications, and the limited armored support available. In addition, Soviet forces rarely exploited penetrations quickly or with determination and often retreated in the face of the vigorous and rapid countermeasures the German Army regularly undertook.

Hitler – the Wild Card

The interference of the Führer became more erratic and damaging during the 1942 campaign and led directly to the loss of the Sixth Army at Stalingrad. The original objective of Blue as set by the High Command, though actually conceived by Hitler, was to capture the vital Soviet oilfields in the northern Caucasus around Maikop. Interestingly, the initial German spring 1942 planning allocated only a low priority to the psychological objective of capturing the city of Stalin's name – Stalingrad. At this point the High Command envisaged that the Blue Offensive would comprise two stages. In the first phase, Axis forces would thrust east and southeast to the Don River, while in the second stage their forces would operate on two separate axes, to drive east toward Stalingrad and to advance south into the Caucasus. As with Barbarossa, however, serious conflict existed within the aims the Germans set for this offensive. For many senior German commanders hoped that the ground operations required to seize this region would also produce the same great "cauldron battle" encirclements seen during Barbarossa. Consequently, in the process of destroying their enemy's economic ability to continue the war, the Wehrmacht might also decisively defeat the Red Army in the field.

If the Wehrmacht did manage to secure a decisive triumph over the Red Army during the course of Blue, Hitler dreamed of exploiting such success by realizing the incredibly overoptimistic schemes developed in 1941 for capitalizing on a successful Barbarossa. These plans envisaged that a successful German advance into the Caucasus could continue through the Middle East. One this advance had linked up with Rommel's triumphant Panzer Group Africa as it pushed north through Palestine, the Third Reich would sit astride the key oil region of the world! Overcautious strategic planning was not a disease that plagued the German High Command during World War II.

On July 16, 1942, Hitler intervened in the unfolding offensive when he diverted Hoth's Panzer Army away from its promising thrust to Stalingrad to help the southeasterly drive of the First Panzer Army toward Rostov. In retrospect, this proved a critical mistake, because it threw away a fleeting opportunity to seize Stalingrad by a surprise attack in mid-July before the Soviets could improvise an effective defense. Hitler, in effect, admitted his mistake on July 30 when he redirected the Fourth Panzer Army, which had by then reached the Don at Isymlyanskaya, back north to resume its attack on Stalingrad. The Führer's erratic

T-34s in the attack. During the struggle for Stalingrad, the Red Army amassed powerful reserves around Stalingrad. To ensure that they could assemble this force of 50 divisions with 1,000 tanks without the Germans discovering their intentions, the Soviets skillfully undertook extensive *Maskirovka* – the deception, security, and concealment actions that Red Army doctrine insisted form a integral part of tactical planning.

orders certainly did not reflect adherence to the classic key military principle of selecting and maintaining an aim. Moreover, during the two-week delay that Hitler's orders had imposed on this formation, and with Paulus's Sixth Army too weak to capture Stalingrad by itself, the Soviets managed to create a powerful defense around the city. In addition, this pointless diversion of Hoth's command consumed large amounts of its scarce fuel stocks, and the resulting shortages hampered the operations his forces subsequently undertook around Stalingrad.

By the third week of July, however, Hitler had grown increasingly frustrated with the failure of an apparently successful Blue to surround and destroy sizable Soviet forces, and this brought his simmering dispute with the Army High Command to boiling point. The Führer's already strained relationship with Army Chief of Staff Halder declined further, and Hitler in addition sacked Bock as commander of Army Group B and replaced him with Weichs, the commander of the Second Army. The Führer preferred to blame Bock for the German failure to

achieve greater success rather than admit that this resulted partly from his own suspect interventions. Then, on July 23, the day that the port city of Rostov fell, Hitler issued new instructions for the development of the offensive in his Directive 45. Hitler made the capture of Stalingrad the key objective of Army Group B, and expanded the goal of Army Group A to include the capture of the Baku oil fields on the Caspian sea coast.

For notwithstanding his frustration that the encirclements already successfully achieved during Blue had not delivered large numbers of Soviet prisoners, the significant territorial advances accomplished during the preceding month still led an overconfident Hitler to assume that the Red Army in the south had been broken. The folly in this assumption should have been clear to the Führer, for he knew that the encirclements already achieved in Blue had netted just 90,000 Soviet prisoners. The principal reason for this disappointing haul was not, as Hitler believed, poor German generalship, or even the adverse impact of his own meddling, but rather the appropriate responses the Soviets made to the offensive.

Hitler reacted to this faltering advance by relieving List on September 9. To replace the commander the Führer appointed himself – incredibly, Hitler attempted to exercise personal command of Army Group A from his own headquarters at Vinnitsa, 900 miles (1,448 km) away from the troops he now directly controlled! Though he promptly ordered the Seventeenth Army to capture the Black Sea ports of Novorossisk and Tuapse, throughout mid-September this army barely managed to advance despite Hitler's direct control on the battle and the copious air support provided by Hans Rudel's Stuka squadrons. Farther east, the First Panzer Army attacked toward Grozny during October, before on November 2 reaching Ordzhonikidze, the most southerly town reached

A German machine-gun position in the snow. By February 17, 1943, the rampaging Soviet spearheads of the Voronezh Front had advanced 60 miles (96 km) beyond Kursk, while Vatutin's Southwestern Front had broken through the Donets River defense line on a 110-mile (177-km) front. The whole of the southern Eastern Front was in danger of being ripped apart.

by the Germans during the war. For during 1942, Stalin, unlike Hitler, had begun to learn from his previous strategic mistakes. His earlier static defense and no withdrawal policies had led to the encirclement and capture of hundreds of thousands of Soviet troops, particularly at Kiev, Bryansk, and Vyazma in 1941. Now during mid-1942, Stalin instead permitted Soviet forces threatened with encirclement to withdraw deeper into the Soviet Union to escape the German pincers. Indeed, during summer 1942, the Soviet forces facing Blue implemented the traditional Russian strategy of trading space to gain time. That, as a result of this policy, the Stalingrad and Southeastern Fronts were far from beaten in August 1942 should have been obvious to Hitler, given that by August 20 the Soviets had halted the Sixth Army in front of Stalingrad. Yet these sobering military realities did not shake the Führer's conviction that through sheer will power his forces could capture both Stalingrad and the entire Caucasus region.

The slim probability that Army Groups A and B could achieve these overambitious objectives was further reduced in mid-August when foolishly Hitler transferred the now available Eleventh Army to Leningrad for an offensive there instead of employing it to reinforce Operation Blue. During the summer of 1942 Hitler's strategy for the Eastern Front failed woefully to implement the classic military principle of concentration of force at the decisive point.

The Failure of the Luftwaffe

At Stalingrad, while the Germans organized a ground relief operation, the air force strove to resupply Sixth Army with all the ammunition, fuel, and rations it needed. Paulus's formation needed to receive 590 tons (600 tonnes) of supplies every day if it was to maintain its combat power. To fulfill these requirements, the air force would have to run 230 successful Ju 52 transport aircraft sorties every day. A critical factor in Hitler's decision that Paulus's Army remained at Stalingrad was the guarantee made by Reichsmarshal Hermann Göring that the Luftwaffe would be able to achieve such a demanding mission. Sadly for Paulus's troops, Göring remained as ignorant of the strategic realities in the East as did his Führer. As Erich von Manstein later stated: "Only if a guarantee of air supplies were given ... could we afford to delay a breakout until the intervention of relief forces improved the army's chances of escape. By refusing to sanction Paulus's request for a breakout ... Hitler had to all intents and purposes already given that guarantee. His refusal had been based on an assurance from Göring.... Nevertheless, Hitler should still have checked up on the reliability of his statements. Besides knowing what sort of person Göring was, he was also well aware of the strength of the Luftwaffe."

The airlift began on November 25, but from the beginning a combination of poor weather, lack of aircraft, and having to run a gauntlet of enemy antiaircraft fire to and from Stalingrad meant it was woefully inadequate. Göring had promised 590 tons (600 tonnes) daily, but the reality was less than a third of that figure (and that was on days when the weather was good). The Luftwaffe's failure at Stalingrad certainly damaged its prestige, but in the immediate aftermath it had more pressing matters to address. It had lost a total of 488 aircraft trying to keep the Sixth Army supplied, the majority of which, ironically, were suffered from poor landings and takeoffs rather than enemy fire. Losses in crews had also been high, especially in instructors sent from Germany to take part in the airlift. This meant that the training of new crews was badly affected; all in all the Stalingrad disaster also had dire consequences for the future of the Luftwaffe.

The Growing Competence of the Red Army

The 1942 campaign did not only mark a turning point in the fortunes of the German Army, it also indicated that the Red Army was becoming more competent. The success of the November 1942 Uranus counterstroke, for example, demonstrated not only that it had outfought the German Army during late 1942 in tactical and operational terms, but also that it had planned unfolding operations more effectively at the strategic level. Unlike Blue, Uranus pursued modest goals – a shallow double envelopment – that remained achievable despite the still modest offensive capabilities that the Red Army had managed to establish by this stage of the war. Clearly, the Soviets had learned from earlier mistakes, particularly the premature overexpansion of the initially successful winter 1941–42 counteroffensive. The success of Soviet operations during late 1942, therefore, owed much to their ability to learn from previous mistakes.

This, though, was a skill that Hitler and his High Command seemed less able to master in 1942. In Blue, for example, the Germans repeated the mistakes they made during Barbarossa. As an overambitious offensive initiated too late in the year, Blue failed to translate tactical success into strategic triumph, extended the German front beyond that logistically sustainable, and left vulnerable flanks that invited a Soviet counterthrust. And in Uranus the Red Army gratefully accepted – with devastating results – the invitation inadvertently issued by the Germans. The failure of the Germans to defeat the Soviets in 1942 did not result from less effective all-arms cooperation, or a slower tempo of exploitation, or ineffective junior leadership, or even declining troop morale, all of which remained reasonably close to their previous 1941 standards. Rather, improving Soviet

German halftracks during Operation Blue in July 1942. Throughout the operations on the Eastern Front in 1942 and the beginning of 1943 the Germans showed a marked superiority over the Red Army when it came to mobile operations. In one large-scale tank-versus-tank engagement that occurred, at Martynovka on July 28, 1942, for example, swifter German reactions, flexible commanders deployed well forward, timely cooperation between all-arms, and superior tank gunnery led to the waiting Soviet armor being outmaneuvered and decimated.

capabilities exploited German weaknesses at the strategic and operational levels. And unfortunately for the hard-pressed ordinary German soldier, Uranus was just the start of a coordinated Soviet strategic riposte across the Eastern Front. The Soviets intended Uranus to be a classic double envelopment that pitted Soviet strength against Axis weakness. However, unlike the "cauldron battles" attempted by the Germans, the Soviets pursued geographically limited objectives to ensure these aims remained achievable.

But senior commanders still launched offensives that were beyond the capabilities of their troops. In autumn 1942 Zhukov simultaneously developed a scheme for an even more ambitious offensive in the center of the Eastern Front. The Soviets conceived Operations Mars and Jupiter as powerful assaults to remove the threat to Moscow posed by the positions held by Army Group Center in the Rzhev salient. In Mars the Kalinin Front attacked the northwestern flank of the Rzhev bulge, while in Jupiter the Western Front hit the east of the salient: between them they aimed to encircle and destroy the Ninth Army, eliminate the salient, and push on to the key junction of Smolensk.

Personally directed by Zhukov, Mars and Jupiter represented the Soviet commander's most significant failure. The experience of these operations exposed how modest Soviet offensive capabilities still remained at this stage of the war when faced with effective German defensive actions. Moreover, these events demonstrated that the still impressive German defensive tactics posed a real threat to any Soviet offensive that had not been able to exploit a strategically undesirable situation created largely by German mistakes at the highest command echelons.

The Red Army underwent a learning process during 1942, though at the end of the year, man for man, it still remained inferior to its German opponent. However, its ability to learn from mistakes did not bode well for the future of the Wehrmacht. Hedgehog defense inadvertently exploited flaws in Soviet organization, leadership, and doctrine, since the Soviets lacked the expertise, firepower, and mobility to encircle and annihilate major Germans forces. Such an offensive was well beyond the depleted Red Army's capabilities, given that Stalin in turn underestimated German defensive power and the powerful obstacle the weather presented to offensive action. Lack of strength and dispersion of effort across the front, enabled the badly weakened but still resourceful German forces to escape annihilation. Without massed artillery, adequate munitions, or effective coordination, the Red Army failed to defeat the stiff defensive resistance offered by the Germans.

German Fighting Quality

Throughout the fighting on the Eastern Front in 1942 the fighting qualities of the individual German soldier remained high. This was undoubtedly bolstered by ideological training. In late spring 1942, for example, the Germans stepped up their efforts to psychologically motivate their frontline soldiers in the East. During May, university lecturers visited the elite *Grossdeutschland* Division – only recently expanded from regimental size – and delivered discussions on the evils of communism. In addition, the division created a new appointment, that of Education Officer, who coordinated all the activities undertaken to bolster the morale and determination of the troops. The officer procured several hundred new propagandistic books for the division's library van, and gave seminars that stressed both the inherent superiority of the German Army and the inevitability of its ultimate victory to "strengthen soldierly qualities" and instill "steadfastness during crises" within the troops. Such effective measures represented the early stages of a trend where increasingly the High Command sought to indoctrinate the troops in order to motivate them to fight effectively despite both the terrible privations experienced in the East and the increasingly unfavorable strategic situation. It was also stressed to the troops that they were fighting an uncivilized "Bolshevik horde" that would wreak death and destruction upon Germany should they fail – a tactic that had some success.

On a wider scale, on July 15 the High Command instructed every division in the East to appoint an Education Officer to coordinate all measures designed to nurture fighting spirit. These appointments proved to be the precursor of the National Socialist Leadership Officers, created in late 1943, who became the chief motivational instrument of the German Army during the last 18 months of the war. Cerebal training in the virtues of National Socialism was also accompanied by hard physical training.

Physical Training

The impressive advances that the Germans achieved in the Caucasus in 1942 were the results of increased levels of "hardness training" received by German replacements arriving in the East during the summer. One recruit for the elite *Grossdeutschland* Division, Guy Sajer, for example, recalled the rigors of his training at Chemnitz barracks in Germany. He and his fellow recruits endured protracted "hardness training" designed to develop their physical and mental stamina to help them endure the appalling conditions likely to be encountered in the East. The trainees undertook numerous day- and night-time live-fire field exercises and drill sessions that placed terrible demands on the exhausted and hungry men. So demanding was this training, and so realistic the battle simulation exercises, that no fewer than 24 out of the 140 recruits in Sajer's group were wounded, four of them fatally. The benefits of training such as this, however unpleasant the experience, were reaped during the German advance across the inhospitable open steppe of the Caucasus. Here, the mentally and physically resilient German soldiers found these qualities tested to the utmost by the vast distances, the oppressive heat and dust, and the dearth of water they encountered (wells were a scarcity in southern Russia, and those that did exist produced water that was often foul tasting; in north, in contrast, there were many wells and their water was cool and pleasant-tasting). The appalling desert and mountainous terrain over which the soldiers of Army Group A operated in order to satiate Hitler's quest for valuable oil resources pushed even these robust soldiers to the very limits of their powers of endurance.

Similarly, during the attempted relief of Stalingrad, on December 19, 1942, after eight days of modest but sustained advances against heavy Soviet resistance, the well-trained troops of LVII Corps reached the Myshkova River some 56 miles (90 km) from their starting positions and just 36 miles (56 km) short of Paulus's perimeter. That the relief effort got this far against fierce resistance and in poor weather conditions owed much to the superior training of the tank crews, the flexible responsiveness of experienced armored commanders like General Rauss and Colonel von Hünersdorff of the 6th Panzer Division, and the bravery of the antitank gunners. As ever the German soldier performed heroics to carry out the orders of his superiors. The tragedy was that those orders were often unrealistic, especially those coming from East Prussia, and resulted in the unnecessary loss of thousands of German lives, losses the Wehrmacht could ill-afford as it prepared for its third summer on the Eastern Front.

PART III

THE NATURE OF THE ARMY

Hitler at War

Portrayed as a lunatic whose inept military decisions led to the unnecessary deaths of hundreds of thousands of German troops, Hitler's military leadership of the German Army was inspired during the early war years, but thereafter was totally disastrous.

As World War II grew in intensity, Adolf Hitler's control of the German war effort became almost total as he resorted to ever-more desperate measures to turn the tide of war in Germany's favor. The Führer's conduct of the war is the subject of great controversy, with many of his generals writing memoirs after 1945 blaming him for Germany's defeat. With Hitler dead in the ruins of his Berlin, it was easy for his generals to shift all the blame for this debacle onto their old boss.

Hitler has been portrayed as a raving madman who doomed hundreds of thousands of German soldiers to death or captivity because of his obsession with not yielding a single inch of territory to the enemy. He is blamed for making huge strategic blunders that included allowing the Allies to gain a foothold in Normandy in June 1944, and the Russians to advance to the gates of Berlin during the following spring. According to many of his generals, if only the Führer had left the conduct of military operations to professional soldiers, Germany would have stood a chance of bringing the Soviet and Anglo-American military juggernauts to a halt and, perhaps, make way for a negotiated end to the war.

To understand why Hitler conducted the war in the way he did it is necessary to look both at his objectives and the man himself. His experiences during World War I, during which he served in the trenches and won the Iron Cross for bravery, moulded his perceptions concerning both warfare and the higher echelons of the army. Throughout World War II he believed that he knew what his frontline troops were thinking in a way that his senior commanders did not, that he knew what they were capable of because he had once been one of them. This view tied in with his rejection of "experts." He was to state: "Instinct is supreme, and from instinct comes faith ... While the healthy common folk instinctively close their ranks to form a community of the people, the intellectuals run this way and that, like hens in a poultry yard. With them it is impossible to make history." His political successes prior to 1939 served to reinforce his view that will and boldness

Hitler the warlord. Though he had a grasp of strategy, his ideological beliefs colored his view of how the war should be conducted. Above all, if Hitler is to be faulted as a war leader on the purely military level it is in his determination to fight a total war to the finish.

could achieve results. He reoccupied the Rhineland and brought Austria and Czechoslovakia into the Reich, all without bloodshed. He began to lose confidence in his senior commanders, especially Field Marshal Werner von Blomberg and Colonel-General Freiherr von Fritsch, who both advised against an aggressive foreign policy. Meanwhile, his successes made him immensely popular with the German people, who regarded him as a greater statesman than Bismarck. This popularity did nothing to lessen Hitler's view of himself as Europe's premier political leader.

From September 1, 1939, Hitler became warlord of Germany when his troops invaded Poland. The string of victories the Germans enjoyed in 1939 and 1940 showed that Hitler had a sound grasp of military strategy, most notably opting for the Manstein plan to attack through the Ardennes in 1940. The defeat of France had two immediate results. First, it convinced Hitler that his grasp of strategy and operational art were equal to, if not better than, his service chiefs (which was not entirely unreasonable, as he had defeated France in six weeks whereas the Imperial German Army and its general staff had spent four years in a vain search for the same result). Second, the widely held view in Germany was that Hitler was a genius. He may not have been the latter but, as the military historian John Keegan states, he did possess "many of the qualitites essential to military success – self-confidence, boldness, intelligence, a hold over his immediate subordinates and a genuine indifference to human suffering."

The conquest of the Balkans in the spring of 1941 and the first few weeks of Barbarossa, the invasion of the Soviet Union, merely reinforced Hitler's belief in his military prowess. Then came the reverse before Moscow in December 1941, an event that marked a turning point in Hitler's relations with his senior commanders. They advocated retreat; he was adamant the troops should stand fast. The troops stayed where they were – and held. Hitler was vindicated in his view. Thereafter he became increasingly disillusioned with his "defeatist" generals, especially when they advocated yielding ground on the Eastern Front.

The Führer's Racial War

Many Western historians have overlooked the importance of the war on the Eastern Front to Hitler. The conflict with Soviet Russia totally consumed the Führer. His every action was driven by his messianic desire to defeat Joseph Stalin's communist regime. This was Hitler's obsession, and he declared in 1942: "If we do not complete the conquest of the East utterly and irrevocably, each successive generation will have war on its hands." He confided to one of his favorite generals, Erwin Rommel, in July 1943: "Germany needs the conquered territories or she will not exist for long. She will win hegemony over the rest of Europe. Where we are – we stay."

In the spring of 1943 Adolf Hitler still believed he would achieve total victory over his enemies, despite the massive defeats suffered by the Wehrmacht in the Soviet Union and North Africa during the previous six months (some 500,000 German troops had been killed or captured in defeats at Stalingrad and El Alamein, and in Tunisia).

Ever the optimist, the Führer maintained a public veneer of confidence that the Third Reich would survive for 1,000 years. Hitler was convinced that he would prevail because his opponents, led by an alliance of Slavs and Jews, were racially inferior to Germany's Aryans. It was just beyond his imagination that the Russian *Untermenschen*, or "sub-humans," could be clever or strong enough to challenge German supremacy (similar to the attitude of European colonialists in the nineteenth century, who believed that African and Asian enemies were not in any way equal opponents).

Hitler did not believe that Slavs and Jews deserved to share the same continent with the German people. They were either to be forced to emigrate, enslaved, or, ultimately, exterminated. For this reason, it was impossible for Hitler to contemplate any kind of negotiated peace with Stalin; either the Soviet Union had to be destroyed or Germany would be destroyed trying. In April 1945, as defeat loomed, he ranted: "I have always been absolutely fair in my dealings with the Jews. I gave them one final warning. I told them that if they precipitated another war they would not be spared."

Hitler with senior Wehrmacht commanders after the successful conclusion of the campaign in Poland in September 1939 (the man immediately to Hitler's right is Franz Halder, chief of OKH). Hitler always retained a distrust of the aristocratic Prussian officer class.

The German defeats at Stalingrad and Kursk in 1943 badly shook Hitler's confidence. He blamed everyone but himself for the disasters that befell the German Army. Incompetence or treason must be to blame, he reasoned, because the Soviets just could not be credited with being able to raise an army capable of fighting the Germans on equal terms.

As it slowly dawned on Hitler that his beleaguered army was unable to hold back the Soviets, his war objectives shifted. His aim was to prolong the war for as long as possible until either Germany's secret V weapons had an impact, i.e. wear down Great Britain's morale and force her to make peace, or the alliance between Stalin and the Western Allies crumbled. The latter scenario was the Führer's favorite, and he remained convinced up until the final days in his Berlin bunker that Germany would soon be allied with the British and Americans against the Russians. On the eve of the Ardennes Offensive in December 1944 he told his generals, "If we can deliver a few more heavy blows, then at any moment this artificially bolstered common front may suddenly collapse."

A negotiated peace was not on Hitler's agenda: he was determined to achieve total victory or face annihilation. The racial struggle between Germany's Aryans and the Slavs became an end in itself. Hitler saw it as a duel to the death. "I shall not give in, I shall never surrender," he repeated time and time again. Not surprisingly, the

Führer's generals became increasingly disillusioned by his war aims as they began to realize that the destruction of Germany was imminent. The Führer was locked into a battle of wills not only with his enemies, but also with his own commanders.

To prepare the German people to meet their destiny, Hitler declared a state of "total war" in January 1943. This was made against the background of the imminent annihilation of the Sixth Army at Stalingrad. Hitler's declaration was followed by a propaganda blitz by Joseph Goebbels, Reich Minister for Propaganda, to prepare German public opinion for bad news and to steel the population for a long and bloody war. Up to this point in the war, the German people had been served an almost daily diet of easy military victories against unprepared and inept opponents. Now Germany had a real fight on its hands.

Total War

A key element of this strategy was the institution of a war economy. No longer was economic planning to be based on the assumption of a short war. Surprisingly, civilian production still dominated the economy, with some six million workers still producing consumer goods, and 1.5 million women working as domestic servants. The average monthly production of tanks was only 136 during 1940, and this had only risen to 257 by January 1943. Albert Speer, Minister of Armaments and War Production, was a capable man, but "total mobilization of the economy" was never attained. In 1942, production of consumer goods was only reduced by 12 percent; even in 1944 it ate up 22 percent of total industrial production.

In February 1943, in one of his last giant public speeches at Berlin's sport's stadium, Goebbels exorted the German people to fight with all their strength. All men up to 65 years and all women up to 45 years were liable to drafting for compulsory war work. Hitler Youth boys were to work on farms or collect scrap metal. Prison labor would be used for war work. At the same time, Hitler drafted a new set of industrialists and military officers to transform war production, which was still bumbling along at levels not much greater that those of 1939–40. Speer and the new head of panzer troops, Colonel-General Heinz Guderian, were tasked with increasing tank production and other weapons programs.

Perversely, the Führer's best ally in his campaign to motivate the German people for total war may have been the British Royal Air Force (RAF). Night after night from March 1943, RAF Bomber Command bombed German cities. This culminated in the death of some 40,000 citizens of Hamburg during a series of raids over six days in July 1943.

Speer and Guderian went to work with a vengeance and were soon producing impressive results. By the middle of 1943, tank production had rocketed to 1,004 vehicles per month, and in 1944 it was averaging 1,538 per month. Peak tank production was achieved in December of that year, when Allied bombing of Germany was at its height. During 1943 and into 1944, German troops fought with great determination on all fronts, indicating that Hitler's efforts to motivate his people were very effective, in spite of the protests by the Führer's generals that he was leading the country to disaster.

To fight his war of delay, Hitler needed to keep enemy troops as far as possible from the Third Reich's borders, to keep Germany's allies on her side and to protect vital industrial and natural resources. This latter point was very important to Hitler, who saw the war in economic terms, believing that technological development and war production were essential factors in defeating the more populous Soviet Union.

Command Posts

As the war dragged on, it became increasingly more perilous for Hitler to visit his troops in the field. Air travel became too dangerous, and the fate of Japanese Admiral Isoroku Yamamoto, who was killed when his aircraft was ambushed by American fighters, was a salutary lesson in the problems caused by the loss of air supremacy by the Luftwaffe.

Hitler retreated into a series of some 21 underground bunker complexes constructed in conditions of great secrecy. They were built around Germany to allow Hitler to remain protected when visiting each of the main battle fronts. Until the Soviets broke through to the Baltic coast in the winter of 1944, Hitler spent most of his time at the famous Wolf's Lair complex in the forests of East Prussia (shown below). Paranoid that the British would drop a division of paratroopers on the complex, Hitler ordered it to protected by huge minefields and a specially trained elite defense unit, the famous *Führer Begleit* Battalion.

During the Ardennes Offensive at the end of 1944, Hitler moved into the Adlerhorst bunker complex in the Rhineland. Deep underground, Hitler was able to receive delegations of his generals and hold court with his Nazi Party favorites. With air travel all but impossible, Hitler moved around his steadily diminishing Reich in his Führer train, which contained communications equipment and was heavily protected by antiaircraft guns.

After the failure of Operation Watch on the Rhine in the Ardennes, Hitler moved his headquarters into the Führer Bunker under the Reich Chancellery in the heart of Berlin. Here he directed, or misdirected according to his generals, the final battles of the war.

The more territory Germany held, the more time Hitler believed he had to divide the Soviets and the Western Allies. This was the heart of Hitler's "hold at all cost" strategy. On many occasions he summed up his strategy with three words, "time, time, time!" He loved to formalize this strategy with orders to defend grandiosely titled defensive positions, such as the Panther Line in Russia or the Atlantic Wall on the French coast. He could use their existence to bully his reluctant generals into standing fast when they wanted to retreat. "I am the greatest builder of fortifications of all time," he declared, "I built the West Wall. I built the Atlantic Wall."

By the summer of 1943, Germany found herself fighting on multiple fronts, with diminishing resources, against enemies that only seemed to get stronger by the month. Hitler was forced to ration the strength of his armies and his attention between these fronts. This approach has been termed "fire fighting," and Hitler's elite Waffen-SS panzer divisions were soon nicknamed the "Führer's fire brigade" because of his keenness to rush them from one crisis to another.

Method of Command

Hitler ran his war by means of a series of formal "Führer directives" and "Führer orders." Directives were wide-ranging strategic plans for specific operations or campaigns, or to say how the war in a specific theater was to be fought. These were issued directly in Hitler's name and were intended to allow military commanders to make long-term preparations. Führer Directive No. 21, Case Barbarossa, issued on December 18, 1940, for example, laid the ground for the invasion of Russia, declaring that the "Wehrmacht must be prepared, even before the conclusion of the war against England, to crush Soviet Russia in a rapid campaign."

As the war progressed and Germany lost the initiative, the scope for such wide-ranging planning was reduced. Hitler resorted to micro-managing the war by means of "Führer orders." These could range from plans for major offensives to ordering a battalion commander to dig extra bunkers.

Führer orders were usually generated as a result of Hitler's daily planning meetings, where he received highly detailed reports on activity from every front and theater of operation. These rambling sessions went on for hours, with Hitler making off-the-cuff instructions to aides for this or that action to be taken.

By this stage in the war, Hitler was distrustful of his "defeatist" generals, men such as Brauchitsch, chief of OKH, Halder, his successor, Rundstedt (who was dismissed and reinstated by Hitler three times during the war), and even Manstein. He was keen to put more backbone into lower-echelon commanders, so in matters he considered particularly important personal emissaries would be dispatched to the far reaches of the Reich to deliver the Führer's orders in person. In some cases, a ranting Führer would immediately reach for the telephone and start shouting orders at particular generals who had incurred his displeasure. "The General Staff Corps ought actually to be disbanded!" he raged in the summer of 1944.

Hitler was a strong believer in imposing his personality on reluctant generals, and was prone to making surprise visits to forward headquarters in Russia. The purpose of these visits was not to find out about the situation on the ground but to bully local commanders into following the Führer's orders to the letter.

In the final two years of the war, Hitler's health and mental stability declined dramatically. The stress of conducting a global war was immense, particularly on a megalomaniac who hated to delegate even the most minor detail to

The bombing of Kiel, May 14, 1943. The bombing of German cities helped to mobilize the population behind Hitler: no longer was the war a remote event that was happening hundreds of miles away on the Eastern Front or in Africa. Every German family was suffering death or hardship in its own home. Nazi propaganda about total war was being directed at a receptive audience.

Hitler with some of Berlin's defenders in April 1945. Increasingly confined to underground bunkers and blacked-out trains, Hitler steadily lost contact with reality toward the end. When not in extended briefings with his generals, the Führer spent his remaining time with a small court of Nazi Party officials. They pandered to his prejudices and fed his paranoia. Even his most outrageous ideas were treated seriously by his cronies, and huge amounts of scarce resources were wasted trying to put them into action.

subordinates. From 1943 onward, he managed only a few hours' sleep each night and by the final months of the war could sleep only with the aid of medication supplied by the Führer's very dubious personal physician, Professor Theodor Morell.

The so-called "final solution of the Jewish problem" was one of the most extreme of the Führer's schemes, while his orders to flatten Warsaw after the Polish Home Army rose in rebellion in fall 1944 was a further example of his mad orders swallowing disproportionate resources. For months after the rebellion was put down, German Army engineers wasted precious time and explosives blowing up every building in the city just to satisfy Hitler's lust for vengeance.

The July 1944 Bomb Plot only served to fuel Hitler's paranoia and distrust of his generals. Increasingly, he turned to the Nazi Party and the Waffen-SS to run things for him. This was best illustrated by the appointment of the head of the SS, Heinrich Himmler, to run the Replacement Army in the days after the bomb plot was foiled. Himmler proved totally inept at running the system of training manpower for the field army and made an even greater mess of things when he was appointed head of Army Group Vistula in January 1945.

And yet Hitler was capable of making sound military judgments. For example, he was correct in believing that the Allies would land in Normandy, whereas his generals were obsessed with the Pas de Calais. He received conflicting advice on how to prepare for the coming invasion of France, with Rommel wanting to fight the key battle on the beaches and Guderian opting for a massive panzer counterattack inland. With the German Army's two best panzer commanders disagreeing on the strategy to defeat the invasion, it is not surprising that the initial response to the D-Day landings was confused and weak. However, in the end such matters are academic, for Hitler was truly the agent of his own and Germany's destruction.

High Command

The German Army contained some of the most gifted generals to see service in World War II, but continual interference from Hitler, who distrusted many of his "defeatist generals," diluted their effectiveness and damaged the German war effort.

The Prussian General Staff was a feared institution in the years leading up to World War I because of its reputation for professionalism and efficiency. After that war it was blamed by the victorious Allies for leading Germany down the road of aggression, and in the 1919 Treaty of Versailles the organization was outlawed.

Hitler's military high command structure was a very different beast from that of Bismarck or Kaiser Wilhelm II. He was determined to retain control over the armed forces, and to do so on February 4, 1938, he set up the Armed Forces High Command (*Oberkommando der Wehrmacht* – OKW) to replace the old War Ministry. With the consent of service chiefs Hitler became supreme commander of the armed forces, and thereafter the German Army High Command (*Oberkommando des Heeres* – OKH) was gradually reduced to being an instrument of the Führer's will, rather than the source of sound military advice and imaginative planning. Through skillful political maneuvering, Hitler watered down the powers of the army general staff because he did not want it to be an alternative power base to his Nazi Party.

"Hitler's most outstanding quality was his will power," commented Colonel-General Heinz Guderian. "By exercise of his will he compelled me to follow him. This power of his worked by means of suggestion and, indeed, its effect on many men was almost hypnotic. At the OKW almost nobody contradicted him: the men there were either in a state of permanent hypnosis, like [Field Marshal] Wilhelm Keitel [OKW chief], or of resigned acquiescence, like [Colonel-General Alfred] Jodl [OKW operations chief]. Even self-confident individuals, men who had proved their bravery in the face of the enemy, would surrender to Hitler's oratory and would fall silent when confronted by his logic, which it was so hard to refute." Another less charitable critic called Keitel "Hitler's unthinking and irresponsible yes-man."

Guderian fails to point out that the officer corps as a whole largely welcomed Hitler and his Nazi Party. Drawn mainly from established military families, from the

Lieutenant-General Paulus directs artillery fire against the city of Stalingrad in 1942. Despite being promoted to field marshal in early 1943, he surrendered what was left of his Sixth Army to the Soviets. Such actions made Hitler lose confidence in what he termed his "defeatist generals."

nobility, or from the professional middle classes, it was traditionally conservative and anticommunist. In addition, senior commanders were loathe to break the oath of loyalty to their Führer, even when the tide of war had turned against Germany. In mid-July 1944, for example, there were over 2,000 generals in the army; only 35 took an active part in the Bomb Plot against Hitler.

In the army, field marshals commanded theaters and army groups, while below them an army was led by a *Generaloberst* (general) or a *General der Infanterie* or *Panzertruppe* (lieutenant-general). A division was commanded by a *Generalleutnant* (major-general) or a *Generalmajor* (brigadier), while individual regiments were led by an *Oberst* (colonel). On paper, the OKW was supposed to coordinate the activities of all different armed services, but it never grew much beyond being Hitler's personal planning staff. The services reported to the OKW on operational matters, but the heads of the services rarely met together except at formal sessions to receive their orders from their Führer. The OKW was not a joint chiefs of staff organization where the service chiefs met and presented agreed planning options or military advice to their head of state. "In democratic states the branches of the armed forces and various aspects of the war economy were firmly coordinated, but in Germany there was a strange separation into independent powers," recalled Major-General F.W. Mellenthin, staff officer. "The army, the navy, the air force, the SS, the Organization Todt, the NSDAP [Nazi Party], the commissariats, the numerous branches of the economy all worked separately, but received their orders directly from Hitler. The reason for this strange and sinister phenomenon was undoubtedly Hitler's craving for power and his distrust of any independent force. The old motto 'divide and rule' was carried to its logical absurdity."

Divide and Rule

Paranoid about threats to his power, Hitler was happy for the air force, army, navy, and industrial barons to be at loggerheads and dependent on him to arbitrate their squabbles. Added to this potent brew of personal and professional rivalries, Hitler created his own private army: the Waffen-SS. By the end of the war it had grown to almost 40 divisions, as well as several independent armies and corps headquarters. In the field the Waffen-SS was subordinate to Wehrmacht tactical headquarters, but had its own logistic, administrative, rank, and promotion systems. It reported direct to Heinrich Himmler's SS organization or personally to the Führer.

Throughout the war generals such as Erwin Rommel, Heinz Guderian, and Erich von Manstein repeated petitioned Hitler to change this chaotic and inefficient command structure to maximize Germany's scarce resources and streamline operational planning. Hitler refused every time to follow this advice. By 1943 he had lost confidence in his generals. He dubbed them either "pisspot strategists" or "defeatists." The July 1944 Bomb Plot further undermined his opinion of the higher echelons of the officer corps. He was convinced that at the first opportunity the generals would try to make a compromise peace with the Allies. Therefore, the only way for Germany to remain locked into his titanic struggle with its opponents was for him to keep total control of the direction of the war, even down to the smallest detail. He was not prepared to be reduced to the status of Kaiser Wilhelm II, who became a tool of the general staff. Germany's supreme warlord was not going to give up the reins of power just because it might help his generals tidy up their frontlines.

Hitler's desire to centralize all decision-making did not stop within the OKW level of command. He divided Europe into a number of operational theaters,

The high command of the German military establishment (from left to right): General Gerd von Rundstedt, army commander in chief General Werner von Fritsch, and Minister of Defense Werner von Blomberg. Both Fritsch and Blomberg were the victims of Nazi-instigated scandals and forced to resign their posts.

commanded by generals who were all working to do down their rivals. The biggest war zone, the Eastern Front in Russia, was nominally run by the OKH. Its area of responsibility was, in turn, carved up into large army groups. The most famous were Army Group North, Center, and South. They respectively looked after the Baltic and Leningrad, the front opposite Moscow, and the Ukraine. Hitler left the OKH staff to deal with routine administrative details, but on strategic matters he dealt directly with the army group commanders. In late 1941, Hitler appointed himself commander in chief of the OKH, effectively formalizing his micromanagement of the war in Russia. The side-tracking of the OKH into the Russian theater command signaled the demise of the old-style general staff. The German Army's leadership was locked into the Eastern Front and the OKW did not

rise to the task of providing an alternative focus for the German armed forces. Indeed, Hitler deliberately designed it that way.

The Mediterranean theater was largely the domain of the Luftwaffe for the last two years of the war, through the appointment of Field Marshal Albert Kesselring as commander in chief of Army Group C in Italy. His success in bogging down tens of thousands of Allied troops meant that Hitler largely left him to his own devices.

From 1942 to 1944, northwestern Europe was the domain of Field Marshal Gerd von Rundstedt. At 67 he was appointed commander in chief West with responsibility for France, Belgium, and the Netherlands. As the Allied invasion drew near in the spring of 1944, Hitler imposed a myriad of layers of command under Rundstedt, which reported directly to the Führer, to ensure that the old field marshal had no real influence over events on the ground.

The Balkans were a major theater of operations for the Germans, soaking up more than 600,000 troops during 1944. For the last two years of the war, Maximilian Baron von Weichs, promoted to field marshal in January 1943, was tasked with keeping a lid on Greek, Albanian, and Yugoslav partisans.

The army groups usually contained a number of armies. They were the real engine houses of Hitler's war machine and were usually located far enough away from the Führer's Wolf's Lair headquarters to allow commanders and their staffs to have a degree of independence in how they conducted operations. Some of the most famous German generals, such as Erich von Manstein, Walther Model, Hans Kluge, and Rundstedt, commanded army groups in Russia.

Army group commanders were, in effect, the first command level where Hitler's "divide and rule" policies started to lose their effect. Luftwaffe, Waffen-SS, and naval forces assigned to an army group commander were under his operational control. Command and personal relationships between senior commanders at this level were generally good, allowing the formulation of coherent plans and efficient conduct of operations.

Within army groups, it was also possible for commanders to conduct operations without overreliance on radios, which were very vulnerable to the British "Ultra" interception and decoding systems. Manstein's success in Russia in 1943 and 1944 is attributed, in part, to his belief in face-to-face briefings with his corps and divisional commanders on future operations. The British lost track of Manstein's counterattack at Kharkov in early 1943 and were unable to provide the Soviets with any warning of the field marshal's plans. The Soviets dangerously overextended themselves and were sent reeling backward, losing Kharkov, thousands of tanks, and tens of thousands of men to Manstein's counterattack.

Manstein built his Army Group South, formerly Army Group Don, headquarters into one of the most effective in the Wehrmacht. Its battles in southern Russia and the Ukraine from December 1943 through to March 1944 achieved

Field Marshal Walther Model (center, with goggles), an able commander who suffered from Hitler's meddling. During the Ardennes Offensive in December 1944 Model led Army Group B, but found that he had little say in any details of the planning for the attack. Hitler and the OKW delivered the plan direct to him and ordered him to get on with it. The Führer even picked the routes that the panzer divisions would take from a map, without any idea of the conditions on the ground. Model, along with a number of his subordinates, strongly disagreed with the scope of the offensive, thinking it overly ambitious, but Hitler took no notice. Only once the offensive was under way did Model regain any influence over events on the ground. This situation did not last long, and Hitler was soon insisting that there be no retreat to the Rhine once it was clear the offensive had failed.

Rommel (seated in center) battled to hold the Allies in their Normandy bridgehead in June 1944, until he was badly wounded when British fighter-bombers strafed his staff car on his way back from a visit to the front. The fact that the army group commander had to spend so much time at the front was a symptom of the weakness of the staff officers he had to rely on in Normandy. Many of his army, corps, and divisional commanders were old, in ill health, or inexperienced in the art of mobile warfare. The shortcomings in his headquarters and subordinate commanders, as well as Hitler's restrictions on the movement of panzer divisions, lay at the root of the confusion in the German command in France in the days after D-Day. These were major factors in the poorly coordinated German response to the initial Allied landings.

almost legendary status. Against seemingly overwhelming odds, time and time again Manstein and his staff saved the southern flank of the Eastern Front from disaster.

By the summer of 1944 Hitler had greatly reined in his army group commanders, with Rommel, for example, finding he had little freedom of action during the Battle for Normandy after the D-Day landings in June 1944. Rommel, as commander of Army Group B, in theory had command of two armies, the Seventh and Fifteenth, but Hitler refused to release the latter to move to Normandy because of his belief that Allied troops were poised to cross the Channel and invade the Pas de Calais. Hitler also issued orders that none of the panzer divisions in France could move without his personal approval. Not surprisingly, the "Desert Fox" believed he was fighting with one arm tied behind his back.

While individual German divisions put up heavy resistance in their respective sectors, Rommel's army group was never able to conduct effective large-scale operations. Though Allied air supremacy played a major part in limiting his freedom of movement, it is also clear that Army Group B never really got into its stride. "Ultra" intelligence also meant the Allies could preempt many of Rommel's moves.

The main frontline field headquarters were army, corps, and divisions. These were usually made up exclusively of German Army units and here the last vestiges of the old general staff tradition lived on. The army and corps were headquarters that could be assigned a variety of types of units, such as panzer, infantry, or panzergrenadier divisions, along with specialist artillery, rocket, or assault gun units. Units would be assigned to these headquarters, depending on the particular mission they were given. They would then be taken away once the mission was completed.

The German staff system operated very differently from its Allied or Soviet counterparts, which placed great emphasis on the role of the commander himself to formulate ideas and issue very detailed orders.

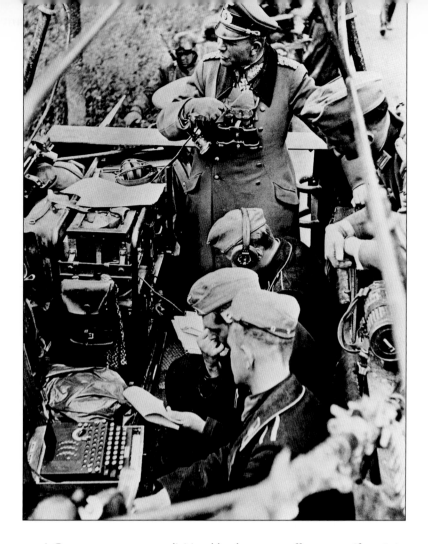

Aggressive frontline leadership was the norm for Germany's generals. On many occasions the day was saved by the prompt intervention of German divisional or corps commanders who were in the right place, at the right time, to order a counterattack or push forward an attack. This was not luck, but what the German Army expected. Commanders were supposed to be present or close to the *Schwerpunkt,* or main effort, of any operation, be it defensive or offensive. Good staff work was all very well, but commanders earned their pay and glory by leading from the front when the situation demanded it. The famous panzer generals, Rommel and Guderian (standing, with binoculars) both made use of armored command post halftracks to follow just behind the first wave of their tanks during major attacks. They always took their Luftwaffe air liaison officer and artillery commander along with them so fire and air support could be summoned up promptly.

A German army, corps, or divisional headquarters staff was a specific unit in its own right, with its own transport, communications, administrative, supply, and protection units. The smooth running of a headquarters depended on the efficiency of these support units, particularly the communications personnel who ensured the staff could remain in contact with higher headquarters and subordinate units at all times.

Personnel were posted to a headquarters for specific tours of duty and they could only serve in key posts if they had passed very demanding staff examinations. Only those officers who had passed the highest level of the general staff corps exam could lead the top staff branches in a division or higher level of headquarters. Throughout the war the army maintained its staff officer career and promotion structure, with officers progressing from one staff job to another, and important interludes where they were posted to command frontline regiments or work as instructors at training depots and staff schools. The Germans tried never to fall into the trap of posting medically unfit or second-rate officers to man the headquarters of frontline armies, corps, or divisions. Attaining a staff posting in a frontline headquarters was a major career ambition for upwardly mobile German officers, and an essential requirement before moving on to high-level command and promotion to the rank of general.

German staff officers were expected to be physically fit and mentally agile. They had to be able to make visits to the frontline to find out what was going on and inspire subordinates by their example. Hiding at a safe rear headquarters was not considered proper officer conduct. Headquarters had to function around the clock, so an ability to do without sleep for long periods of time was a prerequisite for the successful German staff officer!

German headquarters operated a number of staff branches: operations, artillery or fire planning, intelligence, combat engineering, medical, supply, administrative, legal, mapping, and communications. The most important were staff officers for operations and artillery chiefs. The former were responsible for generating operations proposals to the commander and chief of staff. They then formulated specific orders when the commander had decided on the course of action to be taken.

The artillery commander had his own separate command post that was co-located with the army, corps, or divisional headquarters it was supporting. At divisional level, the artillery headquarters was permanently assigned, but in higher-level headquarters it was assigned according to the tactical situation to co-ordinate the fire from a large number of artillery units. It was not the job of the artillery command post to direct the fire of individual gun batteries, but to develop overall fire plans to support any operations. Centralized planning and de-centralized execution was the way the Germans employed their artillery. The artillery commander allocated observation posts to frontline units and then assigned them support from firing batteries. It was up to the observers to call down fire, depending on the situation on the ground. It was the job of the artillery commander's staff to work closely with the operations branch of their parent headquarters to ensure the fire plan met the requirements of the commander's battle plan. The artillery command post controlled its observers and firing batteries by means of a separate radio network or field telephone, to ensure requests for fire received an instant response.

Chief of Staff

The relationship between a commander and his chief of staff was the key to the effective running of a German headquarters. In British, American, and Soviet headquarters the chief of staff was really in charge of little more than the smooth running of the headquarters. In the German Army, he was in many ways the co-equal of his commander. The chief of staff had full authority to take command if his superior was away on leave or out of contact on a visit to the front.

A commander had to work hand-in-hand with his chief of staff to formulate plans and then execute them. The commander would usually spend most of his days at the front visiting units or leading particular operations from a small tactical headquarters, while the chief of staff stayed at the main headquarters monitoring the overall progress of the battle to ensure things went according to plan. During a crisis it was also not unusual for the chief of staff to be sent into the field to command ad hoc battle groups, or to put some "backbone" into wavering subordinates.

To its opponents, the German command system was held in awe. The successes of the Blitzkrieg years created a myth of German invincibility that lasted through to the end of the war. Hitler's generals, particularly those who had masterminded major Allied defeats, such as Manstein in France in 1940 and Rommel in Africa, were seen as sorts of military supermen.

The reality of the German Army command system was less impressive and it was very uneven in quality. Overall strategic direction of the war was totally in the hands of Hitler by 1941. He had sidelined or sacked any senior generals who had tried to interfere in his conduct of the war. He surrounded himself with officers, such as Keitel and Jodl, who were willing to act as his messenger boys. Keitel's justification when passing orders in March 1944 to have 50 British escaped prisoners shot showed his moral bankruptcy: "These escapees must be shot," he told a reluctant subordinate. "We must set an example. We discussed it in the Führer's presence and it cannot be altered."

The OKW organization was never able to operate as a true joint headquarters. Its staff spent most of their time regurgitating reports from the front for Hitler's daily conferences. When called upon to prepare plans for specific operations, it did little more than give the Führer's ideas a veneer of military polish.

When these amateurish orders arrived at frontline headquarters, they were often the subject of great profession derision from the highly trained and experience staff officers who led the German Army. A veteran panzer general, Frido von Senger und Etterlin, recalled that one of Keitel's pep talks to assembled frontline officers in May 1944 received a far from enthusiastic reception. "I was aware that certain officers were anything but enthusiastic at having to listen to such propaganda nonsense at a time when the situation was nothing short of disastrous. But these officers thought it best to conceal their feelings." Fear of revolution had made the die-hard followers of Hitler keep an eye on "unreliable generals."

Frontline Leadership

Out in the field army, professionalism was at the heart of the way the German Army's officer corps conducted military operations. The men who commanded Hitler's armies were all career professionals who had trained their whole lives to lead men into battle. It was a matter of professional pride that they conducted themselves to the best of their ability and their units or headquarters acquitted themselves in a way that enhanced their military reputations. The respect of their peers was very important to German officers.

The German Army may have been outnumbered by its opponents, but it was very rare for its units in the field to be outfought. Free of the Führer's meddling, commanders went about their trade with efficiency and some panache. Efficient staff work was not an end in itself. The German Army believed its purpose was to provide commanders with the ability to judge accurately the flow of battle, make rational decisions, and then execute any measures needed. German headquarters were generally very efficiently run. Commanders were provided with up-to-date battlefield information and were able to have their concepts of operation efficiently translated into workable orders, which were then effectively transmitted to subordinate units.

Below the army group level the army's command system was very robust, proving its worth time and time again, in combat situations that would have led other armies to collapse. Command and control procedures were tried and tested, with every commander and headquarters knowing their missions and responsibilities. This was not just a case of having detailed orders, but of ensuring subordinates had a clear idea of the bigger picture so they could act according to their own initiative if they lost contact with higher headquarters. The famous Eastern Front panzer general Hermann Balck, for example, commander of the 11th Panzer Division, always liked to be present as his counterattacking tanks engaged the enemy to ensure that his subordinates made the most of opportunities when they arose.

As the war progressed, Hitler tried to control his generals to an ever-increasing degree. He blamed them for the increasing number of defeats being

Manstein (right) shakes hands with Hitler. During his time at Army Group South in 1943, Manstein was able to master a succession of crises that would have destroyed other formations. Part of his success was his relationship with Hitler. While Manstein was winning Hitler gave him great latitude, but during the Soviet drive into the Ukraine in the winter of 1943 and into 1944, the Führer began to lose faith in him and began to greatly restrict the field marshal's freedom of action. He finally sacked him in March 1944.

suffered by the German Army, and wanted to ensure the war was fought the way he wanted. In the icy wastes of Russia or in the African desert it would appear to be easy to disobey the "mad orders of the Bohemian corporal." But as the long line of sacked and disgraced generals grew during 1942 and 1944, it was becoming increasingly risky to disobey Führer orders. Careers, salaries, and families were at risk. Manstein estimated that out of 17 army field marshals only one, Keitel, and only three of 36 colonel-generals managed to avoid being sacked during the course of the war. With the execution of some 35 generals and hundreds of more junior army officers after the failed July 1944 Bomb Plot, it was a very brave man who risked the displeasure of Hitler.

There was still a core of German officers who right to the end put the lives of their troops above loyalty to the Führer. When trapped in the Soviet city of Kirovograd with his XLVII Panzer Corps in January 1944, General Fritz Bayerlein, an experienced Africa Corps veteran, simply turned the radios off in his headquarters. He knew that he would receive a "stand-fast" order from Hitler. However, he ordered his troops to break out to the west. "Kirovograd sounds too

much like Stalingrad for my liking," was his comment on the situation as he saved his command from certain destruction. Likewise, General Theodor Busse, Manstein's old chief of staff in Army Group South, ignored orders to fight to the last and broke out of a pocket south of Berlin in the dying days of the war with 40,000 men of his battered Ninth Army, who were mostly ill-equipped and short of ammunition. By then even good staff work was not enough to save Hitler's Thousand Year Reich.

Junior Commanders

Far from being automatons, German junior officers were trained to be adaptable to deal effectively with the enemy and the terrain over which they conducted operations. They were the cement that held the German Army together and kept it fighting.

On the outer ramparts of the Third Reich in the final days of the war, the burden of holding together the battered remnants of the army fell upon the shoulders of a small band of veteran colonels and majors. When divisions were decimated time and again by massive Allied firepower or rolled over by Soviet tank hordes, small groups of German soldiers led by determined commanders formed ad hoc battle groups to try to close the breach in the frontline.

The German Army's junior officer corps, i.e. between the rank of *Oberst* (colonel) and *Leutnant* (2nd lieutenant), was the backbone of Hitler's war machine, and it was the vital link between the Führer, the Wehrmacht's high command, and the ordinary soldiers. It was largely due to the junior officers that Hitler's army kept fighting in spite of the overwhelming odds it faced.

Throughout the war the German Army was keen not to dilute its officer corps by directly promoting noncommissioned officers (NCOs) from the ranks, although in extreme conditions field promotions did occur. All potential officers first served in the ranks prior to selection for officer training before being given the appointment as "aspirant officer." The basic educational qualification was set high, which meant that many NCOs were unable to progress into the officer corps. Potential officers who were selected during their basic recruit training had to have passed the university entrance examination, but more senior potential officers were exempt from this requirement. After serving several months in a unit under supervision, the aspirant officer would be dispatched to the Officer Training School at Doberitz near Berlin for a six-month basic officer training course. The majority of officers commissioned prior to the start of the war were conscripts, who were released to return to civilian life after their two years of national service.

A panzergrenadier squad leader with his men on the Eastern Front in February 1945. On the battlefields of Europe in 1943–45, German field commanders were faced by seemingly insurmountable odds. To keep their troops alive and fighting required commanders to be physically fit, very highly motivated and determined to succeed. Leadership skills of commanders were tested to the limit in the face of unrelenting enemies and extreme climates.

215

In the early war years, the majority of colonels and majors had been professional soldiers in the old *Reichswehr*. They were the last of the old guard, and many were either aristocrats or the sons of career military families. The rapid expansion of the army and first wave of heavy casualties in Russia and Africa in 1941–42 meant that by the time Germany was forced on the defensive after Stalingrad and Kursk in 1943, these men were leading divisions or serving as staff officers at high-level headquarters. As they rose in command their places were taken by men who had risen through the ranks to now lead frontline battalions and regiments.

The burden of leadership thus fell on men who had been commissioned as young lieutenants in the early years of Hitler's rise to power and then progressed through officer training during the 1930s. This infusion of reserve officers after 1943 transformed the German Army officer corps from a peacetime professional force into one that reflected German society as a whole. The reserve officers were almost all from lower-middle-class stock, or university-educated professional classes. Nazi control of the German education system in the 1930s meant that this generation of officers was almost totally indoctrinated with the Führer's racist ideology. In some divisions, this meant that more than a quarter of all officers were members of the Nazi Party.

Mission Command

A major contributing factor to the battlefield success of the German Army was the fact that its officer corps was trained in what is now known as Mission Analysis or *Auftragstaktik*. German officers of all ranks were trained to be able to fight without detailed orders, to make do with just a brief statement of their commander's intentions. The commander told his subordinates what he wanted achieved, not how to do it. Subordinate officers were expected to be able to think on their feet and adapt their brief orders to meet the requirements of the situation on the ground.

German *Auftragstaktik* techniques differed fundamentally from the more rigid command procedures adopted by the Allies. The latter relied on what the Germans called *Befehlstaktik,* or detailed direction of all troops. The differences in command procedures were largely responsible for the ability of the Germans to recover from the brink of disaster time and time again.

After 1943, Allied forces regularly broke through German lines in massive set-piece attacks involving huge artillery barrages and air support. These were tightly choreographed operations and junior subordinates were allowed little freedom of action. However, these attacks invariably became bogged down or deflected. Allied commanders often showed little initiative. They just waited for further orders, for reinforcements, or for new supplies to come forward, leaving the weakened attacking troops vulnerable to counterattack.

This was the point at which the German command doctrine came into its own. It gave the commander on the ground the freedom of action to do what was necessary to stop the attack, without reference to higher command. In many cases, of course, such reference upwards was actually impossible, because the artillery bombardments or air strikes had severed communications with higher headquarters.

For the execution of *Auftragstaktik*, command procedures required highly trained, experienced, and confident commanders. Central to German officer training at this time was the concept that the aspiring commander should be trained to take over the job of his immediate superior. So company commanders had to be ready to take over command of their battalion if its commander was incapacitated. Likewise, platoon leaders had to be prepared to take over from their company commander if he was killed or injured.

Periods of work in staff posts then prepared officers to command a combined-arms battle group or *Kampfgruppe*. A working understanding of how infantry, tanks, antitank guns, artillery, mortars, combat engineers, and aviation could work together was developed through staff training and on maneuvers. Training courses started with instruction on the capabilities of the various arms and equipment found in the Germany Army, then progressed to training exercises without troops where students were given tactical problems to solve, and they walked the ground with instructors discussing the best solution. Students then graduated to full-scale field exercises with demonstration troops. On these exercises students were swapped around between command appointments to give them experience of working with different arms and equipment.

The *Kampfgruppe* concept was so successful for the Germans because it grew from an all-arms combat doctrine, centered on the idea of unity of command, or *Einheit*. The German Army had long since dropped the idea of single-service combat units. Every corps, division, regiment, and battalion contained different types of weapons and sub-units. On the battlefield it was routine for further

A company commander and holder of the Knight's Cross supervises the construction of a defensive point on the Eastern Front in January 1944. Contrary to popular image, German officers were not all career professionals; indeed, more than 80 percent of the wartime German Army officer corps was made up of reservists who had been conscripted in the 1930s and undergone six months of officer training before returning to civilian life. This contrasted with the situation in 1939, when 78 percent of the officer corps was made up of professional soldiers. When the war started, the reservists had not all been called up, and it was not until the campaign in Russia was in full swing in 1943 that all reserve officers were recalled to the colors.

Junior officers planning an attack on the Eastern Front in October 1943. Most junior officers were not professional soldiers, and they had little interest in pursuing military careers after the war. They wanted Germany to win the war as quickly as possible so they could return home to their families and jobs. This meant that they largely remained in frontline units, instead of rising to serve as staff officers in higher headquarters. Their embrace of Hitler and his Nazi Party meant that they were enthusiastic supports of the Führer's war aims. There was little agonizing about Hitler's conduct of the war in the frontline trenches. It was the job of the German Army to kill the Führer's enemies and its junior officers were keen to finish the job they started in 1939. General Frido von Senger und Etterlin witnessed a medal ceremony for junior officers, where the Führer rewarded them for their bravery: "The impression made by Hitler was utterly depressing.... This man was still regarded by many of these young officers as a demigod, a man deserving in complete confidence, whose handshake inspired new confidence."

mixing of weapons and types of unit to occur as *Kampfgruppen* were formed for specific missions and then disbanded when they were completed. In the Allied and Soviet armies the forming of all-arms units was constantly being frustrated by arguments about command relationships, such as tank commanders not wanting to be under the orders of the infantry. In the German Army, the role of the *Kampfgruppe* commander was clear cut: he was the boss, period.

There were well-practiced procedures for establishing *Kampfgruppen* and transferring command of sub-units to them. It was usual to build a *Kampfgruppe* around an existing battalion or regimental headquarters to ensure all the necessary planning and communications capabilities were readily available for the *Kampfgruppe* commander. While a specific *Kampfgruppe* might be centered on a specific battalion or regiment, it was usual for a variety of supporting sub-units to be thrown in the pot to round out its combat capabilities. These generally included combat engineers, communications units, antitank guns, assault guns, medical support, logistic units with additional ammunition and combat supplies, reconnaissance troops, military police for traffic control, intelligence specialists, heavy mortars, rocket launchers, artillery planning staff, and observers. The latter were of particular importance because they determined the level of fire support available for a specific operation.

The most successful German battalion and company commanders were usually in their late twenties or early thirties. They motivated their men by leading from the front, sharing the privations of their frontline troops. Examples of these men included Dr. Franz Bake, who achieved fame as the commander of a *Kampfgruppe* of Panther tanks that led the rescue attempt to open a route to the Korsun-Cherkassy Pocket in February 1944. They also had to convince their troops that they had their interests at heart and were not going to waste their lives in stupid or fruitless operations. But in the extreme conditions on the Eastern Front, commanders also had to act ruthlessly to maintain discipline. The point at which units cracked under pressure was difficult to judge, but if panic was to be nipped in the bud then sometimes waverers had to treated harshly. This was particularly the case when units were in danger of being surrounded. After Stalingrad in 1943, ordinary German soldiers were very frightened of being trapped in pockets, or *Kessels*, and units occasionally collapsed when Soviet troops got behind them. This symptom became known as "Kessel stress," and the Germans thought it had to be dealt with carefully if commanders were to keep their units fighting to give them a chance to break out or launch a counterattack against the enemy.

Maintaining iron discipline to the end: an execution of deserters in April 1945. Even officers with the strongest leadership skills were finding it difficult to keep their men fighting for what was obviously a lost cause at this time. With the Wehrmacht fighting on German soil, it was far easier for soldiers to desert, and the problem started to snowball during the first months of 1945.

Although desertions were rare, especially in Russia where the local population was almost universally hostile to the Germans, officers were regularly urged to take harsh measures against ill-discipline. Field court martials were increasingly common as the war progressed. Junior officers were empowered to shoot on sight any soldiers who wavered in the face of the enemy, or were spotted crossing over to enemy lines. However, at the end keeping the troops fighting was an increasingly difficult task as the ordinary soldier's faith in the Führer started to waver.

The Rank and File

Almost to the very end the German Army recruited and trained individual soldiers who were man-for-man far superior to the soldiers that the Allies could throw at them. They were not Nazi fanatics, but were superbly trained, physically fit, and well motivated.

German infantrymen on campaign in Russia, invariably on foot. At the end of the campaign in North Africa, a British officer wrote: "There is no doubt that the Germans, of all ranks, were more highly professional as soldiers than the British. Their knowledge and practical application of the weapons available to them was in almost all cases superior. ... They were tough, skillful, determined and well-disciplined soldiers. ... Their standard was reached, in a few cases excelled, by some of the British; but a large proportion of the Eighth Army's troops never attained it."

The German Army of World War II was essentially an infantry force. During the war over 700 infantry divisions were raised by the Germans. Granted, many were understrength, especially toward the end of the war. Nevertheless, if the total number of full panzer divisions – 30, plus seven Waffen-SS – is compared to the number of infantry divisions, it can be clearly appreciated the importance that the ordinary infantry played in the Wehrmacht's campaigns between 1939 and 1945. This chapter examines the role of the rank and file, those from the rank of *Schutze* (private) up to *Stabsfeldwebel* (master sergeant) in making the German Army one of the greatest fighting formations in history.

More than anyone else, it was the German infantryman who gave the army the victories in 1939–41, and who conducted a masterful defense in the years thereafter, as he desperately tried to stave off defeat. As the American military historian Colonel Trevor Dupuy has stated: "Except for the careers of a handful of the great captains of history, there is nothing in history – not even the exceptional performance of the German Army in World War I – to match the size, scope, or completeness of the early victories, or the brilliance, versatility, or stubbornness of their performance in defense." Colonel Dupuy also went on to state: "On a man-for-man basis, the German ground soldiers consistently inflicted casualties at about a 50 percent higher rate than they incurred from the opposing British and American troops under all circumstances." Winston Churchill had this to say of the 1940 campaign in Norway: "In this Norwegian encounter, our finest troops, the Scots and Irish Guards, were baffled by the vigour, enterprise, and training of Hitler's young men." Two American psychologists, Edward Shils and Morris Janowitz, who served in the Psychological Warfare Division of General

Eisenhower's headquarters, reinforce the view of the two previous commentators: "Although distinctly outnumbered and in a strategic sense quantitatively inferior in equipment, the German Army on all fronts, maintained a high degree of organizational integrity and fighting effectiveness through a series of almost unbroken retreats over a period of several years. In the final phase, the German armies were broken into unconnected segments, and the remnants were overrun as the major lines of communication and command were broken. Nevertheless, resistance which was more than token resistance on the part of most divisions continued until they were overpowered or overrun in a way which, by breaking communication lines, prevented individual battalions and companies from operating in a coherent fashion. Disintegration through desertion was insignificant, while active surrender, individually or in groups, remained extremely limited throughout the entire Western campaign."

The reasons for the German Army's resistance in the face of overwhelming superiority in terms of men and material were varied – good leadership and defense of the Fatherland in the face of Allied calls for unconditional surrender being the top of the list – but the fighting skills, morale, and discipline of the average German soldier were also of paramount importance. If we reject the idea that Germans are genetically superior to other races, as per Nazi racial theories, or that they are inherently suitable to military life and warmaking, we must scrutinize Churchill's phrase, "the vigour, enterprise, and training of Hitler's young men" more closely. In fact, it was the thorough training that the average German male was subjected to throughout his teenage and young adult life that provided the army with recruits that were physically and mentally superior to those of their Allied adversaries, and also their Axis allies.

Recruits doing basic training. Guy Sajer was an Alsatian who served in the German Army: "The combat course is the most severe physical challenge I have ever experienced. ... We are out of bed at five o'clock. ... Exhausted, soaked to the skin, we fling ourselves onto our mattresses every evening, overwhelmed by a crushing sleep, without even the energy to write to our families." By 1944 there were 305 infantry training battalions, along with 49 panzergrenadier training battalions, 13 tank training battalions, 49 artillery training battalions, and 15 supply training battalions. This was an enormous undertaking, with 128,000 men a month passing through the training system at its peak in 1943–44.

Learning to knock out tanks. The training battalions were manned by experienced veterans who put their charges through some of the most intensive and realistic training then available. Live firing exercises with real ammunition were the norm and there was little squeamishness about casualties in the course of training. Losing a small number of soldiers in training was considered an acceptable cost if the great mass of trainees was better prepared for the rigours of battle. Contrary to popular legend, goose stepping was not on the wartime training syllabus of German soldiers. That remained the domain of certain elite units posted to guard duties in Berlin, or of old prewar units.

From the start of their rule, the Nazis were determined to harness German youth to their cause. Hitler himself believed that a properly educated youth was essential to the survival of his Thousand Year Reich. As he stated: "A violent, active, dominating, brutal youth – that is what I am after. Youth must be indifferent to pain." To achieve his aims he set up two state-controlled organizations in 1933: the Hitler Youth and League of German Girls. The former would have a crucial impact upon the Wehrmacht's combat effectiveness in the 1940s, for it prepared Germany's youth for military service. By 1935 some 60 percent of German youth were members of the Hitler Youth. The process of turning German youngsters into individuals who would be "as swift as the greyhound, tough as leather, and hard as Krupp steel" began at the age of six, when a boy became a *Pimpf*, the equivalent of a wolfcub. At the age of 10 he joined the German Young People, the *Deutsches Jungvolk*, and at the age of 14 went on to join the Hitler Youth proper. The activities of the latter included sports, camping, Nazi ideology, and military training, and by 1938 the Hitler Youth boasted 7,728,529 members.

Far from being a time of grim and remorseless indoctrination, membership of the Hitler Youth was a mostly enjoyable time for German youngsters. Yes, there was indoctrination, but there were also smart uniforms, drill, weapons training, and a host of outdoor activities. The American writer William Shirer lived in Germany during the 1930s, and he witnessed at first hand the activities of the

Hitler Youth: "Though their minds were deliberately poisoned, their regular schooling interrupted, their homes largely replaced so far as their rearing went, the boys and girls seemed immensely happy, filled with a zest for the life of a Hitler Youth. … No one who travelled up and down Germany in those days and talked with the young in their camps and watched them work and play and sing could fail to see that, however sinister the teaching, here was an incredibly dynamic youth movement." And it was a youth movement that was being taught the rudiments of military skills. Thus young males became familiar with small arms, and were taught how to fire them on ranges and maintain them – skills that would be second nature when they joined the army proper. In addition, the boys underwent drill and were brought to a high state of physical fitness by hiking, cross-country runs, and swimming. However ridiculous it may seem with hindsight, the bands of German youths who could be seen scurrying across the countryside and over hills in the 1930s, with a leader clutching a map and a compass, were learning skills that would put them in good stead when they became infantrymen in the army.

Training with the Hitler Youth was divided between two categories: first, ideological training (*Weltanschauung*). At least one evening a week was spent attending lectures given by specially trained leaders who used directives and pamphlets to get their message across. Second, physical training, which was supervised by the *Nationalsozialistischer Reichsbund für Leibesübung* (National Socialist League for Physical Training). Two of the three weekly meetings were usually devoted to physical exercise of a military type: grenade throwing and small arms practice. Summer camp (*Sommerlager*) and Premilitary Training Camp (*Wehrertüchtigungslager*) developed military skills still further.

An award ceremony on the Eastern Front. Maintenance of morale was not just a case of awarding medals. The efficient field postal service was more crucial: postage was free and letters sent from one end of Europe to the other rarely took more than a week. The daily mail call was always one of each day's high points. In addition, men received food and ammunition on a regular basis, which also helped morale. Every effort was made to provide for those wounded in battle: walking wounded made their own way to medical dressing stations, while the seriously wounded were stretchered to rear-area hospitals. Those wounded who required long-term care were shipped back to Germany in hospital trains. In addition, great efforts were made to retrieve the bodies of comrades killed in battle.

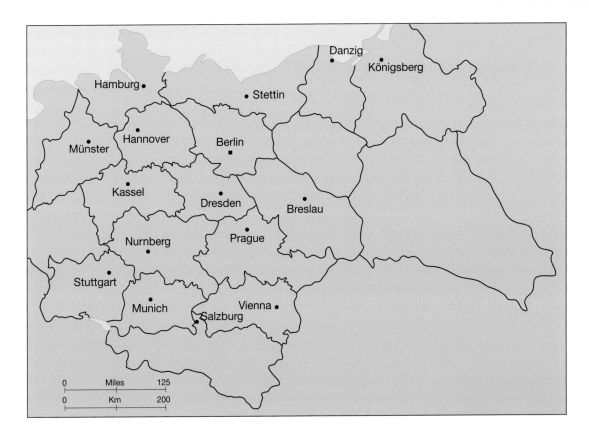

One strength of the German Army was the replacement system. Originally, each infantry regiment that went on campaign left behind at its home base a battalion cadre bearing its own number and known as its *Ersatz* (replacement) battalion. The main task of this battalion was to receive recruits, train them, and then send them to the regiment in the field. In the German Army, every unit in the field army was affiliated for personnel replacement purposes with a specific unit of the Replacement Training Army located in its own *Wehrkreisse* (home base area). Thus each *Wehrkreisse* was home to a number of regiments, which meant that the vast majority of recruits trained and fought in the company of men from their own province. The home base areas are shown above.

Following membership of the Hitler Youth, men aged between 19 and 25 would serve for six months in the *Reichsarbeitsdienst* (RAD – Reich Labor Service). Though the RAD was a measure to reduce Germany's chronic unemployment in the 1930s, members were subject to a strict disciplinary code. Since Hitler regarded the RAD as a necessary step toward rearmament, life for the draftees was highly militarized. Siegfried Knappe entered the RAD in April 1936: "An important function of Labor Service was to free the Army from having to do this very basic type of training. Everyone who went into Labor Service would enter the Army already partially trained. ... We were not permitted out of camp the first four weeks. Our four weeks of training passed quickly with drill, calisthenics, and classes; we were acquiring a general familiarity with military life."

Life in the RAD was spartan: up at 0530 hours, breakfast, followed by drill until lunch. After a 30-minute break the recruits would attend lectures, invariably on the greatness of the Third Reich and how Nazism was good for them and for Germany. More drill followed (though throughout RAD service the recruits shouldered spades, not rifles) until the recruits were discharged for supper. Individuals were expected to maintain their shiny spades and uniforms in their own "free time," which meant there was little opportunity for relaxation by the time lights went out at 2200 hours.

Work details were sent out from RAD camps to help industry and agriculture; the work was invariably hard. Siegfried Knappe describes one open-mining work detail he was assigned to: "One of our first days at work proved to be especially tiring, because the weather was very hot and humid. The work spade had worn blisters on my hands, and sweat poured from my body, making it extremely desirable to gnats, flies, and mosquitoes." On the plus side, food was good, and though many of the instructors had a sadistic streak, the vast majority of recruits reacted positively to the regime under which they were placed. The regime of strict discipline and manual labor turned out young men who were both physically and mentally honed.

After service in the RAD came two years' national service in the Wehrmacht. Thus by the age of 19 or 20, each draftee could have had around 10 years' experience of military drill, discipline, familiarity with small arms, physical fitness regimes, and working as part of small squads. This overall grounding in military skills, including taking orders, meant that Wehrmacht draftees were of a consistently higher caliber than those who entered the French, British, or American armies. They were fitter, which meant they could march longer distances, were well grounded in weapons maintenance and marksmanship, and knew how to work as part of a team, which was essential to success on the battlefield. And whereas the armies of the United States and Western Europe worked to turn raw draftees into soldiers, the Wehrmacht was able to concentrate on turning good recruits into excellent soldiers.

Basic Training

Notwithstanding their chosen arm of service, all recruits faced six weeks of intensive infantry training at the start of their Wehrmacht career. The days were long and physically demanding – up at 0500 hours and almost continuous drills and duties until lights out at 2200 hours.

Following the first six weeks, recruits then began to specialize in the particular arm of service they had opted for: artillery, infantry, or the panzer arm. Nevertheless, the mentally and physically tough regime continued. The German Army of the 1930s traced its traditions and values back to the Prussian Army of the 17th and 18th centuries, especially that of Frederick the Great (1713–86). Frederick once stated: "An army is composed for the most part of idle and inactive men. Unless the general keeps a constant eye over them ... this machine ... will soon disintegrate ... the soldier must be more afraid of his officers than of the dangers to which he is exposed." Frederick's army maintained a routine of harsh discipline and constant practice that was maintained through the subsequent centuries. For example, field exercises were held at least once a month, during which the recruits trained with live ammunition; fatalities were not uncommon.

However, one radical break from Frederician tradition was the delegation of authority to noncommissioned officers (NCOs) and even common soldiers. During the Seeckt era in the 1920s, for example, an important training manual issued to the *Reichswehr* was *Training of the Rifle Squad*, issued in December 1921. The rifle squad, consisting of a squad leader and seven riflemen, was to display initiative and aggression, especially the squad leader. In addition, in the event of several squads combining into a battle group (*Kampfgruppe*), a squad leader had to be ready to assume command and lead it into action.

Between three and four eight-man squads made up a platoon (*Zug*), with three platoons making up a company (*Kompanie*). In German infantry divisions it was also common practice to attach a machine-gun platoon to a company, thus giving a total company strength of around 120 men, though this varied during the war years. A major advantage of German company organization was that each one had a mix of rifles, machine guns, and mortars, and thus companies could be combined on an ad hoc basis without disrupting the balance of arms. A company could also fight as a self-contained unit. In addition, German soldiers were trained to fight under the command of any officer; this contrasted sharply with British units, who preferred to fight under their "own" officers.

A premium was also placed on training junior NCOs to prepare them for frontline service. Soldiers identified as possessing leadership qualities were posted to six-month courses to prepare them for junior command positions as section leaders or platoon sergeants. These were intense battle training courses, with an

"The average German soldier fought for Germany first. He accepted Hitler as leader – he had no choice ... in defeat the German soldier retained at least a modicum of pride and self-esteem. Even when every man became a prisoner, the cities lay in ruins, one-quarter of the population had become refugees, and Germany was occupied, he still knew that he had once belonged to what had been considered the best armed force in the world ... as an individual he had done his duty. He had fought and died with valor." (Charles von Luttichau, Wehrmacht soldier 1939–45)

emphasis on mundane but essential skills such as navigation, preparing and issuing orders, and battle tactics. Until the invasion of Russia these courses were largely taught at special NCO schools but, by 1942, when more than half the German Army was on active service in the East, it became the norm for these training courses to be run by regiments or divisions just behind the frontline.

In the final analysis, the German soldier was a professional par excellence. Siegfried Knappe, whom we met earlier in the chapter, had become the operations officer for LVI Panzer Corps by the war's end. On April 22, 1945, he was serving on the crumbling Eastern Front: "The Russians had torn open the front of the Fourth Panzer Army of Army Group *Schörner* near Guben and Forst and were marching behind us. We had to deal with a breakthrough between the Ninth and Third Armies through which motorized Russian infantry were streaming toward the west without resistance." He and a friend discussed making good their escape, but he realized that this would mean abandoning those men who were still fighting so desperately, and so they both remained at the front. Like tens of thousands of ordinary German infantryman, Knappe and his comrade kept on fighting – until the bitter end.

The Army and Nazism

Following the end of World War II the army liked to claim that it had nothing to do with Nazi atrocities, but the fact is that at worst it was a willing accomplice in Hitler's racial programs, and at best maintained a cowardly silence about Nazi genocide.

Field Marshal Gerd von Rundstedt benefited enormously from Nazi victories, becoming a millionaire during the Blitzkrieg victories. He cynically avoided becoming involved in anti-Hitler movements, though gave tacit support. He made sure he retained his money and privileges.

The relationship between Hitler's Nazi Party and the Germany Army was a complex and evolving one. At the top of the military were the old guard of professional officers who had helped Hitler to power in the 1930s. Many were contemptuous of the Bavarian corporal and his push toward war, but thought they could control him. Once Hitler's political scheming had given him total control of the German state and replaced the army high command with pliable men, these officers started to edge toward using violence to remove Hitler from power.

The German Army senior leadership's attitude to Hitler and his Nazi regime was moulded in the early 1930s. President Paul von Hindenburg, the World War I field marshal and father figure of the *Reichswehr*, was determined to ensure conservative forces in Germany remained in the ascendancy at the expense of left-wing groups. In cooperation with right-wing politicians, leading industrialists, and senior army commanders, Hindenburg thought Hitler and his right-wing National Socialist Party were preferable to any left-wing alternatives. Though they may have been contemptuous of Nazi racial theories and Nazi street politics, they and the army as a whole were receptive to Hitler's plans to expand the armed forces. As the military historian Matthew Cooper states: "The social composition of the Army was, after all, one that had traditionally leaned towards the right in politics. ... [National Socialism] appeared to exemplify the autocratic Germanic spirit, the return of which was eagerly awaited by so many, and to provide an alternative to the decline in the fortunes of the nation and the Army. It stood against the terms of the Versailles Treaty and for general rearmament; against the atmosphere of Marxism, socialism, and pacifism, and for the respect and glory of the Reich and its Army."

Hitler's party did not win a majority of seats in the *Reichstag* (German parliament), but the system of coalition politics meant Hindenburg was able to appoint him chancellor in January 1933. Rather than be a pliant tool of the German political establishment, Hitler set about turning the tables on them. In a series of calculated steps he at first flattered the army, then implicated it in his criminal regime, bound it to him by an oath of loyalty, and then removed any generals who might challenge his leadership. By launching a massive rearmament and expansion program Hitler appeased the generals and distracted them from his project to transform Germany into a Nazi state.

Events gathered momentum in June 1934 with the so-called "Night of the Long Knives," in which scores of Hitler's political opponents, including senior members of the Nazi *Sturmabteilung* (SA) paramilitary group, were murdered by SS firing squads loyal only to him. This was clearly an illegal act, but Hindenburg and the army high command did nothing because it suited their aims to see the SA put in its place. The generals were now accomplices to murder.

Two months later Hindenburg died, and Hitler appointed himself Führer and Reich chancellor. As head of state he bound the army to him by forcing every soldier to swear a personal oath to him: "I swear by God this sacred oath, that I will yield unconditional obedience to the Führer of the German Reich and *Volk*, Adolf Hitler, the supreme commander of the Wehrmacht, and, as a brave soldier, will be ready to lay down my life for this oath." The Germany Army was now tied inextricably to the fate of its Führer.

In 1936–38, as Hitler moved Germany inexorably toward war, he systematically undermined and removed the last senior generals who might be able to mobilize the army against him. He created the OKW to oversee the army, navy, and newly formed Luftwaffe. This move at a stroke undermined the power and influence of the army general staff, the OKH, which had traditionally been the preeminent service and hub of military power in Germany. The army commander in chief, General Werner von Fritsch, and war minister, Field Marshal Werner von Blomberg, were both forced to stand down after being smeared in trumped-up sex scandals. Hitler loyalists were appointed in their place. Blomberg had at first been an enthusiastic supporter of Hitler, and in 1934 had called upon all officers to take a personal oath of loyalty to the Führer. However, following a meeting at the Reich Chancellery on November 5, 1937, at which Hitler outlined his plans for a war to gain living space in the East (the

Field Marshal Wilhelm Keitel (above, left), Hitler's chief military adviser in World War II. He stated: "At the bottom of my heart I was a loyal shield-bearer for Adolf Hitler." He was hanged in 1946 as a war criminal.

Field Marshal Ritter von Leeb (above, center) commanded an army group during the invasion of the Soviet Union in 1941. He received a large sum of money from a grateful Führer in 1940, who then sacked him for urging a retreat in Russia after Barbarossa's failure.

Retired Army Chief of Staff General Ludwig Beck (above, right) and General Henning von Tresckow, the leaders of the anti-Nazi movement in the army, were convinced that the only way to prevent Germany being destroyed as a result of Hitler's war was to remove him from power. Beck was killed after the failed 1944 Bomb Plot.

notes taken at which later became known as the Hossbach Memorandum), he became disillusioned with Nazism. Fritsch was also at the meeting, and was equally appalled by Hitler's plans for war. Both said so, and effectively ended their military careers.

With his chosen men now controlling the army, Hitler was free to start his campaign of aggression. The Rhineland was reoccupied in 1936 and Austria seized in March 1938. Hitler's next target was Czechoslovakia's Sudetenland. As Hitler blustered and bullied the East European country into handing over the Sudetenland with its ethnic German population to him, a small group of senior officers led by General Ludwig Beck, OKH chief of staff, prepared for a coup if the crisis threatened to embroil Germany in a war with Great Britain and France. In September 1938, Great Britain and France caved in to Hitler and signed the Munich Agreement, which forced the Czechs to surrender the Sudetenland. The coup plot fizzled out.

For the next four years, as Hitler and his army rode a tide of victory, opposition to the Führer and his regime seemed hopeless. Hitler's victories in Poland, Denmark, Norway, Holland, Belgium, France, Yugoslavia, Greece, and Russia up to 1942 were the basis of the Führer's reputation for infallibility. His generals had time and again cautioned that Hitler was leading Germany to disaster, but he repeatedly emerged victorious. He was a magician who could seemingly summon victory against almost impossible odds, which made him immensely popular among the German population and the army rank and file.

Medals and Money

From 1939 to 1943 Hitler continued his drive to ensure the total loyalty of his generals. One of his aides summed up Hitler's attitude. "He [Hitler] requires from generals and officers that they are politically subservient to the state and that they carry out orders without questions. It would be easier for the men concerned – even against their inner convictions – if they received appropriate honors from the head of state and therefore felt obliged to the state."

The Führer was generous in victory. Medals were dispensed like confetti, but promotions and money were the real weaknesses of Hitler's generals. Weeks after the defeat of France, on July 19, 1940, he created 12 field marshals, the first of 23 men he would appoint to the highest rank in the Germany Army. With the rank came honor, privilege, and wealth. The annual salary of a field marshal was the equivalent of $200,000 in 2000 prices. On top of this, the new field marshals received tax-free cash sums to help them buy estates. Gerd von Rundstedt and Wilhelm Keitel received initial payments worth the equivalent of $1 million, and Ritter von Leeb benefited from a $500,000 equivalent payment. Keitel later received another payment worth more than $3 million. These were huge sums for officers who had had to endure paltry salaries during the days of the Weimar Republic. The amounts must also be compared with the average monthly salary of a Germany industrial worker, which at this time was the equivalent of $140.

The number of generals in Hitler's army had reached 2,242 by 1944, not including 150 Luftwaffe generals and the senior commanders of the Waffen-SS. Some 40 army and 10 air force generals were promoted to colonel-general, or four-star rank. High rank in the Wehrmacht meant good salaries: the equivalent of $100,000 went with the rank of major-general. Large houses and estates were also showered on the Führer's favorites. Heinz Guderian, the famous father of the panzer force, was promised an estate for his services to the Reich by the Führer. In spite of sacking him during the retreat from Moscow, Hitler kept his word, and in January 1943 the general was installed in a 947-hectare estate in eastern Germany

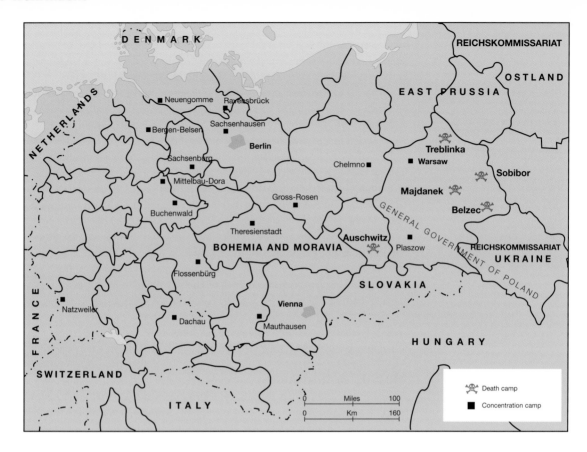

(now part of western Poland). A grateful Führer even paid for all the general's furniture and farm machinery. Not surprisingly, Guderian was eager to return to Hitler's service in 1943 as inspector general of panzer troops. In the wake of the July 1944 Bomb Plot he served Hitler as OKH chief of staff. He then called on his fellow generals to stay loyal to the Führer.

Being assigned to occupation duties in Western Europe was another perk of rank, with the best French châteaux being pressed into service as German headquarters. Field Marshal Gerd von Rundstedt lived for more than two years in a huge villa at St-Germain-en-Laye near Paris while he oversaw the German occupation of France. The cynical old field marshal took life very easy, and was not even stressed with having to make any important command decisions: they were all made at the Führer's headquarters. Rundstedt joked that he could not even change the guard at the front of his château without the permission of the "Bohemian corporal." In spite of his opposition to the Führer's conduct of the war, Rundstedt refused to join the resistance to Hitler.

Hitler also went to great lengths to implicate his generals fully in his criminal war in the East to exterminate the Jews and Slavs. The Commissar Order to deny some captured Soviet soldiers the protection of the Geneva Convention, so-called scorched-earth policies, and cooperation with the SS *Einsatzgruppen* murder squads (who had murdered 500,000 Jews by the end of 1941) were all channeled through the OKW and OKH chains of command. Hundreds of generals and senior staff officers saw these orders and signed them, before passing them on to their subordinates for action. In the East, German generals saw for themselves the fields full of starving Soviet prisoners and mass graves full of massacred Jews. Almost to a

The concentration camp network was a vast and complicated enterprise. Thousands of people were involved in the machinery of genocide, and it is inconceivable that all ranks of the army did not know what was happening to European Jewry. However, the Wehrmacht, to its eternal shame, stayed silent.

man, they chose to ignore the unpleasant side of Hitler's Reich. It was not their business to get involved in "politics" or to interfere in "local administrative issues."

Serving the Führer was not risk-free: by 1944 more than 500 German generals had been killed in action or captured by the enemy. Arbitrary dismissal was the norm for any generals who displeased Hitler. Some 35 corps and divisional commanders were dismissed after the retreat from Moscow in 1941, and after that it became almost a weekly occurrence for German generals to suffer the indignity of being removed from their command on the orders of the Führer. The lucky ones packed their bags and returned to their families to see out the war in obscurity. For those who really upset Hitler, there was the risk of imprisonment, or worse. Although executions of sacked generals did not take place until after the Bomb Plot in 1944, Hitler was no longer concerned about placating the victims' peers. He wanted revenge.

In the wake of Operation Barbarossa, the enormity of what Hitler had done by launching his invasion of Russia slowly began to dawn on a number of mainly aristocratic and professional German officers. A number of like-minded civilians, including churchmen and city mayors, began to discuss the possibility of overthrowing Hitler in a coup and negotiating a peace with the Allies.

During 1941 the conspirators began approaching senior military figures to gauge their attitude. There were few signs of support, but none of the conspirators were betrayed to Hitler's feared secret police, the Gestapo. This was a sign of things to come. The generals were notoriously fickle. On the one hand they loved to complain about Hitler's military ineptitude, but they could not bring themselves to do anything about it. They would be more than happy if someone else removed the "Hitler problem," but few generals were prepared to make the first move. The common excuse was that they were bound by their oath of loyalty. Then there was their fear of dividing the nation and army, while Germany was fighting for its life. Major-General F.W. Mellenthin's views were common: "The frontline soldiers – and we officers for the Army General Staff are proud to belong to them – were disgusted to hear of the attempt on Hitler's life and indignantly refused to approve of it: the fighting soldier did his duty to the bitter end."

Bomb Plots

Some generals also expressed horror at the idea of an unconstitutional coup in case this undermined the political neutrality of the army. At the heart of the problem was the fact that many German generals had grown rich and powerful thanks to Hitler, and felt they owed him their loyalty. In January 1943, in the wake of the defeat at Stalingrad, the conspirators approached Guderian for his support, but went away empty handed. The general was in the middle of negotiating with Hitler a gift of the equivalent of several hundred thousand dollars with which to buy an estate.

The conspiracy gathered momentum in early 1943, when the first serious attempt was made to kill Hitler as he flew to a meeting with senior generals in Russia. General Henning von Tresckow's adjutant, Dr. Fabian von Schlabrendorff, placed a bomb disguised as a bottle of brandy on Hitler's aircraft, but the fuse malfunctioned and the bomb did not explode. Fortunately the bomb was not discovered and the conspiracy remained a secret from the Gestapo, which was in the process of arresting and torturing anti-Nazi groups in civilian society, and Admiral Wilhelm Canaris, the chief of the *Abwehr*, German military intelligence.

There then followed the Suicide Bomb Plots, in which the conspirators planned to kill Hitler by getting close to him and detonating bombs concealed in their uniforms. Several attempts were made, but they all failed.

The Wehrmacht

Tresckow was now joined by Colonel Count Claus von Stauffenberg in his efforts to organize a more widely based coup. The colonel was chief of staff to the head of the Replacement Army, which controlled all the army units in and around Berlin. The military governor of France, Colonel-General Heinrich von Stulpnagel, agreed to join the plot and seize control of Paris. Field Marshal Hans von Kluge, commander in chief in the West, offered lukewarm support.

When ordered to the Wolf's Lair in East Prussia for an OKW conference on July 20, 1944, the colonel packed a suitcase with captured British explosives. With supreme coolness, Stauffenberg managed to smuggle the briefcase into the conference room and place it a few feet from Hitler. Fate intervened and a large table leg absorbed most of the blast. Four officers were killed, but the Führer only received minor injuries. In Berlin, units loyal to Hitler quickly regained control and many of the conspirators were summarily executed. Others took their own lives – they were the lucky ones.

Now in charge of the OKH bunker complex in Zossen, south of Berlin, Guderian was given the dubious task of demonstrating the army's loyalty to its Führer. The Nazi salute was adopted by the army. Formation of the *Volkssturm* home guard was entrusted to Martin Bormann and the Nazi Party. Nazi indoctrination of the troops was intensified. Given Hitler's thirst for vengeance after the Bomb Plot, Guderian and other generals, such as Rundstedt, who had to serve on the Honor Court, had little choice but to do their master's bidding. The whole episode cast a black stain on the reputations of those involved. However, it removed once and for all the illusions that the German Army was a nonpolitical organization. It was now thoroughly Hitler's army, from the bottom to the very top. And it is as well to remember that the various attempts against Hitler's life were carried out by a small minority of German officers. The vast majority of the army remained loyal, turned a blind eye to atrocities, and continued to serve their maniacal leader.

A wounded Hitler clutches his arm following the abortive assassination attempt in July 1944. The aftermath of the July Bomb Plot was disastrous for those officers caught up in it, and for many more only tenuously associated with the plan. In the following days the Gestapo rounded up thousands of suspects, including several hundred army officers. Hitler ordered his newly appointed OKH chief of staff, Guderian, to hold so-called Honor Courts to dismiss conspirators from the army. The victims were then handed over to Nazi Party courts, headed by the notorious demagogue Judge Roland Freisler. This was a classic show trial, and defendants, including a number of field marshals, had to stand in court holding up their trousers because their belts and suspenders had been removed. Their false teeth were also confiscated, adding to their humiliation. All the accused were found guilty. The bulk, including 35 army generals, were executed in August 1944 in a grisly circus. Stripped naked, they were hanged on piano cable in front of movie cameras that recorded the spectacle for later viewing by the Führer.

PART IV

THE YEARS OF DEFENSE

Triumph of Improvisation

Field Marshal Albert Kesselring's campaign in Italy was a masterful exercise of defense at the strategic, operational, and tactical levels. With limited equipment and manpower levels, he was able to tie down hundreds of thousands of Allied troops in a grim war of attrition.

The Italian campaign was by far the German Army's most successful prolonged defensive effort of the war. From the first British and American landings in Sicily in July 1943 to just before the final surrender in May 1945, the outnumbered German units, led by the redoubtable Field Marshal Albert Kesselring, always held the line and prevented the Allies achieving a decisive breakthrough.

After the surrender of 275,000 German and Italian troops in Tunisia in May 1943, the next target for the Allies was Italy. At the Casablanca Conference in January 1943, Allied leaders decided to begin preparations for amphibious operations to land troops in Italy with the aim of knocking Germany's Axis ally out of the war. This would open up the Mediterranean for Allied shipping and draw German troops away from the Eastern Front. By attacking in Italy it was hoped to answer Soviet calls for a second front in the West. Operation Husky began on July 10 with a massive airborne and amphibious landing by 180,000 British and American troops on the island of Sicily. Waiting to repulse the invasion were 130,000 Italian and 30,000 German troops. The latter were veterans of the 15th Panzergrenadier and *Hermann Göring* Panzer Divisions. The Italian troops put up half-hearted resistance, but the German troops, led by General Frido von Senger und Etterlin, gave the Allies a bloody nose. German airborne forces joined the battle along with General Hans Hube's XIV Panzer Corps. Italian troops started surrendering en masse, and this was soon followed by a *coup d'état* that overthrew the fascist dictator Benito Mussolini. American troops led by Lieutenant-General George Patton outflanked the German defenses, and Kesselring, then the German commander in southern Italy, ordered a withdrawal to the mainland in early August. A skillful retreat allowed the bulk of the German forces, 60,000 troops,

German artillery in a vineyard in southern Italy in September 1943. In general, German units and commanders reacted more rapidly to changing situations than did their Allied opponents. In this way they were able to slow the Allied advance north.

to escape with their equipment. Kesselring's men inflicted almost 20,000 casualties on the Allies, but 134,000 Italians surrendered.

Italian disatisfaction with the Axis cause culminated with the overthrow of Mussolini on July 25, 1943. A temporary, and ostensibly pro-Axis, regime was established under Marshal Pierto Badoglio, but it capitulated to the Allies on September 8. For their part, Hitler and Kesselring were aware of the wavering support of the Italians, and had been steadily moving troops into the country to preempt any Italian desertion. British troops crossed the Straits of Messina from Sicily and headed north up the "toe" of Italy." In the first week of September the Germans struck, seizing key points in Rome and throughout the country, while the Allies landed their Fifth Army south of Naples at Salerno on the 9th to try to cut off the retreat of Kesselring's troops northward to Rome.

The Germans reacted quickly, sealing off the Allied beachhead with panzer troops and then almost pushing the British and American troops back into the sea. Only a last-ditch defense backed up with fire support from Allied battleships offshore stopped Kesselring's attack. Although the Allies managed to hold on by their fingertips, the Germans had gained valuable time to withdraw the bulk of their forces in good order to the Gustav Line south of Rome.

Holding the Line

Kesselring's troops held the Gustav Line position until late May 1944 against an almost continuous series of Allied attacks. Time and again the Allies were repulsed with heavy casualties. Monte Cassino was the key to the German defenses, and it proved a particularly tough nut for the Allies to crack. To break the stalemate, the Allies tried to bypass the Gustav Line by staging another amphibious landing at Anzio in January 1944. This was the last major amphibious operation the Allies were to mount in Italy because of the need to move the bulk of their specialist craft and shipping to England to support the planned Normandy landings.

Again, Kesselring was able to muster forces to contain and then attack the new Allied bridgehead. Allied troops were never able to advance to seize Rome in the days after the initial landing. The Italian capital would have to wait five months, until the Gustav Line was cleared, for its liberation.

Kesselring, as always, was one step ahead of the Allies and he had already begun preparing a series of fall-back positions to the north. The Allies made a major attempt to break through Kesselring's Gothic Line in September 1944, but the result was another bloody stalemate until the winter weather brought the fighting to a halt. The concentration of the Allies on northwest Europe during the winter of 1944 meant their forces in Italy were not able to contemplate another offensive until the spring of 1945.

When the Allies attacked on April 9, the Germans again put up strong resistance, but British tanks finally broke through their lines south of the Po River. The British 6th Armoured Division led the pursuit of the now demoralized German forces, who were retreating northward as fast as they could. This time there was no defensive line to fall back on. The road to the Austrian border was open, while Italian partisans staged an insurrection and seized Milan and Venice.

Kesselring had by this point been posted to the Rhine, so his successor, Heinrich von Vietinghoff, opened surrender negotiations with the Allies. On April 29 the surrender was concluded, a day before Hitler's suicide in Berlin, and a million German soldiers in Italy, the Balkans, and Austria were to lay down their arms by May 2.

A major factor in the thwarting of Allied plans for a swift victory in Italy was the quality of German generalship throughout the campaign. Under the overall leadership of Kesselring, the German army in Italy was led by a number of very talented and effective generals.

Kesselring was an unlikely figure to emerge as one of Germany's most successful ground commanders. Known to his men as "Smiling Albert" because

Field Marshal Albert Kesselring (far right), German commander in Italy. It was during the defense of Sicily in July 1943 that Kesselring came into his own. Hurling furious counterattacks against the Allied invasion beaches, he at first contained the British and Americans. Then, through improvised ferries across the Straits of Messina, Kesselring bolstered his defenses with panzer reinforcements. On the Italian mainland he continued to conduct a skillful defense against great odds.

of his eternal optimism and cheesy smile, he had served as an artillery officer during World War I and rose to be a *Reichswehr* divisional commander during the early 1930s. His career was not going anywhere, so in 1933 he transferred to the newly formed Luftwaffe. Success leading the Second Air Fleet during the invasion of France led to promotion to field marshal in July 1940. Further successes in Russia during 1941 brought Kesselring to the attention of Hitler and a number of senior officers close to the Führer, including Colonel-General Alfred Jodl, chief of the OKW operations branch. Having friends in high places helped Kesselring's career, and in December he was appointed commander in chief South, to run the war in North Africa and the Mediterranean theater. Despite having good relations with Erwin Rommel, the commander of the famous Africa Corps, the campaign against the British Eighth Army was constantly dogged by interference from Hitler, culminating in the Führer's decision to reinforce Tunisia in early 1943, which resulted in the loss of over 200,000 men.

When the Allied material and manpower supremacy began to wear down his defense on Sicily, Kesselring organized a deliberate retreat through a series of prepared positions. The Allies tried to bypass his defense lines with a series of amphibious landings, but he was constantly one step ahead of them. He also began organizing the withdrawal of his troops from Sicily, despite Hitler's usual insistence on fighting to the last man. Thanks to his influence with the Führer, Kesselring was at last able to persuade him of the necessity of pulling out the outnumbered Germans from Sicily. General Hube, who only six months earlier had been one of the last men to be flown out of the doomed Stalingrad Pocket in Russia, took charge of the evacuation and ferried 40,000 German troops, 9,905 vehicles, 47 tanks, 94 artillery pieces, and 17,000 tons (17,272 tonnes) of ammunition to safety on the Italian mainland.

Over the next month, political intrigues with the Italians, who were on the verge of changing sides, preoccupied Kesselring. He was now appointed commander of Army Group C in central and southern Italy. In cooperation with Rommel, who was now in charge of a reserve army group based in the Austrian Alps, Kesselring organized a series of coups to seize control of Italy before the Allies. His planning was thorough and took the Italians totally by surprise, and his paratroopers manage to seize airfields around Rome as the Italian government was locked in meetings with Allied peace emissaries.

The September 9 landings at Salerno also prompted a rapid response by Kesselring, who quickly realized the importance of containing the Allies if German forces in southern Italy were not to be cut off. In a matter of hours, Kesselring had issued orders for a panzer corps to be dispatched to reinforce the German troops ringing the invasion beaches. Within three days Kesselring had six panzer and panzergrenadier divisions in the line around the bridgehead. This rapid improvisation totally confounded the Allies. Their troops were soon fighting for their lives and Lieutenant-General Mark Clark, the American commander of the bridgehead, even issued orders to prepare to evacuate his men. For the next two days it looked as though the Germans would succeed in driving the Allies into the sea. When it was clear the counterattack was not going to succeed, Kesselring ordered another of his famous deliberate withdrawals.

The Battle for Rome

Kesselring's troops were able to escape again, and within weeks the Allied advance was stopped dead in its tracks at the Gustav Line in December 1943. The battle to defend Rome was perhaps Kesselring's finest hour. The Italian capital was held for another six months, thanks to his prompt action to seal off the Allied bridgehead at Anzio. In a repeat performance of the Salerno battles, Kesselring mobilized the German Fourteenth Army, with eight infantry and five panzergrenadier divisions, to destroy the bridgehead within four days of the first landings on January 24, 1944. When Allied troops eventually advanced out of the bridgehead on January 29 they were met with a hail of artillery and machine-gun fire. Within a week, Kesselring's 125,000 troops were counterattacking. The attacks were led by a number of panzer units, including a company of 11 Ferdinand super-heavy assault guns, a regiment of 76 Panther tanks, a battalion of 45 Tiger tanks, and more than 85 assault guns.

Any idea that the Allies were going to be in Rome in a matter of days was now out of the question. Nazi propaganda rejoiced in telling the world that the bridgehead was now a "death head." The German attack could not totally destroy the bridgehead, but a bloody stalemate ensued for months. Given the strategic situation, this was a major success for the outnumbered and outgunned German forces in Italy. Allied casualties were enormous: the US Fifth Army lost 30,000 men, the British some 12,000. The Germans lost 25,000 men.

In the end it was steady pressure on the Gustav Line at Monte Cassino that broke the German defense. With his troops about to be cut off around Monte Cassino, Kesselring ordered another withdrawal. This time he paused at a series

American B-25s on their way to bomb German positions at Anzio, February 1944. Inhospitable terrain and lengthy periods of static warfare went a long way to reducing the effectiveness of Allied air superiority in Italy.

of delaying positions both south and north of Rome, until his troops were safe in the Gothic Line to the south of Bologna in mid-August. Allied troops followed closely on the heels of Kesselring's men, but he managed to evade every attempt to trap them.

The delaying actions of his troops bought Kesselring time to turn the Gothic Line into a death trap for Allied troops. It boasted 30 emplaced tank turrets, 100 steel shelters, 23,786 machine-gun posts, 479 antitank guns, and 75 miles (120 km) of barbed wire in a 10-mile (16-km) deep minefield and obstacle belt. Allied troops began their attack on the Gothic Line on August 26. The British Eighth Army looked close to making a breakthrough, but Kesselring managed to deploy three divisions from other sectors to seal the breach in the line. Three weeks later the attack had bogged down into another stalemate, with the British losing 14,000 dead, wounded, or missing, along with 200 destroyed tanks. These battles ensured that the Allies would not be able to break into the Po Valley before winter and threaten the Austrian border. It would be eight months before Kesselring's troops would finally be defeated.

Fortunately for Kesselring, Hitler took little interest in the Italian campaign and generally left his subordinate to run things how he felt best. The Führer's most famous interventions were during the Anzio battles, when he micromanaged one attack that ended in a bloody debacle. During the April 1945 battles along the Po Valley Hitler was quick to issue his orders to fight to the last man, but by this point in the war such instructions made little difference to the situation on the ground.

The field marshal was also fortunate to have under his command some of the German Army's best field commanders and staff officers. Kesselring benefited

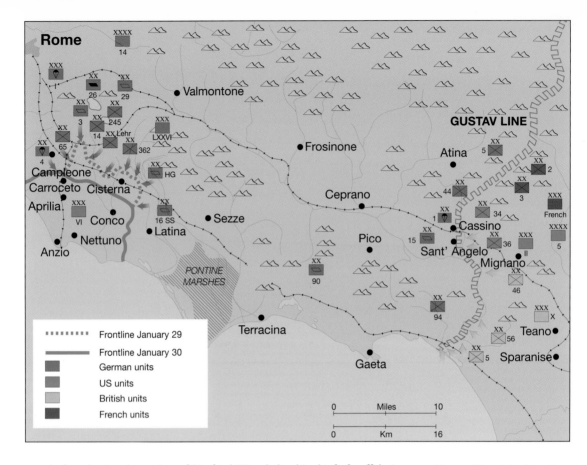

Frontline January 29
Frontline January 30
German units
US units
British units
French units

greatly from having the services of Siegfried Westphal as his chief of staff during the period from mid-1943 through to the spring of 1944. This superb staff officer was one of the main reasons why Kesselring was about to achieve many of his battlefield "conjuring tricks."

General Heinrich von Vietinghoff, commander of the Tenth Army, was a solid, if not ostentatious, former Prussian guardsman. He led the attack on the Salerno bridgehead that very nearly drove the Allies back into the sea. Later he masterminded the defense of the Gothic Line against the British attack in September 1944. The general was a by-the-book officer who was ruthlessly efficient. His attack and defense tactics were methodical, which was just what was required during the German retreat up the Italian peninsula.

One of Kesselring's most talented subordinates was the one-armed Hans Hube. His evacuation of Sicily was masterful, and he later repeated the exercise in southern Italy after the British crossed the Straits of Messina. He held up the Allies for several weeks, giving Vietinghoff time to hammer the Salerno bridgehead.

Hube was replaced as commander of XIV Panzer Corps by Senger in October 1943, just as the Monte Cassino battle was starting to hot up. Senger was a daring panzer commander who had earned his spurs on the Eastern Front and soon turned the Gustav Line around Cassino into a veritable fortress. The Gustav Line was, in fact, an in-depth defensive position with a number of sub-positions, such as the Winter and Bernhard Lines. Senger became the master of defense, forcing the Allies to waste precious time and casualties assaulting these sub-positions before they could even get near the main position. An American frontal river

The position at Anzio and Cassino in early 1944 following the landings on January 22. Major-General John Lucas was probably too cautious during the first six days of the Anzio landing. In those vital days the road to Rome was wide open with no Germans to be seen, but Lucas spent the time building up his supply dumps. When he did move forward on January 29, his troops ran into hastily assembled German troops. The result was a massacre, and the Anzio enterprise was set to degenerate into a bloody stalemate that lasted four long months.

assault across the Rapido on January 20, 1944, was repulsed for the loss of 400 dead and 500 prisoners among the 36th (Texas) Division.

Not only were senior German officers in Italy of high quality, but divisional commanders were also among some of the most talented in the Wehrmacht. The 90th Panzergrenadier Division was led in 1943–44 by the eccentric Ernst Baade. He defended the Cassino Front during the first phase of the battle with great skill. His troops loved his foibles, such as going into battle wearing a Scottish plaid kilt, or radioing his American opponents across the line to wish them a Happy New Year.

Baade's successor in command of the Cassino Front was Richard Heinrich, commander of the Luftwaffe's 1st Parachute or *Fallschirmjäger* Division. Its defense of Cassino was legendary and its success was in no small part due to Heidrich's leadership and skill.

Veteran Troops

As well as excellent commanders, Kesselring benefited from possessing a number of veteran divisions that were better trained, equipped, and led than their Allied opponents. Kesselring took great pains to ensure that his troops and divisions were not destroyed in battles of encirclement, as had happened in France or on the Eastern Front. Until the final battles along the Gothic Line, casualties among his divisions had generally been replaced. In late 1944 and the spring of 1945, however, the Italian Front was stripped of a number of key units, and losses incurred during the fall were not replaced.

The most powerful German division to see service in Italy was Luftwaffe's *Hermann Göring* (HG) Panzer Division. It was named after the flamboyant chief of the Luftwaffe, and its presence in Italy had much to do with his political support for Kesselring as the only Luftwaffe officer who commanded a major theater of operations. The prestige of the Luftwaffe was at stake in the Mediterranean, and Göring was keen to ensure his protégé was not short of men and equipment.

The original *Hermann Göring* Regiment was expanded to divisional strength in January 1943 as part of Göring's contribution to solving the German Army's manpower shortage because of losses on the Eastern Front. This expansion took place at the same time that Göring ordered the raising of the Luftwaffe field divisions. The latter formations proved to have limited fighting abilities, but the HG Division was a very different beast. It was an all-volunteer force rather than press-ganged aircraft mechanics, and developed a formidable combat reputation. Some elements of the division were sent to Tunisia and lost during the first half of 1943. By the time of the invasion of Sicily those units not sent to Africa had been reinforced to allow the formation of two powerful *Kampfgruppen* (battle groups) to be put into the field to oppose Operation Husky. One *Kampfgruppe* was formed around the HG Panzer Regiment, which fielded three battalions, containing 29 assault guns, 46 Panzer IIIs, and 32 Panzer IVs. A company of the army's 508 Heavy Panzer Battalion was attached with 17 Tiger I tanks. The other *Kampfgruppe* contained a strong contingent of 88mm Flak guns, which were deadly when employed in the antitank role against thinly armored Allied tanks.

Many of the recruits to the division had never seen action before, and in its first engagement with the Americans some troops panicked, but swift action by Lieutenant-General Paul Conrath, their commander, calmed the situation. For the rest of the Sicilian campaign the division fought well and soon gained a good reputation. One of its attacks inflicted heavy casualties on the US 1st Division,

Special Weapons at Anzio

To Allied troops hunkered down in the precarious Anzio beachhead during January 1944, she was known as "Anzio Annie." To German troops pressing to eliminate the Allied toehold on the Italian coast, the Krupp K-5 280mm-caliber railway gun was affectionately nicknamed "Slim Berthe."

The German commander in Italy, Field Marshal Albert Kesselring, was determined to drive the Allies back into the sea, so he ringed Anzio with massive firepower to support a series of determined ground offensives. "Anzio Annie" was a major part of Kesselring's fire plan and operated from a tunnel in the Alban Hills, south of Rome. It was wheeled out at night to fire deadly barrages into the bridgehead before retreating underground during daylight to avoid detection and destruction by Allied reconnaissance aircraft and bombers.

Everything about the weapon was staggering. The gun and its carriage alone weighed 218 tons (221 tonnes). Each shell weighed in at 561 lb (255 kg) and could be fired up to a range of 38 miles (61 km).

"Anzio Annie" was part of a major German interdiction campaign to bring the whole Allied beachhead under fire and allow its beleaguered defenders no respite from fire. The tactics had been used to great effect on the Russian Front during the sieges of Sevastopol (1941–42) and Leningrad (1941–44).

At the height of the fighting for the bridgehead in January and February 1944, Allied troops were hanging on precariously to an area 12 miles (19.2 km) wide by 6 miles (9.6 km) deep on the Italian coast. With some Allied units suffering more than 50 percent casualties, morale was starting to crumble. When combined with regular salvos from "Anzio Annie" at beach landing zones, which were the bridgehead's only lifeline, Allied morale sank even further.

The Germans were not content with merely hitting land targets at Anzio, and so the Luftwaffe was called into action, with its new guided 3,300-lb (1,500-kg) Fx-1400 or Fritz X and 1,100-lb (500-kg) Henschel Hs 293 glider bombs, to devastate the Allied armada supporting the landing force. An operator in the launch aircraft, usually a Dornier Do 217 bomber, guided the bomb to its target by radio command signals. The first attacks on January 23 sank a British destroyer and a hospital ship.

Frontline Allied positions were attacked by robot bombs, called Goliaths. These remote-controlled tracked vehicles were sent forward from German positions with command signals issued down a 6,561-ft (2,000-m) cable that trailed out behind the 2-ft-high (60 cm) Goliath. Once in position, the operator detonated the vehicle's 200-lb (91-kg) warhead. After the initial surprise of seeing the Goliaths, Allied troops soon learned to counter them with light antitank weapons or concentrated heavy machine-gun fire.

and its Tigers broke through to the sea and exchanged shots with an American destroyer! The division, invariably outnumbered, suffered heavy tank casualties in engagements with Allied Shermans, and by the time it pulled back to the mainland it had lost half its tanks and assault guns. Only one of the Tigers could be ferried back to Italy. The division was rebuilt to near full establishment in time to play a leading part in the counterattack at Salerno.

During the Gustav Line battles, Kesselring kept the HG Division in reserve near Rome to counter any Allied amphibious operations aimed at bypassing defensive positions. After the landing at Anzio the division was dispatched to contain and then smash the bridgehead. Its 35 Panzer IIIs, 27 Panzer IVs, and 14 StuG III assault guns were in the forefront of the German attacks that rained down on the Allied lines in February 1944. The boggy terrain meant the German armor was not able to operate freely, however, and the battle degenerated into costly duels with emplaced Allied Shermans.

With the Anzio beachhead stalemated, Kesselring pulled the division out of the line to refit and act as his reserve near Rome in case of another Allied amphibious landing. It was ordered south in late May to act as a rearguard to allow the Tenth Army retreating northward from Cassino to escape past Rome. It was badly shot up by Allied fighter-bombers while moving southward in daylight and suffered heavy losses holding the so-called Caesar Line south of the Italian capital. After the fall of Rome the HG Division joined the retreat northward. The success of the Soviet offensive in the central sector of the Russian Front in June forced Hitler to cull Kesselring's command for reinforcements, and the HG

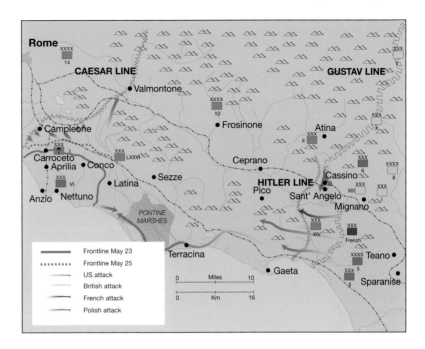

The breaking of the Gustav Line. The victory was an incomplete one because Lieutenant-General Mark Clark, commander of the US Fifth Army, allowed most of Kesselring's troops to escape from the Cassino Front in 1944. When a two-pronged assault finally broke through at Anzio and north of Cassino, the bulk of Kesselring's elite troops, including his 1st Parachute Division and all his panzergrenadier divisions, were at the mercy of Allied pincers. Rather than take a key road junction and block the German's escape route, Clark ordered his armor to head for Rome on June 5. The American general was keen to gain the glory of capturing the first Axis capital before the D-Day landings, which began on the following day, totally eclipsed the importance of the Italian theater. Without these German troops that had escaped safely, the defense of the Gothic Line would have been impossible.

Division was packed on trains for East Prussia. Denied powerful units such as the HG Division, Kesselring's command was badly weakened.

Other effective units under Kesselring's command were his two parachute divisions, the 1st and 4th. The 1st Parachute Division was the Luftwaffe's elite unit and many of its regiments had spearheaded the invasion of Crete two years before. It was formed as the OKW strategic reserve, based in southern France, and was held ready to intervene throughout the Mediterranean theater. It was still fully jump-trained, and one of its regiments actually parachuted into action during the Sicilian campaign. Under the command of the famous General Heinrich, it was in continuous action during the retreat to the Gustav Line, acquitting itself very well. One battalion was detached to fight at Salerno, force-marched to the front in a day, and then captured more than 2,000 British troops.

Elements of the division were first committed to defend Monte Cassino in February 1944, alongside the 90th Panzergrenadier Division. Heinrich's elite troops assumed full responsibility for defending the key sector of the Gustav Line during March, and for two more months the paratroopers held off an overwhelming force of Allied troops, inflicting tens of thousands of casualties on the attackers. Cassino was an epic battle. The German defenders endured daily bombardments by thousands of guns and waves of bombers, hiding by day in caves and deep bunkers before emerging at night to rebuild their fortifications or mount counterattacks.

The 4th Parachute Division was not fully jump-trained but was formed during late 1943 out of cadres from the 2nd Parachute Division and batches of new recruits. It fought well at Anzio, spearheading many of the attacks against the bridgehead. Both of the parachute divisions remained in Italy for the remainder of the war, putting up strong resistance in the battle for the Gothic Line, thanks to the strong cadres of veterans who remained in their ranks to stiffen up the thousands of new recruits who were sent to them.

Two army panzer divisions were sent to Italy, the 16th and 26th. The 16th Panzer Division made only a brief contribution to the Italian campaign during the fall of 1943, although its stout defense of Salerno before the arrival of

Kesselring's main counterattack force arrived is credited with containing the Allied bridgehead. The action cost it two-thirds of its tanks. The 26th Panzer Division was a permanent feature of Kesselring's command, fighting at Salerno, Anzio, and on the Gothic Line. It boasted a very strong panzer regiment with 80 Panzer IVs, 23 Panzer IIIs, and 14 StuG III assault guns in January 1944.

The remainder of Kesselring's armored units were made up of panzergrenadier divisions, which boasted a battalion of either panzers or assault guns, though they rarely mustered more than 40 fully operational tanks or assault guns at any one time. The 3rd, 15th, 29th, and 90th Panzergrenadier Divisions, along with the 16th SS Panzergrenadier Division, were all hard-fighting units that put up good performances whenever Kesselring called them into action. While the 15th and 90th Divisions played key parts in the defense of the Monte Cassino position, Kesselring's other panzergrenadier divisions were thrown into the Anzio battles. During the summer and fall of 1944, the 3rd and 15th Divisions, along with the 16th SS Division, were ordered to the Western and Eastern Fronts, reducing Kesselring's armored force by more than half. At the end of the war only the 26th Panzer and the 29th and 90th Panzergrenadier Divisions were in Italy, and they lacked the strength to counter the British armored breakthrough to the Po Valley in April 1945.

Kesselring was also fortunate to have a solid backbone of 12 to 14 German infantry and mountain divisions available to him throughout the campaign. These were professional outfits, and in the final year of the war only three had been denuded of men to form Volksgrenadier Divisions. Unlike in other theaters of war, German forces were never caught in pockets in Italy because Kesselring was always able, at the last minute, to pull his troops out of Allied encircling moves. This meant that, despite suffering heavy casualties, German divisions in Italy were always able to retain intact their core cadre of commanders and

German paratroopers on their way to the Anzio bridgehead. Kesselring had much going in his favor in Italy: high-quality troops and commanders, plus a terrain and climate beneficial to defense, but he was also fortunate not be facing overwhelming Allied forces. The Allied troops in Italy were also of very mixed quality, and only a fraction of the troops facing the Germans during 1944 could be considered top of the line. By the time of the battles along the Gustav Line in early 1944, the majority of the veteran divisions that had spearheaded the invasion of Sicily and southern Italy, such as the famous British "Desert Rats" 7th Armoured Division, had been pulled back to Great Britain in preparation for the D-Day invasion of northwest Europe.

Airborne Operations

During the 1943 defensive battles in Italy and Greece the Germans made use of airborne forces on a number of occasions to make strategic interventions. During the spring of 1943, the Luftwaffe concentrated a strategic reserve of airborne troops in southern France ready to counter expected Allied landings throughout the Mediterranean region.

The Allied landings in Sicily in July 1943 provided the first opportunity for the airborne forces to show their strategic utility. The 3rd *Fallschirmjäger* (Parachute) Regiment parachuted into Sicily to seize Catania, which was being threatened by a British armored thrust. Two days later British paratroopers were dropped behind their German counterparts' positions, leading to heavy fighting between the two elite forces.

Barely a month later, the Italian dictator Benito Mussolini was overthrown in a coup, prompting German intervention to seize Rome and other key cities in Italy. Under the leadership of the father of Germany's airborne forces, General Kurt Student, strategic reserve airborne units were flown to seize key airfields around Rome. A surprise parachute drop also overwhelmed the Italian army headquarters on the outskirts of the Italian capital, achieved with minimal casualties.

In another *coup de main*, a German parachute battalion seized the island of Elba, capturing 10,000 bemused Italian soldiers in the process. The culmination of these operations was the rescue of Mussolini himself by German paratroops under the command of the *SS-Hauptsturmführer* Otto Skorzeny from his mountain-top prison at Gran Sasso.

To take advantage of the chaos caused by the Italian surrender, British Prime Minister Winston Churchill ordered British troops to seize the Dodecanese islands on the eastern fringe of the Aegean Sea from their now nominally pro-Allied Italian garrisons. The Americans refused to support the British move with their strong Mediterranean air forces, so the newly seized islands were vulnerable to German countermoves. In battalion-sized air drops, German paratroopers landed on first Kos and then Leros ahead of larger amphibious forces. In a repeat of the 1941 battle for Crete, the German paratroopers suffered heavy losses – more than 60 percent during the initial landings – but were soon able to turn the tables on isolated British contingents.

Antipartisan operations in Yugoslavia were a major concern of the German commanders in the Mediterranean because of the country's position, astride their lines of communications to Greece. Ever-increasing numbers of Axis troops were sucked into the war against Tito's communist partisans. In May 1944, the German High Command tried to wipe out Tito's headquarters at Drvar in a surprise airborne raid by 900 SS paratroopers. The daring raid inflicted heavy casualties on the partisans, but Tito eluded the Germans during the confusion after the battle. Nevertheless, it was another daring example of the use of airborne units.

specialists, particularly artillery men, so that the formations could be quickly rebuilt with new drafts of troops from training depots in Germany. This was essential to retaining the fighting power of infantry divisions.

Kesselring's most important ally during the Italian campaign was the country's unforgiving terrain and climate. Throughout the two-year campaign the German defenders were able time and again to skillfully exploit Italy's mountain ranges, river valleys, and waterlogged lowlands to delay and frustrate Allied attempts to create a decisive breakthrough. The Germans were further assisted by Italy's climate, which at crucial points during the campaign intervened to close down the Allied advance.

For the Allied troops leading the invasion of Italy in the summer of 1943 the country's terrain came as a big surprise. Their previous combat experience had been in the deserts of North Africa, where tanks had been able to undertake wide outflanking maneuvers. It took them many months to adapt to the Italian terrain, and during that time the Germans were able to inflict heavy casualties and, in many cases, dictate the course of battle. Italy, however, is geographically a very diverse country, and the Allies soon learnt that tactics that worked in Sicily did not work in the mountains south of Rome, forcing them to reassess constantly their battle plans. This constant learning process worked in the Germans' favor because they always retreated to defensive positions on terrain of their own choosing, giving them an advantage over the Allies, who were always advancing into unfamiliar terrain.

Defensive Lines

Italy's mountainous terrain was ideally suited to the defensive tactics employed by the Germans to hold back Allied forces trying to penetrate the Third Reich's "soft underbelly." With names like Gustav, Bernard, Rome, Caesar, Albert, and Gothic, the German defensive positions in Italy were treated with great respect by the Allied soldiers and commanders who had to attack them.

Unlike the famous Siegfried Line and West Wall in northwest Europe, German positions in Italy never had the same amount of material resources devoted to them. German commanders had to make maximum use of the terrain, minefields, and earthwork defenses. Improvisation was the name of the game, with the turrets of disabled Panther tanks pressed into service as fixed pillboxes.

The key to the success of the German defensive lines was the skillful sighting of positions along natural obstacles, such as rivers and high mountain ridges. Every approach route was blocked by minefields and covered by artillery or machine guns. Control of the high ground meant that German artillery fire was always expertly directed onto its targets.

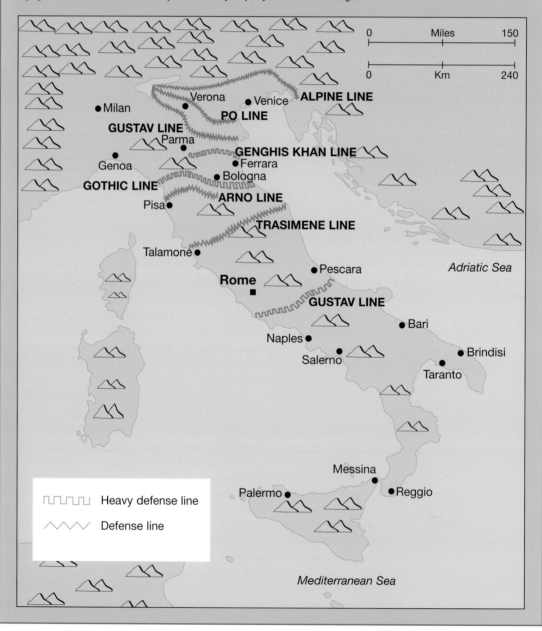

British troops examine the turret of a German Panther tank that has been dug into the ground as part of the Gothic Line defenses. Note the excellent view it commands of the surrounding terrain.

The Allied landing at Salerno ran straight into the German 16th Panzer Division, which was positioned in the heights above the invasion beaches. This was the first time the Allies had faced quality troops in an opposed beach landing, and it taught them many lessons that were put to use the following year during the D-Day landings. The German troops held a ring of high ground around the British and American invasion beaches, and positioned their artillery observers to good advantage. Allied troops were met with a hail of artillery fire as they struggled inland, then waves of panzers and panzergrenadiers stormed forward to counterattack, hidden from view and from Allied artillery fire by a series of winding gullies. Only when the Germans reached the edge of the landing beaches were they exposed to Allied naval gunfire and stopped in their tracks.

Monte Cassino rises 1,968 ft (600 m) above the Liri Valley. It dominated the route north from Naples to Rome, effectively blocking the Allied advance to the Italian capital. Kesselring turned the mountain, which had a Benedictine monastery perched near its summit, into the center of the Gustav Line. In front of the mountain was the town of Cassino, which lay in the Garigliano Valley. This wide river was downstream of the Rapido River, which, as its name suggests, flowed very fast during the winter months. In the first months of 1944, when the Cassino battles were at their height, the Garigliano/Rapido was in full flood and provided an almost uncrossable obstacle to Allied troops trying to begin their assault on the Gustav Line. Allied assault boats were swept downstream by the river and engineers were unable to build assault bridges to bring across tanks and artillery. Bridging sites in the deep river gorges were rare and easily pinpointed by German artillery observers, which only added to the difficulties facing Allied troops trying to cross fast-flowing water in freezing winter conditions.

Once the Allied troops had crossed the river they found Kesselring's troops dug in on top of a series of open ridges, from which came a relentless hail of German machine-gun, mortar, and artillery fire. The steep hillsides also prevented Allied tanks from keeping up with the assault infantry, further hindering the pace of the advance. A few miles behind the main German position at Cassino was Monte Cairo, which rose more than 3,280 ft. (1,000 m) above the Liri Valley and provided German artillery observers with a superb view of Allied positions, ensuring the defenders were never taken by surprise.

The Allies tried to counterattack German defenses by employing overwhelming firepower, but the mountain side was covered in deep caves and gullies that allowed the German defenders to seek cover from even the heaviest artillery barrages and bomber raids. After several weeks the Allies' dependence on their firepower started to suffer diminishing returns. The town of Cassino and the monastery on the hill behind it were reduced to ruins that provided even more cover for the Germans and only added to the problems of the Allied infantry, who had to clear every ruined building of German machine-gun posts and snipers. The rubble allowed the defenders plenty of cover to keep their forward positions supplied and offered easy escape routes.

German Tactics

Even at Anzio, where the Allies thought they would have open country for their tanks to drive northward to Rome, the terrain proved more favorable to the defenders. The low-lying bridgehead was prone to flooding, making large stretches of the front impassable to Allied tanks, channeling them into "killing zones" that were dominated by German antitank guns. In addition, Allied armor was not helped by the railroads and raised roads that crisscrossed the battlefield. The waterlogged terrain turned the frontline positions into muddy hell holes, which the combatants compared unfavorably to the conditions endured in Flanders during World War I.

After the fall of Rome, the plains of Tuscany and Umbria gave the Germans plenty of opportunity to stall the Allied pursuit. The extensive agricultural cultivation of the region, with terraced fields and irrigation canals, made crosscountry movement by tanks difficult, forcing the Allies to stick to roads. Over the 120 miles (192 km) north from Rome to the Gothic Line were some 60 major road bridges, not counting the hundreds of culverts and "side cuts," where a road passes under a cliff. German engineers planted demolition charges on almost all of them, creating havoc among the pursuing Allied troops. Every bridge had to be approached with caution because of the fear of booby traps and snipers. In the 107 days of pursuit to the Gothic Line by the British 6th Armoured Division, for example, its engineers had to build 50 bridges, with spans totalling 6,561 ft (2,000 m) in length.

Once the Allies reached the Gothic Line they found the terrain even more demanding. There were yet more river lines to cross, but the direction of advance was channeled into steep, open gorges, which became killing zones for German antitank guns and machine-gun teams. Allied hopes to use the flat coastal plain along the Adriatic Sea to bypass the German mountain defenses of the Gothic Line were also dashed by large marshlands that bogged down whole armored regiments. With no breakthrough by the end of fall 1944, the Allied armies had to endure a freezing winter in the northern Apennine mountains, where the terrible terrain and weather meant that the bulk of their effort was directed at

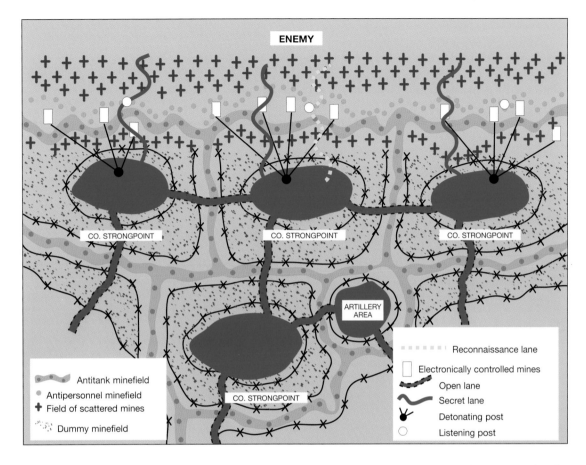

ENEMY

CO. STRONGPOINT

CO. STRONGPOINT

CO. STRONGPOINT

ARTILLERY AREA

CO. STRONGPOINT

Reconnaissance lane
Electronically controlled mines
Open lane
Secret lane
Detonating post
Listening post

Antitank minefield
Antipersonnel minefield
Field of scattered mines
Dummy minefield

Diagrammatic representation of a German reinforced battalion strongpoint. The use of mines, well-placed artillery and machine-gun nests acted as powerful force multipliers and meant Allied units had to devote large amounts of resources to knock out each one.

keeping troops in forward positions alive, let alone building up supplies for another major offensive. It would be more than six months before the Allies overcame the Italian climate to launch their final offensive of the war.

Italy was a defending commander's dream and Kesselring did not miss any opportunity to exploit one of his few advantages. Preparations for the Gustav and Gothic Lines began well before the Allies landed in Sicily, with survey teams examining the ground and developing plans to deploy and site defenses in the most effective locations. German defensive tactics were methodical and very effective. Every position on the Gustav and Gothic Lines was held in depth. For each division manning the frontline, another was set to work behind it building reserve positions and on call for counterattacks.

The Germans were always critically short of frontline infantrymen, with most battalions never mustering more than 400 men, and in the midst of major battles it was common for their frontline strength to drop below 200 men. They therefore never had enough men to man a continuous line of trenches. Accordingly, the front was held by a series of strongpoints positioned on key terrain that had a commanding view of the battlefield. In daytime they could dominate their sector of the frontline with machine-gun or mortar fire. If possible, they were sited along river lines to ensure the whole of the front was covered by overlapping fields of machine-gun fire, so there was no chance of Allied troops using a gap in the "wall of German fire" to make a secure bridgehead on the opposite bank. The Germans were particularly keen to set up enfilade fire positions so machine guns could sweep whole lengths of a river, rather than just a narrow field to their front.

At night, fighting patrols would be sent out to man ambush positions and prevent Allied troops infiltrating behind the strongpoints. German commanders spread out their scarce manpower into as many strongpoints as possible to reduce the risk of Allied bombardments killing or injuring a large number of their soldiers in one strike. Each strongpoint usually numbered about 40 men and was sited in natural cover, such as a gully or cave. Fire positions had to be gouged out of the rock with explosives, crowbars, and other tools. Shovels proved useless against the hard Italian rock.

Early experience of Italian mountain warfare made some German commanders wary of siting their strongpoints on top of ridge lines because they tended to attract a disproportionate amount of enemy fire. But as the Germans became more experienced they realized that ridge-line positions had natural advantages. Allied artillery fire was not as effective against ridge positions as against those in valleys. In most cases the fire either overshot or fell short because Allied gunners had to fire uphill. Ridge positions were also easier to keep supplied and evacuate wounded from because the rear slope behind the position was not observed by the enemy and could not be brought under aimed fire.

Counterattacks

The Germans in Italy were expert at making prompt counterattacks. German corps and divisional commanders, such as Senger, were keen to counterattack in overwhelming force to defeat decisively enemy penetrations of defensive positions. Specially positioned reserves, normally not less than battalion strength, would be kept just behind the line for this job rather than stripping out troops from strongpoints (the strongpoint garrisons were never numerous enough to have a decisive impact against a major enemy incursion). On the Cassino Front the Germans usually counterattacked in regimental strength, with the aim of wiping out enemy bridgeheads on river banks. They succeeded in this on several occasions, particularly against poorly motivated US troops.

Italy was one of the few theaters where the Germans decided not to concentrate their armor for counterattacks. With the terrain all but preventing the movement of large armored formations, German commanders broke up their tanks, assault guns, and antitank guns into small units, usually pairs, and posted them to forward strongpoints or with counterattack teams. In the Italian terrain, a handful of heavy weapons could provide firepower out of all proportion to their small number. During the Cassino battles, a handful of StuG III assault guns and Marder III self-propelled 75mm antitank guns operating with forward German paratroop strongpoints made it impossible for the Allies to try to spearhead their infantry assaults with tanks. During rearguard operations, small groups of tanks also proved very effective at forcing Allied troops to deploy to mount assault operations. The Germans would then quickly retreat once they had achieved their aim – delaying the advance – before their line of retreat became threatened.

The Italian theater benefited greatly from the fact that Kesselring, a Luftwaffe field marshal, was able to draw on the resources of his service in a way that army commanders were never able to. The Luftwaffe was never totally driven from Italian skies, and was able to provide him with aerial reconnaissance at strategically vital moments during the campaign: for example, just before and during the Salerno and Anzio landings. Armed with information about the movement of Allied shipping, Kesselring was able to judge the right moment to commit his scarce reserves. With only a few ports available to Allied shipping, it

Monte Cassino

The Allies' four-month battle to gain control of the Benedictine monastery was at the time dubbed the "Stalingrad of the Italian campaign." Soldiers from every continent of the world were committed to the battle that cost the Allies more than 115,000 dead, wounded, or missing. Losses among the German defenders totaled more than 20,000 dead.

From January 1944 the Allies launched a series of frontal assaults against formidable German defenses around Monte Cassino that guarded the route northward to Rome. The first phase involved a series of bloody attacks against the Rapido and Garigliano River lines. Tens of thousands of American troops were killed or wounded in the confused and chaotic river crossings against strong and well-positioned German defenses.

In February, the Allied high command ordered the "carpet" bombing of the monastery itself, in one of the most controversial decisions of the war. Allied commanders thought the Germans were using the historic building to house artillery observers. Whatever the truth, German paratroopers from the 1st Parachute Division then transformed the ruins of the monastery and the nearby town of Cassino into a fortress. For four months the *Fallschirmjägers* held at bay a vastly superior force of Allied troops drawn from the United States, Great Britain, Poland, Canada, New Zealand, France, Algeria, India, and Nepal.

In turn, Allied divisions were thrown against the seemingly impregnable Cassino position. Time after time, a huge air and artillery barrage would pound the German lines prior to a frontal infantry assault. But every time the *Fallschirmjägers* would emerge from their bunkers and trenches to repel the Allied advance. Often it only took a handful of defenders to hold up the Allied troops in the numerous steep gullies and bombed-out village streets that lay on the path up the mountainside to the monastery (the artillery fire and bombs also churned up the ground). If the Allied troops did gain ground, small groups of *Fallschirmjägers* were mustered to counterattack them before their gains could be consolidated.

By early May, the meat-grinder tactics of the Allies were beginning to pay off, with French and British troops creating important breaches on the *Fallschirmjägers*' eastern and western flanks. With the Anzio beachhead now also showing signs of going critical, Field Marshal Kesselring ordered the *Fallschirmjägers* to pull out of the Cassino Front on May 17. A day later Polish troops had the dubious honor of putting the seal on the Allies' pyrrhic victory by occupying the ruins of the Monte Cassino Monastery.

was not difficult to work out when a major amphibious operation was imminent, and once the assault force was at sea it was relatively easy to deduce the likely target.

A staggering 350 Luftwaffe Flak guns were mustered to provide an antiaircraft barrage to protect the evacuation of German troops from Sicily, which it was claimed was "heavier than over the Ruhr." Hundreds of Junkers Ju 52 transports were also mustered to ship in the intervention force that preempted the Italian defection to the Allies, and enabled Kesselring to contemplate defending the Gustav Line through to the middle of 1944. Luftwaffe strike aircraft scored some major successes against Allied shipping off Anzio and Salerno, hampering the buildup of British and American reinforcements. Stuka dive-bombers even reappeared over the Anzio battlefield in February 1944 to provide close air support for advancing German troops. The largely static nature of the war also negated, to a certain extent, Allied air power, because there were few columns of German vehicles, especially tanks, to attack. With the pace of operations relatively slow, German reinforcement columns could be moved under the cover of darkness. With limited resources, Field Marshal Kesselring frustrated Allied strategy in a key theater of conflict until the final weeks of the war and showed how a strategic defense should be conducted.

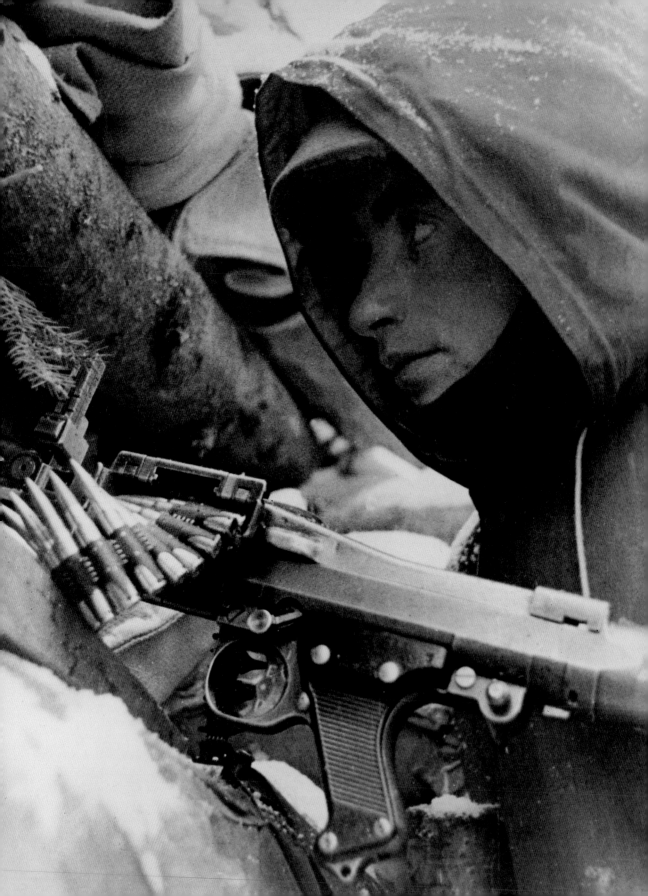

Defense in the East 1943–45

The Germans managed to stabilize the Eastern Front following the disaster at Stalingrad, but any chance the Wehrmacht had of achieving victory in the East ended with defeat at Kursk. Thereafter, the army fought a fighting withdrawal to the borders of the Reich.

Germany's war against the Soviet Union was the decisive theater of battle during World War II. It was a titanic struggle between two totalitarian regimes led by ruthless warlords. Both Hitler and Stalin saw the conflict as a life or death struggle against an alien political system. In the summer of 1943 this conflict reached its climax during the Battles of Kursk, where the elite armored forces of both sides were committed to action against each other. The German Blitzkrieg was blunted and the Soviets launched an offensive that would take them to the gates of Berlin some 21 months later.

The scale of the war on the Eastern Front was unprecedented. In 1943 the Soviets put 400 divisions into the field to take on some 120 German divisions, more than half of Hitler's army. The material spearhead of Stalin's offensive consisted of 8,000 Soviet tanks, 60,000 artillery pieces and the Red Air Force's 5,000 combat aircraft. To hold back the Russian steamroller, Hitler sent 3,000 tanks, 37,000 artillery pieces and 2,000 combat aircraft to the Eastern Front in 1943. In 1944, Stalin kept over six million men in uniform throughout the year, compared to 3.5 million Axis troops at the beginning of the year, and some 2.5 million German troops by its end.

The cumulative totals for losses on the Eastern Front make for sobering reading. The Red Army lost 13.7 million dead between 1941 and 1945, compared to two million dead German soldiers; while 11 million Russian civilians lost their lives compared to two million German civilians. The scale of destruction was awesome. Every major town and city between Berlin and Moscow was ravaged by the fighting. Few roads, railroad lines, bridges, tunnels, factories, and power stations escaped this orgy of destruction. Millions of homes were devastated and

A German soldier waits for the next Soviet attack in the winter of 1943–44. Within German Army units, fear of Soviet retribution was almost universal. It meant that there were few desertions or mass surrenders. There was nowhere to run to in the wastes of Russia, in any case, with partisans roaming behind the lines killing any stray Germans.

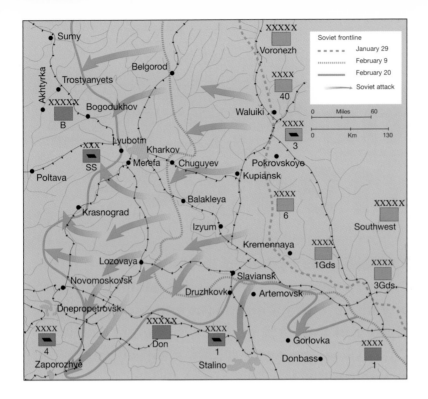

The Soviet offensive into the Ukraine in early 1943. Two Red Army fronts ripped a hole in the German frontline and threatened the whole of the Ukraine. However, as the Soviet spearheads headed farther west tanks began to run short of fuel and ammunition, and their supply lines became dangerously overstretched.

tens of millions of people forced to flee for their lives from one army or another as the war ebbed and flowed across Eastern and Central Europe.

At the beginning of 1943 it appeared that the Red Army would destroy Army Group South. Following the disaster at Stalingrad, Stalin ordered an offensive that threatened Germany's hold in southern Russia: the Hungarian and Italian satellite armies were disintegrating, and Soviet assaults in front of Rostov threatened to cut off the retreating First Panzer Army. Between February 2–20, Soviet spearheads threatened Kharkov and approached the Dnieper. Another Stalingrad loomed, but Manstein, the army group commander, abandoned the city then launched a devastating counterattack (see maps on these pages) against the overextended Soviet armored units. He recaptured Kharkov on March 14 and stabilized the front.

The Genius of Manstein

Field Marshal Erich von Manstein can lay claim to the status of the German Army's master strategist during World War II. He devised the daring "Sickle" plan to push panzer columns through the Ardennes forest that defeated France in the spring of 1940. This established Manstein's reputation with Hitler as an unconventional general who was prepared to play for high stakes to win victory. Manstein regained the attention of the Führer with the methodical attack that captured the besieged Soviet city of Sevastopol in July 1942. Manstein's greatest hour came in the dark days after the defeat of the German Sixth Army at Stalingrad in January 1943, however. Showing that he had not lost his touch for maneuver warfare, the commander of Army Group Don (formerly South) skillfully concentrated his weak and scattered forces, recaptured Kharkov (though 11,500 German troops were killed in street fighting in the city), and restored the southern sector of the Eastern Front to some semblance of order.

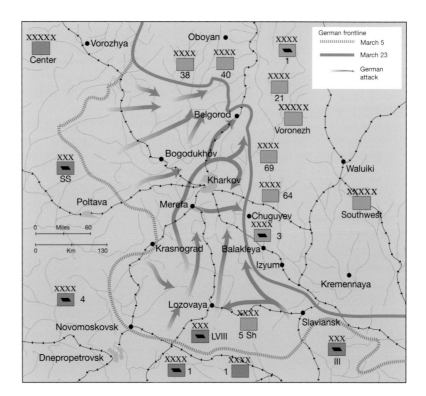

German frontline
- IIIIIIIIII March 5
- ▬▬▬ March 23
- → German attack

Manstein's brilliant counterattack in March 1943 that effectively destroyed any hopes Stalin may have had to retake the Ukraine in early 1943. The Soviet Fifth Shock Army was destroyed, while the SS Panzer Corps recaptured Kharkov.

The field marshal's role in the ill-fated Kursk Offensive is still controversial. In his memoirs, *Lost Victories*, he claimed that Operation Citadel failed because of interference from Hitler. First, asserts Manstein, Hitler delayed the offensive to allow the new Panther and Elephant tanks to participate, allowing the Soviets crucial time to rebuild their defenses around the salient. Then, Hitler called off the offensive just as it looked as if II SS Panzer Corps was about to break through the Soviet lines. More recent studies of the Kursk battles, based on German and Soviet records, however, paint a different picture of Manstein's leadership. The Soviets on several occasions duped both Manstein and Hitler with effective deception tactics. The extensive Soviet defensive lines at Kursk defeated German panzer tactics, preventing a decisive breakthrough, while the subsequent Soviet offensive toward Kharkov unhinged Manstein's defenses and he was not able to recover the situation.

In the winter battle along the Dnieper River, Manstein proved himself again to be the master of improvisation. He successfully extracted his troops from Soviet encirclement in the Kirovograd, Cherkassy–Korsun, and Kamenets Podolsk Pockets in 1944. The latter operation was a major success for Manstein, who managed to save 200,000 Germans from captivity. Hitler was less impressed with the commander of Army Group South's conduct of the battle. Manstein got some more medals but was out of a job. "The time for operating is over – what I need now is men who stand firm," commented an ungrateful Führer. The field marshal spent the rest of the war in retirement, and afterwards served three years in a British jail for having command responsibility for regions of Poland and the Soviet Union where war crimes were committed.

For three brief months up to July 1943 the Eastern Front was strangely quiet as both the Germans and Soviets rebuilt their forces after the heavy fighting during the previous winter. The Kursk salient in the centre of the front was the

The Wehrmacht

focus of attention for Hitler and Stalin. The large bulge of Soviet-held territory jutted into the German line for more than 50 miles (80 km) to the east of the small and hitherto unknown town of Kursk. It had been left hanging exposed after the German counteroffensive that retook Kharkov in March 1943 ground to a halt in a sea of Russian spring mud.

Hitler's generals proposed Operation Citadel to the Führer as a way to regain the initiative on the Eastern Front by destroying the Kursk salient. If the Soviets tried to intervene with their strategic armored reserves, so much the better, because they would be destroyed by panzers in battles of encirclement, or so thought German commanders. With the Red Army defeated, the Russian people might rise in revolt as in 1917 to overthrow Stalin, and give the Germans a free hand against the Allies in the West.

A huge effort was put into rebuilding the German forces on the Eastern Front to ensure Citadel was a decisive success. More than 900,000 men were concentrated against the northern and southern shoulders of the salient, with some 2,400 tanks and assault guns to spearhead the offensive. In addition, the new Panther tanks and Ferdinand heavy assault guns would make their debut during the battle.

Warned by British intelligence and their own spies inside the Wehrmacht, the Soviets were lying in wait for the elite of Hitler's army (though even without this intelligence it was obvious that the Kursk salient represented a tempting target for the Germans). Crammed into the salient were 54 rifle divisions, 12 tank corps, and 16 mechanised brigades. More than a million men were set to work digging bunkers, laying minefields, and emplacing thousands of antitank guns in the

The Battle of Kursk (right), July 1943. The hollow purple arrows represent the German plan to link up the two pincers at Kursk. The solid purple arrows show the actual progress of German forces during the seven-day battle, and the effectiveness of the three Soviet defensive belts that protected the Kursk salient.

A Waffen-SS Tiger I during the Battle of Kursk. The density of Soviet minefields and antitank defenses exhausted the strength of the German panzer divisions.

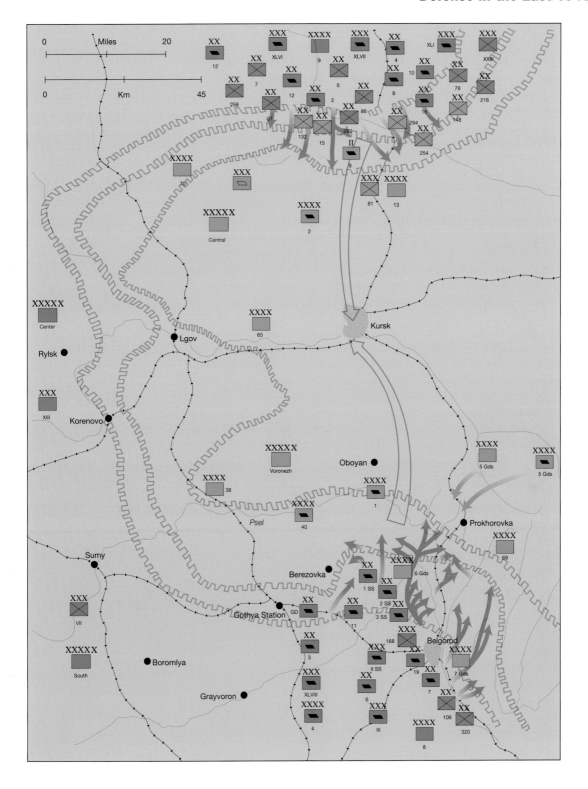

months leading up to the offensive. Behind five prepared defense lines were armored reserves with more than 3,000 tanks. Some 20,000 field guns were ready to rain shells on the Germans as they tried to push northwards. As time progressed the Soviet defenses grew stronger, but Hitler was determined to have his great strategic victory in the East.

A Lost Cause?

The influence of Hitler on the course of the final two years of the war in Russia was significant. His orders to fight to the last man and bullet consigned thousands of German soldiers to fruitless deaths in surrounded pockets. However, it is less clear that it would have turned the tide in Germany's favour even if Hitler had heeded calls by his generals for a more mobile defense.

Hitler's critics blame him for the failure of Operation Citadel, because he called it off just as Manstein's attack on the southern axis was reaching its climax. During the next eight months, Hitler was constantly ordering German troops to stand and fight in the Ukraine, leading to hundreds of thousands being trapped in pockets. Up to April 1944, Manstein was able to pull his men out of these pockets. After his dismissal, the Führer usually got his way, with predictable results. The Crimea fell with the loss of 75,000 in May and hundreds of thousands were lost in the collapse of Army Group Center in June and July, when Hitler ordered the cut-off troops to form fortresses and to fight to the last man.

Hitler was not alone in misjudging how to deal with the resurgence of the Red Army after the defeat of the German Sixth Army at Stalingrad, however. Hitler was not the originator of the plan to attack at Kursk: it was first suggested by the German Army chief of staff, Colonel-General Kurt Zeitzler. Some generals, including Guderian, objected, but Manstein and Model were keen exponents. "Whenever I think of this attack my stomach turns over," Hitler told Guderian in May 1943.

Every German offensive on the Eastern Front had succeeded in breaking through Soviet lines and routing the hapless Russians. It was just not imagined that Operation Citadel could fail. The Germans had ample intelligence on the state of Soviet field fortifications around the salient but went ahead regardless. It was an act of supreme arrogance.

This was symptomatic of German attitudes to their enemy throughout the war in Russia. The Russians were regarded as Slav sub-humans. From 1941 onward, the occupied territories were systematically looted to support the German war effort, Jews and Russians alike were massacred, and more than three million Russian prisoners of war were allowed to starve or died of neglect. Not surprisingly, the Soviet population united against a common enemy and German attempts to undermine Russian morale proved hopeless.

The Germans, both Hitler and his generals, when they launched Operation Barbarossa in 1941 were totally unprepared for a conflict of such scale and intensity. "We only have to kick in the door and the whole rotten structure will come crashing down," was the Führer's considered opinion on the level of resistance the Soviets would put up.

They were intoxicated by their Blitzkrieg victories in the West, and Germany was not prepared for a "total war." This was not just a case of Wehrmacht quartermasters not ordering enough winter clothing. Until 1943, the German economy was still largely on a peacetime footing. War production was minimal compared to the Soviets, and Germany's population was not prepared for sacrifice.

Field Marshal Erich von Manstein shakes hands with German soldiers on the Eastern Front. A master of mobile armored warfare, he saved Army Group South from certain destruction at the beginning of 1943.

From the summer of 1941, Stalin put his country on a war footing. Every Soviet citizen and all its natural and industrial resources were to be mobilized. Whole towns and factories were relocated out of reach of German bombers to the east of the Urals to rebuild Russia's industrial base. By 1942, Soviet annual tank production was running at 24,000 compared to Germany's 4,000. Russian industrial production was running in high gear from the start; the Germans never caught up. The seeds of the defeats of 1943 onward were sewn well before Operation Citadel even got underway.

The Battle of Kursk began on July 5, 1943, and reached a climax on July 12, when II SS Panzer Corps clashed head on with the Soviet's strategic armored reserve, the Fifth Guards Tank Army. After the biggest tank battle in military history, the Waffen-SS panzers were held and Hitler decided to call off Citadel. Allied troops had invaded Sicily, Soviet forces had launched a major offensive to the north of the Kursk salient that forced back the German line, and far to the south another Soviet offensive had punched through the Eastern Front. Panzer divisions were dispatched to plug the gaps, but in early August more than 2,000 Soviet tanks burst through the depleted German front in the center around Kharkov. The German Army Group South was lucky to escape annihilation, before a reluctant Hitler agreed to a strategic withdrawal to the Dnieper River line in September. After a fighting retreat, the Germans turned and faced their pursuers during late October and November, in a series of limited counteroffensives with fresh panzer reserves from the West.

Huge Soviet tank armies carved further chunks out of Army Group South during December 1943. A series of swirling tank battles ensued as the Germans tried to hold them back. One panzer corps was briefly trapped in Kirovograd during January 1944 before it escaped, but by February the Soviets had encircled two German corps in the Cherkassy–Korsun Pocket, to the south of Kiev.

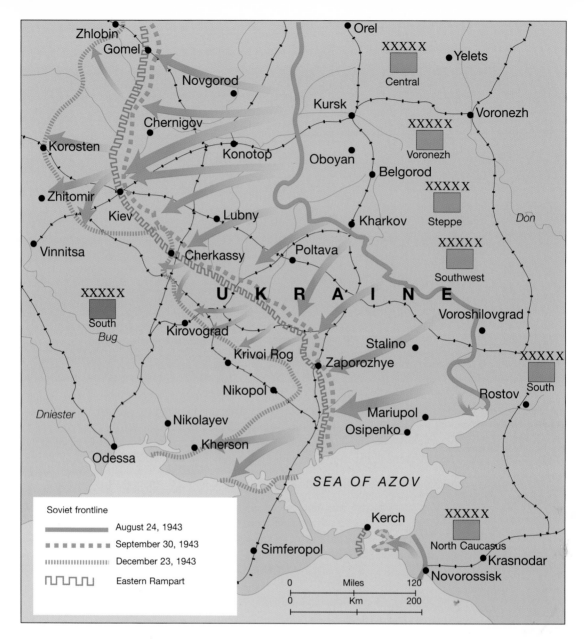

Soviet frontline

———————	August 24, 1943
▪ ▪ ▪ ▪ ▪ ▪	September 30, 1943
▨▨▨▨▨▨	December 23, 1943
⊓⊔⊓⊔⊓⊔	Eastern Rampart

Around half the 60,000 men trapped escape, but they left behind all their heavy equipment. Barely a month later, the Soviets trapped the First Panzer Army in another pocket, and it was lucky to be able to fight its way out.

Huge German withdrawals were made by their Army Groups Center and North during the autumn and winter of 1943, to try and keep the Eastern Front in line with the fluid frontline in the Ukraine. A major Soviet offensive in January 1944 broke the German ring around Leningrad, ending the two-year siege of the Soviet Union's second city. Soviet troops also landed in the Crimea and destroyed the German Seventeenth Army. Except for a huge bulge in Belorussia occupied by Army Group Center, German troops had largely been driven out back to beyond their 1941 start lines. During April and May 1944, a series of vicious battles took place as the frontline stabilized in the western Ukraine and along the

The speed of the Soviet advance in the Ukraine in the second half of 1943 disrupted German plans for a defense in depth. The so-called Eastern Rampart was an illusion.

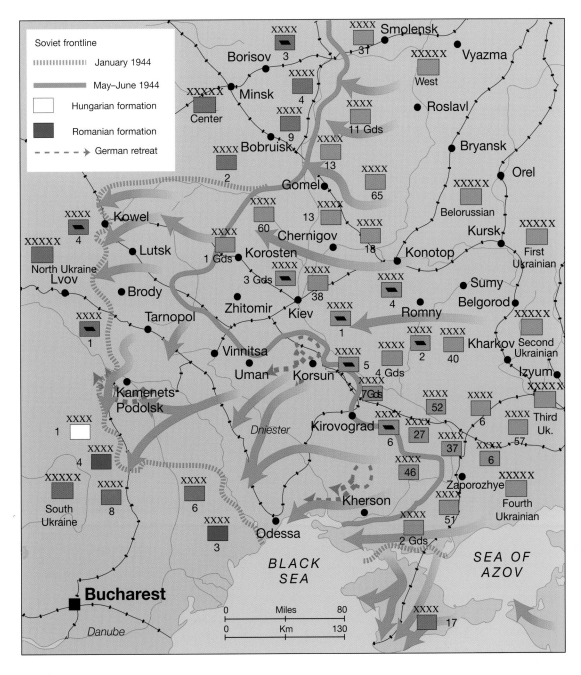

Soviet frontline

|||||||||||||| January 1944

May–June 1944

☐ Hungarian formation

■ Romanian formation

- - - - → German retreat

XXXX
3

XXXX
31

XXXX
Smolensk

XXXXX
West

Vyazma

Borisov

XXXXX
Center

Minsk

XXXX
4

Roslavl

XXXX
9

XXXX
11 Gds

xxxx Bobruisk

XXXX
2

XXXX
13

Bryansk

Gomel

XXXX
65

Orel

XXXXX
Belorussian

XXXX
Kowel

XXXX
4

XXXX
13

Kursk

XXXXX

XXXXX
North Ukraine
Lvov

Lutsk

XXXX
60

Chernigov

XXXX
18

Konotop

XXXXX
First
Ukrainian

XXXX
1 Gds

Korosten

XXXX
3 Gds

Brody

XXXX
38

Zhitomir

Kiev

XXXX
4

Romny

Sumy

Belgorod

XXXX
1

Tarnopol

XXXX
1

XXXX
2

XXXX
40

Kharkov

XXXXX
Second
Ukrainian

Vinnitsa

XXXX
5

XXXX
4 Gds

Izyum

XXXXX

Uman

Korsun

XXXX
7 Gds

XXXX
52

Kamenets-
Podolsk

XXXX
1

Kirovograd

XXXX
27

XXXX
6

XXXX
Third
Uk.

Dniester

XXXX
6

XXXX
37

XXXX
57

XXXX
4

XXXX
46

XXXX
6

XXXXX
South
Ukraine

XXXX
8

XXXX
6

Zaporozhye

XXXXX
Fourth
Ukrainian

XXXX
3

Kherson

XXXX
51

Odessa

XXXX
2 Gds

**BLACK
SEA**

*SEA OF
AZOV*

Bucharest

0   Miles   80

0   Km   130

XXXX
17

Danube

**The clearing of the Ukraine
was a hard fight for the Red
Army, not least because
German commanders
conducted a skillful defense.**

Romanian border as German reserve panzer divisions tried to tidy up the line, and cut off a number of small Soviet incursions and salients.

That Army Group South held together at all from August 1943 through to April 1944 was due to the efforts of its commander, Manstein, who believed in mobile defense rather than holding cities or other geographic features. Manstein went to great efforts to maintain the freedom of action and fighting power of his small number of divisions. This, for example, involved using panzer divisions as hard-hitting reserves, to either preempt Soviet offensives or cut into them after they had made penetrations in the German lines. Once they had achieved their mission, destroying the bulk of the Soviet tank force, Manstein would

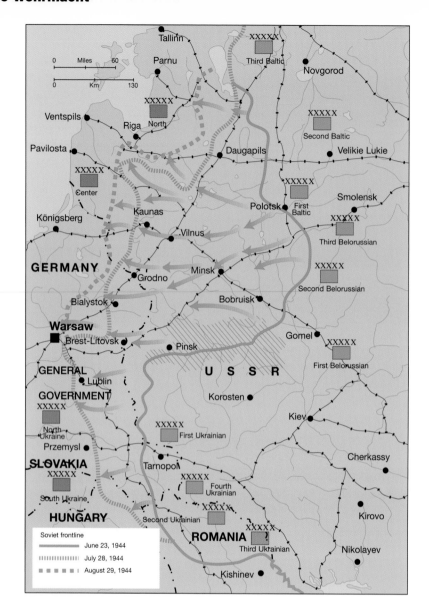

Operation Bagration, the Soviet offensive that smashed Army Group Center. Stalin committed 1,254,000 men, 2,715 tanks, and 1,355 assault guns to the offensive, which was a stunning success.

immediately pull them back into reserve, so they would not fritter away their precious tanks in futile defensive operations to hold specific towns or river lines.

While this tactic was eminently sensible from an operational point of view, it was also very good for the morale of his troops. They had confidence that their efforts were achieving something and their lives were not being put unnecessarily at risk. The fear of being trapped in a pocket and becoming a prisoner of the Russians was at the forefront of the minds of all German soldiers on the Eastern Front. So Manstein's efforts to ensure they were not caught in pockets, or promptly rescued if they were surrounded, maintained fighting spirit. Not surprisingly, he was highly regarded by senior officers and frontline troops alike.

Manstein's first success in the defensive battles during the summer of 1943 was when he rescued the situation after the massive breakthrough by Soviet troops north of Kharkov in August 1943. Outnumbered three to one by 650,000 Soviet troops, the German defenses quickly cracked and 2,300 Soviet tanks streamed southward after brushing aside the 300 panzers in their path. Manstein pulled in a powerful force of six Waffen-SS and army panzer divisions to contain and then attack the Soviet incursion. Once the crisis had passed he concentrated his panzer force to defend Kharkov and organize an orderly withdrawal to the Dnieper.

During November 1943 Soviet troops broke over the Dnieper line, took Kiev, and then spread southward threatening to turn Army Group South's northern flank and surround the bulk of Manstein's forces in the Ukraine. Using panzer reinforcements from the West, Manstein pushed back the Soviets until the outflanking threat was neutralized, destroying or capturing 700 Soviet tanks and 668 antitank guns as he did so.

A swirling tank battle of massive proportions developed in the last week of December when more than 1,000 T-34s were launched at the heart of Manstein's now understrength panzer reserve. This was the first of a series of jabs into his defensive positions that slowly chipped away at his hold on the Ukraine.

The Cherkassy Pocket

A month later the Soviets were able to cut off two German corps in the Korsun or Cherkassy Pocket. Manstein saw this as an opportunity and deployed his panzers to break through to the trapped troops, while at the same time turning the tables on the tank units leading the Soviet offensive. A rapid thaw turned the Ukraine into a mud trap for Manstein's panzers, and all ideas of a counterattack were shelved. The operation instead focused on rescuing as many of the trapped troops as possible.

In March 1944, two giant Soviet pincers sliced into Manstein's now shaky army group, effectively trapping the 200,000 men of the First Panzer Army. Again, Manstein was not content with just getting his men out of the pocket, but maneuvered them westward in such a way that they blocked any Soviet attempt to exploit the huge gap in the German line to advance into Poland. For his efforts, Hitler sacked him in March 1944.

Manstein's replacement was Walther Model, who was a totally different character to his cerebral and well-respected predecessor. An ardent Nazi, Model was fanatically loyal to his Führer, and had none of the manners expected of the old school of Prussian generals. He bullied subordinates and expected his orders to hold to the last bullet to be obeyed. Model was a born improviser, but lacked the vision of Manstein. He was not surprisingly nicknamed the "Führer's fireman," because Hitler had picked him to salvage desperate situations.

His finest hour was perhaps rescuing the Eastern Front after the destruction of Army Group Center by the 1944 summer offensive, Operation Bagration, launched on June 22. With more than 2,000 Soviet tanks heading westward virtually unopposed, Model calmly gathered in a strong panzer reserve and halted the Russians in a series of effective counterattacks. By mid-August the Red Army had been kept out of Warsaw. The battering handed out by Model's panzer divisions, which decimated several Soviet tank corps and scores of infantry divisions, forced the Soviets to remain on the defensive in central Poland for the remainder of the year.

Model's successful counterattacks could not, however, disguise the scale of the disaster that the Wehrmacht underwent in the summer of 1944. More than two million Soviet troops, spearheaded by several thousand tanks, smashed into the 400,000 men of Army Group Center. The sheer scale of the offensive just overwhelmed the defenders. Whole German divisions and army corps were trapped in a series of pockets throughout the battle zone. There was no coordinated defense or effort to relieve the pockets, which either surrendered or were eliminated. By July 8, 28 divisions out of Army Group Center's 37 divisions had ceased to exist. More than 200 tanks and 1,300 artillery pieces were lost. At least 285,000 Germans were either killed or captured and, in an act of supreme humiliation, 57,000 captured Germans headed by 19 Wehrmacht generals were paraded through the center of Moscow. This was a worse defeat than Stalingrad and the heaviest defeat for the German Army in World War II.

The Red Army had punched a massive hole more than 200 miles (320 km) wide in the German Eastern Front. It took superhuman efforts by Model to create a frontline just to the east of Warsaw during the middle of August. Barely had Model stabilized the front in the north than the Soviets opened a new offensive in the south, which ripped through into Romania. Within days, Romania had changed sides, and Bulgaria followed suit in September. A major retreat from the Balkans was ordered by Hitler, with Crete, Greece, and Albania being abandoned. German troops held open a corridor through Yugoslavia long enough for the Greek garrison to escape northward during November.

Soviet spearheads pushed through Romania during October and penetrated into Hungary, before a lightning panzer counterattack at Debrecan sent them temporarily reeling backwards. The Hungarians were now wavering, and a German coup was staged to removed pro-Allied elements from the country's government. In November, the Soviet offensive in Hungary was back in high gear and Budapest was surrounded, trapping 70,000 German and Hungarian troops.

Soviet operations in the Baltic succeeded in forcing the surrender of Finland and, in spite of strong German counterattacks, the Soviets were able to isolate the 22 divisions of Army Group North in the Courland peninsula.

In the final days of 1944, the German forces holding the Eastern Front were a mere shadow of those that had tried to cut off the Kursk salient in July 1943. German frontline divisions were lucky to muster a couple of thousand men. Tanks and artillery were in short supply. A year before, the German Army had been firing 1.5 million tank and artillery shells a month on the Eastern Front, but in January 1945 only 367,000 reached frontline troops. Spares and fuel were now precious commodities. Holes in the ranks were filled with old men, medical cases, or teenagers. Nazi Party officials and Gestapo personnel made their presence felt at army headquarters to ensure obedience to the Führer's orders to fight to the last man. The smell of decay and defeat was everywhere. German soldiers along the length of the Eastern Front could only wait in their freezing trenches for the final Soviet offensive to come.

Hard Fighting

The defeat of Hitler's army in Russia was no walkover, though. The Wehrmacht put up ferocious resistance. Soviet victories were paid for in huge quantities of blood. The Red Army suffered some five million battlefield casualties and a further two million from non-battle causes during 1944 alone. This was supposed to be the year of its greatest victories, but Russia's losses were on a par with those suffered in 1941. The Germans lost 1.1 million battle casualties and some 700,000 non-battle casualties during 1944.

Time and again during 1943 and into early 1944, the Germans were able to salvage their battered front from disaster and keep on fighting. In the face of the overwhelming odds they faced this was a remarkable achievement. This

Scorched Earth

As the tide of war turned against Germany on the Eastern Front in the summer of 1943, Hitler was increasingly preoccupied with what he saw as the "economic struggle" with the Soviets. With his armies being forced back along the length of the front, the Führer was determined to deny his enemies the economic resources of the regions being abandoned.

In September 1943, he instructed Reich Marshal Hermann Göring to issue orders for a scorced-earth policy in southern Russia. No foodstuffs, industrial raw materials, livestock, factories, agricultural machinery, railroady rolling stock, motor vehicles, or anything that could help the Soviet war effort was be left behind as German troops pulled back to the Dnieper River. What could not be moved was to be destroyed.

Behind the German rearguards, massive columns of 200,000 cattle, 153,000 horses, and 270,000 sheep were herded toward the Dnieper. More than 3,000 trains carried off foodstuffs and industrial goods. Squads of German engineers roamed the Donets basin region blowing up factories, bridges, power stations, and government buildings.

German military commanders were far from enthused with Hitler's policy. They had more important things to do, and thought the Scorched Earth policy was a distraction from their efforts to save what was left of Army Group South from the Soviet advance.

In the end, much of the Scorched Earth effort proved to be of little effect. The Russians beat the Germans to many of the Dnieper crossings, and large quantities of the looted booty had to be abandoned.

After the war, several senior German Army officers, including Field Marshal Erich von Manstein, were tried and convicted for breaching the rules of war by participating in Hitler's Scorched Earth policy.

performance was possible for a number of reasons: the quality of German field commanders, the quality of German units, particularly panzer divisions, the fighting spirit of German officers and soldiers, and shortcomings in the Red Army's tactical skills and capabilities.

German Army commanders and staff officers on the Eastern Front during 1943 and 1944 almost always conducted their combat operations with great professionalism, and some displayed the old dash of the Blitzkrieg years. Hans Hube, for example, is considered by many to have been the best panzer army commander of the war. A panzer division commander in 1941 and a panzer corps commander during the ill-fated attack on Stalingrad the following year, Hube proved to be a master of defense during the invasion of Sicily in July 1943, and later in southern Italy. Posted to command the First Panzer Army under Manstein in October 1943, he inflicted massive losses on the Soviets as they tried to seize the Dnieper Bend region of the Ukraine. Time and again, with a handful of understrength panzer divisions he kept the Soviets at bay until the end of the year. In late January 1944, Hube was put in charge of the Cherkassy–Korsun rescue operation, getting to within three miles (4.8 km) of the trapped troops and holding open a tenuous corridor long enough to allow a breakout.

A month later Hube found that his First Panzer Army was trapped behind Soviet lines. A survivor of the Stalingrad Pocket, where he was flown out at the last minute on Hitler's orders, he was determined that his troops would not share the fate of Paulus's doomed command. The one-armed panzer general organized his troops into a mobile pocket, moving steadily westward to freedom. Luftwaffe air supply flights were made to roads and specially prepared airstrips along the

StuG IIIs of a battle group on the Ukrainian steppe in November 1943. The German system of forming ad hoc all-arms battle groups, or *Kampfgruppen*, to deal with specific tactical situations was another example of the sophistication of their battle tactics and organization. *Kampfgruppen* could be formed at a few hours' notice, and usually contained all the types of unit needed to deal with a wide range of tasks, such as combat engineers to clear mines or build bridges, antitank guns to deal with enemy tanks, armor to spearhead assaults, and infantry to hold ground. Red Army units of battalion and regimental level were single arm, either tanks, infantry, artillery, antitank, or engineer. This meant their attacks usually bogged down if they came across unexpected problems that required specialist support. Long delays resulted if Soviet infantry needed engineer or tank support, as the infantry commander went up the tortuous Red Army chain of command to get help. While this was happening the Germans were often able to launch a counterattack.

army's route. By skillfully dodging the main Soviet encircling force, Hube's men were never pinned down. This kept up morale and ensured the Soviets could not seal in his troops and concentrate their overwhelming strength against them. Once they were free, Hube was summoned to an audience with the Führer to receive a well-earned promotion to colonel-general. However, his aircraft crashed and he was killed.

Hermann Balck was one of Manstein's most effective panzer corps commanders during the battles south of Kiev in November and December 1943. He led XLVIII Panzer Corps in the successful counterattack that retook Zhitomir, and then destroyed several Soviet tank corps and divisions in the forests north of the town. Panzer columns pressed deep into the forests to bypass and then surround large pockets of Soviet resistance. Balck's lightning attacks totally confused his Soviet opponents, who were left reeling and disorientated by the "phantom" panzer columns that emerged from the forests in the darkness, firing on the move.

When the Soviets counterattacked in strength a few weeks later, Balck again saved by the day by maneuvering his forces around the flanks of the huge columns of T-34s, and then attacking from surprise positions.

Calmness in a crisis and strong nerves were often needed to save the day. General Ferdinand Schörner's retreat out of the Nikopol Pocket at the extreme eastern edge of the Dnieper Bend in January 1944 was an example of outstanding leadership in a crisis. When Soviet troops broke through on the flanks of the pocket, threatening to trap Schörner's XL Panzer Corps, he quickly organized

Kampfgruppen (battle groups) to hold open the last escape route. He went from one antitank gun position to the next, motivating his troops to keep fighting to allow the bulk of the corps to escape, in defiance of Hitler's orders to fight to the last man. Once all the wounded had been evacuated, Schörner successfully evacuated his rearguard.

These great tactical feats by German army and corps commanders were not chance but the result of careful planning and coordination by many staff officers. Behind every German general was a hardworking chief of staff, who ran their headquarters, translated the commander's intention into orders and, in time of crisis, acted in the name of their superior. Manstein's faithful chief of operations and later chief of staff, Theodor Busse, from the siege of Leningrad to the field marshal's sacking in April 1944, was instrumental in ensuring the success of many Army Group South operations. He even flew into the Stalingrad Pocket to pass on Manstein's plan for a breakout to the beleaguered Paulus. When Manstein was summoned to the Führer's headquarters to account for another of his "tactical withdrawals," it was Busse who was left to deal with any crises.

Balck's right-hand man during the panzer battles south of Kiev was F.W. Mellenthin, a veteran of the African campaign. Mellenthin controlled the corps from its headquarters when Balck was at the front, and on occasions was sent to act as a troubleshooter when crisis threatened.

Divisional Commanders

In Hitler's army, divisional commanders were battlefield commanders, not staff officers who sulked in the safety of rear headquarters far from the enemy's guns. A prime example of the dynamic and charismatic characters who rose to lead German panzer divisions was Hasso von Manteuffel. During the retreat in the Ukraine he led the 7th Panzer Division, Rommel's old outfit, known as the "Ghost Division" because it moved so fast, from the turret of his command tank. Success at Balck's side south of Kiev in November 1943 saw him rewarded with command of the *Grossdeutschland* Panzergrenadier Division.

Manteuffel's style of command was simple. He positioned himself at the *Schwerpunkt*, or main effort, of his division's battle and made all the crucial decisions about the conduct of the battle based on what he saw with his own eyes, not some garbled radio message from a frontline trench.

Grossdeutschland was the German Army's elite fighting formation, and in 1944 was superbly equipped with battalions of Tiger and Panther tanks. The high point of his tour of command came in May 1944 when 400 Soviet tanks bore down on the division's positions at Targul Frumos on the Romanian border. Manteuffel waited until his 88mm Flak guns had done their worst, destroying 25 of the new Soviet Joseph Stalin II heavy tanks, and then launched his Tigers and Panthers in a counterattack. From the turret of his Panther, Manteuffel led his panzer crews forward again and again until the Russians were fleeing the battlefield. When the battlefield was inspected, the burning hulks of 250 Soviet tanks were found by the victorious *Grossdeutschland* troops.

General Fritz Bayerlein was the exact opposite of the flamboyant and aristocratic Manteuffel, and had to overcome very different challenges. His 3rd Panzer Division was a line unit that received little in the way of replacement men or equipment. He was a cunning tactician and thorough planner, who was on his first posting to the Eastern Front. In January 1944, Bayerlein's division was surrounded, along with three other divisions of his panzer corps, in the Ukrainian

German Fortress Towns

Hitler was well known for his love of ordering German troops besieged by Soviet encirclement "to fight to the last man and last bullet." The results were usually disastrous for the soldiers trapped by vastly superior Soviet forces.

The Führer's first employment of "do or die" orders was during the Soviet offensive outside Moscow in the winter of 1941–42. After a fashion the tactics worked, and the German front held together to fight another day. Experience countering the massive human-wave charges and deep encircling moves during this period led the Germans to develop specific tactics to defend the massive length of the Eastern Front.

There were just not enough troops to hold the whole length of the front, so a system of strongpoints and fortified zones was developed. These acted as fire bases, around which the Soviets would be allowed to pass. Artillery and mortars would sweep the areas not held by the Germans and then panzer columns would be sent to seal any breaches in the front. The attacks would then be cut off and destroyed. Up to the spring of 1943 these tactics proved themselves time and again, but in the last years of the war the Wehrmacht was so outnumbered that it was no longer able to muster the mobile forces necessary to turn the tables on the Russians.

Time after time during 1944, Hitler ordered cut-off German forces to form what he termed "fortress towns." He believed they would tie down scores of Soviet divisions that would otherwise be free to rampage westward. In reality, with no panzer reserves available to ride to the rescue, the fortress towns became death traps for their garrisons. The Soviets simply surrounded the fortress towns and waited for the Germans to run out of food and ammunition.

The Soviet offensive that destroyed the German Army Group Center in June and July 1944 demonstrated the bankruptcy of the Führer's ideas. Within a few weeks the Russians had surrounded several German army corps in isolated pockets at Vitebsk, Orsha, Mogilev, and Bobruisk. Hitler ordered them to fight to the last man. When he at last allowed them to break out it was too late. Only a few thousand managed to escape. More than 150,000 Germans were killed and some 100,000 were captured. The prisoners were later paraded through the streets of Moscow by the victorious Soviets.

city of Kirovograd. Bayerlein was Rommel's old chief of staff from North Africa and was not inclined to wait to be annihilated. Taking advantage of a breakdown in radio communications to ensure no orders to the contrary were received from the Führer's headquarters, Bayerlein formed his division into an attack formation, panzers at the front, and broke out of the pocket. "Kirovograd sounds too much like Stalingrad for my liking," was his comment to an aide. Once he had regained his freedom of movement, Bayerlein turned his tanks around and led them back to defeat the besieging Russian troops. In a panic at seeing tanks in their midst, the Soviet troops fled, opening an escape route for the remainder of the German garrison still trapped in Kirovograd.

Throughout the war on the Eastern Front, German Army units were far more combat effective than Soviet units of an equal size or role. German units were better trained and their commanders more experienced than their Soviet counterparts. The German Army's tactics, unit organization, and battle procedures were always far more sophisticated than those of the Red Army. This was the main reason for the enormous casualties the Germans were able to inflict on the Russians.

At divisional and battle group level, the Germans always had far better communications to enable them to react very quickly on the battlefield. Every German tank or armored vehicle, for example, had a radio, allowing panzer commanders to employ very complex tactics. The Russians, on the other hand, had nowhere near as many radios. In Soviet tank battalions only the commander usually had a radio, and he had to communicate with his subordinates by means of colored flags. Unsurprisingly, once a Soviet tank battalion was committed to battle it either drove the Germans off or was shot to pieces.

German command and control procedures also allowed them to employ their limited artillery assets to great effect, rapidly switching fire to crisis zones under

By the end of August 1944 the Red Army had cleared the Germans from the Soviet Union and had thrust into Poland. By this period of the war on the Eastern Front it was supply problems as much ast the Wehrmacht that slowed the Soviet advance.

the direction of artillery observers on the frontline. Soviet artillery, on the other hand, relied on weight of fire, centrally directed.

German officers were fully trained in the principles of *Auftragstaktik*, or Mission Analysis, that allowed them to make rapid decisions in response to Soviet attacks. Low-level Soviet commanders were never allowed the freedom of action of their German counterparts. The dead hand of communist control was felt far down the Soviet chain of command, leading to very inflexible and uninspired tactics on the battlefield. Meticulous staff planning characterized most Soviet offensives, but once they got underway things started to go wrong, sometimes badly, as the Germans reacted, launching counterattacks or delaying the timetable of the operation. Soviet officers, even up to major-general level, were used to being issued with very detailed orders for every aspect of their mission. If unexpected German responses occurred, Soviet officers would have to consult their superiors for orders. When outflanked and if communications were cut, Soviet officers often floundered and could not decide what to do.

Under Manstein in the Ukraine and Model in Poland, German commanders were allowed plenty of freedom of action to achieve their objectives as best they saw fit. This meant that the German "decision-making cycle" was always shorter than the Soviet one, resulting in many setbacks for the Soviets at the hands of the two field marshals' army groups. Once Hitler's Nazification of the German Army gathered momentum in the late summer and fall of 1944, it became tied to the Führer's detailed instructions, which stifled freedom of action.

In spite of being driven back to the borders of the Reich in the last days of 1944, German troops on the Eastern Front could not be accused of lacking fighting spirit. The panzer spearheads at the Battle of Kursk in July advanced with all the elan of the Blitzkrieg days, and German defensive lines were then held with grim determination, against overwhelming odds.

The reasons for the fierce resistance of German troops were varied. On the orders of Hitler and the army high command, the Nazi indoctrination of the rank and file troops was massively intensified during 1943. Hitler's declaration of "total war" in January 1943 was used to reinforce the motivation of frontline troops to fight the Slav and Jewish sub-humans in the East. With Allied bombing raids on German cities now a daily occurrence, it was not difficult for Nazi propaganda films, books, newspapers, and radio broadcasts to convince ordinary German soldiers that they were locked in a life-or-death struggle with their enemies.

Morale ebbed and flowed with the military situation, with the period before the launching of Operation Citadel being a period of rising expectations. The assault troops were made aware of the high stakes involved and, when the battle ended without a decisive German victory, morale slumped. The long retreat in the Ukraine by Army Group South during September and October did little to improve things. Manstein's counterattack south of Kiev was a major boost for his troops. The capture of thousands of poorly equipped and motivated Russians convinced many German soldiers that they might just be bleeding the Soviets at a greater rate than they could sustain. Mellenthin said this was a "flicker of hope" for the troops of Army Group South. "It was clear the limits of Soviet manpower were being reached: the Russians could not continue to suffer these losses indefinitely." German officers started to think in terms of a repeat of 1917, when huge losses had precipitated the Russian Revolution. This, however, was wishful thinking. Stalin's war machine did not break apart. In 1944, it redoubled its efforts, and poured even more men and material into battle against the Germans.

The Bolshevik Horde

The collapse of Army Group Center brought the Red Army to the borders of the Reich, threatening the very existence of Germany. Senior German officers, such as Heinz Guderian who was appointed army chief of staff in July 1944, talked in terms of the Eastern Front "tottering on the edge of an abyss from which it was necessary to save millions of German soldiers and civilians."

German officers and soldiers had seen the way Red Army troops and partisans had brutally treated German prisoners of war, as well as "liberated" civilians. They feared for the fate of their families if Soviet troops broke into the heart of Germany. With East Prussia, Silesia, and Pomerania within artillery range of Soviet troops at the end of 1944, this threat was considered very real. The hated Soviet enemy was literally at the gates of the Reich.

There was also a realization that the Soviets would exact a bloody revenge on Germany and the German people for the ruthless and brutal occupation of Russia. Eastern Front officers knew that Hitler's war against Russia was unique. If the Soviets won, then Germany would receive the treatment that had been meted out by Hitler. The social order would be destroyed, industry put at the disposal of the Soviet economy, agricultural production organized to feed Russia, and followed by mass deportations of manpower to the Soviet Union. For the German professional officer class, their role in Germany's future looked forlorn if the Soviets prevailed. Nazi leaders, SS officers, and party members realized they

Hasso von Manteuffel (left) was an accomplished panzer commander on the Eastern Front. He eventually commanded a panzer army in the ill-fated Ardennes Offensive in December 1944.

could expect no mercy from the Soviets. Hitler's orders to execute captured commissars meant the Soviets treated their ideological opponents in the same way.

On the frontline, German soldiers were subjected to harsh discipline. If troops wavered, then German officers were empowered to take desperate measures to maintain discipline. Officers could shoot on sight anyone deserting their post in battle. Court martials dispensed harsh sentences on offenders. This kind of thing was rare in veteran combat units during 1943–44, which relied on the loyalty to well-known officers and friends to ensure unit cohesion. In the chaos of the last half of 1944, as more and more poorly trained new units were thrown into battle, draconian measures were more necessary to keep troops fighting. This became an increasing problem as German units found themselves deployed on home territory, where the opportunities for desertion were much higher.

Despite their superior leadership, tactics, organization, and motivation, the German Army suffered its worst defeats in its history at the hands of the Red Army. Its victory at Kursk was decisive, and for the next 21 months it held onto the initiative on the Eastern Front. It was a question of numbers. At the start of 1944 the Red Army outnumbered German forces by two to one, but by the end of the year it had risen to three to one.

The Soviets had a much larger pool of manpower to draw on, with 45 million men aged between 20 and 59 in 1941, compared to only 25 million Germans of comparable age. Throughout 1943 and 1944 the Soviets were able to keep the size of the Red Army constant at just over six million men. The German Army's

The Wehrmacht

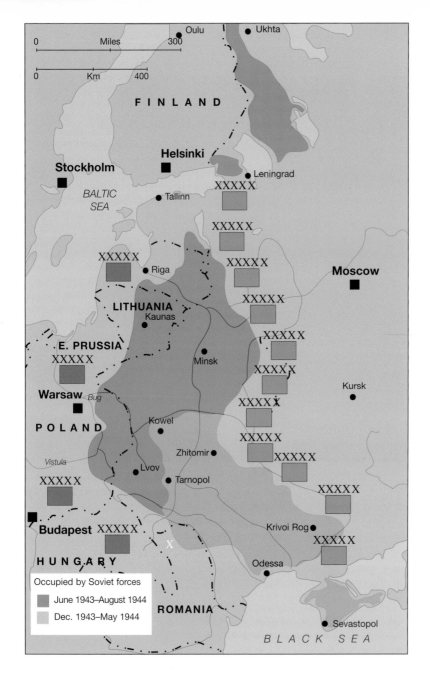

The scale of German losses in the East between June 1943 and August 1944 was massive. In addition, as can be seen, the Wehrmacht could deploy only four army groups against 11 Soviet fronts, and all the German army groups were short of men, equipment, and ammunition.

peak strength on the Eastern Front was 3.3 million men in June 1941, but by the end of October 1944 was down to 2.5 million. Its cumulative losses in the East in 1944 were just over a million men. Units were 500,000 men below strength at the start of the year, but the German Army's replacement system could only generate 128,000 new recruits a month. Not all these replacements were sent to the Eastern Front. Between July and August 1943, the German Army in the East suffered 654,000 casualties, but only received 279,000 replacements.

This was nowhere enough to keep pace with losses in Russia, but during 1944 the Germans lost more than 500,000 men in the West and the Balkans. With those level of losses there was no way the Germans could maintain the strength of their depleted existing divisions. The hammer blow came in June and July 1944 when Army Group Center and the Normandy Front collapsed. In Belorussia 285,000 Germans were dead, wounded, or captured, and 440,000 suffered a similar fate in Normandy. To fill the frontlines, desperate measures were required. The German training system was culled of its instructor cadres to establish a raft of new divisions. These were the men that fought in the Battle of the Bulge and during the Hungarian offensives. With no one left to train the next wave of recruits, the fate of the German Army was sealed.

War of Production

On top of its superiority in human resources, the Soviet Union was also able to bring its human, natural, and industrial resources to bear to build tanks, artillery, small arms, and other war matériel on a scale that Germany could not match.

During 1943, Soviet factories churned out 24,000 tanks and assault guns compared to only 9,500 in Germany. The following year, German production surged to a wartime high of 17,000 tanks and assault guns, but the Russians were able to boost their production to 29,000 heavy armored vehicles. Battlefield losses on both sides were staggering, with the Soviets losing 23,000 tanks in both 1943 and 1944, compared to some 7,500 German tank losses in 1943 and 7,600 in 1944. In spite of German efforts the huge losses made little impact on the frontline tank strength of the Red Army. At the start of 1943, it boasted 20,000 tanks, a year later it was 24,000 and as it was poised to strike at Berlin, the Red Army mustered an amazing 35,000 tanks and assault guns. The German Army on the Eastern Front put more than 2,000 tanks and assault guns into the field for Operation Citadel. From then on it was downhill. This ratio of production was similar for artillery, aircraft, and other equipment.

The inability of the German Army to break through the Soviet defenses around Kursk was a turning point in the war. Not only did the ordinary soldiers of the Red Army prove they could stand and fight on equal terms with the Wehrmacht, but Stalin's generals showed they were the masters of strategy on the Eastern Front.

The Red Army High Command (STAVKA) masterminded a brilliant defensive battle, and then went effortlessly over to the offensive once the German attack had run out of steam. Strategic tank reserves were moved forward under conditions of great secrecy and their intervention against II SS Panzer Corps on July 12 1943 at Prokhorovka totally surprised the Germans. STAVKA then choreographed diversionary offensives elsewhere on the Eastern Front to draw off Manstein's panzer divisions. When they were committed to action elsewhere, the Soviets launched another massive surprise offensive that ripped open Army Group South north of Kharkov, throwing the Germans back to the Dnieper.

The same strategy was used time and again over the next 21 months, to draw off German reserves and then strike elsewhere to devastating effect. Hitler's generals had to "firefight" against Soviet offensives with an ever-diminishing reserve of panzer units. There were never enough forces to plug the holes in the Eastern Front. Stalin's STAVKA recognized that its tactical forces were never going to be the equal of their German counterparts. It was therefore willing to incur huge losses on secondary fronts if it served the greater aim of making other German forces vulnerable to decisive attack. In the final two years of the war, STAVKA developed a number of specialist formations that were perfectly suited to this type of warfare. They created tank and mechanized corps which each boasted more than 200 tanks. The Germans had no answer to these units.

Arming Hitler's Army

Under Albert Speer's direction Germany's armaments industry produced some of the most effective weapons in military history – such as the Panther tank and Me 262 jet fighter – but ultimately failed to turn the war in Germany's favor.

A column of Tiger I tanks on the Eastern Front. In the key area of tank building, Germany was never able to compete with Soviet tank and assault gun production rates of 24,000 in 1943 and 29,000 in 1944, or the American rate of 29,000 tanks in 1943 and 17,000 in 1944. The scale of disparity between German tank production levels and those of its enemies can be gauged from the fact that Americans built some 88,410 tanks in World War II, the Soviet Union some 93,000, Great Britain 24,803, and Germany only 24,350.

One of the enduring images of the German Army is that of huge columns of tanks racing through Europe from one conquest to another. The newsreel footage of the Blitzkrieg years has forever immortalized the power and superiority of the German Army's tanks and other weapons.

During World War II the German armaments industry produced weapons that were far in advance of those used by Germany's enemies. As rapid advances in technology occurred during the war, the Germans more than kept match with their opponents, for example fielding the superlative Panther tank to counter the Soviet T-34.

If the German Army had an Achilles' heel, it was that its weapons were too complex and sophisticated to be easily mass-produced. As the war developed into a struggle between rival industrial systems, the Germans had to move from almost hand-made methods of construction to mass-production methods. Under the weight of relentless Allied bombing and horrendous frontline losses, however, the Germans could only lose the production war.

Hitler had a fascination with science and technology. He liked to surround himself with scientists, such as Dr. Ferdinand Porsche, who designed versions of the Tiger tank and Dr. Werner von Braun, the creator of the rocket-powered V weapons. These men worked at the cutting edge of science and engineering. Their results were far in advance of what their Allied or Soviet counterparts achieved. They had been encouraged in their work by Hitler when he launched Germany's rearmament campaign in the 1930s. Thanks to the Reich's largesse their employers, such as Krupp, Heinkel, Messerschmitt, Dornier, Henschel, MAN, Rheinmetall-Borsig, and Daimler-Benz, grew rich on armaments contracts in the run-up to war. These companies set up their own research and development departments and allowed their design teams to work on newer and even more advanced weapons, safe in the knowledge that the Führer would purchase the best for his Wehrmacht.

Products of the prewar period included the Panzer III and IV series tanks, MP-38 submachine gun, MG 34 machine gun and 88mm Flak gun. All these weapons far outclassed their rivals in design and quality of production.

Once the war began, the German Army's Ordnance Office started to generate requirements from frontline commanders for new equipment to counter the enemy's latest weapons or to equip new types of units. During the Blitzkrieg years the demand was mainly for modifications to existing weapons arising from their combat use. The shock caused by the first engagements against the new Soviet T-34s during the summer of 1941 led to the first major effort by the German Army to develop new weapons specifically in response to its enemy's technological advances. The T-34, with its sloped armor, 76mm gun, diesel engine, and simple design, rendered the 1930s-vintage Panzer IIIs and IVs obsolete overnight. Only the intervention of Stuka dive-bombers or 88mm Flak guns in the antitank role could neutralize T-34s effectively. As a stopgap the Panzer IV was equipped with a long-barrel 75mm main gun until a more permanent solution to the T-34 threat could be found.

New Tanks

Colonel-General Heinz Guderian, the father of the panzer force and then a senior commander on the Eastern Front, initially suggested that Germany should just start building copies of the T-34 because he could find little to improve upon its basic design. In November 1941, contracts were issued by the Army Ordnance Office for the development of the tank that eventually became known as the Panther from a design originally conceived by MAN. Few Allied tanks stood any chance of penetrating the Panther's armor unless they could close to within suicidal ranges, while its 75mm gun could pick off Shermans and Cromwells at ranges in excess of 6,561 ft (2,000 m). Even the mighty T-34 was outclassed by its German "clone," and its arrival in strength on the Eastern Front in the autumn of 1943 did much to ensure the survival of Manstein's Army Group South during the retreat into the Ukraine. The first appearance of a full battalion of Panthers in the East in August 1943 outside Kharkov was instrumental in the blunting of an attack by a whole Soviet tank army, with the Waffen-SS *Das Reich* Division's Panthers accounting for the majority of 184 T-34s knocked out in a single day.

Prototypes of the Tiger I tank were already being developed before the war, but with little urgency until the T-34 appeared. Hitler was fascinated by heavy tanks and for a time was taken with the design being proposed by his favorite designer, Dr. Porsche. This resulted in the bizarre situation that Porsche began building his version of the Tiger even before the Army Ordnance Office had selected its final design. A rival design by Henschel was eventually judged the best and put into production. The 90 Porsche Tigers were remanufactured into Elefant tank destroyers. In late 1942, as the Wehrmacht was starting to encounter new Allied tanks, such as the Sherman, Churchill, up-gunned T-34 and KV-1 heavy tank, the Army Ordnance Office began to lay plans for a successor to the Tiger I. Again Porsche and Henschel competed for the contract to build the new King Tiger or Tiger II, which combined the Panther's sloped lines with the Tiger I's new high-velocity 88mm gun and heavy armor. Production contracts were placed in January 1944.

Henschel's Tiger I was literally a mobile pillbox. Few Allied or Soviet tanks stood any chance of penetrating its 3.9-in (100-mm) frontal armor, even at very close range. The Tiger allowed the Germans to use their famous *panzerkeil* or wedge tactics at Kursk. Tigers would be posted to the front of an attack formation to absorb the deadly fire of dug-in Soviet 76.2mm antitank guns. Being impervious to this fire, which harmlessly bounced off their frontal armor, the Tigers would then be able to pick off the Soviet gun positions, clearing the way for less well-protected Panzer IVs and troop-carrying halftracks to pass through and exploit the breach in the now devastated Russian lines.

Weapons Crisis

While German Army field commanders were now happy that they were getting the quality of weapons needed to defeat the best the Allies or Soviets could produce by the spring of 1943, the Wehrmacht was in crisis. German industry just could not produce weapons and ammunition in quantities needed to fight a "total war." Tank production was one of the worst areas. In November 1942 when the Battle for Stalingrad was reaching its height, only 113 Panzer IVs rolled off the Krupp production lines. Henschel only built 17 Tiger Is and the Panther was months away from entering production. In the same month the Soviets built 900 T-34s. Panzer divisions in Russia were suffering massive losses and receiving only a handful of replacement tanks, while the Soviets seemed to have an unlimited supply of tanks.

This state of affairs had arisen for a variety of reasons. A major factor was the fact that the Nazi state encouraged rivalry and competition rather than coherent

A Tiger I on the production line. Strangely, the main tank production and assembly centers were never a top priority for Allied bombers, though they were still protected by antiaircraft gun defenses, mockups to confuse the bomb aimers, search lights to illuminate night raiders, electronic jamming, and giant smoke generators to obscure them from view if enemy aircraft appeared overhead.

direction of the economy. The German air force and navy controlled their own production. The big armaments companies and their designers had direct links to Hitler and were not adverse to using them to advance their pet projects, as the confusion over the Tiger project showed. "For street fighting Hitler ordered the construction of three Ram-Tigers," commented Guderian. "This 'knightly' weapon seems to have been based on the tactical fantasies of armchair strategists." This made things difficult for Hitler's war minister up to February 1942, the able Dr. Fritz Todt. After Todt's death in an air crash, Hitler picked his favorite architect, the 36-year-old Albert Speer, to head up the Armaments Ministry with a mandate to sort things out.

Speer knew little about weapons production but he was what would be known today as an expert in management theory, and soon set about reorganizing his new empire on more rational lines. He was a great believer in integrated teams or committees to bring together users, designers, and production experts to solve a problem. The over-sophistication and complete design of many German weapons was a major problem, even in apparently simple weapons such as small arms. Speer took drastic action: the MG-34 machine gun, which was considered the best weapon of its class in the world, was superseded by the MG-42 which was cheaper and easier to make because the majority of its parts were mass-produced stampings that could be assembled by unskilled labor.

Speer had limited effect on tank production because of continuing disagreements with the army high command about armored vehicle production requirements. The artillery wanted priority given to armored assault guns and self-propelled antitank guns. In December 1942, for example, all production of Panzer III chassis was switched to StuG III manufacturing. Even before Tiger and Panther

The Panther was by far the best all round tank fielded by any side in World War II. It borrowed the sleek lines of the T-34's sloped armor, which gave it excellent protection, and combined it with the deadly hitting power of the long-barreled Rheinmetall-Borsig 75mm L70 cannon.

production had increased to substantial levels in February 1943, the high command ordered Panzer IV production to be terminated in favor of the new vehicles.

The imminent collapse of the panzer force seemed to be near. Hitler recalled Guderian at the end of February 1943 from his enforced leave after being sacked during the failed attempt to take Moscow in December 1941 and appointed him inspector general of panzer troops, with sweeping powers to do something about the chaos in tank production. In modern management terms, Guderian sorted out the requirements or customer side of the problem, while Speer was now able to deliver what was required.

Guderian said that the scraping of Panzer IV production "would have certainly led to the defeat of the German Army in the near future." The decision was reversed as part of the first integrated and coherent plan for the equipping and organization of the panzer force. Realistic targets were set for Panzer IV, Panther, and Tiger production, testing, and development schedules. Designs were to be streamlined to ease production, proper systems established for the training of tank crews to use the new tanks, and requirements issued for supporting light armored vehicles, such as reconnaissance and troop-carrying halftracks and self-propelled antitank guns. He set out requirement for future research and development, with priority given to work on self-propelled antitank vehicles armed with the L70 long-barreled 75mm cannon. In spite of not being able to wrest control of assault gun production, except for heavy assault guns, from the artillery branch, Guderian's plan was the basis for the rebuilding of the panzer divisions during 1943 and into 1944.

Production Surges

Speer and Guderian worked wonders during the early part of 1943 to boost production of tanks and deliver them to the frontline panzer divisions. During 1943 Krupp and Nibelungenwerk turned out 3,023 Panzer IVs. MAN, MNH, DEMAG, Henschel, and Daimler-Benz produced 1,845 Panthers and Henschel delivered 643 Tiger Is. Some 200 of the new Panthers were even delivered in time for the Kursk Offensive in July 1943, although it became clear that the tank still had serious teething troubles. Assault gun production leaped from only 695 in 1942 to 3,041 in 1943 and more than 1,300 self-propelled antitank guns were built or converted including 345 of the 88mm-armed Nashorn.

Armored vehicle production reached its peak in 1944, at just the time when battlefield losses were reaching their height. Panzer IV production rose only marginally to some 3,800, but Panther production surged ahead to 3,584, production of 623 Tiger Is was augmented by the building of 376 Tiger IIs, StuG III and IV production reached nearly 6,000, and some 2,357 of the new Panzerjäger IV with the L70 cannon were built along with 226 of the 88mm-armed Jagdpanther. These figures need to be considered against total losses in 1943 of nearly 8,000 tanks and assault guns, and over 9,000 in 1944. This production surge allowed the frontline units to just keep their heads above water and gave Rommel a fighting chance of defeating the D-Day landings in June 1944.

Speer's methods were bearing fruit on such a spectacular scale that the Luftwaffe swallowed its pride and turned over responsibility for aircraft production to his ministry. Fighter production would quickly double. Speer soon became the key figure in the battle with the Royal Air Force (RAF) and US Army Air Force (USAAF) heavy bombers that were raiding German cities in increasing numbers. The Allied air commanders were convinced they could knock Germany out of the war if they could destroy its industrial base, so reducing the supply of

The Wehrmacht

weapons to her armies to a trickle. The British under Air Chief Marshal Arthur "Bomber" Harris attacked at night and used area bombing, primarily incendiaries, to create fire storms to de-populate cities of their industrial work force. The Americans, led by General Carl Spaatz, aimed to knock out key links in the German production chain, such as ball-bearing factories, with precision daylight bombing. Hitler tasked Speer with ensuring that the Reich's factories kept turning out vital war matériel in the face of daily raids by more than 600 bombers from August 1943 onward.

Speer first ordered increased anti-aircraft protection. Then, as the weight of attacks increased and the Americans inflicted heavy damage on the key ball-bearing factory at Schweinfurt in August 1943, cutting production by 35 percent, Speer devised a plan to relocate vital factories to safer areas in the east at the extreme range of Allied bombers. As the raids intensified so-called "unique manufacturing" sites had to be protected by huge concrete casements or moved into underground caverns. V weapon and Me 262 jet fighter production was moved underground during 1944. Speer also set up special committees to coordinate the decentralization of the production chain of key industries, so damage to one would not cripple any one type of weapons manufacturing.

Thanks to Speer's efforts, until early 1944 German industry largely weathered this storm and production levels were surging ahead of existing records. Almost 4,000 aircraft were built in 1944 compared to 2,000 in 1943, and in other sectors, such as armored vehicles and synthetic oil, record production levels were achieved. RAF area bombing was not adversely affecting morale, and the Luftwaffe was still shooting down large numbers of American B-17 bombers. Then, in January 1944, the USAAF began escorting its bombers with P-51

During the autumn of 1944, the Allies increased the pressure by systematically bombing the German railroad network, extending the campaign that had so successfully hamstrung Rommel's supply lines during the summer campaign in Normandy. It became almost impossible to move raw materials to factories or finished products to the fronts. A surge in refugees into the heart of Germany from the East further added to the dislocation of the transport system. In February 1945, Hitler put Speer in charge of the transport system to see if he could work his organizational magic again. He drafted in two million workers to repair the damage, but as they rebuilt one section of rail line, another was destroyed. By March 1945 the Reich's industrial base had been destroyed.

Mustang long-range fighters. More than 2,000 German fighters were shot down in February 1944, and a similar number were lost the following month. The Americans then switched to bombing aircraft factories to prevent the Luftwaffe replacing its losses. Aircraft production dropped by 60 percent. For two weeks in March 1944 the Americans struck a series of devastating blows against the synthetic oil sector. Repeat attacks in April and May were a hammer blow. Further attacks in the summer prevented the rebuilding of the key factories and

A Luftwaffe fighter factory following an RAF raid in 1943. Speer recalled: "From May 12, 1944, all our fuel plants became targets for concentrated attacks from the air. This was catastrophic: 90 percent of the fuel was lost us from that time on. The success of these attacks meant the loss of the war as far as production was concerned: our new tanks and jet planes were of no use without fuel."

German fuel production in September 1944 was only eight percent of the April level. The Luftwaffe was all but grounded for lack of fuel and the panzer divisions were running on empty tanks.

Speer's superhuman efforts apart, Germany was just not capable of matching the combined industrial weight of the Soviet Union, United States, and British Empire. They proved more adept at molding their economies for the requirements of total war. During the first four years of war the German economy was not geared up for total war, while the Americans, British, and Russians had at least a two-year head start. By the time Speer came on the scene it was probably too late.

The Allied bombing campaign never specifically targeted the German Army's tank, artillery, and small arms factories or caused major disruption to production. However, the decision to aim the focus of Allied bombing at the Luftwaffe, fuel supplies and, finally, the transport system had a devastating effect on Germany's fighting potential. Finally, the hammering of the rail network starved the frontline troops of new equipment and ammunition during the final battles on the borders of the Reich. The industrial front was the key to victory during World War II; Germany lost it and with it the war.

Partisan War

During the first two years of the war there was no partisan resistance to the German Army. However, following the invasions of Yugoslavia and the Soviet Union, the partisan problem exploded and began to tie down tens of thousands of German soldiers.

A female Soviet partisan keeps watch while her comrades rest. One reason why the Soviet partisan movement was so successful was the treatment meted out to Slav "sub-humans" by their Nazi overlords, as described by Major-General F.W. Mellenthin: "The Russians hoped for a Russian government to oppose Stalin and his clique but nothing was done to fulfill their hopes. Hitler liberated them from their communist commissars and gave them Reich commissars instead."

At its height in October 1942, Hitler's Third Reich stretched from the Bay of Biscay to the Caucasus mountains in southern Russia, and from the North Cape of Norway to El Alamein in Egypt. Some 150 million people in Western Europe and a further 70 million in the Soviet Union fell under the control of the Führer and his Nazi regime.

This was an empire that had only one purpose: to serve the needs of the Thousand Year Reich. Hitler ordered the crushing by physical force of any political, economic, or military resistance to his rule. Any man, woman, or child who refused to submit to the New Order was an enemy of the Reich and was to be arrested, deported for service as a slave laborer, or put to death.

In Führer Directive No. 33, issued in July 1941, Hitler summed up his attitude to resistance in the occupied territories. "... if the occupying power meets resistance, [it is be met] not by legal punishment of the guilty [but] by striking such terror into the population that it loses all will to resist. The commanders concerned are to be held responsible, together with their troops at their disposal, for quiet conditions in their areas. They will contrive to maintain order, not by requesting reinforcements, but by employing suitably draconian methods."

Those who failed Hitler's bizarre racial standards were classed as *Untermenschen*, or "sub-humans," and marked down for eventual death. Alongside the six million Jews, more than three million Russian prisoners of war, and at least a similar number of civilians in Eastern Europe and the Balkans were allowed to starve to death, or died of neglect on forced labor projects. Nazi rule in Western Europe was not as overtly brutal, but any flicker of resistance was crushed instantly.

With Germany military power at its zenith in the summer of 1941 as Hitler's armies seemed to heading for a swift conquest of the Soviet Union, resistance seemed futile. In Western Europe this was limited to isolated acts of sabotage, with which the German secret police, the Gestapo, were more than capable of dealing.

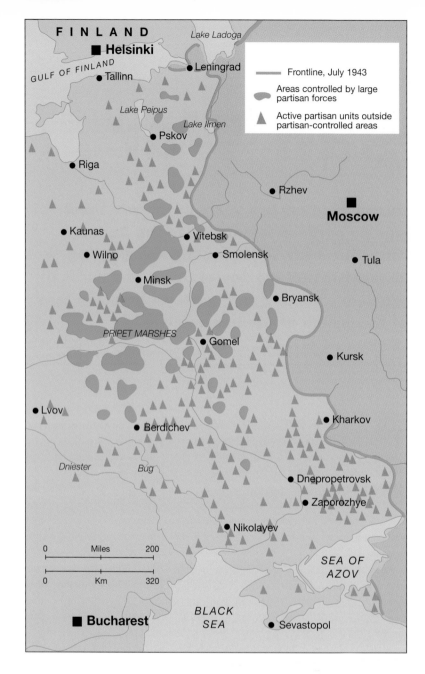

The scale of partisan activity behind German lines in mid-1943. Apart from diverting huge numbers of men from the frontline, the partisans had a highly damaging effect on German morale. Their random and deadly attacks made ordinary soldiers paranoid and increased their fear of the local population, who they could never be sure were not harboring partisans. Once the Soviets started to drive the Germans back after the Battle of Kursk in July 1943, the partisans also served as a pool of willing manpower for the hard-pressed Red Army. In newly liberated areas, for example, thousands of partisans would flock to fill the ranks of Soviet units advancing westward.

Only in Yugoslavia, where Tito's partisans were regrouping after the country's occupation by the Germans in April, was there any overt armed resistance.

The dramatic German advances into Russia during the summer of 1941 and the subsequent disintegration of most of the Soviet armies in the border regions was the genesis of a partisan movement that would eventually tie down scores of German divisions behind the Eastern Front. With Hitler's armies advancing eastward toward Moscow, hundreds of thousands of Soviet soldiers were left behind in the huge forests of the northern Ukraine, Belorussia, and the Baltic. The Germans tried to seal off these troops in pockets, but they just did not have enough men to trawl the wooded areas. The more determined and motivated Red

Partisan Front

While the partisans never inflicted a decisive military defeat on the Germans, except perhaps in Yugoslavia, the activities of the millions of men and women who took up arms against Hitler's tyranny in the Balkans and the Soviet Union tied down a huge portion of the Wehrmacht's fighting power at crucial stages in the war.

Russian and Yugoslav partisans alone tied down millions of German and Axis troops for years in fruitless garrison duties. The campaign against German communications before the Battle of Kursk and the Normandy landings are also credited with interrupting the Wehrmacht's supply lines, at a time when its troops were fighting the decisive engagements of the war.

The partisan war was a predictable side effect of Hitler's policy of racial war and economic exploitation, particularly in Russia where German troops were at first treated as liberators in some areas. Once it became clear that the Germans had an agenda of oppression and exploitation, the Russian people quickly rallied to Stalin's call to fight a "patriotic war" against the Nazi invaders. With the population alienated, there was just no way the 2.5 million German troops on the Eastern Front stood a chance of holding down a popular revolt by 70 million Russians, while at the same time fighting the six million troops of the Red Army. "If one single factor played a predominate part in the collapse of National Socialism and of Germany it was the folly of this racial policy," recalled Heinz Guderian.

The battle for the hearts and minds of the Russian people was perhaps the most crucial battle lost by Hitler during the war, and made defeat in the East inevitable. There would not be a repeat of the 1917 October Revolution to knock Russia out of the war. Hitler's Third Reich was eventually overwhelmed by the full might of 200 million vengeful Russians.

Army soldiers formed the nucleus of the huge partisan armies that would soon be harrying the Germans. The first resistance to the Germans was spontaneous and uncoordinated. Stalin and the Soviet leadership were preoccupied with forming a front to defend Moscow. In addition, the Soviet dictator and his secret police chief Lavrenti Beria were deeply suspicious of any armed force of Russians outside the control of the Communist Party. As increasing reports started to trickle into Moscow during the autumn of 1941 of the first partisan attacks on isolated German detachments, Stalin decided to send cadres behind enemy lines to take control of the resistance movement. The first coordinated attacks took place during the winter of 1941–42 in a bid to cut German communications as Red Army troops struck to throw Hitler's armies back from Moscow. In May 1942 the Soviets set up their Central Partisan Staff to control the operations of the estimated 142,000 partisans operating behind German lines. Huge areas of territory were outside German control, and the numbers of recruits only increased every time Axis troops resorted to harsh measures, such as collective punishments and mass executions, in increasingly desperate attempts to put an end to resistance.

In the buildup to the Battle of Kursk in the summer of 1943, the Central Partisan Staff directed that all partisan activity be aimed at disrupting German communications to the vital sector of the Eastern Front. In June and July 1943 there were more than 2,500 partisan attacks on German railroads, which destroyed at least 44 bridges, 298 railroad locomotives, and 1,223 railroad wagons. The Soviets claimed their partisans killed 300,000 Germans during the first two years of the war.

To keep their lines of communications open, the Germans had to deploy increasing numbers of troops. In 1942, some 25 special security divisions, 30 regiments, and over 100 police battalions were hunting partisans in western Russia. A year later half a million Russian, Ukrainian, and Baltic auxiliaries were recruited to fight off the partisans and help in the "Final Solution." Antipartisan operations and mass killing of Jews and other "sub-humans" were closely coordinated, with a series of ruthless SS officers, such as Erich von dem Bach-Zelewski, earning a notorious reputation in the process. Large numbers of Germany Army units were closely involved in these operations.

Increasingly the Germans resorted to more drastic actions to end partisan activity. Whole regions were laid waste to deny the partisans supplies and recruits. The population was deported to Germany as slave labor, livestock confiscated, crops destroyed, and buildings razed to the ground. From 1943 the size and scope of partisan operations had become such a threat to German communications that frontline divisions, including panzer units, were having to be pulled back to keep roads and railroads open. Typical antipartisan sweeps involved in excess of 10,000 men and they were launched on almost a monthly basis during 1943.

The partisans were now being resupplied by air, had their own artillery and mortars, antiaircraft guns, and an inexhaustible supply of recruits thanks to the Germans' misguided attempts to "pacify" Russia. Fanatical resistance was now put up against these major German search and destroy operations. One of the largest operations involved two panzer divisions, three German infantry divisions, a Hungarian division, SS units, and locally recruited forces.

Operation *Kottbus* was launched between May and July against a major partisan stronghold in the Borissow–Lepe area. It ended in an orgy of killing. A 16,000-strong force of Germans and renegade Russians found itself surrounded in a series of villages by the very partisans they were sent to eliminate. Minefields were laid by the partisans to trap the Germans, who resorted to forcing hundreds of local civilians to run through the minefields to open an escape route. The Germans owned up to a body count of 13,000, but only 950 rifles were seized, indicating the ratio of civilians to partisans killed by the German troops taking part.

Outside Russia, the main theater of partisan activity was the Balkans, with Yugoslavia, Greece, and Albania being the centers of resistance to German rule in

Suspects are rounded up during a German antipartisan sweep in Russia. Antipartisan operations in Russia were a mix of static defense and mobile offensive sweeps. Key bridges and major stretches of railroads could only be secured by the physical building of fortified support points, manned by a platoon of 20 to 30 men. Battalion-sized reaction forces were then based at regular intervals to patrol the main roads and railroads, ready to take the offensive against any partisan raids. Armored trains and small tank detachments were used to give security units overwhelming firepower. Air reconnaissance was used to regularly check railroad lines and roads for mines and other acts of sabotage. Areas of known partisan activity were ringed with support points to try to contain and stop the spread of hostile actions. Small patrols of *Jagdkommando*, or hunter, units were used to penetrate into partisan territory to gather intelligence and raid their bases. The services of the Gestapo were employed on captured partisans or their relatives to make them betray their comrades by leading German troops to their bases.

Offensives against Tito's partisans

1   Sept.–Dec. 1941

2   January 1942

3   June 1942

4   Jan.–March 1943

5   May–June 1943

By the fall of 1943 Tito's partisan movement had survived no less than five Axis offensives against it.

the region. The demise of the Serbian Royalist regime in Belgrade opened the way for the Germans and Italians to split Yugoslavia into rival spheres of interest. Serbia and northern Slovenia were incorporated directly into the Reich. Albania and Kosovo came under Italian control along with most of the Dalmatian coast. Hungary and Bulgaria were allowed to annex chunks of the country as well. A puppet *Ustashi* regime was set up in Zagreb, controlling most of Croatia and Bosnia.

The German presence in the Balkans was initially only a token effort of two divisions, with the bulk of garrison duty falling on 38 Italian divisions to release German forces for the Eastern Front. Resistance at first was fragmented, with Royalist elements in Yugoslavia, Albania, and Greece initially receiving backing from the British. The fragile nature of the support they had among their populations became increasingly clear as new partisan groups, led by communists, started to lead the resistance to brutal Nazi dominance in the region. Marshal Tito's communist partisans in Yugoslavia were by far the most successful in battle and in attracting popular support, so much so that in 1944 the Germans had 700,000 troops in the Balkans in an effort to destroy the partisan movement.

The Army and the Waffen-SS

The elite divisions of the Waffen-SS made a valuable contribution to the German war effort. However, many of their members took part in atrocities, while many of the second-rate Waffen-SS divisions were little more than criminal organizations.

The Waffen-SS crew of a Tiger I take advantage of a rare lull in the fighting on the Eastern Front for a wash and a shave in the summer of 1943. The personnel of the Waffen-SS panzer divisions were generally well led, motivated, and generously equipped with the latest weapons and equipment.

Like most dictators, Hitler was obsessed with threats to his rule, either real or imaginary. He saw the SS (*Schutz Staffel* – Protection Squad) as the guarantor of his control of power in Germany. It was the SS that had slaughtered the leaders of the Nazi paramilitary SA (*Sturmabteilung* – Brown Shirts) in 1934, and throughout the early years of his rule Hitler built up the SS to ensure that he had a totally loyal group of armed men. It became the Third Reich's Praetorian Guard.

Throughout the 1930s the SS, under the trusted henchman Heinrich Himmler, was expanded from being Hitler's elite bodyguard into a massive police, prison, intelligence, and security organization. It was a state within a state, loyal only to Hitler. Several *Standarten* (regiments) of paramilitary SS were formed initially for guard and security duties in Berlin. By the late 1930s they included the *Leibstandarte Adolf Hitler*, and were fully fledged combat units equipped with machine guns, light antitank guns, antiaircraft weapons, and artillery. In 1940 they became the Waffen-SS (Armed SS). They were to be the fourth branch of the Wehrmacht, alongside the army, navy, and air force. Rapid expansion soon followed. In 1939 the SS *Verfügungsdivision* was formed to take part in the Polish invasion, and thereafter the Waffen-SS was expanded into three fully fledged motorized divisions: the *Leibstandarte*, *Das Reich*, and *Totenkopf*.

Hitler and Himmler were determined to protect the racial purity of their creation and thus only specially selected volunteers were allowed into its ranks. These men were to be the core of the Waffen-SS throughout the war, providing the officer and noncommissioned officer cadres for the 38 Waffen-SS divisions that were formed over the next five years. Everything about the SS was unique: its budget was separate from other branches of the Wehrmacht, it was administered by the SS organization, and it had separate recruitment and training centers. The Waffen-SS also had a different uniform and rank system from the Wehrmacht, and used the "Heil Hitler" salute rather than the army one.

But the Waffen-SS needed professional military men to guide and mold it. Disillusioned army generals and officers, such as Paul Hausser, were attracted to it by its wealth, reputation, and political influence within the Nazi regime. In turn they transformed the organization, training, and outlook of the Waffen-SS. During the 1930s army officers dismissed the Waffen-SS as "asphalt soldiers," in a reference to their employment on ceremonial duties in Berlin. By the end of the Greek campaign in 1941, the three new Waffen-SS divisions had won their spurs in action and army commanders were glowing with praise.

As the war in Russia stalled at the end of 1941, Hitler blamed the setbacks on the German Army's lack of fighting spirit. He sacked 35 high-ranking army officers and set in train plans to massively expand the Waffen-SS. Its three elite divisions were to be formed into panzer corps, and a number of Waffen-SS panzergrenadier, cavalry, mountain, and police divisions were to be formed to put National Socialist resolve into the war on the Eastern Front. In 1941 there were 150,000 men in the Waffen-SS; within three years this figure had jumped to 600,000. The final number of Waffen-SS divisions was 38, including seven panzer divisions. Over a million men served in the ranks of the Waffen-SS, and more than a third of them were killed in action.

Foreign Legions

Its heavy casualty rate resulted in the Waffen-SS having an insatiable appetite for manpower. The losses during the heavy fighting in southern Russia in the winter of 1942–43 were too much for the SS system to cope with. The need to fill the ranks of the growing numbers of divisions meant recruitment was expanded to include so-called ethnic Germans from Eastern Europe. As casualties mounted during 1943, the Waffen-SS started to turn to Nazi sympathizers in occupied countries to fill its ranks. These were Hitler's so-called "foreign legions," which contained in their ranks a very diverse group of men. They ranged from Scandinavian, Dutch, French, and Belgian Nazi collaborators, who were used to fill out elite panzer units, to Ukrainian Catholics, Bosnian and Albanian Muslims, Hungarians, Italians, Latvians, and Estonians, who were employed in antipartisan units. There was even a British Waffen-SS unit, the British Free Corps, recruited from renegade prisoners of war, as well as an Indian Legion which recruited 2,000 prisoners of war in to its ranks.

This wholesale recruitment of foreigners was one of the main differences between the Waffen-SS and the Wehrmacht, which was restricted to recruiting only citizens of the Reich. In spite of this foreign recruitment campaign, the Waffen-SS and Wehrmacht were still in competition to find suitable German recruits to fill their ranks. The elite Waffen-SS panzer and panzergrenadiers divisions needed well-educated and motivated recruits, as did the Wehrmacht.

In the run-up to the Battle of Kursk in July 1943, the Waffen-SS had to resort to diverting Luftwaffe personnel into the ranks of II SS Panzer Corps, because the pool of "racially pure" volunteers had been exhausted. And every time the Waffen-SS panzer divisions were rebuilt over the next 18 months the net had to be spread wider to find enough men to make up losses. The air force and navy were regularly culled for manpower, and soon army draftees were being diverted to the Waffen-SS as well. In late 1943, a special recruitment drive was made to attract teenagers from the Hitler Youth movement into a new Waffen-SS division.

Many of the Waffen-SS divisions recruited from Eastern, Central, and Southern Europe were of little use beyond low-level police operations against poorly equipped partisans. These units operated in Yugoslavia and the huge forests of western Russia. Their performance was mixed. On the one hand they knew the ground they were fighting on and had a good understanding of their enemies, but motivation and discipline were big problems. The Latvians and Estonians were highly motivated to fight the Soviets because of Stalin's brutal occupation of their countries in 1940. They were also some of the most zealous exterminators of Jews in the whole of the SS. The Croatian and Bosnian *Handschar* Division was equally brutal but was a poor fighting unit, and was eventually disarmed by army troops who needed its weapons and equipment. The

A machine-gun team of I SS Panzer Corps during the fighting in Kharkov, March 1943. Hausser's men fought a bitter battle to retake the city, and suffered 11,500 killed achieving their victory. The recapture of Kharkov convinced Hitler that his SS soldiers could be relied upon to retrieve any seemingly hopeless situation in the East.

most bizarre foreign unit of the Waffen-SS was the so-called Vlasov Free Russian Army under the captured Soviet general, Andrei Vlasov. In 1944 Himmler formed two divisions from anticommunist Russian prisoners in the vain hope of stirring a revolt among Stalin's troops. It was too little, too late. After spending three years trying to kill as many Slavs as they could, the idea of the SS being allies of the Russian people was clearly ludicrous. The ranks of the Russian Waffen-SS divisions were filled with prisoners of war who had faced starvation and death in Himmler's concentration camp system; they naturally took the easy option. It was not until May 1945 that Vlasov's ragtag force saw action, fighting alongside Czech partisans against the Waffen-SS garrison of Prague.

Fire Brigade

The Waffen-SS fought in every theater on mainland Europe, and became indispensable to Hitler's war effort from 1943 onward. The seven elite Waffen-SS panzer divisions became known as the "Führer's fire brigade" because he rushed them from one crisis front to another to "extinguish" enemy breakthroughs. To equip them for this role, they received the best equipment the Reich's weapons factories could turn out. They were also top of the list for the replacement of destroyed or damaged tanks, field guns, and armored vehicles. In addition, every effort was made to keep them up to strength with trained manpower.

The majority of the other Waffen-SS divisions were employed on less-crucial fronts, in largely static defense roles or on counter-partisan duties. The reputation of these units was mixed, to say the least. The divisions that fought with Army Group North besieging Leningrad and later defending the Baltic States, such as the *Nordland* Panzergrenadier Division, acquitted themselves well. This division played a key role in saving the Eighteenth Army from encirclement at Riga in September 1944. The SS *Nord* Mountain Division fought for three years in the Arctic as part of the German thrust to capture the Russian port of Murmansk, establishing an excellent reputation alongside the army's elite mountain units.

To senior German Army commanders, the Waffen-SS was a mixed blessing. There was resentment that Hitler's private army was siphoning off its best recruits and had the pick of the production from the Reich's armament factories. However, field commanders grew to value the fighting qualities of the mainstream Waffen-SS divisions, in particular the panzer units. Waffen-SS units usually came with superb equipment and lavish supplies of ammunition, making them a powerful addition to the fighting power of any army headquarters that had them assigned to it. For their part, Waffen-SS commanders were keen to win their spurs in battle and regularly offered up their units for tasks that army officers had refused. This rivalry became legendary, and no Waffen-SS officer wanted to be seen to fail any battlefield mission. The more glory the Waffen-SS could gain at the expense of the army, the better.

Hausser's efforts to professionalize the Waffen-SS officer corps was largely successful in the panzer divisions. This was one of the main reasons that army commanders soon came to value having Waffen-SS panzer units under their command. Waffen-SS staff officers were trained to army standards and doctrine, so their divisions could easily be taken under command by army headquarters.

However, there were tensions and disputes, which mainly stemmed from the fact that several favored Waffen-SS commanders, such as Hausser and Sepp Dietrich, commander of the *Leibstandarte*, had direct communications to the Führer. During the Battle of Kharkov in March 1943, for example, these tensions came to the fore when Hausser ignored the orders of his direct army superior to besiege the city and mounted a costly, but ultimately successful, direct assault. This was necessary to regain face with Hitler after Hausser had earlier pulled out of the city rather than risk encirclement, in direct contravention of a Führer order.

Hausser's decision to pull out of Kharkov when he realised that the Führer's orders were senseless was the beginning of a rift between Hitler and his senior Waffen-SS commanders. As the latter rose to command divisions, corps, and armies, these men saw the folly of the Hitler's "fight to the last man and last bullet" orders. They grew closer to their army counterparts, such as Erich von Manstein, Heinz Guderian, and Erwin Rommel, who tried to limit the Führer's interference in operational and tactical matters.

As the war went on, Waffen-SS panzer commanders increasingly ignored the Führer's more bizarre orders. Kurt "Panzer" Meyer was the youngest German general of the war, rising to command the Hitler Youth division at 34 years of age in 1944, on account of his combat record. At the height of the fighting in Normandy during July 1944, he was regularly ignoring the Führer's orders to fight to the last man. "We were meant to die in Caen but one just couldn't watch those youngsters being sacrificed to a senseless order," was Meyer's assessment.

Dietrich was openly sceptical of the chances of Operation Watch on the Rhine decisively defeating the Americans in December 1944. A few months later, commanding the Sixth SS Panzer Army, he pulled his troops back from Hungary rather than risk encirclement by Soviet forces. The Führer was livid and ordered his once-favored Waffen-SS panzer units to be stripped of their honorific *Adolf Hitler* sleeve cuffs.

If the Waffen-SS panzer units eventually became kindred spirits of their army counterparts thanks to their shared experiences at the front, some elements of the organization were nothing more than murderers in uniform. The Waffen-SS units led by Erich von dem Bach-Zelewski, Jürgen Stroop, and Dr. Oskar Dirlewanger were only good at slaughtering innocent civilians. The one time Dirlewanger and his troops were entrusted with fighting at the front they deserted their posts, with their commander leading the race to safety, leaving

SS-Obergruppenführer und Generaloberst der Waffen-SS Paul Hausser. An ex-*Reichswehr* general, he joined the armed SS in 1934 and was appointed its inspector two years later. A competent commander, he was commander of the *Das Reich* Division, the SS Panzer Corps, and ended the war as commander of Army Group G. Known affectionately as "Papa" to his men, Hausser's greatest contribution to the Waffen-SS was ensuring it was instilled with sound military military principles (that it so patently lacked in the 1930s). He was not above ignoring Hitler's more extreme orders, such as holding Kharkov in February 1943. To do so, as Hausser recognized, would mean the destruction of the SS Panzer Corps. He therefore cut his radio link to Führer headquarters and evacuated the city. Hitler was infuriated, but Hausser's recapture of the city the following month redeemed him in Hitler's eyes.

army units to restore the frontline. Army officers shunned them, and even Waffen-SS panzer officers regarded them with contempt. Hitler and Himmler, however, realized that these men had their uses.

Stroop graduated from the *Totenkopf* and *Leibstandarte* Divisions to command of the SS in Warsaw in April and May 1943. In response to the uprising in the city's Jewish ghetto, Stroop mustered a force of 820 Waffen-SS, 200 SS police, and 350 Ukrainian and Latvian SS men to put down the revolt. It took almost a month for Stroop's butchers to comb the ruins of the ghetto and

clear its 56,000 residents. Stroop reported 5,000 Jews killed in explosions and fires, 7,000 in the course of the fighting, and a further 7,000 during the transportation of the ghetto's former residents to Treblinka extermination camp. Every building in the ghetto was then flattened. Colonel-General Alfred Jodl, head of the OKW operations staff, accused Stroop of being a "dirty arrogant SS swine" after he produced a book about his "glorious victory."

Dirlewanger was a convicted child rapist and drunkard who was at one point thrown out of the Waffen-SS for drunkenness. The brigade, later a division, that bore his name was largely recruited from violent criminals and earned notoriety during the Warsaw Uprising.

Bach-Zelewski was put in charge of putting down the revolt in the Polish capital in August 1944 by Himmler. The Waffen-SS general's pedigree for this task was his command of the 1st SS Motorized Infantry Brigade in the Minsk area during 1942, where it conducted large-scale killings of Jews and alleged partisans. "Von dem Bach has been entrusted with the task of pacifying Warsaw, that is to say he will raze it to the ground," remarked Himmler.

During the brutal battle for Warsaw, Himmler let loose Dirlewanger's troops and a brigade of turncoat Ukrainian prisoners under the command of a very

A Panzer IVH of either the *Totenkopf* or *Wiking* Divisions on the Eastern Front in 1944. There were seven SS panzer divisions in total, and their intervention was decisive at certain points in the war in preventing a major German defeat: in southern Russia in early 1943, outside Warsaw and in Normandy in mid-1944, and at Arnhem in September 1944.

unsavory character named Kaminski. Army and even Waffen-SS officers in Warsaw were outraged at the behavior of these units. Bach-Zelewski took the precaution of having Kaminski and a number of other subordinates executed to cover up the evidence of their crimes.

After the war Waffen-SS officers tried to claim that their units were separate from the mainstream SS, that they and their men were just "soldiers like other soldiers," and the likes of Bach-Zewelski were "rotten apples". The evidence suggests otherwise.

Heinz Lammerding, commander of the *Das Reich* Division in Normandy and a high-profile Waffen-SS combat veteran, was Bach-Zelewksi's chief of staff during antipartisans operations in the Pripet Marshes in 1943, which produced a body count of 15,000 dead Russian civilians. In France the following year his "combat" troops publicly hanged 94 suspected resistance fighters, and he ordered that the village of Oradour-sur-Glane be raised to the ground after a resistance ambush killed one of his officers. More than 400 people were burned alive after being locked inside the village's church by *Das Reich* troops.

The Waffen-SS was also thoroughly implicated in the actions of the SS *Einsatzgruppen* in Russia, particularly the *Totenkopf* Division which was closely linked with the SS concentration camp organization that was responsible for putting Hitler's "Final Solution" of the Jewish question in action. Senior officers and ordinary soldiers of the *Totenkopf* Division were regularly posted back to the concentration camps throughout the war.

The ugly side of the Waffen-SS: rounding up Jews in the Soviet Union. The *Einsatzgruppen* were special detachments of SS troops whose sole purpose was to find and kill Jews. They followed up behind the main army groups during the summer of 1941, and began to systematically kill any "sub-humans" they could find. First they made do with machine gunning their victims, but when this became time-consuming and messy they moved onto gassing them in special sealed buses. During their operations, the *Einsatzgruppen* managed to kill an estimated 500,000 Jews. There is ample documentary evidence of Waffen-SS participation in *Einsatzgruppen* operations, with more than two-thirds of *Einsatzgruppe* A, which operated in the Baltic States in 1941, being made up of Waffen-SS men.

A *Totenkopf* veteran, Friedrich Jeckeln, was placed in command of *Einsatzgruppe* C in the Ukraine, during July and August 1941. His efforts resulted in the death of 100,000 Jews. Promoted to a command in the Baltic during late 1941 and into 1942, Jeckeln was responsible for the murder of more than 100,000 Jews. During this time he set up a special warehouse to store the looted possessions of his victims. This was then used to supply the *Totenkopf* Division. Whatever they may have said, Waffen-SS men were certainly not just soldiers.

Fighting the Materialschlacht

In the West in 1944 the Allies could call upon massive firepower, but the Germans showed them how to conduct defensive battles against overwhelming odds and under threat of air attack, and how to make an enemy pay dearly for ground in blood.

Although the Allied invasion of Normandy on June 6, 1944, caught the German Army by surprise on the day, in terms of timing and location the Wehrmacht had been making extensive preparations to fight the Western Allies in France for several months.

The campaign in northwest Europe saw Hitler's army ground down against the huge material resources of the Americans and British. The Germans now faced a technologically advanced enemy that had control of the air in a large-scale battle. However, the ability of the Wehrmacht to fight against these odds was enormously to its credit as a military machine.

A key factor in holding the Normandy front together for most of June and into July was the leadership of Erwin Rommel, the hero of North Africa and commander of Army Group B. While the lower level and divisional commanders were of good quality, higher up the chain of command was not so impressive. Friedrich Dollman of the Seventh Army was a far from inspiring leader, and other senior officers, including Hans Speidel, Rommel's own chief of staff, were preoccupied with the preparations for the Bomb Plot against Hitler.

The competent officers were being killed or injured at an alarming rate. One corps commander was killed in an air raid and three divisional commanders also fell victim to roving Allied fighter-bombers. The entire staff of Panzer Group West was killed in a huge bombing raid designed to obliterate its headquarters. In the first month of the battle some 96,000 Germans were killed, wounded, or taken prisoner in Normandy. Only 6,000 replacements and 17 new tanks were able to weave their way through the ruins of the French transport system to the front. Supplies of ammunition and fuel were also running short.

Weary German soldiers during Operation Watch on the Rhine in December 1944. This was the last great offensive in the West in World War II. Within five months of its failure, Hitler's Third Reich had collapsed.

Amid this carnage, Rommel was everywhere. He drove up to the front on almost every day of the battle, giving morale-boosting talks to the young troops who idolized him, backslapping tired divisional commanders, and cajoling wavering corps commanders. He would then return to his headquarters and spend the night pleading with Hitler, and anyone who would listen back in Germany, for more troops, tanks, and supplies. Rommel may not have been able to pull off one his dramatic panzer outflanking maneuvers during the Normandy battles, but he proved himself to be a master of improvisation, using his armored units to plug gaps in the line, time and time again inflicting heavy losses on the Allies. It was a solid and professional defense.

There has been a lot of speculation that Rommel was involved in or at least forewarned of the Bomb Plot. The truth is difficult to establish, but it was clear that by mid-July 1944 he was convinced that the great gamble had failed. His army was not strong enough to throw back the Allies into the sea. This could only mean the defeat of Germany. Some sources have suggested he was preparing to negotiate an armistice with the Allies if Hitler refused to bring an end to the war. Whatever the truth of the matter, Rommel was seriously injured when his car was shot up by an RAF Typhoon on July 16. He was in hospital when the Bomb Plot failed and could not influence events. As Hitler took his revenge on the conspirators, Rommel was offered the choice of suicide or an appearance before a People's Court. He took the cyanide capsule and was dead soon afterward.

Hitler now cleared out the plotters from the German headquarters in France and installed men who would follow his orders to the letter. Field Marshal Walther Model, one of the Führer's favorites from Russia, was installed as commander in chief in the West. Model quickly made his views on the way the battle for Normandy was being fought clear to Fritz Bayerlein, commander of the *Panzer Lehr* Division, when the latter asked permission to make a tactical withdrawal. "My dear Bayerlein, in the East our divisions take their rest in the frontline," barked Model. "And that's how things are going to be done here in the future. You will stay with your formations where you are."

The Normandy battle was now micromanaged by the Führer from his bunker in East Prussia. "No retreat" orders were issued almost daily. Within weeks the front had collapsed, and the bulk of the army Rommel had built to repel the Allied invasion was in ruins.

Defeat Inevitable?

The German defeat in Normandy turned on a number of events and factors, many of them out of the control of Rommel and his troops battling to stem the tide of Allied men and machines pouring off the invasion beaches.

The major failure of German strategy in Normandy was the confusion in the Wehrmacht chain of command. No one would take responsibility to order the launching of an immediate counterattack by the units, including the 21st Panzer Division, to hit the Allies hard before they consolidated their bridgehead. This had worked in Italy, where prompt action by commanders on the spot had turned the Anzio and Salerno landings into bloodbaths for the Allies. No single commander had authority over the panzer reserves and, as a consequence, nothing happened because no one at the Führer's headquarters was willing to interrupt Hitler's meetings with the Hungarian prime minister. As a result vital hours were lost.

Hitler and Rommel's obsession with the Pas de Calais also meant only five of the 10 reserve panzer divisions were within a day's drive of Normandy. The U.S.

The Atlantic Wall

As Allied aerial photographic interpreters pored over images of the French coastline during the spring of 1944, they became increasingly alarmed at the scale of the construction work underway on the Third Reich's western rampart. They were observing the results of Field Marshal Erwin Rommel's crash program to turn the coastal defenses along the Atlantic coast and English Channel into a real obstacle for any Allied amphibious invasion.

After a tour of the dilapidated German defenses from the Bay of Biscay to Holland in December 1943, Rommel wrote a report calling for the fortifications to be revamped. For his efforts, the hero of the Africa Corps was appointed commander of the coastal region of France. He immediately ordered a huge construction effort to strengthen what soon became known as the Atlantic Wall. All major coastal towns and ports were turned into veritable fortresses, with huge concrete pillboxes and gun emplacements positioned to protect them (a typical example is shown below). The monster gun positions in the Pas de Calais symbolized this effort to create "concrete battleships" at key parts along the Atlantic Wall to prevent the Allies seizing a port intact. These efforts were complemented by extensive engineering work to turn likely invasion beaches into a death trap for any Allied amphibious or airborne assault. Explosive tipped steel and concrete traps were placed out at sea, below the waterline, to penetrate the hulls of approaching landing craft.

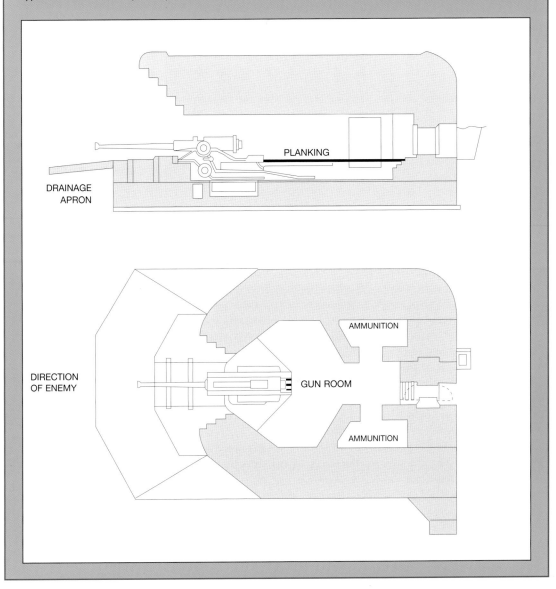

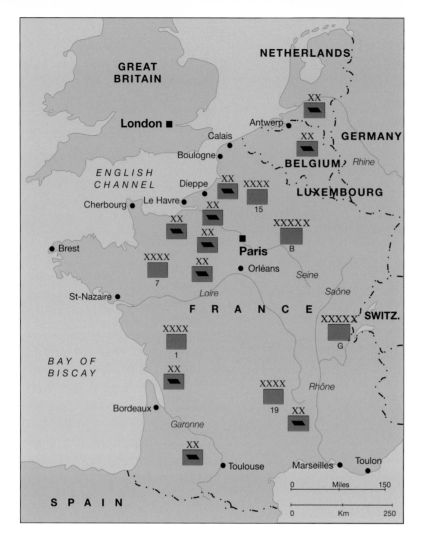

landing on Omaha beach was, in effect, held by the German defenders for most of June 6, but there were no armored reserves anywhere near to counterattack. A golden opportunity to repeat Salerno was lost.

Once established ashore, the Allies and Germans became locked in a war of attrition: *Materialschlacht*. During June the Germans and Allies both put a million men each into the battle for Normandy. Seven weeks after D-Day, the Allies had 1.45 million men ashore, along with 2,000 tanks. The Germans had lost nearly 200,000 men and 400 tanks. This was a similar number of men to the losses incurred by the Allies; however, a month later the Allies had two million men in France, and the Germans were down to 600,000 with only 100 tanks. Not surprisingly, the Germans were soon retreating to their homeland.

Apart from the imbalance between the Germans and the Allies in western France, two other factors critically affected the battle for Normandy. Firstly, the collapse of Army Group Center meant there was a more pressing need for reinforcements in the East. Panzer divisions in Italy and elsewhere that had been promised to Rommel were diverted to Poland to shore up the Eastern Front. Secondly, the Allied air forces had effectively isolated Rommel's troops in Normandy. The entire French railroad network was pounded into oblivion by Allied bombers.

The disposition of German armies and panzer divisions on the eve of the Allied invasion of Normandy. French beaches along the Atlantic coast were sewn with millions of antitank and antipersonnel mines. Farther up the beaches, large concrete roadblocks were built to close any vehicle routes inland. Behind the beaches likely parachute and glider landing zones were also mined and covered with obstacles to prevent landings. Not content with physically blocking any Allied landing, Rommel insisted that every beach be covered by machine-gun, mortar, and artillery positions. Rommel wanted to stop the invaders on the beach and then kill them there, before they had time to establish a firm bridgehead. Once the beach defenses had done their work, Rommel wanted reserve panzer divisions to be quickly brought forward to deliver the coup de grâce against what remained of the Allied invasion force.

The *bocage*

Normandy's distinctive terrain is known as the *bocage*. The small fields, hedgerows, and villages that make up the *bocage* to the west of Caen quickly became a bloody battlefield in June 1944 as Allied and German forces struggled for supremacy.

Modern intensive farming had yet to arrive in Normandy, with agriculture following much the same pattern as it had for hundreds of years before. Small farm holdings predominated, and this produced an interlinked network of small fields separated by ancient hedgerows. Crucially, these hedgerows had grown into thick barriers, reinforced by very high and thick earth banks. Even the biggest German or Allied tank found the Normandy hedgerows almost impossible to pass through or over. Without specialist engineering or demolition equipment, the hedgerows proved impassable.

Tank movement was effectively channeled along the few roads, making it easy for enemy antitank gunners to delay and hold up advances for hours and days at time. The control of villages and their crucial crossroads became an imperative for both sides.

It was up to the Allied infantry to move forward systematically and clear every hedgerow or village. Tanks could only be used in ones or twos to support infantry attacks. There were no dramatic tank advances in the *bocage*.

For the German defenders the *bocage* was an amazing advantage. The hedgerows not only provided superb obstacles to movement, they were ideal for digging in machine guns and antitank weapons. Earth-roofed bunkers provided much-needed overhead protection from Allied artillery and mortar fire. Every village was turned into a fortress, roads were blocked, houses hid snipers and machine-gun teams, and tanks disappeared into barns and industrial buildings.

Intermingled between the fields and villages was a series of small but thick woods. These also helped channel movement toward German defensive positions. Another favorite German tactic was to post snipers high in trees, allowing them to pick off Allied officers at long distance. This made Allied junior commanders very wary and hesitant.

The *bocage* effectively turned the battle for Normandy into a bloody war of attrition. With decisive maneuver denied to them, the Allies had to resort to wearing the Germans down, throwing more men and equipment into the battle until the enemy's material, physical, and psychological ability to resist had collapsed.

Every road and railroad bridge between Normandy and the German border was damaged. Whole regions of France rose in revolt, further complicating the Germans' attempts to keep their precarious lines of communications open. At the same time, German naval and air force units were successfully neutralized by Allied air and maritime supremacy. The Luftwaffe was unable to intervene in any meaningful way to stop the huge Allied buildup. When one American general complained to a U.S. Army Air Force commander that his headquarters had been bombed, the American airman just produced aerial photographs of the German and Allied rear areas. On the German side of the lines there was nothing moving, only downed bridges and broken railroad lines. Across the lines the roads were crammed with nose-to-tail truck convoys heading for the front. The Allies won the *Materialschlacht*.

The Atlantic Wall

Hitler loved to order the pouring of thousands of tons of concrete into the many defensive lines built by Organization *Todt* construction engineers during the war. The mere act of creating huge "facts on ground" gave him a warm feeling. Concrete bunkers could not "retreat" during the mobile battles his generals were so keen on. Not surprisingly, the Führer had great hopes for his Atlantic Wall. Once the Allied invaders were trapped on France's beaches by the mines, booby traps, and machine-gun posts of the Atlantic Wall, he would order his carefully nurtured panzer reserves to finish them off.

The reality was less impressive. Few of the 50 or so infantry divisions garrisoning the Atlantic Wall were top-rate units; the majority were made up of former Russian prisoners of war or medically substandard German troops. Away from the coast, the 10 panzer and panzergrenadier divisions held in reserve were also of mixed quality. Many were in the process of being rebuilt after suffering

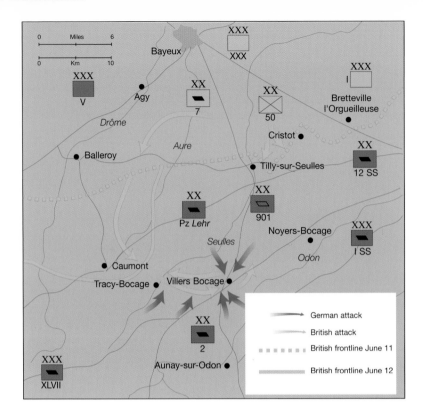

A prime example of German armored tactical and technical superiority. The British 7th Armored Division launched an attack toward Villers Bocage in an effort to outflank the Panzer *Lehr* Division. However, the heavy tank battalion of I SS Panzer Corps, commanded by tank ace Michael Wittmann, struck back and stopped the British advance.

heavy losses on the Eastern Front. There was also a question mark over the leadership of German armies in France, which was seen as a comfortable backwater, far away from the horrors of Russia. The arrival of Field Marshal Erwin Rommel at the end of 1943 as commander of the invasion defenses shook much of the complacency out of the German forces in France, but he was far from finished in his work when the Allies finally launched Operation Overlord.

The German reaction to D-Day was lethargic. Many key commanders, including Rommel himself, were away from their headquarters on June 6. Counterattacks by the troops in Normandy were halfhearted, and Hitler delayed releasing the panzer reserves because of continuing fears of another landing in the Pas de Calais. It was not until June 7 that the first significant counterattack got underway, when the *Hitlerjugend* Division slammed into the Canadians north of Caen.

British and Canadian troops came ashore on the eastern flank of the Allied invasion, under the command of General Bernard Montgomery, Rommel's nemesis from North Africa. His object was to capture Caen swiftly and then push his armored divisions inland to complete the German rout. Rommel had other ideas.

For the next six weeks Montgomery launched his troops forward in a series of set-piece battles of growing intensity, as more forces poured into the bridgehead and became available to him. First he sent forward the 7th Armored Division, the famous Desert Rats, on a daring outflanking attack to the west of Caen. German Tiger tanks ambushed the force and sent it reeling back to the bridgehead (see map on this page). Next the British XXX and VIII Corps began Operation Epsom to envelop Caen, but four Waffen-SS panzer divisions concentrated to hammer them hard. Into July, Montgomery continued to chip away until his infantry were at the gates of Caen. He then launched Operation Goodwood to outflank the town from the east. Three British armored divisions, with almost 900 tanks, backed by

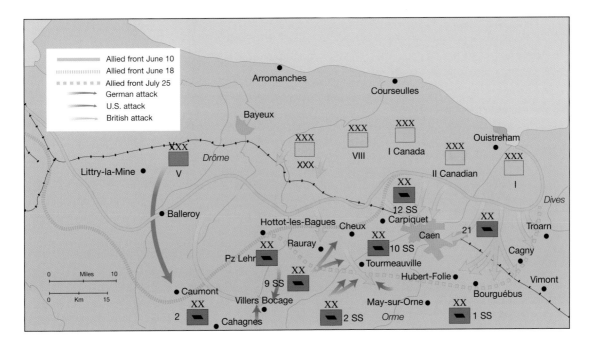

The fighting around Caen was part of Montgomery's plan to draw as much German armor as possible to wear it down. The Germans were worn down, but their tenacity also cost the Allies thousands of men and hundreds of tanks.

10,000 infantry, 700 guns, and 2,000 heavy bombers, were to smash through the now weak German lines and break into open country.

The Germans weathered the massive bombardment, and an improvised line of Tiger tanks and 88mm Flak guns ripped the British attack force apart. Confusion reigned in the British ranks, and the attack stalled without breaching the German lines. Some 270 burning hulks of British tanks littered the battlefield.

The Villers Bocage, Goodwood, and other battles showed up the tremendous technological superiority of German tanks over their Allied opponents. The Tiger I, Panther, and, to a lesser extent, Panzer IV all had far greater range, hitting power, and armored protection than the American Shermans or British Cromwells and Churchills. A Tiger or a Panther could survive frontal hits from Allied tanks' guns at ranges greater than 984 ft (300 m). The long 75mm on the Panther or the 88mm in the Tiger could cut through the thin armor of a Sherman at 6,561–9,842 ft (2,000–3,000 m). Allied tanks had to close to within suicidal ranges of German tanks to stand even the remotest chance of knocking them out. Only the British Sherman Firefly, which had the excellent high-velocity 17-pounder installed, could take on the Germans on anything like equal terms. This, however, was still in short supply during the Normandy battles.

The success of German defensive tactics in Normandy was due to a combination of factors. Great importance was placed on integrated defense plans, with tanks, antitank guns, artillery, and infantry all playing a part. The main defensive positions were held in strength by infantry armed with handheld antitank weapons, *Panzerfausts, Panzerschrecks,* and Tellar mines. They were occasionally reinforced by towed antitank or 88mm Flak guns (this was not considered wise because Allied artillery fire could easily find and knock them out). Artillery had an important role to play in German defensive plans, not as a tank-killer, but as a means to force Allied commanders to close down inside their tanks, thereby reducing their visibility. A rain of high explosives also forced Allied infantry to take cover and often led to British and American tanks being separated from their supporting troops. This further increased the ability of

Camouflage

To German troops in France in 1944, Allied Typhoon and Mustang aircraft were known as *Jabos* or fighter-bombers. With the Luftwaffe a mere shadow of its former glory, the only defense against intensive strafing and rocket attacks by Allied aircraft was to disappear under a canopy of camouflage.

France's rolling and wooded countryside proved to be the German Army's only ally during the bitter fighting after the D-Day landings in June 1944. German divisions became expert at dispersing themselves in woods, farm buildings, tunnels, mines, and industrial sites. All vehicles would be adorned with huge amounts of foliage to break up their shapes and make them merge with local vegetation.

The Germans, however, were determined to avoid being paralyzed by Allied air supremacy and developed techniques to allow them to remain hidden and still fight. A system of camouflage hides or laagers was developed, under which German units would operate from camouflaged bases in woods or industrial buildings, just behind the frontline. Units would emerge at night to reinforce and resupply frontline positions. Strict track discipline would be imposed, so armored vehicles would only use prepared routes in and out of the hide, on metaled roads so aircraft could not spot tank tracks across fields.

If major route marches were needed to redeploy units over long distances, then moves would ideally be made at night with vehicles parking up during daylight in preprepared hides in woods, buildings, or tunnels. This system broke down in the days after D-Day, when reserve panzer divisions were ordered to move in daylight toward the invasion beaches. Not surprisingly, prowling Allied fighter-bombers soon found the columns, and many panzer units suffered up to 50 percent casualties.

While German camouflage was usually effective at making it difficult for Allied pilots to spot enemy tanks and vehicles, the Allies soon found that their radio-interception and direction-finding assets were able to pinpoint the position of German units. In the days after D-Day the headquarters of Panzer Group West was located in this way and devastated by air strikes, spreading confusion among its units for several crucial days.

German tank-hunting teams to employ their short-range weapons successfully against isolated Allied tanks.

German armor and mobile antitank guns were usually held in reserve behind the main defensive position. Once large concentrations of Allied armor was on the move, small groups of German vehicles would either be maneuvered to intercept and block the enemy advance or positioned on flanks to inflict maximum damage. The aim was to create a "killing zone" where Allied tanks could be engaged from multiple directions, confusing the hapless victims and making it more difficult for them to organize a coherent response. Keeping out of range of the Allied tanks was important because it meant the Germans could husband their own precious tanks.

The effectiveness of these tactics can be gauged from the fact that in the first month of battle in Normandy the Germans knocked out almost 550 Allied tanks. Some 227 were destroyed by panzers, 61 by assault guns or self-propelled antitank guns, 105 by Flak guns or towed antitank guns, 36 by artillery fire, and 108 in close combat with infantry. In the same period the Germans lost just over 300 panzers and assault guns, of which at least 100 were hit in Allied air strikes. The kill ratio of two to one was impressive, but it was nowhere near that achieved on the Eastern Front.

German commanders made excellent use of the Normandy terrain to delay and hold up the Allied advance. In the west of the bridgehead the *bocage* hedgerows stalled the American advance and forced them to fight small-scale infantry battles to clear every field and village. The quality of the U.S. Army's untried infantry left a lot to be desired, and they had to learn the hard way how to prize out the Germans from the bunkers and trenches.

Farther east, the British and Canadians had to contend with more rolling and open terrain. Here, the control of high ground dominated the battle. Artillery observers were able to use the series of ridges each side of Caen to rain down fire

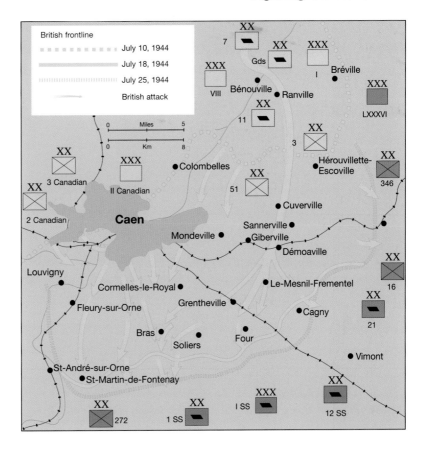

Operation Goodwood, Montgomery's attempt to open a route to Falaise. Three armored divisions made the attack, but were halted by a combination of Tiger tanks and 88mm antitank guns. The operation cost the British 400 tanks.

on Allied concentrations. The superior range of German tank and antitank guns meant that, by placing them on high ground, they could break up Allied massed armored attacks at long range before they even got close to German lines. With their tank support shot up, the Allied infantry soon faltered and was unwilling to press on to engage the German frontline infantry. The ridges also afforded the Germans a measure of protection from the huge Allied artillery batteries and naval gunfire support.

For the majority of the Allied troops who engaged the German Army in battle in the fields and villages of Normandy, the experience was their first taste of combat. They may have endured weeks and months of intensive training in England before they were shipped to France, but nothing could prepare them for what they were to face.

British, American, and Canadian divisional, brigade, and battalion commanders were all less experienced in all-arms mechanized warfare than their German counterparts. At first they all employed rigid tactics, which led to thousands of Allied casualties in fruitless frontal assaults on German positions. They believed their firepower would overcome the Germans, and that there was no need to use the terrain to cover their movement or to try to infiltrate behind centers of resistance.

The Allies also still relied on top-down command procedures that meant their inability to react to surprise German moves was a weakness. When key officers were killed or communications with higher headquarters did not work, Allied attacks often broke down because there was no one to take the initiative and lead the remaining troops forward. During the Goodwood battle, the British corps

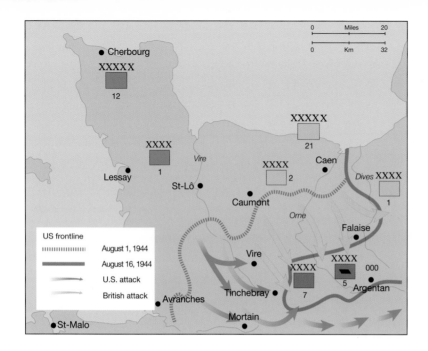

As the German front crumbled in Normandy, British and American forces advanced east and south to close a ring around Wehrmacht units west of Falaise and Argentan.

commander, Lieutenant-General Sir Richard O'Connor, insisted on directing the battle from a command post far to the rear, and was trying to control the action of every battalion in his command. He often overruled subordinates who were with the vanguard of his armored force. Any opportunities to exploit what British success there was were missed, since O'Connor insisted on ordering his troops to stop and reorganize before assaulting the numerous German strongpoints in their line of advance. Not surprisingly, what should have been a dynamic armor breakthrough turned into a confused and disjointed slogging match.

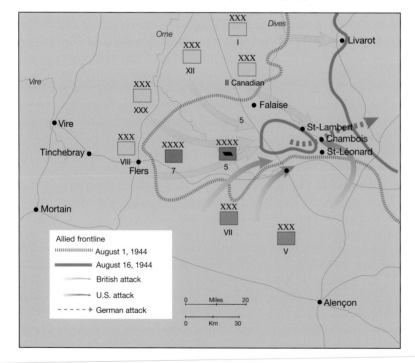

Over 10,000 Germans died in the Falaise Pocket, while 50,000 others went into Allied captivity. The Allies now had a free hand to advance beyond Normandy toward Paris.

To the west the Germans were also giving the Americans a hard time in the difficult *bocage* country. Rommel was desperate to prevent the Allies capturing the port of Cherbourg, which would considerably ease their logistical problems. The defense was led by veteran German parachute and Waffen-SS divisions, but there were not as many German tanks facing the Americans as the British.

By the end of July the Americans had broken through the German line, thanks to Operation Cobra, which overwhelmed the worn-out frontline defenses. Hitler ordered six panzer divisions to counterattack and seal the front. After almost two months of continuous fighting, these divisions were little more than weak regimental battle groups. Allied fighter-bombers caught the German tanks in the open and the attack collapsed in chaos. This was the cue for Lieutenant-General George Patton to launch his recently activated Third Army into action, breaking through and racing eastward for the Seine River.

The Falaise Pocket

Hitler forbade his troops to even contemplate retreat. Patton's tanks were now closing a huge trap around the German forces that were being driven into a pocket south of Caen. By mid-August the remnants of more than 20 German divisions were pinned into the pocket, with the only escape route being a narrow corridor to the east. On August 20 the pocket was locked shut. Allied aircraft and artillery pounded the pocket for days until resistance ceased. There was no formal surrender or breakout. Individuals made their own choices. The scene Allied troops found as they combed the ruins of the German Army in Normandy was truly apocalyptic. They found 567 tanks, 950 artillery pieces, 7,700 vehicles, and the bodies of 10,000 Germans and the carcasses of tens of thousands of horses. Some 50,000 Germans surrendered, and 20,000 others made their escape on foot through the Allied ring. Of the 38 German divisions committed to the Normandy Front, 25 had ceased to exist. The German Army had lost almost half a million men.

There were now only 70 German tanks and 36 artillery pieces between the Normandy Front and the Rhine! What remained of the German forces in France were in full retreat from the victorious Allied forces. Additional landings in southern France in mid-August completed the rout of Hitler's armies in the West. For a month the pursuit was unrelenting, and by mid-September almost all of France and Belgium had been liberated. Montgomery argued for a narrow advance into Germany, but Eisenhower, the supreme Allied commander, maintained a broad front strategy which gave the Germans some respite. In addition, a fuel crisis forced the Allies to rein-in their tank columns to regroup and reorganize before they could begin the final offensive to smash into the heart of Hitler's Reich.

In spite of being five years into a long and bloody war, the Wehrmacht put up an amazing fight in Normandy. While some of the German Army's generals were disaffected with the Führer and were actively plotting to kill him, the rank and file of the fighting troops still believed in Germany's cause. Rommel's infectious enthusiasm rubbed off on the troops being trained to repel the invasion. He was famous for his victories against the British and Americans in North Africa, and many of his troops, along with the divisional officers, were convinced of the logic of Hitler's claim that if the Allied invasion could be thrown back into the sea, then Germany would be able to turn its attention eastward to finish off the Soviets. "When the enemy invades in the west it will be the moment of decision in this war," said Rommel. "And the moment must turn for Germany's advantage."

The Wehrmacht

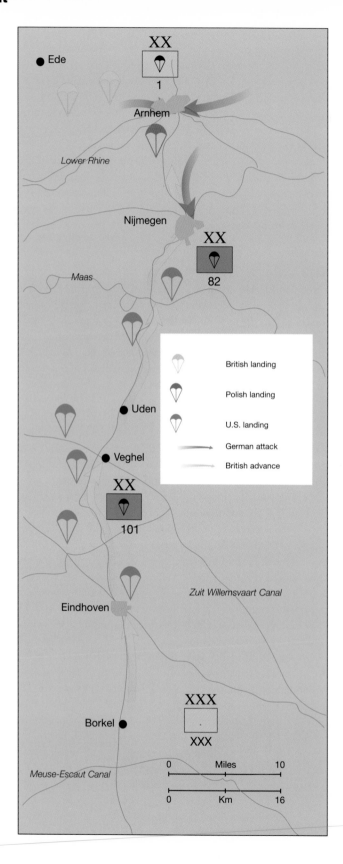

The defeat of the Allied airborne landings in Holland during September 1944, codenamed Market Garden, was the one unambiguous German victory in the West during 1944. Montgomery may have claimed that his Operation Market Garden was 90 percent successful, but the point of the enterprise was to seize the key Rhine bridge at Arnhem and open a route for Allied tanks into the heart of Germany's Ruhr industrial region. In this aim Montgomery quite clearly failed. The defeat can be put at the door of the prompt reaction of Model and the German commander in the Arnhem region, Waffen-SS General Willi Bittrich and his II SS Panzer Corps. By sheer luck he had been dispatched to the supposed backwater of Arnhem to refit his two divisions, the 9th and 10th SS Panzer Divisions which had been badly mauled in the retreat from Falaise. Allied intelligence blundered and missed the movement of Bittrich and his panzers to Arnhem. Once the British 1st Airborne Division started landing outside Arnhem, Bittrich formed a series of emergency battle groups from his corps and army units in the area. Within a day he had the British troops penned into their drop zones, apart from one battalion that had managed make it to the bridge. This was not before Bittrich had ordered Nijmegen bridge to the south to be held at all costs by a Waffen-SS panzer unit, effectively blocking the relief of the British paratroopers by Montgomery's armor.

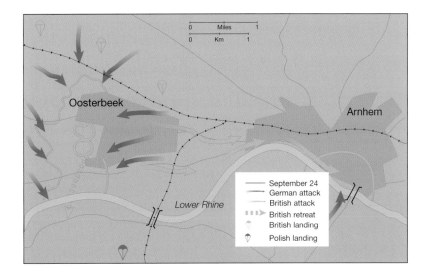

The end at Arnhem. In 10 days of heavy fighting the British paratroopers north of the Rhine were forced into a small pocket. Unable to open a supply route across the river, the battered remnants of the 1st Airborne Division, fewer than 2,000 men, swam for their lives across the Rhine.

Given that the Germans had almost thrown back Allied landings at Salerno and Anzio during the Italian campaign, Rommel's optimism was not misplaced. While after the event Allied generals tried to portray the Normandy campaign as a foregone conclusion, it is clear that many Allied leaders, such as the British Chief of the Imperial General Staff Field Marshal Sir Alan Brooke and Supreme Allied Commander General Dwight Eisenhower, shared Hitler's assessment that the course of the war would turn on the outcome of the invasion.

By September 1944 the Allies were convinced the war was won. The normally cautious Montgomery ordered an ambitious airborne operation to seize a series of strategic bridges in Holland, to allow the Allies to gain a foothold over the Rhine at Arnhem. Within days of the British and American paratroopers landing at Arnhem, Nijmegen, and Eindhoven, the German commander in the West, Field Marshal Walther Model, had contained the weak airborne forces and placed panzer forces to block their relief by Allied armor advancing north from Belgium. Waffen-SS units surrounded the British paratroopers at Arnhem, eventually

British bombers attack German tanks in France in 1944. The Allies were able to call upon massive firepower during the campaign in the West. During Operation Goodwood in July, for example, the British pounded the German frontline east of Caen on the morning of July 18 with 8,000 tons (8,128 tonnes) of bombs and more than 300,000 shells. The bombardment had a devastating effect, killing and wounding hundreds of Germans, or driving some mad, and knocking out dozens of tanks.

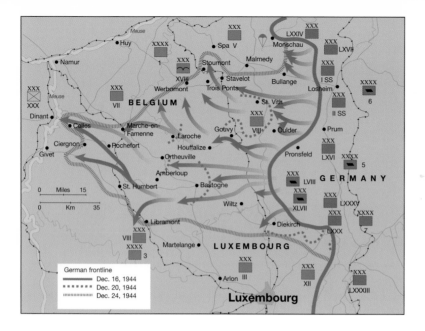

In nine days in December 1944 the Wehrmacht inflicted the biggest defeats on the U.S. Army during the Western campaign. Within days of Operation Watch on the Rhine on December 16, a U.S. division was surrounded and more than 7,000 men were captured. A further 8,000 would be captured in the coming days as two U.S. corps were sent reeling back from the German border in panic. By the end of the offensive more than 81,000 Allied troops had been killed, wounded, or captured. Over the next week panzer spearheads punched nearly 60 miles (96 km) toward Antwerp and another U.S. division was surrounded in Bastogne, where it was holding on grimly in the face of constant German attacks.

forcing them to pull back across the Rhine, leaving 8,000 dead and prisoners behind. Model successfully prevented Montgomery from securing his bridgehead across the Rhine.

All along Germany's western frontier, the Wehrmacht was rallying and turning back Allied spearheads. In the Hurtgen Forest south of Aachen the U.S. Army got bogged down in a series of battles of attrition. Far to the south Patton's Third Army found itself fighting costly engagements around Metz, but could not smash open the German border defenses.

Behind this now solid front Hitler ordered one final effort to rebuild his battered armies to inflict a decisive defeat on his enemies. "We gamble everything," he told his generals. The attack would punch through the mountainous Ardennes region to capture the Belgian port of Antwerp, splitting the British in Holland from the

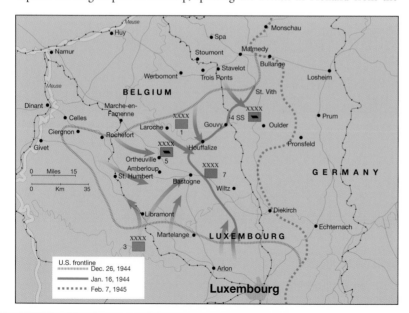

As the weather began to clear, the German advance ground to a halt south of the River Meuse, 60 miles (96 km) from Antwerp. Patton pushed an armored column into the southern flank of the German panzer forces. More than 120,000 German troops were killed, wounded, or captured, along with some 800 panzers destroyed, and by the end of January 1945, the Germans were back on their start lines inside Germany.

Siegfried Line

As Allied columns raced eastward from Normandy in the fall of 1944, the newly appointed German commander in chief in the West, Field Marshal Walther Model, was desperate to pull together a defensive line along Germany's western border (ironically, the Allies had outrun their fuel supplies and their tanks literally ground to a halt; Model had more time then he realized to put together an effective defense against the enemy).

Hitler told Model to make use of the old Siegfried Line defenses to bolster the new Western Front. The Siegfried Line had been built in the 1930s in response to the French building their famous Maginot Line. The German line stretched from the Swiss border northward to near the Dutch border. In the "phoney war" period of the late 1930s, the Siegfried Line had taken on almost mystical proportions, as both the French and Germans attempted to out-do each other in the propaganda war, claiming their respective lines were stronger, bigger, and more impregnable than that of their opponent. In reality, the German line was never as strong as its French counterpart, being more a series of field fortifications for army units rather than a "concrete battleship" in the style of the Maginot Line. The Siegfried Line boasted long lines of concrete dragon's teeth antitank obstacles, pillboxes, and huge barbed-wire entanglements. Crucially, the Germans garrisoned the line with 19 well-equipped and trained infantry divisions.

In the fall of 1944, the Siegfried Line was a shadow of its former self. Much of the line had been dismantled and shipped to the Atlantic coast to bolster the anti-invasion defenses earlier in the war. The concrete shell of the line remained, but there was little wire, few mines, and none of the gun emplacements had artillery pieces in them.

More importantly, the human resources available to Model were pitiful. Hitler provided the field marshal with 100 so-called "Fortress Battalions" made up of old men and walking wounded. The Führer believed that the Siegfreid was strong enough to meet any attack, but he was living in a dream world. Rundstedt called the defensive line a "shameful fabrication." General Westphal, Rundstedt's chief of staff, had stated: "The West Wall [Siegfried Line] was no longer in a defensible state because of the removal of weapons, ammunition, wire, and mines ... sometimes even the keys for individual emplacements were missing." He also went on to say that not a single bridge over the Rhine had been prepared for demolition.

Fortunately, the rapid speed of the Allied advance worked in Model's favor. As mentioned above, the Allied tanks were only stopped in their tracks short of the Siegfried Line when they outran their fuel supplies. But the breaching of the Siegfried Line would be only a formality when the time came.

Americans in France. This was to be a repeat of the 1940s Ardennes offensive that had smashed the Anglo-French forces in a matter of days.

In conditions of great secrecy, some 500,000 men in 28 divisions, including 11 panzer and panzergrenadier divisions, were reorganized and retrained. Almost all Germany's production of war matériel, including 1.25 million tons (1.27 million tonnes) of ammunition, 100,000 machine guns, 9,000 artillery prices, and 1,500 tanks and assault guns, was diverted to support the offensive along with more than 1.32 million gallons (5 million liters) of precious fuel. This was an amazing feat, considering the losses of the previous six months and the damage inflicted on Germany's industrial base by round-the-clock Allied bombing.

Operation Watch on the Rhine took the Allies totally by surprise, and initially it swept away the weak American forces holding the frontline in the Ardennes. For almost a week the bad weather kept Allied air units on the ground and the German panzers were able to race westward. German commandos wearing Allied uniforms added to the panic among the green GIs trying to hold back the surprise Blitzkrieg.

Hitler's plan was daring and, for a few days, looked like it might just cause the Allies major problems. Once the Allies recovered their composure and brought their airpower and armored reserves to bear, however, Watch on the Rhine was doomed. The best that can be said is that it delayed the Allied push to the Rhine by a few weeks. However, on the debit side the offensive had cost the German Army nearly 120,000 men and large quantities of irreplaceable hardware. There were now no reserves left.

Valor Not Enough

The German Army's last reserves had been used up in the abortive Ardennes Offensive, and at the beginning of 1945 the enemy was on German soil. Defeat was now inevitable, but while Hitler still lived the army did not abandon its oath to him.

Germany's strategic position in January 1945 was hopeless: in the West the Allies were approaching the Rhine, in the East the Red Army mustered over 400 divisions for the drive on Berlin, and in the south Soviet forces were besieging the Hungarian capital, Budapest. Only in Italy was the front stable.

The once-proud Wehrmacht was a mere shadow of its former self. Seven million Germans may have been under arms, but they were short of ammunition and equipment and morale was crumbling. Only in the East was the army prepared to fight with any degree of vigor, and only then as a means to allow escape to the West.

In his Berlin "Führer Bunker," buried deep below the Reich Chancellery, however, Hitler refused to contemplate defeat. He continued to believe that as long as his armies kept fighting there was a possibility that the Western Allies and Soviets would fall out. It was totally illogical, of course, but Hitler was on the brink of a mental and physical breakdown. He dismissed intelligence reports of the Soviets' overwhelming strength on the Eastern Front as "idiotic," and suggested that the German Army's intelligence chief, Major-General Reinhard Gehlen, be sent to a lunatic asylum. The estimates were, however, the most accurate ever produced by Gehlen's "Foreign Armies East" organization. Hitler could not grasp that German Army's divisions were now so weak that many were little more than regimental strength.

The Führer's will to keep fighting was unrelenting, though. Hitler ordered the arrest of scores of senior officers who failed to follow his orders, while others were demoted and sent to fight at the front as lieutenants or privates. Regional Nazi officials, *Gauleiters*, were given authority over the defense of their local areas, with

German prisoners taken by the Americans in April 1945. During that month the Western Allies took no less than 1,650,000 Germans prisoner – there was no fight left in the Wehrmacht. Only in the East did the Germans continue fighting, and that was only to allow the British and Americans to reach Berlin first.

authority to remove any army officers who showed signs of disloyalty. They reported directly to Martin Bormann, Hitler's trusted henchman, and regularly interfered in military matters, often just to prove they were in charge.

But the army kept on fighting, mainly because of the personal oath of loyalty to Hitler taken by both officers and men. As professional soldiers they could not contemplate the shame of deserting their country in its time of need. Erwin Rommel summed up the feeling of the officer corps in October 1944, as he waited to hear his fate after being suspected of being involved in the July 1944 Bomb Plot. He told his son: "Our enemy in the East is so terrible that every other consideration has to give way before it. If he succeeds in overrunning Europe, even only temporarily, it will be the end of everything which has made life appear worth living. Of course I would go."

The German Army in Ruins

In January 1945 a final attempt was made to try to rebuild the Wehrmacht for the defense of the Fatherland. A plethora of orders were issued, calling for the formation of scores of new panzer divisions, infantry divisions, artillery units, and antitank brigades. Most of the units existed only on paper, or were made up of only a handful of half-trained battalions. The *Clausewitz* Panzer Division, the last armored division formed, for example, had only 39 tanks and a few thousand men. Hitler hoped that by giving these new units stirring titles from Germany's glorious military past, their members would be motivated to fight to the end. However, finding trained officers and troops to man these new units was almost impossible: the German Army's training system had long since broken down – there were no longer any instructors or training camps. Every German division found itself having to press-gang old men and boys from the *Volkssturm* (Home Guard). Though willing, they lacked training, rifles, or ammunition.

German war production was grinding to a halt under the weight of Allied bombing and a shortage of raw materials. Tank and aircraft production stopped in February 1945; synthetic fuel production was reduced to a trickle (Soviet troops had cut Germany off from fuel supplies in Romania and Hungary); and the railroad system was on the verge of collapse as Allied bombers destroyed key bridges and marshalling yards.

The last significant armored reserve available to Germany were the five Waffen-SS panzer divisions of the Sixth SS Panzer Army. They were pulled out of the Western Front in the middle of January 1945. As they had suffered heavy losses during the Ardennes Offensive, they were given what few armored vehicles were rolling off the production lines. Chief of Staff Colonel-General Heinz Guderian wanted them to defend Berlin, as the 12 panzer or panzergrenadier divisions on the Eastern Front each had, on average, less than 40 operation tanks. They had little prospect of holding back the 6,000 Soviet tanks poised to break into Poland. But Hitler wanted this elite panzer force and its 400 tanks to go to Hungary to break the siege of Budapest and secure the country's oil supplies. Guderian's protests that Hungary was a sideshow were in vain; only one of the Waffen-SS divisions was sent to defend the front in Poland.

The first Soviet hammer blow fell on the German Army on January 12. Two million Red Army troops swarmed over the 400,000 Germans holding the front in central Poland. Within a week Warsaw was free and the Germans had lost 50,000 killed, wounded, or captured. The situation would have been far worse but for the efforts of General Walther Nehring, who formed his panzer corps of

Hitler's ill-conceived offensive in Hungary in March 1945. It used up what little tank reserves the German Army had, and achieved nothing.

The encirclement of Field Marshal Walther Model's Army Group B in the Ruhr Pocket. It took 18 days to reduce the pocket, after which 370,000 German troops entered captivity. Model himself committed suicide.

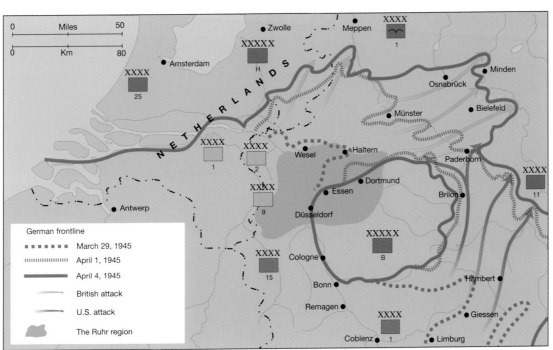

The area held by the German Army in March 1945. Its forces in Italy, Austria, Czechoslovakia, and Yugoslavia were effectively cut off from the main battle in Germany.

three divisions into a "roving pocket" and led them on an 11-day, 156-mile (250-km) march through woods to German lines at Breslau on the Oder River. Airlifted petrol kept his vehicles moving, and a rescue force from the *Grossdeutschland* Panzer Corps held open a bridgehead for Nehring's beleaguered command and thousands of civilians who joined the march.

Soviet tank spearhead armies ignored the remnants of German frontline defenses and raced westward for the Oder and Baltic Sea. By the beginning of February Soviet troops were only 35 miles (56 km) from Berlin and had cut off East Prussia from Pomerania, trapping the remnants of 40 divisions. A further 25 divisions were cut off in Courland on the Baltic coast. Hitler ordered both of these commands to fight to the end rather than reinforce the Berlin sector.

In February the Soviets launched another series of offensives, and by the end of March they held a stretch of front from Stettin on the Baltic coast to Görlitz on the Czech border. They were now poised for their all-out assault on Berlin.

Hitler's offensive in Hungary was a predictable fiasco. It failed to relieve Budapest, and only 785 Germans out of the 70,000-strong garrison managed to escape. After almost a month of trying to battle through the Soviet lines, the Waffen-SS panzer army was reduced to less than 100 operational tanks. A Soviet offensive on March 25 shattered the German front on the Danube. The Waffen-SS panzer divisions retreated into Austria; by early April Vienna was being assaulted by Red Army tanks.

Allied troops in the West waited until February 8 to launch their push to the Rhine. Six armies attacked along the whole length of the front from the Netherlands to Switzerland. German troops put up local resistance, but a coordinated defense was beyond the capabilities of the battered armies west of the Rhine. Within a month the Allies were at the river and preparing to strike into the heart of the Reich. In the northern sector of the front, 52,000 German troops were captured.

The first bridgehead was established over the Rhine on March 7, and Allied troops began major amphibious operations to breach the water obstacle on the 22rd. Field Marshal Walther Model's Army Group B was cut off in the Ruhr Pocket on April 1. Just over two weeks later, 370,000 German troops surrendered amid the ruins of the Reich's industrial heartland. Model decided he did not want to achieve the dubious distinction of being the second German field marshal to be captured, and so committed suicide.

The Soviet offensive to take Berlin was both massive and well planned. In addition to being outnumbered and outgunned, German units were suffering crippling shortages of fuel.

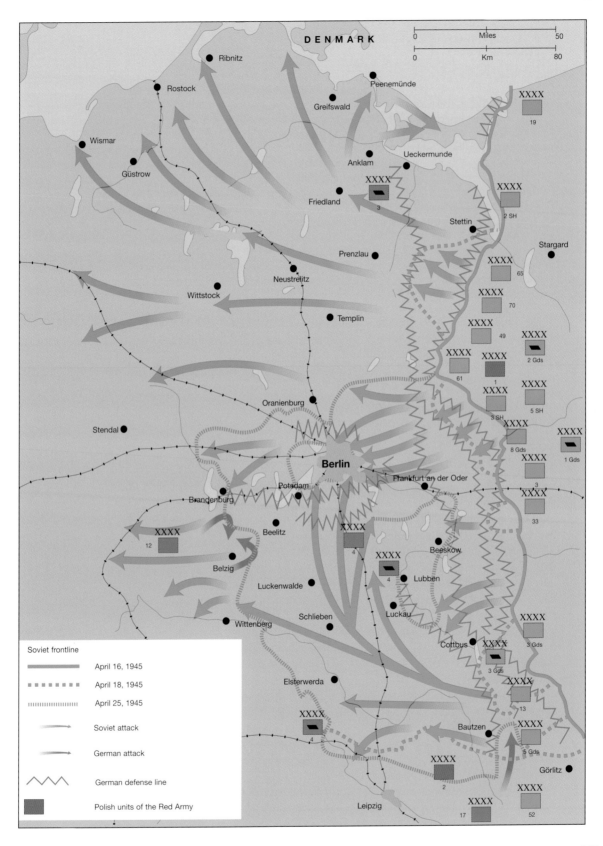

DENMARK

Miles
0   50
0   Km   80

Ribnitz

Rostock

Peenemünde

Greifswald

Wismar

Güstrow

Anklam

Ueckermunde

XXXX
19

Friedland

XXXX
3

Stettin

XXXX
2 SH

Stargard

Prenzlau

Neustrelitz

XXXX
65

Wittstock

XXXX
70

Templin

XXXX
49

XXXX
2 Gds

XXXX
61

XXXX
1

Oranienburg

XXXX
5 SH

Stendal

3 SH

XXXX
8 Gds

XXXX
1 Gds

Berlin

Frankfurt an der Oder

XXXX
3

Potsdam

Brandenburg

XXXX
33

Beelitz

XXXX
4

XXXX
12

Beeskow

Belzig

XXXX
4

Lübben

Luckenwalde

Luckau

Schlieben

XXXX
3 Gds

Wittenberg

Cottbus

XXXX
3 Gds

XXXX
13

Elsterwerda

XXXX
5 Gds

Bautzen

XXXX
4

Görlitz

XXXX
2

XXXX
52

Leipzig

XXXX
17

Soviet frontline

——— April 16, 1945

••••••• April 18, 1945

||||||||||||| April 25, 1945

⟶ Soviet attack

⟶ German attack

∧∧∧∧ German defense line

▨ Polish units of the Red Army

Monster Panzers

Hitler's love of hi-tech wonder weapons is well known, and in the field of armored vehicles he authorized the production of a number of "monster tanks." In spite of the Führer's predictions, the small number of these vehicles failed to turn back the Allies.

The most heavily armed armored vehicle to see frontline service was the Jagdtiger. Based on the chassis of the famous Tiger II tank, the Jagdtiger was built from April 1944 onward. Some 150 were eventually produced, but only 70 of the 68.9-ton (70-tonne) vehicles were deployed to two frontline *Panzerjäger* (antitank) battalions.

They saw action during the Ardennes Offensive in December 1944, inflicting heavy losses on the unfortunate Allied tank units to cross their path. But the Jagdtigers suffered at the hands of allied airpower during the retreat from the Ardennes, which meant that only a handful were available to resist the Allied advance into Germany during 1945.

The heaviest tank produced by the Germans, and possibly the heaviest tank ever produced, was the *Maus*, which weighed in at a massive 186 tons (189 tonnes). Described by the father of the German panzers, Colonel-General Heinz Guderian, as a "gigantic offspring of the fantasy of Hitler and his advisors," the *Maus* never saw combat.

Dr. Ferdinand Porsche persuaded Hitler to allow him to start work on the *Maus* in the summer of 1942. Everything about the tank was big. It was to have the biggest gun ever mounted in a German tank turret, a 128mm cannon, along with a 75mm secondary armament. The first field trials of the two prototypes got under way in late 1944, but they were never anywhere near being ready for service by the time the Soviets overran the tank testing range at Kummersdorf in 1945. The prototypes were ordered to be destroyed, but rumors persist that at least one *Maus* was captured by the Soviets.

A third super-heavy tank, the E-100, was being developed when the war ended. It was intended as a replacement for the Tiger II, and was armed with a 128mm cannon. The E-100 was intended to be the first of a series of six types of tanks ranging from 4.9 tons (5 tonnes) to 138 tons (140 tonnes) in weight. One example of the 138-ton (140-tonne) tank was captured by the Americans in the Henschel factory in Paderborn, but work was at a very early stage.

Allied troops now advanced across western Germany, with British troops heading for the Baltic coast in the north and the Americans driving southwest to deal with the so-called Nazi "National Redoubt" in the Alps, which proved to be another of Hitler's flights of fancy. Other U.S. troops headed into the heart of Germany and into Czechoslovakia. By prior agreement, the Americans and Soviets met up on the banks of the Elbe River. In Italy Allied troops at last punched through to the Po Valley and began driving north toward the Austrian Alps and into Yugoslavia to link up with Marshal Tito's partisans. German resistance in the West was now half hearted.

The final Wehrmacht battle began on April 16, 1945. Hitler had managed to scrape together almost a million men to hold the Oder, though more than half were press-gang civilians of the *Volkssturm*. The core of the defense rested on some 850 tanks and assault guns that had been collected from various depots, reinforced by over 500 antiaircraft guns from Berlin's air-defense batteries. A series of six defense lines had been rapidly dug between the Oder and Berlin, directed by Colonel-General Gotthard Heinrici, the new commander of the Oder Front. He faced more than 2.5 million Red Army soldiers, with 41,000 artillery pieces, 6,000 tanks, and 7,500 aircraft.

The Soviets launched two giant pincers to encircle Berlin. The Germans fought fanatically, and briefly held the Soviets on the Seelow Heights to east of the city. Nine days into the offensive, the Soviets closed the ring around the German capital. The 200,000-strong remnants of the troops defending the Oder Front were trapped in a pocket to the south of Berlin, under the command of General Theodor Busse, Manstein's old chief of staff.

In Berlin, Hitler ordered every man to fight to the last round. It took the Russians four days to battle through the ruined city's streets to the gates of Hitler's bunker. Meanwhile, outside the city, Heinrici, with the cooperation of his

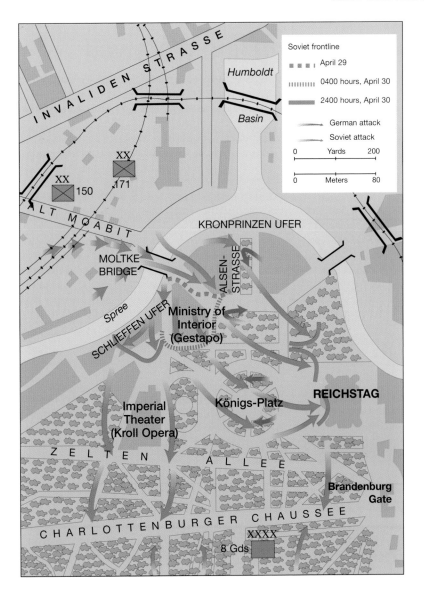

Legend:
Soviet frontline
▪ ▪ ▪ April 29
‖‖‖‖‖ 0400 hours, April 30
▬ 2400 hours, April 30

→ German attack
→ Soviet attack

0 — Yards — 200
0 — Meters — 80

INVALIDEN STRASSE
Humboldt
Basin
XX 171
XX 150
ALT MOABIT
KRONPRINZEN UFER
MOLTKE BRIDGE
ALSEN-STRASSE
Spree
SCHLIEFFEN UFER
Ministry of Interior (Gestapo)
REICHSTAG
Königs-Platz
Imperial Theater (Kroll Opera)
ZELTEN ALLEE
Brandenburg Gate
CHARLOTTENBURGER CHAUSSEE
XXXX 8 Gds

The last great drama of the Third Reich: the battle for the Reichstag.

subordinate generals ordered a retreat to the west to reach Allied lines. Hitler ranted in his bunker about this "treason," but there was nothing he could do. Busse, together with 100,000 troops and 300,000 German civilians, crossed the Elbe to reach American lines. In the north, tens of thousands of German troops led by Hasso von Manteuffel also reached the Americans.

Hitler took his own life late on the evening of April 30. The following day the German Army's last chief of staff, Colonel-General Hans Krebs, who had taken over after Guderian had been sacked by Hitler on March 28, began surrender negotiations with the Soviets. Halfway through the negotiations Krebs committed suicide, along with Joseph Goebbels and other Nazi leaders. It was left to a German Army officer, General Helmuth Weidling, the last commander of the Berlin defense zone, to formally surrender the city to the Soviets at 1300 hours on May 2.

The intensity of the fighting can be gauged by the fact that 304,000 Russian soldiers died in Berlin. Their victory put an end to Hitler's murderous rule. At least 100,000 German civilians were killed in the battle, along with a similar

Volkssturm and Werewolf

With the Allies on the Rhine and Soviets at the gates of Berlin in the spring of 1945, Hitler ordered the German population to be mobilized en masse for a final *Götterdämmerung.* The German people would emerge victorious or die fighting, declared the Führer.

Despairing of the Wehrmacht and the even the Waffen-SS, he turned to the Nazi Party to raise, organize, equip, and lead the new *Volkssturm* militia. Often compared to the British Home Guard, the *Volkssturm* was a similar desperate measure. Old men, boys, and foreign refugees were thrown together with few weapons and little idea how to use them, while many of the local Nazi leaders of the *Volkssturm* had little military experience. According to Colonel-General Heinz Guderian: "The brave men of the *Volkssturm* prepared to make any sacrifice, were in many cases drilled busily in the proper way of giving the Hitler salute, instead of being trained in the use of weapons of which they had no previous experience."

In the dying days of the Reich they put up some resistance, but by May 1945 Germany Army commanders were ordering *Volkssturm* units to disband rather than get caught up in the general capitulation of the Wehrmacht.

The Werewolf was very different beast. It was intended to be a stay-behind resistance organization to continue the fight even after the Allies and Soviets had occupied Germany. Only fanatical Nazis were allowed to join, and they were provided with arms and explosives for storage in secret caches. A number of acts of sabotage were committed, but ruthless Allied action against captured Werewolves – they were executed – and war weariness prevented a Nazi resistance movement taking off.

In the dying days of the Reich the Werewolf movement gained much notoriety, along with stories that Hitler was preparing for his last stand in the so-called "mountain rampart" in southern Germany. The Werewolves were also linked with rumors of secret networks to smuggle Nazi and SS leaders out of Germany to exile in Spain and South America. As with all these stories there was more myth than reality, although they probably played a part in the Allied decision to push into southern Germany to finally crush German resistance once and for all, rather than race to beat the Soviets to Berlin.

number of German soldiers. In the last six months of the war the Wehrmacht suffered an estimated two million dead, wounded, or captured. The Soviets claimed the capture of 134,000 Germans in Berlin on May 2 alone, and some 480,000 in total since they began their drive to the Reich's capital on April 16.

Hitler's death immediately released the German Army from its oath of loyalty. All over Europe, German commanders started to enter into surrender negotiations with their enemies. Six days of confused negotiations then took place until Colonel-General Alfred Jodl signed documents for the unconditional surrender of the German people and armed forces at Rheims, France on May 7.

The Wehrmacht now began the process of laying down its arms. Some six million men surrendered, the vast majority to the Allies in Germany, Italy, Austria, Holland, Denmark, and Norway. German troops in Berlin, Courland, East Prussia, and Czechoslovakia fell into Soviet hands.

The bulk of these men were herded into large improvised prisoner-of-war camps until their captors worked out what to do with them. In the West, hundreds of thousands of ordinary soldiers were just told to take off their uniforms and go home to help rebuild their ruined country. For the majority of those who remained in captivity, life was far from pleasant. Food was scarce in Europe in 1945–46, and German soldiers were hardly a top priority. It took a couple of years for many to return home because hundreds of thousands were kept as forced laborers in Britain, France, and other West European countries. By 1948 most had returned home. Senior officers were held for longer, pending their investigation for war crimes. Some passed their time writing their memoirs or contributing to Allied analytical studies of the performance of the Wehrmacht.

The 2.38 million German and 600,000 Axis soldiers who fell into Soviet hands had a far tougher time. Most became slave laborers in Stalin's gulags in Siberia. More than a million, including at least 450,000 Germans, died in captivity before the rest were released in1955. Thousands of Waffen-SS officers and Nazi Party officials were executed out of hand, as were tens of thousands of Russians who had served in Hitler's armies.

At the War Crimes Tribunal at Nuremberg Field Marshal Wilhelm Keitel, chief of the OKW and Jodl, OKW chief of operations, were sentenced to death for their part in the formulation, transmission, and execution of Hitler's illegal orders to murder three million Soviet and dozens of British prisoners and laying waste to much of Europe. Other generals prosecuted included Rundstedt, Brauchitsch, Strauss, Kesselring, Manstein, and Hoth. Kesselring was sentenced to death for ordering the execution of Italian partisans; the others to long terms of imprisonment for war crimes. The Luftwaffe field marshal had his sentence commuted and the others were eventually released when the Cold War no longer made it fashionable to imprison Germans who had fought the Soviets. Waffen-SS officers shared a similar fate, and more than 80 top SS commanders were convicted for their part in the murder of American prisoners of war during the Ardennes Offensive. The guilty men, sentenced to death, were reprieved and later served time in jail.

By 1955, the Cold War was at its height. Germany was a key battle ground between East and West. The British and Americans rehabilitated many former German generals and officers to form the nucleus of the new democratic *Bundeswehr* (West German Army). Some Wehrmacht veterans, captured by the Soviets, found their way into the ranks of the East German People's Army. Hitler's generals had found new masters.

The division of Germany and Austria by the victorious powers following Wehrmacht defeat in May 1945. Stalin proceeded to create a communist-controlled buffer between the West and the Soviet Union, which was interpreted in the West as dangerously expansionist.

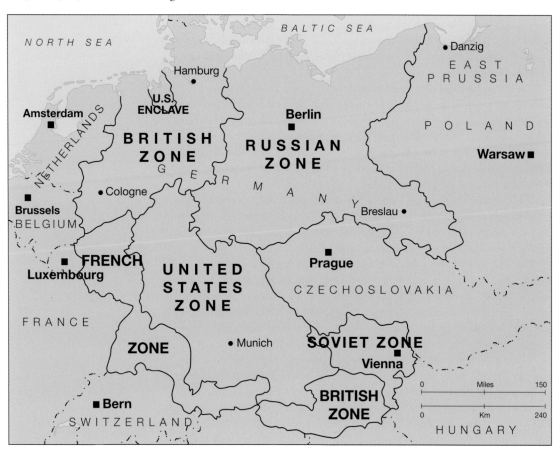

The Legacy of the Wehrmacht

In six years of war, the German Army had conquered most of Western Europe and the coast of North Africa, before being destroyed in the ruins of its Führer's "Thousand Year Reich." Between September 1939 and November 1941, the Polish, Norwegian, Dutch, Belgian, French, British, and Soviet armies were all defeated by the Wehrmacht in a series of crushing defeats. In a matter of months the German Army achieved what had been impossible in four years of bloody attrition during World War I.

Heinz Guderian boasted: "Twice after the loss of a World War, the General Staff has been dissolved on the orders of the victors. Both these actions show the unwilling respect in which our enemies hold that most excellent organization."

For Hitler's generals this was the pinnacle of their professional careers. They had backed his rise to power because he promised to restore Germany's greatness. In turn, they created one of the most effective fighting machines in military history. Once unleashed, it initially swept all before it. In their hour of victory, Germany's soldiers were feted by a grateful nation and the Führer handsomely rewarded them for their efforts.

The Blitzkrieg swept all before it for a variety of reasons. The Wehrmacht was far ahead of its rivals in adopting new technology. Its tanks and aircraft were technologically more advanced than those of its rivals. Paratroopers, assault gliders and dive-bombers were just some of the new tactics and weapons pioneered by the Germans. On top of this, the German general staff proved better at integrating these combat units with well-proven assault tactics and battle procedures.

The German officer corps was one of the most professional in the world, and it was ruthless in its pursuit of military perfection. Its logic and clear thinking ran rings around its more pedestrian opponents, who were not psychologically or physically prepared to meet the Wehrmacht in battle.

The Blitzkrieg victories made Hitler and the Wehrmacht over-confident, though. They had not expected their opponents to fold so quickly and they soon became "drunk" on success. Operation Barbarossa was a folly of monumental proportions, and once they had begun to murder Jews and Russians on an industrial scale there was no going back. However, Germany was in no position to match the industrial and human resources of her enemies.

When Hitler launched his "total war" in January 1943, the Wehrmacht threw itself into the defensive phase of the war with a new-found determination to fight the Soviets and Allies to a draw. Thanks to superlative efforts to rebuild the Germany Army during early 1943 for Operation Citadel (the attack at Kursk), and again to counter the Allied invasion of France in 1944, the Wehrmacht was able to fight effectively against superior odds. Germany's generals and soldiers gave their all for their Führer and Fatherland, but it was not enough. The Allies and Soviets just ground the Wehrmacht down in a series of massive defeats in June and July 1944 from which it could not recover.

The Wehrmacht's Blitzkrieg victories, however, served an evil cause and in territories it conquered Hitler's henchmen soon began a reign of terror, enslaving whole peoples and exterminating those who did not fit into the Führer's warped racial view of Europe's future.

Hitler's generals and soldiers were willing participants in this murderous enterprise, and fought hard to ensure it prevailed. Germany's barbarous rule in occupied Russia sowed the seeds of a vengeful whirlwind that grew during 1942 and 1943 to stop and turn back Hitler's armies at Stalingrad and Kursk. With Soviet and Allied forces resurgent in Russia, North Africa, Italy, and France, the Wehrmacht was forced onto the defensive.

Some of Hitler's former generals claimed that Germany's defeat was not their fault, suggesting that if only the Führer had taken their professional military advice, disaster could have been avoided. Others point to their role in the 1944 Bomb Plot as proof that they had Germany's interests at heart.

They are the classic symptoms of a group of men trying to shift responsibility to a conveniently dead Hitler. Germany's generals sold their souls to Hitler in the years of victory and, when things went wrong, they blamed everyone but themselves. If some tried to undo the damage, it was far too late to recover the situation. They had sworn to give their lives for their Führer and, in the years of defeat, he held them to their oath. Some tried to limit the damage of the Führer's increasingly deranged orders by continuing to serve him. This proved increasingly difficult as Hitler took greater control over his war machine. Some German officers decided to kill Hitler, but they made a such a bad job of it that most of them ended up dead at the hands of the Führer's lackeys. Hitler ran rings round his generals. They proved to be political pygmies compared to Hitler.

While the political weaknesses of Germany's generals could perhaps be excused, their moral bankruptcy is more difficult to explain. After the war they tried to claim that they had only been professional soldiers, and the atrocities of the Nazis and SS were nothing to do with them. The enthusiasm with which they and their troops cooperated with SS murder squads in Russia showed how far they had become active participants in Hitler's racist campaigns to exterminate Jews and other Slav "sub-humans."

Lord Justice Geoffrey Lawrence, one of the judges who preceded at the Nuremberg Trials held after the war, was scathing in his condemnation of Germany's generals: "They have been responsible in large measure for the miseries and suffering that must have fallen on million of men, women and children. They have been a disgrace to the honourable profession of arms. Without their military guidance the aggressive ambitions of Hitler and his fellow Nazis would have been academic and sterile .... Many of these men have made a mockery of the soldier's oath of obedience to military orders. When it suits their defence they say they had to obey: when confronted with Hitler's brutal crimes, which are shown to have been within their general knowledge, they say they disobeyed. The truth is they actively participated in all these crimes, or sat salient and acquiesced."

Germany's generals and soldiers were not alone in falling under the evil spell of Hitler. The whole German nation backed him in his pursuit of his destiny, which brought ruin and destruction to the world between 1939 and 1945.

Early Panzer Divisions

The 1st Panzer Division was formed on October 15, 1935, in Weimar from the 3rd Cavalry Division. Its organization is typical of the panzer divisions of the early war years.

Organization on September 1, 1939

1 Motorized Brigade Headquarters (I/,II/Motorized Infantry Regiment 1 and
    Motorcycle Battalion 1)
1 Panzer Brigade Headquarters (I/,II/Panzer Regiment 1 and I/,II/Panzer Regiment 2)
I/,II/Artillery Regiment 73 (motorized)
Reconnaissance Battalion 4 (motorized)
Antitank Battalion 37 (motorized)
Engineer Battalion 37 (motorized)
Signals Battalion 37 (motorized)
Supply Troop 81 (motorized)

Organization on June 22, 1941

1 Motorized Brigade Headquarters
I/,II/Motorized Infantry Regiment 1
I/,II/Motorized Infantry Regiment 113
Motorcycle Battalion 1
I/,II/Panzer Regiment 1
I/,II/,III/Artillery Regiment 73 (motorized)
Reconnaissance Battalion 4 (motorized)
Antitank Battalion 37 (motorized)
Engineer Battalion 37 (motorized)
Signals Battalion 37 (motorized)
Supply Troop 81 (motorized)

Sources

Barker, A.J. *Hitler's Forces – Panzers at War*. London: Ian Allan Publishing, 1998.
Chamberlain, Peter, and Doyle, Hilary. *Encyclopedia of German Tanks of World War Two*.
London: Arms & Armour, 1999.
Macksey, Major K.J. *Panzer Division: The mailed fist*. New York: Ballantine Books, 1968.
Nafziger, George F. *The German Order of Battle: Panzers and Artillery in World War II*.
London: Greenhill Books, 1999.
Perret, Bryan. *Panzerkampfwagen III*. Oxford: Osprey Publishing, 2001.

Later Panzer Divisions

The winter battles in the Ukraine on the Eastern Front during late 1943 and into 1944 bled the elite of the panzer divisions white. Instead of receiving large reinforcements in the spring of 1944, most of Germany's tank production was switched westward to equip divisions preparing to fight off the impending Allied invasion of France.

By mid-1944, the German Army's panzer divisions on the Eastern Front were a shadow of their former glory. On paper they were powerful formations with two battalions of tanks, usually one of 88 Panzer IVs and one of 88 Panthers, but battle losses and delays in delivering replacement vehicles meant that divisions on the Eastern Front were lucky if they mustered on average more than 50 working tanks, of both types.

The panzer division was also supposed to boast four panzergrenadier battalions, one of which was to be equipped with armored Sdkfz 251 halftracks. In reality these "battalions" were often little more than over-sized companies, while the armored panzergrenadier battalion was lucky to muster more than a dozen halftracks.

A desperate situation was made even more critical by the destruction of Army Group Center in June and July 1944. With no respite available on either the Western or Eastern Fronts, it was no longer possible to pull worn-out panzer divisions out of the line for reequipping and refitting. More drastic measures were needed.

In July 1994, the first of 10 new so-called panzer brigades were formed to fill the gaps in the German battle line. These were basically strong regimental *Kampfgruppen* (battle groups) made up of a panzer battalion, with around 40 Panthers and a weak panzergrenadier battalion mounted in armored halftracks. The experiment was short-lived, and by the late autumn they had been used to beef-up depleted panzer divisions.

By the spring of 1945, the panzer divisions on the Eastern Front were on their last legs. A new order organization was issued in March 1945 reducing panzer divisions to a single battalion of tanks, but this was largely an academic exercise. Most could only muster a couple of dozen tanks, backed up by an equal number of assault guns or armored self-propelled antitank guns.

Sources
Barker, A.J. *Hitler's Forces – Panzers at War*. London: Ian Allan Publishing, 1998.
Chamberlain, Peter, and Doyle, Hilary. *Encyclopedia of German Tanks of World War Two*. London: Arms & Armour, 1999.
Doyle, Hilary. *Panther Variants 1942–1945*. Oxford: Osprey, 2001.
Jentz, Thomas L. *Panzertruppen: The Complete Guide to the Creation and Combat Employment of Germany's Tank Force 1943–1945*. Atglen, PA: Schiffer, 2000.
Macksey, Major K.J. *Panzer Division: The mailed fist*. New York: Ballantine Books, 1968.
Nafziger, George F. *The German Order of Battle: Panzers and Artillery in World War II*. London: Greenhill Books, 1999.
Perret, Bryan. *Panzerkampfwagen III*. Oxford: Osprey Publishing, 2001.

Panzergrenadier Divisions

Panzergrenadier divisions of the later-war period were the successors of the motorized infantry divisions that had followed in the wake of the panzer divisions during the Blitzkrieg years.

Contrary to popular legend, panzergrenadier divisions were not equipped with hundreds of armored Sdkfz 251 troop-carrying halftracks. These were almost exclusively concentrated in either army panzer divisions or Waffen-SS panzergrenadier, later panzer, divisions.

The 1943–44 panzergrenadier divisions were essentially motorized infantry formations, but reinforced by the allocation of either a panzer or an assault gun battalion. Lucky divisions might also boast an armored reconnaissance battalion, equipped with armored cars or halftracks, along with a self-propelled antitank battalion. By 1944 tank losses meant that the panzergrenadiers lost their panzer battalions, and had to rely on Sturmgeschütz (StuG) III or IV assault guns for armored support.

The fighting power of the panzergrenadier division was found in its two grenadier regiments. These each had three infantry battalions, supported by their own integral mortar, light gun, antiaircraft, and assault pioneer companies.

All troops in a panzergrenadier division were provided with motorized transport to give the division either strategic or operational-level mobility. The division's infantry did not use their trucks to drive them into battle. The truck's main purpose was to get the panzergrenadiers to just behind front, then they would go into action in much the same way as conventional infantry: on foot.

The one major exception to this situation was the famous *Grossdeutschland* Division which, although being designated a panzergrenadier division from June 1943 onward, usually fielded three times as many tanks as the average army panzer division. At one point it even boasted four panzer battalions, including both Tiger 1 and Panther tanks. Its infantry regiments were superbly equipped as well, with one of its infantry battalions being mounted in halftracks. The majority of the specialist support units, such as reconnaissance, artillery, antitank, and antiaircraft units were equipped with armored vehicles. Unlike other units, the *Grossdeutschland* Division was provided with a regular stream of reinforcements to ensure it remained up to strength.

In the final months of the war, heavy losses forced the German military authorities to no longer differentiate between panzer and panzergrenadier divisions. Henceforth, both types of units would be scaled for the same numbers of men and equipment, although by this point in the war such matters were largely academic.

The 3rd Panzergrenadier Division provides a typical example of how these formations were organized.

Organization on September 1, 1943

I/,II/,III/Grenadier Regiment 8 (motorized)
I/,II/,III/Grenadier Regiment 29 (motorized)
Panzer Battalion 103
I/,II/,III/Artillery Regiment 3 (motorized)
Panzer Reconnaissance Battalion 103
Engineer Battalion 3 (motorized)
Army Antiaircraft Artillery Battalion 312 (motorized)
Signals Battalion 3 (motorized)
Supply Troop 3 (motorized)

Sources
Nafziger, George F. *The German Order of Battle: Panzers and Artillery in World War II.*
London: Greenhill Books, 1999.
Scheibert, Horst. *Panzer-Grenadier: Motorcycle & Panzer-reconnaissance Units 1935–1945.* Atglen, PA:
Schiffer, 1991.

Motorized Infantry Divisions

On the battlefield the motorized infantry divisions were created to keep up with fast-moving panzer divisions, and thus were completely equipped with motor vehicles. The first four motorized infantry divisions (2nd, 13th, 20th, and 29th) were directly upgraded from infantry divisions during 1937 to 1939. They therefore kept most of the features of their parent units. Each motorized infantry division had three motorized infantry regiments, one motorized artillery regiment, and supporting units components.

Organization of a typical motorized infantry division, 1939

Division Headquarters (motorized)
Infantry Regiment (motorized)
Infantry Regiment (motorized)
Infantry Regiment (motorized)
Artillery Regiment (motorized)
Reconnaissance Battalion (motorized)
Antitank Battalion (motorized)
Engineer Battalion (motorized)

The motorized infantry division had a total of nine motorized infantry battalions, supported by three motorized light artillery battalions and one motorized heavy artillery battalion.

Sources for this page and page 331
Davies, W.J.K. *German Army Handbook 1939–1945*. London: Military Book Society, 1973.
Lucas, James. *German Army Handbook 1939–1945*. Stroud: Sutton Publishing Limited, 1998.
Nafziger, George F. *The German Order of Battle: Infantry in World War II*. London: Greenhill Books, 2000.
US Handbook on German Military Forces. Washington: US War Department, 1945.

Infantry Divisions

Typical organization of a 1939 infantry division was as follows:

Division Staff Company
Mapping Platoon (motorized)
Three Infantry Regiments
    Each with three battalions
        Each with three rifle companies
        Machine Gun Company
        Infantry Gun Company

    Reconnaissance Battalion
        Mounted Squadron
        Bicycle Squadron
        Heavy Squadron
        Antitank Platoon (motorized)
        Infantry Gun Platoon
        Armored Reconnaissance Troop

Artillery Regiment
    Artillery Regimental Staff and Staff Battery
    Three Light Artillery Battalions
    Artillery Battalion Staff and Staff Battery
        Three Batteries
    Heavy Artillery Battalion
    Artillery Battalion Staff and Staff Battery
        One Battery
    Observation Battalion (motorized)

Panzerjäger Battalion
    Three *Panzerjäger* Companies (motorized)
    Heavy Machine Gun Company (motorized)

Pioneer Battalion
    Two Pioneer Companies

Signals Battalion

Replacement Battalion

Plus bakery, butcher, medical, and veterinary support

Volksgrenadier Divisions

Hitler coined the name *Volksgrenadier* division in the late summer of 1944. It appealed to his sense of drama and his need for "struggle." The *Volk*, or "German People," had mythical connotations for the Führer, who saw World War II as a racial struggle between the German master race and Jewish and Slav "sub-humans," or *Untermenschen*.

In reality the *Volksgrenadier* divisions were little more than underequipped and undermanned line infantry divisions, repackaged with a new politically correct title. There were 13 "new" *Volksgrenadier* divisions, but dozens more were reformed from the remnants of line units.

The manpower strength of a *Volksgrenadier* division was nearly a third less than a 1939-era infantry division, with only 10,000 men compared to 16,500 men in the old type of unit. The frontline strength was badly hit, with the new divisions only having six infantry battalions, as opposed to nine infantry battalions in the earlier type of division. Improvements in firepower were made, however, with the new divisions on paper boasting more than 500 machine guns.

Volksgrenadier divisions were of very mixed quality. Those based on old formations were generally of better quality than those formed from scratch. The first big test of the new divisions was during the Ardennes Offensive in December 1944. Many of them were specifically reinforced for the offensive with assault gun battalions, and other specialist units. They were at the center of the action along the front and most acquitted themselves well.

The 18th *Volksgrenadier* Division played a pivotal role in the destruction of the US 106th Infantry Division in the opening days of the Battle of the Bulge. Using classic infiltration tactics, the *Volksgrenadiers* were able to push through American lines, spreading panic and confusion among the inexperienced G.I.s. In total, some 8,000 Americans surrendered to the division in perhaps the most serious US military defeat on mainland Europe in World War II.

For the remainder of the war, the *Volksgrenadier* divisions did not taste victory again. The majority were posted to the East to hold the line in Poland, Czechoslovakia, and Hungary, where they were destroyed.

Sources

Davies, W.J.K. *German Army Handbook 1939–1945*. London: Military Book Society, 1973.

Lucas, James. *German Army Handbook 1939–1945*. Stroud: Sutton Publishing Limited, 1998.

The Editors of *Command Magazine*. *Hitler's Army: The Evolution and Structure of German Forces*. Pennsylvania: Combined Publishing, 2000.

Waffen-SS Panzer Divisions

The Waffen-SS panzer divisions were among the most effective formations fielded by the Wehrmacht in World War II. The 12th SS Panzer Division *Hitlerjugend* was fairly typical of the SS panzer divisions.

Organization in October 1943

25th SS-Panzergrenadier Regiment *Hitlerjugend*
26th SS-Panzergrenadier Regiment *Hitlerjugend*
12th SS-Panzer Regiment
12th SS-Artillery Regiment
12th SS-Motorcycle Regiment
12th SS-Reconnaissance Battalion
12th SS-Tank-Hunter Battalion
12th SS-Rocket Artillery Battalion
12th SS-Antiaircraft Battalion
12th SS-Engineer Battalion
12th SS-Panzer-Signals Battalion
12th SS Divisional Support Units

Sources
Nafziger, George F. *The German Order of Battle: Waffen-SS and other units in World War II*. Pennsylvania: Combined Publishing, 2001.
Reynolds, Michael. *Steel Inferno: I SS Panzer Corps in Normandy*. Staplehurst: Spellmount, 1997.
Reynolds, Michael. *Sons of the Reich: The History of II SS Panzer Corps*. Staplehurst: Spellmount, 2002.
Reynolds, *Men of Steel: I SS Panzer Corps: The Ardennes and Eastern Front 1944–45*. Staplehurst: Spellmount, 2002.

Divisional Strengths

Strength of the most important division
types of the German Field Army in 1939

	Inf. Div.	Mot. Inf. Div.	Pz. Div.	le. Div.
Officers	500	500	400	400
Officials	100	100	100	100
Non-Commisioned Officers	2,500	2,500	2,000	1,600
Enlisted Man / Crews	13,400	13,400	9,300	8,700
Total Strong	16,500	16,500	11,800	10,800
Machine Guns	500	500	220	460
Mortars	140	140	50	60
Infantry Guns	25	25	10	10
37mm Pak Guns	75	75	50	50
Howitzers & Cannons	48	48	28	24
20mm Flak Guns	12	12	12	12
Armored Scout Cars	3	30	100	100
Tanks	-	-	324	86
Trucks	500	1,700	1,400	1,400
Passenger Cars	400	1,000	560	600
Motorcycles	500	1,300	1,300	1,100
Sidecars	200	600	700	600
Horses	5,000	-	-	-
Covered Vehicles (Wagons)	1,000	-	-	-

Inf. Div. – Infantry Division
Mot. Inf. Div. – Motorized Infantry Division
Pz. Div. – Panzer Division
le. Div. – *Leichte* (Light) Division

Sources
Chamberlain, Peter, and Doyle, Hilary. *Encyclopedia of German Tanks of World War Two*.
London: Arms & Armour, 1999.
Davies, W.J.K. *German Army Handbook 1939–1945*. London: Military Book Society, 1973.
Deighton, Len. *Blitzkrieg: From the Rise of Hitler to the Fall of Dunkirk*. London: BCA, 1979.
Hogg, Ian V. *German Artillery of World War Two*. London: Greenhill Books, 1997.
Macksey, Major K.J. *Panzer Division: The mailed fist*. New York: Ballantine Books, 1968.
Nafziger, George F. *The German Order of Battle: Infantry in World War II*. London: Greenhill
Books, 2000.

Tank Strength of Panzer Divisions

Time Period:	Number of Tanks:
1939/1940	324
1941/1942	150–200
1943	170
1944	120–140

Note: These are ideal numbers that usually did not reflect the strength of frontline units.

Sources

Barker, A.J. *Hitler's Forces – Panzers at War*. London: Ian Allan Publishing, 1998.

Chamberlain, Peter, and Doyle, Hilary. *Encyclopedia of German Tanks of World War Two*. London: Arms & Armour, 1999.

Jentz, Thomas L. *Panzertruppen: The Complete Guide to the Creation and Combat Employment of Germany's Tank Force 1943–1945*. Atglen, PA: Schiffer, 2000.

Macksey, Major K.J. *Panzer Division: The mailed fist*. New York: Ballantine Books, 1968.

Nafziger, George F. *The German Order of Battle: Panzers and Artillery in World War II*. London: Greenhill Books, 1999.

Perret, Bryan. *Panzerkampfwagen III*. Oxford: Osprey Publishing, 2001.

German Tank Strengths

June 1941 to January 1945

Date:	Quantity:	Date:	Quantity:
06/1941	5,639	06/1944	9,148
03/1942	5,087	09/1944	10,563
05/1942	5,847	10/1944	11,005
11/1942	7,798	11/1944	12,236
03/1943	5,625	12/1944	13,175
08/1943	7,703	01/1945	13,362

Note: Numbers do not include APCs and armored cars.

Sources

Barker, A.J. *Hitler's Forces – Panzers at War*. London: Ian Allan Publishing, 1998.
Chamberlain, Peter, and Doyle, Hilary. *Encyclopedia of German Tanks of World War Two*.
London: Arms & Armour, 1999.
Cooper, Matthew and Lucas, James. *Panzer: The Armoured Force of the Third Reich*. New York:
St Martins Press, 1976.
Doyle, Hilary. *Panzerkampfwagen IV Ausf. G, H and J 1942–45*. Oxford: Osprey Publishing, 2001.
Jentz, Thomas L. *Panzertruppen: The Complete Guide to the Creation and Combat Employment of
Germany's Tank Force 1937–1942*. Atglen, PA: Schiffer, 1996.
Jentz, Thomas L. *Panzertruppen: The Complete Guide to the Creation and Combat Employment of
Germany's Tank Force 1943–1945*. Atglen, PA: Schiffer, 2000.
Jentz, Thomas L. *Germany's Tiger Tanks: Tiger I & II: Combat Tactics*. Atglen, PA: Schiffer, 1997.
Macksey, Major K.J. *Panzer Division: The mailed fist*. New York: Ballantine Books, 1968.
Nafziger, George F. *The German Order of Battle: Panzers and Artillery in World War II*.
London: Greenhill Books, 1999.
Perret, Bryan. *Panzerkampfwagen III*. Oxford: Osprey Publishing, 2001.
Mitcham Jr., Samuel W. *The Panzer Legions: A Guide to the German Army Tank Divisions of World War
II and Their Commanders*. Westport, CT: Greenwood Press, 2001.
Stolfi, R.H.S. *Hitler's Panzers East: World War II Reinterpreted*. Norman: University of Oklahoma Press,
1993.

Antitank Tactics

German antitank tactics on the Eastern Front involved a mix of offensive and defensive actions. Central to these was the need to commit heavy antitank weapons, either towed guns or self-propelled guns, en masse to achieve decisive effects.

Antitank weapons were concentrated at regimental and divisional level, and strict orders were issued against these high value assets being committed in ones or twos to bolster frontline infantry positions. They had to rely on mines, hollow-charge grenades, or manportable rocket launchers, such as the *Panzerschreck* or later the single-shot *Panzerfaust*, for protection.

Heavy antitank or *Panzerjäger* units were usually held in reserve until concentrations of Soviet tanks were detected. German commanders then positioned their antitank units in the best place to halt the Soviet advance in what was termed a "killing zone." Antitank gun batteries covered the killing zone with overlapping arcs of fire, so there would be no escape for any Soviet tanks that entered the zone.

From the Battle of Kursk onward, Soviet tank attacks were pressed home in such numbers that the average divisional antitank unit, with at most a dozen 75mm antitank guns, was unable to cope. Divisional *Panzerjäger* units would therefore be combined in *Kampfgruppen*, or battle groups, with tank battalions.

It would be the job of the *Panzerjägers* to act as the anvil of the defense, absorbing and slowing down the momentum of the Soviet attack. Meanwhile the hammer, the panzer battalion, would be maneuvering around the flanks of the Soviet tank formation to gain a good position to engage it in a decisive attack.

Poor Soviet command and control procedures, along with a shortage of radios, often meant that even small German combined antitank gun and armored forces could usually outmaneuver and devastate much larger Soviet forces. After a major breakthrough south of Kiev in December 1943, for example, a well-led German panzer corps was able to position its antitank units and tank battalions in such a way that it decimated an 800 tank Soviet formation. The Soviet tank armada was so massive that its commanders totally lost control of it, and the German gunners were able to take pot shots at its flanks without any effective counteraction being taken.

Sources

Carell, Paul. *Scorched Earth*. New York: Ballantine, 1971.

Fugate, Bryan I. *Operation Barbarossa: Strategy and Tactics on the Eastern Front, 1941*. Novato, CA: Presidio, 1984.

Lucas, James. *War on the Eastern Front: The German Soldier in Russia 1941–45*. London: Greenhill, 1979.

Mellenthin, F.W. von. *Panzer Battles 1939–45: A Study in the Employment of Armor*. London: Cassell, 1955.

Newton, Steven H. *German Battle Tactics on the Russian Front 1941–45*. Atglen, PA: Schiffer, 1994.

German Ranks

Heer Rank	Luftwaffe Rank	Kriegsmarine Rank	Waffen-SS Rank
Grenadier	*Flieger*	*Matrose*	*SS-Schütze*
Obergrenadier			*SS-Oberschütze*
Gefreiter	*Gefreiter*	*Matrosengefreiter*	*SS-Sturmmann*
Obergefreiter	*Obergefreiter*	*Matrosenobergefreiter*	*SS-Rottenführer*
Stabsgefreiter	*Hauptgefreiter*	*Matrosenhauptgefreiter*	
	Stabsgefreiter	*Matrosenstabsgefreiter*	
Unteroffizier	*Unteroffizier*	*Mät*	*SS-Unterscharführer*
Unterfeldwebel	*Unterfeldwebel*	*Obermät*	*SS-Scharführer*
Fähnrich		*Fähnrich zur See*	
Feldwebel	*Feldwebel*	*Feldwebel*	*SS-Oberscharführer*
Oberfeldwebel	*Oberfeldwebel*	*Stabsfeldwebel*	*SS-Hauptscharführer*
Hauptfeldwebel		*Oberfeldwebel*	*SS-Stabsscharführer*
Oberfähnrich		*Oberfähnrich zur See*	
Stabsfeldwebel	*Stabsfeldwebel*		*SS-Sturmscharführer*
		Stabsoberfeldwebel	
Leutnant	*Leutnant*	*Leutnant zur See*	*SS-Untersturmführer*
Oberleutnant	*Oberleutnant*	*Oberleutnant zur See*	*SS-Obersturmführer*
Hauptmann	*Hauptmann*	*Kapitänleutnant*	*SS-Hauptsturmführer*
Major	*Major*	*Korvettenkapitän*	*SS-Sturmbannführer*
Oberstleutnant	*Oberstleutnant*	*Fregattenkapitän*	*SS-Obersturmbannführer*
Oberst	*Oberst*	*Kapitän zur See*	*SS-Standartenführer*
		Kommodore	*SS-Oberführer*
Generalmajor	*Generalmajor*	*Vizeadmiral*	*SS-Brigadeführer*
Generalleutnant	*Generalleutnant*	*Konteradmiral*	*SS-Gruppenführer*
General der...	*General der...*	*Admiral*	*SS-Obergruppenführer*
Generaloberst	*Generaloberst*	*Generaladmiral*	*SS-Oberstgruppenführer*
Generalfeld-marschall	*Generalfeld-marschall*	*Grossadmiral*	*Reichsführer-SS*
	Reichsmarschall		

Rank Equivalents

German Army	U.S. Army
Schütze	Private
Oberschütze	Private 1st Class
Gefreiter	Acting Corporal
Obergefreiter	Corporal
Unteroffizier	Sergeant
Unterfeldwebel	Staff sergeant
Fähnrich	Officer candidate
Feldwebel	Technical sergeant
Oberfeldwebel	Master sergeant
Oberfähnrich	Senior Officer candidate
Stabsfeldwebel	Sergeant Major
Leutnant	2d Lieutenant
Oberleutnant	1st Lieutenant
Hauptmann	Captain
Major	Major
Oberstleutnant	Lieutenant-Colonel
Oberst	Colonel
Generalmajor	Brigadier General
Generalleutnant	Major-General
General der Infanterie (etc.)	Lieutenant-General
Generaloberst	General
Generalfeldmarschall	General of the army

Sources for this page and page 338

Hohne, Heinze. *The Order of the Death's Head: The Story of Hitler's SS*. London: Penguin Books, 2000.
Lucas, James. *German Army Handbook 1939–1945*. Stroud: Sutton Publishing Limited, 1998.
US Handbook on German Military Forces. Washington: US War Department, 1945.

Casualty Figures

German Population
German Population in 1933: 66,000,000+
German Population in 1938: 78,000,000+
German Population in 1939: 80,600,000+

Gender and Age
German Men in 1939: 38,900,000+
German Men aged 15–65 in 1939: 24,620,748
German Men aged 15–20 in 1939: 3,137,429
German Men aged 21–34 in 1939: 8,885,775
German Men aged 35–44 in 1939: 5,695,510
German Men aged 45–65 in 1939: 6,902,034
German Women in 1939: 41,700,000+
German Women aged 15–65 in 1939: 27,960,000+

Wehrmacht (German Armed Forces)
In Wehrmacht Service, 1939: 4,722,000+
In Wehrmacht Service, 1940: 6,600,000+
In Wehrmacht Service, 1941: 8,154,000+
In Wehrmacht Service, 1942: 9,580,000+
In Wehrmacht Service, 1943: 11,280,000+
In Wehrmacht Service, 1944: 12,070,000+
In Wehrmacht Service, 1945: 9,701,000+
Total in Wehrmacht Service 1939–45: 17,893,200

Total Wehrmacht KIA, 1939–45: 2,230,324
Total Wehrmacht MIA, 1939–45: 2,870,404
Total Wehrmacht WIA, 1939–45: 5,240,000
Total Wehrmacht Casualties, 1939–45: 10,340,728

German Army
In German Army Service, 1939: 3,737,000+
In German Army Service, 1940: 4,550,000+
In German Army Service, 1941: 5,000,000+
In German Army Service, 1942: 5,800,000+
In German Army Service, 1943: 6,550,000+

In German Army Service, 1944: 6,510,000+
In German Army Service, 1945: 5,300,000+
Total in German Army Service, 1939–45: 13,000,000+

German Army KIA/MIA, 1939–45: 1,600,000+
German Army WIA, 1939–45: 4,175,000+
German Army Casualties, 1939–45: 5,775,000+

Waffen-SS
In Waffen-SS service, 1939: 35,000+
In Waffen-SS service, 1940: 50,000+
In Waffen-SS service, 1941: 150,000+
In Waffen-SS service, 1942: 230,000+
In Waffen-SS service, 1943: 450,000+
In Waffen-SS service, 1944: 600,000+
In Waffen-SS service, 1945: 830,000+
Total in Waffen-SS service, 1939–45: 1,000,000+

Waffen-SS KIA/MIA, 1939–45: 250,000
Waffen-SS WIA, 1939–45: 400,000
Waffen-SS Casualties, 1939–45: 650,000+

Key
KIA: killed in action
MIA: missing in action
WIA: wounded in action

The figures on these two pages are reproduced with the kind permission of Jason Pipes, who has extensively researched the units of the German Army and Waffen-SS in World War II. His excellent website—www.feldgrau.com—contains a vast wealth of information, which has been painstakingly amassed over a number of years. It is well worth a visit. In addition, there are a number of German governmental organizations that provide information on German military and civilian losses in World War II. Readers are advised to contact them direct for casualty figuers pertaining to specific German armies, divisions and regiments:

Bundesarchiv – Militärarchiv
(Federal Records Office – Military Archive)
Postfach, 79024 Freiburg
Wiesentalstrasse 10
79115 Freiburg
Germany

Deutsche Dienstelle (WASt)
(Wehrmacht Information Office for War Losses and POWs)
Postfach 51 06 57
D-13400 Berlin
Germany

Volksbund Deutsche Kriegsgräberfürsorge
(German War Graves Commission)
Werner-Hilpert Strasse 2
D-34112 Kassel
Germany

Glossary

A

Abteilung depending on its usage, this term could mean detachment, department, or battalion, but the vast majority of the time *Abteilung* meant battalion. *Abteilung* was used for battalion-sized units in the Panzer, *Kavallerie*, and *Artillerie* branches. Well-known exceptions to the word meaning battalion were *Armee-Abteilung* and *Korps-Abteilung*, in which army detachment and corps detachment were the meanings, respectively.

Armee a term meaning army. An organizational formation made up of corps units.

Armee-Abteilung a term meaning army detachment. Usually larger than a single corps but smaller than a full *Armee*. Sometimes formed by grouping corps in an *Armee* together.

Armeegruppe army grouping. By 1943 these were usually two or three adjacent armies, possibly but not always one German and one German-allied, with one of the *Armee* HQs (usually the German) temporarily placed in command over the others. An *Armeegruppe* was always subordinate to the local *Heeresgruppe*.

Artillerie artillery.

Artillerieführer artillery officer.

Artilleriekommandeur artillery commander.

Aufklärung reconnaissance.

B

Bataillon battalion. An organizational formation made up of *Kompanien* and usually attached to a regiment.

Batterie battery. An organization equal to a *Kompanie*, but used in place of that term for units of similar size but composed of artillery or antiaircraft weapons. An *Infanterie-Bataillon* was composed of three or four *Infanterie-Kompanien*, while an *Artillerie-Abteilung* was made up of three or four *Artillerie-Batterien*.

Baupionier construction engineer.

Befehlshaber der commander of ...

Bewährung This term means punitive or literally "probation." When speaking of actual units, this type of formation was used as a punishment unit for soldiers guilty of serious violations of German military law. If a soldier broke a military law, disobeyed an order, or otherwise was found guilty of a crime or criminal act, he could be sent to this type of unit. If he served well and survived, he could be rehabilitated back to a regular unit.

Bodenständige static, used to indicate certain units were not fully field-mobile.

Brigade brigade. Means the same in German as in English. An organizational unit usually made up of two or more *Regimenter*. Brigade-sized units served either as independent units or as an organic part of a division. Sometimes they served as an organic part of a corps in place of a division. Early in the war, many *Divisionen* consisted of one or more *Brigaden*, each consisting of a number of *Regimenter*, along with the usual attached and organic units.

C

Chef des Generalstabes the chief of the general staff.

D

Division division. Means the same in German as in English. An organizational unit made up of *Regimenter* and usually controlled by a corps.

E

Einheit detachment or unit.

Eisenbahn railroad.

Ersatz replacement.

F

Fahrtruppen fast troops.

Fallschirm parachute. Used in conjunction with other unit types.

Feld field. Used occasionally to designate certain rear-area units when they were deployed in the combat zone (although usually as rear-area security and not in the frontline).

Feldgendarmerie field police.

Feldkommandantur field command, equivalent to a regiment in importance.

Feldlazarett field hospital.

Festung fortress.

Flak (*Fliegerabwehrkanone*) antiaircraft. Completely: antiaircraft gun. Originally, *Flak* were larger-caliber guns.

Flieger flyer.

Fliegerabwehrkanone antiaircraft gun.

Freiwillige volunteer. Used mainly

by the Waffen-SS to denote units composed of foreign volunteers. For a while, it was applied to non-German but Germanic volunteers, such as Norwegians and Danes. Later it was applied to denote non-Germanic units, such as Ukrainians.

Fusilier infantry or heavy infantry. An infantry formation with some reconnaissance abilities that replaced an infantry division's reconnaissance battalion in mid-war (when the Germans reduced the number of standard infantry battalions in their divisions from nine to six).

G

Gebirg mountain.

Generalkommando general headquarters.

Generalstab des Heeres army general staff.

Geschütz gun.

Grenadier In 1942, the Germans needed to reinforce their field forces in some way. Since they didn't have the men or equipment to send out in quantity, they decided to reinforce the morale of their field forces, by resurrecting traditional military terms and thereby recalling Germany's glorious military past. The most significant resurrection was *Grenadier*, a traditional term for a type of infantryman. Other resurrected terms were *Fusilier* and *Musketier*.

Granatwerfer mortar.

Gruppe group.

H

Heer army. The regular German Army.

Heeresgruppe army group. An organizational formation made up of a number of *Armeen*. The largest single German organizational formation during World War II.

Usually consisted of hundreds of various units and a few hundred thousand men, all of which operated in a far-ranging geographic region of the front. An example would be *Heeresgruppe Afrika* which controlled all units fighting in North Afrika at the time of its formation.

J

Jagd- literally "hunting." Used in conjunction with another word to signify a unit's role. Also applied to weapons, i.e. *Jagdtiger* was the special tank-hunter version of the Tiger tank.

Jagd-Kommando hunting command. In theory, a commando outfit that, when the enemy overran an occupied area, would remain behind enemy lines and carry out sabotage and other guerrilla actions. They did not operate as such and were taken over by the SS and used as frontline troops in 1944–45.

Jäger light infantry.

-jäger 1) -infantry. Used in conjunction with other unit types, it indicated the infantry component of that general type. *Fallschirmjäger*: Parachute Infantry.

2) When used in its hunting sense, -jäger did not necessarily imply infantry. Thus, *Panzerjäger* meant antitank ("tank hunter") and not armored infantry.

K

Kavallerie cavalry.

Kettenkrad tracked motorcycle.

Kommandeur a person commanding a unit (*Divisionskommandeur*: divisional commander). Other uses were rare, except for the artillery branch. An *Artillerie-Kommandeur* (abbreviated *Arko*) was a numbered HQ used to control artillery assets

at corps level. Later in the war, the Germans created the *Höherer Artillerie-Kommandeur* (abbreviated *Harko*) to control artillery assets at army level.

Kommando 1) A command in the sense of a geographical area of authority.

2) A headquarters. The HQ of an army group was a *Heeresgruppe Kommando*; an Army HQ was an *Armee Oberkommando*. German corps came in several varieties, of which a *Generalkommando* was a general corps HQ and a *Höhere Kommando*, a "higher" HQ.

Kompanie company.

Korps corps.

Korps-Abteilung corps detachment. On the Eastern Front, the Germans took to grouping sets of three burnt-out divisions (each about regimental strength) in a formation equivalent to a division. It was called a *Korps-Abteilung* because the Germans for a while had hopes of rebuilding the divisions.

Krad (*Kraft-Radfahrzeug*) motorcycle.

Kradschütze motorcycle soldier.

Kriegsmarine the German Navy.

L

Legion legion, often used for units comprised of foreigners in German service. Used by both the German Army and Waffen-SS. A legion had no fixed size and usually ranged in size from a battalion to a brigade. Often preceded by *Freiwillgen* to denote the volunteer status of the unit.

Leicht light. When used with another unit type, it meant a light version of the unit type. A *Leichte* division was a motorized/armored formation. In 1939, light divisions were similar to panzer divisions but had fewer tanks. In 1941, the 5th

Light Division had as many tanks as a panzer division but only half the infantry (it later was redesignated a panzer division).

Luftlande air landing.

Luftwaffe the German Air Force.

M

Maschinengewehr machine gun.

Materialschlacht war of attrition

Motorisiert motorizied.

N

Nachrichten signals/communication.

Nachschub supply.

Nebelwerfer rocket artillery. *Nebelwerfer* was originally a term for a chemical smoke mortar. The *Nebel* units were subsequently used for the rocket artillery.

O

Oberfeldkommandantur High Field Command, equivalent roughly to a division in importance, used for security purposes in occupied territory.

Oberkommando der Wehrmacht (OKW) German Armed Forces High Command.

Oberkommando des Heeres (OKH) German Army High Command.

P

Pak antitank. Short for *Panzerabwehrkanone*, antitank gun.

Panzer armor/armored.

Panzerabwehr antitank.

Panzergrenadier armored infantry. Panzergrenadier units were not necessarily armored – most used trucks, as German industry was incapable of producing sufficient halftracks for all units.

Panzerjäger tank-hunter.

Panzerzerstörer tank-destroyer.

Pionier engineer.

R

Reserve reserve. a training and/or replacement unit that could handle security and combat duties.

S

Sanitäts medical.

Schlacht battle.

Schutzstaffel literally, Protection Force or Defense Squad. The SS consisted of three parts, the *Allgemeine-SS*, the *SS-Totenkopfverbände*, and the Waffen-SS.

Schwer heavy.

Sicherung security.

Stab HQ or staff.

Standarte regiment.

Sturm assault. Used with other unit types, supposedly meant a skilled, offensive formation.

Sturmartillerie assault gun. Literally, assault artillery, the early war term for the assault guns.

Sturmgeschütz assault gun. Not all assault guns were in assault gun units. It was also used partly (or completely) in various antitank units and as replacements for tanks in panzer units.

Sturmpionier assault engineer.

T

Totenkopf death's head.

Totenkopfverbände Death's Head Organization, the organization formed as a sub-unit of the political SS early in the 1930s, initially to guard the concentration camps. The *Totenkopfverbände* would later go on to form the 3rd SS Panzer Division *Totenkopf*.

V

Volksgrenadier Infanterie people's infantry. *Volk* was a morale term used to encourage the idea that the conflict was a people's war.

Volkssturm Home-defense units pulled together because of the crumbling situation on the Eastern Front toward the end of the war.

W

Waffen armed.

Waffen-SS term for the armed units of the political organization of the SS, the German *Schutzstaffel*. The Waffen-SS is often mistaken for the SS itself, but in fact it was a frontline fighting organization that would grow to well over 900,000 members by the end of World War II. Though it did commit atrocities, the Waffen-SS was not directly responsible for the Holocaust as is often misinterpreted.

Wehrmacht armed forces. German term which encompassed the three major groupings of the German military, the *Heer*, *Luftwaffe*, and *Kriegsmarine*.

Werewolf German guerrilla fighters dedicated to harass the rear areas of the invaders of Germany.

Werfer Rocket artillery units.

Bibliography

Addington, Larry. *The Blitzkrieg Era and the German General Staff, 1865–1941*. New Brunswick, NJ: Rutgers University Press, 1971.

Alexander, Martin S. "The Fall of France." *Journal of Strategic Studies 13, No. 1* (March 1990): 10–44.

Alexander, Martin S. "In Lieu of Alliance: The French General Staff's Secret Cooperation with Neutral Belgium 1936–40." *Journal of Strategic Studies 14, No. 4* (December 1991): 413–27.

Assmann, Kurt. *The German Campaign in Norway: Origin of the Plan, Execution of the Operation, and Measures Against Allied Counterattack*. London: Naval Staff, Admiralty, 1948.

Barker, A.J. *Hitler's Forces – Panzers at War*. London: Ian Allan Publishing, 1998.

Barnett, Corelli. *The Desert Generals*. London: Allen & Unwin, 1983.

Bartov, Omer. *Hitler's Army: Soldiers, Nazis and War in the Third Reich*. Oxford: Oxford University Press, 1992.

Beevor, Antony. *Crete: The Battle and the Resistance*. London: Penguin Books, 1992.

Bethell, Nigel. *The War Hitler Won: The Fall of Poland 1939*. New York: Holt, Rinehart & Winston, 1972.

Bloch, Marc. *Strange Defeat*. New York: Norton Library, 1968.

Bond, Brian. *Britain, France, and Belgium, 1939–40*. New York: Brassey's, 1990.

Boog, Horst *et al.* (eds.). *Germany and the Second World War, Vol. IV: The Attack on the Soviet Union*. Oxford: Clarendon, 1998.

Brett-Smith, Richard. *Hitler's Generals*. London: Osprey, 1976.

Buchner, Alex. *Narvik: die Kämpfe der Gruppe Dietl im Fruhjahr 1940*. Neckargemünd: K. Vowinckel, 1958.

Buckley, Christopher. *Greece and Crete 1941*. London: HMSO, 1977.

Carell, Paul. *Hitler Moves East, 1941–1943*. Boston: Little, Brown & Co., 1964.

Carell, Paul. *Scorched Earth*. New York: Ballantine, 1971.

Chamberlain, Peter and Doyle, Hilary. *Encyclopedia of German Tanks of World War Two*. London: Arms & Armour, 1999.

Clark, Alan. *The Fall of Crete*. London: Anthony Bland, 1962.

Cooper, Matthew, *The German Army, 1933–1945: Its Political and Military Failure*. New York: Random House, 1978.

Cooper, Matthew, and Lucas, James. *Panzer: The Armoured Force of the Third Reich*. New York: St Martin's Press, 1976.

Cooper, Matthew, and Lucas, James. *Panzer*. London: Macdonald, 1976.

Cooper, Matthew, and Lucas, James. *Panzergrenadier*. London: Macdonald and Jane's, 1977.

Cooper, Matthew, and Lucas, James. *Hitler's Elite*, London: Grafton, 1990.

Corum, James S. *The Roots of Blitzkrieg: Hans von Seeckt and German Military Reform*. Lawrence, KS: Kansas University Press, 1992.

Corum, James S. "The Luftwaffe and Coalition Air War in Spain, 1936–39." *Journal of Strategic Studies 18, No. 1* (March 1995): 68–90.

Creveld, Martin van. *Command in War*. Cambridge, Massachusetts: Harvard University Press, 1987.

Creveld, Martin van. *Hitler's Strategy 1940–1941: The Balkan Clue*. Cambridge: Cambridge University Press, 1973.

Creveld, Martin van. *Supplying War: Logistics from Wallenstein to Patton*. Cambridge: Cambridge University Press, 1977.

Cross, Robin. *Citadel: The Battle of Kursk*, London: Michael O'Mara, 1993.

Davies, W.J.K. *German Army Handbook 1939–1945*. London: Military Book Society, 1973.

Davis, Brian L. *German Ground Forces: Poland and France, 1939–40*. London: Almark, 1976.

Deighton, Len. *Blitzkrieg: From the Rise of Hitler to the Fall of Dunkirk*. London: BCA, 1979.

Deist, Wilhelm. *The Wehrmacht and German Rearmament*. Toronto: Toronto University Press, 1981.

Deist, Wilhelm *et al.* (eds.). *Germany and the Second World War, Vol. 1: The Build-up of German Aggression*. Oxford: Clarendon, 1998.

Dinardo, R.L. *Germany's Panzer Arm: (Contributions in Military Studies)*. Westport, Connecticut: Greenwood Publishing Group, 1997.

Dinardo, R.L. "German Armour Doctrine: Correcting the Myths." *War in History 3, No. 4* (November 1996): 384–98.

Doughty, Robert A. *The Seeds of Disaster: The Development of French Army Doctrine, 1919–39*. Hamden, CT: Archon, 1985.

Doughty, Robert A. *The Breaking Point: Sedan and the Fall of France 1940*. Hamden, CT: Archon, 1990.

Doughty, Robert A. "The Maginot Line." *MHQ: The Quarterly Journal of Military History 9, No. 2* (Winter 1997): 48–59.

Downing, David. *The Devil's Virtuosos*. London: New English

Library, 1976.

Doyle, Hilary. *Panther Variants 1942–1945*. Oxford: Osprey, 2001.

Doyle, Hilary. *Panzerkampfwagen IV Ausf. G, H and J 1942–45*. Oxford: Osprey Publishing, 2001.

Dunnigan, James. *The Russian Front*. London: Arms and Armour, 1978.

Dupuy, Trevor N. *A Genius for War: The German Army & General Staff, 1807–1945*. London: Macdonald and Jane's, 1977.

The Editors of *Command Magazine*. *Hitler's Army: The Evolution and Structure of German Forces*. Pennsylvania: Combined Publishing, 2000.

Edwards, Jill (ed.). *El Alamein Revisited*. Cairo: AUC Press, 2000.

Edwards, Roger. *Panzer: A Revolution in Warfare, 1939–45*. London: Arms & Armour, 1989.

Erickson, John. *The Road to Stalingrad*. New York: Harper & Row, 1976.

Forty, George. *German Tanks of World War Two*. London: Blandford Press, 1987.

Forty, George. *The Armies of Rommel*. London: Arms & Armour, 1997.

Fugate, Bryan I. *Operation Barbarossa: Strategy and Tactics on the Eastern Front, 1941*. Novato, CA: Presidio, 1984.

Glantz, David M. *Zhukov's Greatest Defeat: The Red Army's Epic Disaster in Operation Mars, 1942*. Lawrence, KS: University of Kansas Press, 1999.

Glantz, David M., and House, Jonathan. *When Titans Clashed: How the Red Army Stopped Hitler*. Lawrence, KS: University of Kansas Press, 1995.

Glantz, David M., and House, Jonathan. *The Battle of Kursk*. London: Ian Allan Publishing, 1999.

Guderian, Heinz (transl. Christopher Duffy). *Achtung-Panzer!* London: Arms & Armour, 1992.

Guderian, Heinz. *Panzer Leader*. London: Joseph, 1952.

Gunzberg, Jeffery A. *Divided and Conquered: The French High Command and the Defeat in the West, 1940*. Westport, CT: Greenwood, 1979.

Gunzberg, Jeffery A. "The Battle of Gembloux, 14–15 May 1940: Blitzkrieg Checked." *Journal of Military History 64* (January 2000): 97–140.

Hastings, Max. *Overlord*. London: Michael Joseph, 1984.

Haupt, Werner. *Assault on Moscow 1941*. Atglen, PA: Schiffer, 1996.

Haupt, Werner. *Army Group Center*. Atglen, PA:, Schiffer, 1998.

Hitler, Adolf. *Hitler's Table Talk*, London: Weidenfeld & Nicolson, 1953.

Hogg, Ian V. *German Artillery of World War Two*. London: Greenhill Books, 1997.

Horne, *Alistair. To Lose a Battle: France 1940*. London: Macmillan, 1969.

Hubatsch, Walter. *Die deutsche Besatzung von Danemark und Norwegen 1940*. Göttingen: Musterschmidt, 1952.

Irving, David. *The Trail of the Fox: The Life of Field Marshal Erwin Rommel*. London: Weidenfeld & Nicolson, 1977.

Jars, Robert. *La Campagne de Pologne (Septembre 1939)*. Paris: Payot, 1949.

Jentz, Thomas L. *Panzertruppen: The Complete Guide to the Creation and Combat Employment of Germany's Tank Force 1937–1942*. Atglen, PA: Schiffer, 1996.

Jentz, Thomas L. *Panzertruppen: The Complete Guide to the Creation and Combat Employment of Germany's Tank Force 1943–1945*. Atglen, PA: Schiffer, 2000.

Jentz, Thomas L. *Germany's Tiger Tanks: Tiger I & II: Combat Tactics*. Atglen, PA: Schiffer, 1997.

Kennedy, Robert M. *The German Campaign in Poland 1939*. Washington, D.C.: Office of the Chief of Military History, 1956.

Kessler, Leo. *The Iron Fist*. London: Futura, 1977.

Kleine, Egon, and Kuhn, Volkmar. *Tiger*. Stuttgart: Motorbuch Verlag, 1990.

Knappe, Siegfried. *Soldat: Reflections of a German Soldier, 1936–1949*. New York: Dell Publishing Co., 1993.

Kurowski, Franz (transl. Joseph G. Walsh). *Deadlock Before Moscow: Army Group Center, 1942–43*. Atglen, PA: Schiffer, 1992.

Lehman, Rudolf. *The Leibstandarte*. Manitoba: JJ Fedorowicz, 1990.

Lewin, Ronald. *Rommel as Military Commander*. London: Barnes & Noble, 1999.

Liddell Hart, Capt. B.H. (ed.). *The Rommel Papers*. London: Collins, 1953.

Lucas, James. *Panzer Army Africa*. London: MacDonald and Jane's, 1977.

Lucas, James. *Grossdeutschland*. London: MacDonald and Jane's, 1978.

Lucas, James. *German Army Handbook 1939–1945*. Stroud: Sutton Publishing Limited, 1998.

Lucas, James. *War on the Eastern Front: The German Soldier in Russia 1941–45*. London: Greenhill Books, 1979.

Lucas, James. *Hitler's Mountain Troops: Fighting at the Extremes*. London: Arms & Armour, 1992.

Luck, Colonel Hans von. *Panzer Commander: The Memoirs of Hans von Luck*. Westport, CT: Praeger, 1989.

MacDonald, Charles. *The Battle of the Bulge*. London: Weidenfeld & Nicolson, 1984.

MacDonald, Charles. *The Lost Battle: Crete 1941*. London: Macmillan, 1993.

Macksey, Kenneth. *The Crucible of Power: The Fight for Tunisia, 1942–43*. London: Hutchinson, 1969.

Macksey, Major K.J. *Panzer Division: The mailed fist*. New York: Ballantine Books, 1968.

Manstein, Erich von. *Lost Victories*. Chicago: H. Regency Co.,

1958.

Mellenthin, F.W. von. *Panzer Battles 1939–45: A Study in the Employment of Armour*. London: Cassell, 1955.

Mitcham Jr., Samuel W. *The Panzer Legions: A Guide to the German Army Tank Divisions of World War II and Their Commanders*. Westport, CT: Greenwood Press, 2001.

Mitchell, Samuel. *Hitler's Legions*. London: Leo Cooper, 1985.

Müller, Rolf-Dieter, and Ueberschär, Gerd R. *Hitler's War in the East 1941–45: A Critical Assessment*. Oxford: Berghahn, 1997.

Müller, Rolf-Dieter, and Volkmann, Hans-Erich. *Die Wehrmacht: Mythos und Realität*. München: Oldenbourg, 1999.

Nafziger, George F. *The German Order of Battle: Panzers and Artillery in World War II*. London: Greenhill Books, 1999.

Nafziger, George F. *The German Order of Battle: Infantry in World War II*. London: Greenhill Books, 2000.

Nafziger, George F. *The German Order of Battle: Waffen-SS and other units in World War II*. Pennsylvania: Combined Publishing, 2001.

Newton, Steven H. *German Battle Tactics on the Russian Front 1941–45*. Atglen, PA: Schiffer, 1994.

Nipe, George. *Decision in the Ukraine*. Manitoba: JJ Fedorowicz, 1996.

O'Neill, Robert J. *The German Army and the Nazi Party 1933–39*. London: Cassell, 1966.

O'Neill, Robert J. "Doctrine and Training in the German Army 1919–1939." in Howard, Michael (ed.). *The Theory and Practice of War*. New York: Praeger, 1965: 158–85.

Ottmer, Hans-Martin. *Weserübung: der deutsche Angriff auf Danemark und Norwegen im April 1940*. München: Oldenbourg, 1974.

Overmans, Rüdiger. *Deutsche militärische Verluste im Zweiten Weltkrieg*. München: Oldenbourg, 1999.

Pallud, John Paul. *France 1940: Blitzkrieg in Action*. London: Battle of Britain, 1991.

Perret, Bryan. *Panzerkampfwagen III*. Oxford: Osprey Publishing, 2001.

Pimlott, John. *The Historical Atlas of World War II*. New York: Henry Holt and Company, 1995.

Reynolds, Michael. *Steel Inferno*. Staplehurst: Spellmount, 1997.

Reynolds, Michael. *Men of Steel*. Staplehurst: Spellmount, 1999.

Reynolds, Michael. *Sons of the Reich: The History of II SS Panzer Corps*. Staplehurst: Spellmount, 2002.

Ryan, Cornelius. *A Bridge Too Far*. London: Hamish Hamiliton, 1974.

Sadarananda, Dana. *Beyond Stalingrad*. New York: Praeger, 1990.

Sadkovich, James J. "Of Myths and Men: Rommel and the Italians in North Africa, 1940–42." *International History Review 13, No. 2* (1991): 284–313.

Sajer, Guy. *The Forgotten Soldier*. Sterling, VA: Brasseys, Inc, 2000.

Salisbury, Harrison. *The 900 Days: The Siege of Leningrad*. New York: Da Capo Press, 1985.

Scheibert, Horst. *Panzer-Grenadier: Motorcycle & Panzer-reconnaissance Units 1935–1945*. Atglen, PA: Schiffer, 1991.

Schreiber, Gerhard *et al.* (eds.). *Germany and the Second World War, Vol. 3: The Mediterranean, South-east Europe and North Africa 1939–41*. Oxford: Clarendon, 1995.

Seaton, Albert. *The Russo-German War, 1941–45*. New York: Praeger, 1970.

Seaton, Albert. *The German Army, 1933–1945*. London: Weidenfeld & Nicolson, 1982.

Senger und Etterlin, General Frido von. *Neither Fear Nor Hope*. London: Greenhill Books, 1989.

Soviet General Staff. *The Battle for Kursk 1943* (eds. David Glantz and Harold Orenstein). London: Frank Cass, 1999.

Spaeter, Helmuth. *Die Einsätze der Panzergrenadier-division Grossdeutschland*. Friedberg: Podzun-Pallas-Verlag, 1986.

Stadler, Silvester. *Die Offensive gegen Kursk 1943*. Osnabrück: Munin Verlag, 1980.

Stolfi, R.H.S. "Equipment for Victory in France 1940". *History No. 55* (February 1970): 1–21.

Stolfi, R.H.S. *Hitler's Panzers East: World War II Reinterpreted*. Norman: University of Oklahoma Press, 1993.

Stroop, Juergen. *The Stroop Report*. London: Secker & Warburg, 1979.

Sydnor, Charles. *Soldiers of Destruction: The SS Death's Head Division, 1933–1945*. Princeton, NJ: Princeton University Press, 1977.

Toppe, Maj-Gen. Alfred. *German Experiences in Desert Warfare during WWII*. Washington, D.C.: Dept. of the Navy, USMC, 1990.

Trew, Simon. "The Battle for Crete: The Pyrrhic Victory," in Badsey, Stephen (ed.). *The Hutchinson Atlas of World War Two Battle Plans*. Chicago: Fitzroy Dearborn, 2000.

US Handbook on German Military Forces. Washington: US War Department, 1945.

Watson, Bruce Allen. *Exit Rommel: The Tunisian Campaign 1942–43*. Westport, CT: Praeger, 1999.

Wilmot, Chester. *Struggle for Europe*. London: Collins, 1952.

Young, Desmond. *Rommel: The Desert Fox*. New York: Harper & Row, 1950.

Ziemke, Earl F. *The German Northern Theater of Operations, 1940–1945*. Washington, D.C.: GPO, 1959; CMH, 1989.

Ziemke, Earl F. *Moscow to Stalingrad*. Washington, D.C, GPO, 1987.

Ziemke, Earl F. *Stalingrad to Berlin*. Washington, D.C., US Government Printing Office, 1968.

Index